Drama

This book is dedicated to my brother, Tom.

OXFORD
UNIVERSITY PRESS

Drama

Learning connections in primary schools

Barbara Poston-Anderson

OXFORD
UNIVERSITY PRESS

253 Normanby Road, South Melbourne, Victoria 3205, Australia

Oxford University Press is a department of the University of Oxford.
It furthers the University's objective of excellence in research,
scholarship, and education by publishing worldwide in
Oxford New York

Auckland Cape Town Dar es Salaam Hong Kong Karachi
Kuala Lumpur Madrid Melbourne Mexico City Nairobi
New Delhi Shanghai Taipei Toronto

With offices in

Argentina Austria Brazil Chile Czech Republic France Greece
Guatemala Hungary Italy Japan Poland Portugal Singapore
South Korea Switzerland Thailand Turkey Ukraine Vietnam

OXFORD is a trademark of Oxford University Press
in the UK and in certain other countries

National Library of Australia Cataloguing-in-Publication data

Poston-Anderson, Barbara.
Drama: learning connections in primary schools.

Bibliography.
Includes index.

ISBN 9780195560435 (pbk.).

1. Drama - Study and teaching (Primary). I. Title.

372.66044

Edited by Chris Wyness
Cover and text design by Mason Design
Typeset by Mason Design
Proofread by Liz Filleul
Indexed by Russell Brooks
Printed by Ligare Book Printers, Australia

Brief Contents

Contents

List of Boxes

Activity boxes

Each box includes a description of a drama activity followed by mentor notes and often variations and extensions.

Concept boxes

Each concept box includes either a visual to reinforce a point in the text or guidelines, procedures or explanatory diagrams.

From the Classroom boxes

Each segment provides a vignette of how drama was used with primary school children.

Story and Script boxes

Each box contains a summary or full text of a story or a partial or full script.

Preface

This book aims to identify and explore educational approaches to drama, while at the same time recognising drama's value as an art form. To achieve this goal, both a theoretical and a practical approach to creating, performing and responding to drama in educational settings are taken. Boxed materials including concepts, activities, experienced-based vignettes from the classroom, and stories and scripts support the underlying theories and principles in the text and provide in-depth examples. The overall aim of this approach is to help educators learn how to work effectively with drama to meet children's social, affective, aesthetic and cognitive learning needs.

The text is divided into two major sections, each of which has a different emphasis. The first section, Drama in Learning Contexts, explores how drama can be situated within the overall educational curriculum of the school and the individual classroom program. Planning for drama and drama's potential as a catalyst for integrating learning and for developing social skills among students are the main emphases in this section.

The second section, Drama Building Blocks for Learning, concentrates on drama as a creative process enumerating its key elements and identifying selected drama forms. For each of these elements and forms, in-depth examples are provided, often accompanied by reflections from student teachers on the benefits they have found for the various approaches and exercises suggested.

This book is intended for pre-service primary school teachers as an introduction to drama theory and practice. Although many of the drama strategies and exercises can be used across the grade levels, specific indications of those that are particularly appropriate for older students (i.e. upper primary) are provided within the Activity Boxes. Also, in the second section of the book, a separate discussion is provided in each chapter that identifies applications of drama concepts and activities for middle school students (i.e. years 7-9).

Although this book can be read consecutively, chapter by chapter, it may also be a useful strategy to use the exercises in the second section of the text to explicate theories in the first section, as is appropriate. Some users of this book may also prefer to read the second section, Drama Building Blocks for Learning, before the first section, Drama in Learning Contexts. In short, this book is designed to accommodate a range of approaches to drama study.

About the Author

Associate Professor Barbara Poston-Anderson, who has her doctorate in Primary Education, is the Creative Scholar and a drama specialist at the Centre for Research and Education in the Arts in the Faculty of Education at the University of Technology, Sydney. Much of her previous research and teaching has explored the potential that drama and other creative arts have for student learning. She is also a storyteller, playwright, director of children's plays, and a co-author of books on storytelling and readers' theatre.

As an educator at the tertiary level, who also has taught in both primary and secondary schools, she bases her view of learning on those educational theories that hold that active participation in a socio-cultural context plays a central role in how children learn. This social constructivist position gives priority to individual students' sensory experiences and uses guided learning through an interactive approach as the means for assisting students to develop beyond what they could achieve on their own.

The author, who recognises the situated context of learning through drama, promotes an eclectic approach that encourages mentors to draw on drama elements, forms, and processes as appropriate to meet student needs and interests and curriculum outcomes. The spiral approach to curriculum in which there is a return to ideas in increasingly more depth over time is also part of the author's orientation. The author also recognises that student identification of their own values and respecting those of others is at the heart of learning through drama.

Acknowledgments

'Nothing comes from nowhere.'

(Margaret Drabble, *The Red Queen*)

The author wishes to acknowledge and express appreciation to the numerous drama theorists and educational practitioners who inspired this book. Their expertise and insight illuminated the many complementary pathways available through drama education. This current work builds on the solid foundations that they have laid and on the shared drama experiences that the author has had over the years with students in tertiary, secondary and primary school classrooms.

In particular, the author thanks her husband, Keith, for his ongoing, generous support. His valuable suggestions and artistic contributions are much appreciated.

She also wishes to thank her colleagues, especially Associate Professor Rosemary Ross Johnston, Dr Lesley Ljungdahl and Dr Paul March, for their encouragement over the many months it took to write this book.

Her sincere appreciation is expressed to the student teachers studying drama in the Faculty of Education at UTS past and present for their enthusiastic participation in workshopping ideas in this book and for their valuable feedback.

Appreciation is also expressed to the UTS Alumnae Theatre Company (CREA) and to the UTS Youth Theatre Company (CREA), particularly to Cassandra, Claire, Lucy and Michael, who always showed dedication to and flair for drama.

Finally, the author thanks staff and students at Kuyper Christian School, Leonay Primary School and Toongabbie Christian Community School for participating and responding in various ways to the drama activities in this book.

Also, a sincere thank you to: The Centre for Research and Education in the Arts (UTS) for permission to use selected photographs; Sarah Borsellino for performance photographs of *A Midsummer Night's Dream* and *Sense and Sustainability*; and The State Library of New South Wales, Mitchell Library for background and source material about Vincent Patrick Taylor, a.k.a. Captain Penfold.

Every effort has been made to trace the original source of copyright material contained in this book. Notice of any errors or omissions should be directed to the publisher.

Drama in Learning Contexts

Section One, consisting of Parts One and Two of this book, focuses on describing drama and examining drama's role in learning.

Part One (Chapters 1 and 2) introduces drama, emphasising its cultural traditions in society and its learning connections in education. Drama's benefits as a learning medium for students are stressed; so, too, are the ways a teacher can learn to function effectively as a drama mentor.

Part Two (Chapters 3, 4 and 5) focuses more in-depth on drama as a learning medium, emphasising programming and lesson planning for drama within the broader context of curriculum development. The role that drama can play in integrated learning is also addressed, as is the way that drama can serve as a catalyst for social learning.

The overall aim of Section One is to position drama within society, and more particularly within education, as a valuable resource, effective method for student-centred learning, a recognised product of artistic endeavour, and an object of study in its own right. Far from being mutually exclusive, these drama orientations can combine in innovative ways to transform students' learning.

Preview

Section One: Drama in Learning Contexts consists of Parts One and Two.

Part One: Introducing Drama: Parameters and Possibilities consists of Chapters 1 and 2.

Chapter 1: Describing Drama considers drama's contributions to society as an art form and to education as a learning medium. Particular emphasis is given to drama's benefits for students and its role in learning.

Introducing Drama:
Parameters and Possibilities

Objectives

By the end of this part you should be able to:

- Appreciate the role of drama in history, culture and learning;
- Identify the benefits of drama for students and for their learning; and
- Understand the role of the teacher as a drama mentor.

Drama can be viewed from many perspectives, including historical, cultural, social and educational. Part One introduces students to the role that drama has played in various times and cultures, in addition to presenting a number of key concepts that relate to drama in learning. How the teacher can become a mentor for students in drama is also considered, with suggested areas for knowledge and skill development.

Describing Drama

'True drama for discovery ... is about journeys and not knowing how the journeys may end' (Heathcote 1975).

Drama traditions

Concept Box 1.1

Drama traditions:
From classic plays to children's theatre

Figure 1.1 The chorus comforts Antigone in the Greek tragedy *Antigone* by Sophocles

Figure 1.2 Strega Nona, her cat, and Antonio in *A Celebration of Italian Folktales*

Figure 1.3 Witches foresee the future in Shakespeare's *Macbeth*

Within human consciousness there is an impulse for **drama**—that urge that the classical writer, Aristotle, called an instinct 'lying deep in our nature' (1961, p. 55). From the earliest times, indigenous peoples throughout the world performed cyclical rituals for the propagation of crops and the regeneration of life using song, dance and re-enactment. Remains of theatres at Delphi, Aspendos, Pergamon, Ephesus, Myra and other ancient sites attest to the central role that dramatic ritual and re-creation played for ancient cultures. These special purpose community spaces nestled into steep hillsides were the places where tragedies, dramatising the rise and fall of heroes and their relation to the gods, and satiric comedies, holding a mirror to society and its foibles, were once enacted. To spark the imagination, provoke thought, inform, challenge, persuade and educate are all functions of the dramatic traditions passed down to us from diverse times and cultures that now form part of our human heritage.

In contemporary society, however, the understanding of what constitutes drama extends well beyond the bounds of formal theatrical performance. Recent developments in drama theory (e.g. **performativity**) hold that 'drama pervades life' (Courtney 1990, p. 4); in fact, life itself is regarded as a drama to be performed (Conrad 2004). In a range of fields, from theatre studies to philosophy, psychology, sociology, anthropology, cultural studies and folklore, drama terms and concepts have been used to explain social and cultural phenomena; for example, 'social drama' (Turner 1982) and 'cultural performance' (Singer 1959) are terms used in social anthropology to describe types of life events. Drama terminology is not only used in the area of drama itself, but has 'slipped into common parlance' (Courtney 1990, p. 5) in other specialised fields of study and in the 'performativities' of daily life (Watson 2000).

Perhaps one reason why drama is so often used as a 'metaphor for non-theatrical manifestations' (Carlson 1996, p. 21) is that human values expressed through emotions and actions are central to both drama and life. Drama mirrors the human condition reflecting what people feel and the ways in which they express these feelings. No matter how, where, or in what ways drama is experienced, enacted, or used, this central element is the linchpin that connects the dramatic endeavours of the present with those of the past; the performances on the world stage with those in the professional theatre; and the dramas that take place on a busy street corner with those in the school classroom. Although the ways in which drama can be approached and the contexts in which it can be used are unlimited, this book focuses on approaches for helping children learn through drama in educational settings.

Drama and learning

In Australia, a study commissioned by the Australia Council (Saatchi & Saatchi 2000) found that a majority of Australians surveyed (i.e. 85 per cent) agreed that the arts should be 'an important part' of every child's education (p. 86). Drama is one of these arts that educators describe as an expressive and creative art and is regarded as an important way of knowing that can illuminate children's learning (Henry 2000; Board of Studies NSW 2000; Cattanach 1996; Courtney 1990; Heathcote 1975; McCaslin 1974). Drama, seen as 'basic' and 'central' to the curriculum (Bolton 1986, p. 230), cuts across subject boundaries enabling students to delve into issues in depth and to integrate their learning. Educators place particular significance on the 'change of attitude and understanding' that can result as students participate in drama (Fleming 2000, p. 39).

Despite general agreement about drama's educational value, there is still ongoing discussion about the most appropriate terminology to use. Over the years a number of terms have competed for acceptance, including: child drama, creative drama or dramatics, educational drama, developmental drama, drama in education, process drama, participatory drama, and the more general term drama, which this book uses. How this term is viewed is explained in Drama Description (Concept Box 1.2).

Concept Box 1.2

Drama description

Drama is a collaborative process of sense making in which participants engage in imagined, yet authentic experiences using their creative and critical thinking abilities, verbal and non-verbal communication skills, and empathic responses. Participants reflect on these shared experiences during or after these interactions in order to grow in their understandings of themselves, others, and their world. As children involve themselves in learning through drama they assume various roles that can include: character-in-role, expert, storyteller, communicator, performer, puppeteer, listener, group participant and audience member. They also create, perform and respond.

Drama is both an interactive process and an area of study in its own right.

Drama can be integrated with the other arts (e.g. music, visual arts, dance, media) and/or integrated with other areas in the curriculum (e.g. literature, human society, maths, science, technology).

This book does not attempt to settle the long-standing debates about what the emphasis in drama should be (e.g. whether drama is primarily a medium for learning or an art form and whether drama is by its nature process-oriented or product-oriented); instead, underlying the description of drama used in this book is the view that what governs the approach to drama needs to be what is appropriate for the students and the situation. At any one time, drama can be any or all of these (e.g. art, medium of learning, process, product). As Nicholson (1995) states, 'to accept that there is one, unitary vision of reality is to marginalise others' (p. 36). This book is consistent both with Bolton's claim that drama is 'multi-faceted' (1986, p. 235) and with Simons's view (1992) that, in drama education, there need to be 'interactive' paradigms rather than 'oppositional' ones (Arnold & Taylor 1995, p. 22). Based on these premises, this book links a range of dramatic elements, forms and problem-solving processes to form an integrated view of drama.

Drama's benefits for students

Within educational settings, drama has numerous benefits for the child who participates as enumerated in Drama's Benefits for Students (Concept Box 1.3).

Concept Box 1.3

Drama's benefits for students

Drama is:

- *Self-affirming*: Students gain positive self-concepts of themselves as they build confidence in their knowledge and communication skills and have their ideas valued by others.
- *Social:* Students gain competence in interacting and communicating with others as together the group builds a 'community of imaginers' (Cremin 1998, p. 223).
- *Empathic:* Students learn to understand and respect other people's perspectives and feelings—which, according to Abbs (1989, p. 43), consist of 'emotions, intuitions, judgments and values'. Bolton (1986) calls these 'feeling-values' (p. 66) and Cremin (1998) contends that it is through 'empathetic engagement' that 'significance is found' (p. 224).
- *Symbolic*: Students develop higher order thinking skills as they employ double vision—what Henry (2000) calls 'double awareness' (p. 51) and what Boal (1995) and Bolton (1984) refer to as **metaxis**, which in the case of drama means that participants belong to two worlds at the same time, one—the actual here-and-now and the other—the imaginary.
- *Transformative*: In the context of drama, students experience situations in drama that in their actual lives would not be possible. These meaningful interactions engage their cognitive, affective and aesthetic selves. Through participating in the drama process and reflecting on it, they 'come to know' (Courtney 1990, p. 25), become 'empowered (Bayliss & Dodwell 2002, p. 47), and as Woods (1993) suggests, they experience 'significant changes in the way they regard themselves and others' (Bayliss & Dodwell 2002, p. 46).

Increasing confidence, developing awareness, deepening understanding, and becoming empowered are all benefits that children can gain from drama participation.

Drama's benefits as a learning medium

In addition to the benefits that flow to children from their participation in drama experiences, there are benefits for the educational program. This is because drama by its nature has characteristics that promote learning. Drama is engaging and motivating, holistic and integrating, and inclusive and community building. Each of these complementary concepts will be discussed in turn.

ENGAGING AND MOTIVATING

The medium of drama has the potential to captivate learners because it builds on the spontaneity and make-believe action of dramatic (i.e. symbolic) play. As young children play they often pretend, taking on various roles (e.g. shopkeeper, fire fighter, parent) that help them learn about their world. The 'now-ness' of the situations (Bolton 1986, p. 264) and the active imaginative involvement that characterise children's symbolic play are also evident in drama. The 'make-believe' of play provides a direct link to the **'as if'** of drama.

Another reason why drama is motivating is because it focuses on particulars at the concrete level rather than on abstractions (Bolton 1986, p. 36). Learning through drama is contextual; for example, instead of asking children to explain a concept, such as freedom, students may first experience the idea within an imagined situation. To understand what is meant by freedom, students may take on the roles of First Fleet convicts transported to Australia. As they identify with and reflect on the plight of these individuals whose freedom was restricted, they make the action of the drama personally meaningful. In this way, children engage in 'critical learning by doing' (McCullough 1998, p. 173). It is through this process of direct participation and critical reflection that they come to understand what is meant by the concept freedom. The personal involvement that initially engages and motivates students in their learning can lead to the development of broader understanding through 'generalising and making connections' (Fleming 2000, p. 40).

HOLISTIC AND INTEGRATING

In using drama as an approach to learning, the child's cognitive, affective, social and aesthetic development become the centre of concern. As children participate in the problem-solving processes that are at the heart of drama, they make use of their **multiple intelligences**. Gardner (1985, 1983) describes intelligence as 'the ability to solve problems or to create problems that are within one or more cultural settings' (p. x) and enumerates these abilities as: linguistic (verbal); logical-mathematical (using number and pattern); musical (using rhythm, melody, pitch, tone through music and dance); visual/spatial (using images and pictures); bodily-kinaesthetic (using the body to express ideas); interpersonal (understanding and working with others); intrapersonal (capacity to understand one's self); naturalistic (having a strong connection with the environment) and existential (having a concern for universal truth) (Gardner 1999, 1993). Children may draw on any of their intelligences as they integrate their learning through drama experiences.

However, when using drama as a learning medium, not only is the child viewed holistically as a complex individual but so, too, is knowledge. The process of considering alternatives, communicating and empathising with others, making decisions and assessing the consequences of their actions within the 'communal imaginative' context of drama (Cremin 1998, p. 216) depends on children being able to see situations from multiple perspectives and being able to integrate ideas, understandings, and knowledge in order to gain a holistic picture of the problem. As Bolton (1986) points out, the concepts explored in drama 'are more fundamental than subject classification will allow' (p. 239). Students are eclectic in drawing on whatever will help them fill the gaps in their sense making. In doing this they cut across subject boundaries as they attempt to consolidate knowledge, rather than compartmentalise it.

In drama the immediacy and relevance of personalised learning and the formal objectives of the educational program converge when teachers begin where children are, motivating them to learn for themselves. Through 'as if' activities, such as role play and improvisation, augmented by the mentor's skilful questions and guided reflection, children discover what they already know and learn how to extend this knowledge in meaningful and integrative ways. When mentors provide guidance through **scaffolding**, they assist children to extend their learning beyond where they started and to reach their own level of understanding, what Vygotsky (1978) calls the **zone of proximal development**.

INCLUSIVE AND COMMUNITY BUILDING
'Developing people' is at the core of a drama approach to learning (Way 1967, p. 7). Because in this medium students can engage at their own level and from their own perspectives, drama has value for all learners including second language learners, disadvantaged students and those with other special needs (Cattanach 1996; Hoyt 1992). Because drama employs a range of communication systems that draw on children's verbal and non-verbal abilities and skills, students are able to experience information through several different channels and, in this way, reinforce their learning.

There is also a sense in which drama develops a community among all learners (Bayliss & Dodwell 2002, p. 46), what social anthropologists (e.g. Turner 1982) call 'communitas' (Courtney 1990, p. 59). As children work together they learn about each other and develop the understanding and empathy that enables them to move forward in a 'communal imaginative direction' and to interact meaningfully in 'a shared fictitious world' (Cremin 1998, pp. 216, 212).

In summary, the use of drama in the learning environment has many benefits both for the children who participate and for the educational programs in which they are involved. The developmental process of drama enables learners to find out more about themselves and others, and to acquire knowledge in a motivating, integrating and communal way.

Making connections

Participant roles, drama structures and contextual characteristics are all factors that shape the drama experience for participants. These interconnecting factors will be discussed in turn.

PARTICIPANT ROLES
In drama, the child's interests and developmental needs are paramount. Pioneer dramatists, including Peter Slade (1954) and Brian Way (1967),

emphasised that the child's self-development was the main reason for doing drama. Contemporary drama educators also emphasise the child, who is now described as a learner, and the process of drama as being learner-centred. In drama's student-based approach, the classroom teacher takes on the role of a 'facilitator' who provides a scaffold for learning; a 'coach' who supports and encourages, but does not direct (Hoyt 1992, p. 582); and a 'mentor' who provides input and guidance when appropriate, but must ultimately 'let go' (Prior 2001). **Mentor** is the main term that is used in this book for the person who works with children in drama.

To achieve and maintain these learner and mentor roles, power sharing becomes a necessary component of drama interactions. A central question becomes: Who owns the drama? If it is not the children, a lack of commitment on their part can result in surface rather than deep learning. As Prior (2001, p. 27) points out, 'for participants to fully benefit from process drama, students must be endowed with decision-making roles within the work'. Drama educator Dorothy Heathcote (1984) demonstrated one effective way of achieving this by empowering students using the **mantle of the expert** technique. In other words, students 'took on' the role of 'experts' and shared this expert knowledge within the context of the drama. Such empowerment is regarded as one of the 'strengths of process drama' (Prior 2001, p. 23).

During drama sessions, then, the students and the mentor become coparticipants. Sometimes the mentor steps into role alongside the students, which is called **teacher-in-role** (Heathcote 1984). This shared role playing, during which participants frequently shift between actual and 'as if' worlds, builds strong interpersonal relationships that result in a partnership in which children and adults interact, cooperate, and share power (Warren 1993).

DRAMA STRUCTURES

Choices about how to structure drama for learning are influenced by the underlying **metaphors** for drama that the mentor (who is usually the one who does the structuring) holds, either consciously or unconsciously. Metaphors that 'combine two thoughts in order to create a new meaning' (Courtney 1990, p. 65) are important because they affect thinking and action (Lakoff & Johnson 1980). In Definitional Metaphors for Drama (Concept Box 1.4) some metaphors that have been used to describe drama are listed and explained.

Concept Box 1.4

Definitional metaphors for drama

Drama as:

A grab-bag

Drama is seen as a collection of unrelated activities that can be used at a moment's notice to motivate children, fill a gap in the educational program, build group rapport, or have fun. These activities are viewed as having little or marginal relationship to the rest of the educational program and are usually regarded as 'one-off' experiences.

A performance

Drama involves a presentation for an audience. Presenters, called actors (alone or as part of a group), use their verbal and non-verbal skills to enact a prepared dramatic piece (e.g. play, musical, dance drama). The artistic product that results can be assessed according to criteria ranging from personal preference to set standards.

A language

Drama has a grammar and a structure of its own consisting of elements (e.g. dramatic tension, space, time), physical forms (e.g. mime, puppetry) and contexts (i.e. social and cultural) that can be combined in different ways to make meaning. For this reason, drama is sometimes described as another 'literacy' (Pascoe 1999).

A catalyst

Drama is a stimulus that brings about change in the participants' cognitive and affective understandings; it 'unearths knowledge and understanding which will be of use to its owners' (Warren 1992).

In Structural Metaphors for Drama (Concept Box 1.5) some ways that have been used to visualise drama and its structure are presented.

Concept Box 1.5

Structural metaphors for drama

Drama as:

A continuum

Drama consists of forms of drama that can be grouped along a line from the more unstructured, process-oriented on one end, such as dramatic play, role play and improvisation, to the more structured, product-oriented, such as readers' theatre and play performance, on the other end.

A process

Drama consists of planned developmental activities, sometimes organised by stages or phases, which help children grow in their understandings of self, others and the world.

A cycle

Drama consists of procedures that flow in a circular pattern from preparation and initiation through to implementation and evaluation. Reflection may occur at any point, with the potential for final evaluation to stimulate the start of the sequence again.

A spiral

Drama centres on the child who is first introduced to concepts and techniques at a basic level. As the child's understanding and skill increase, these concepts and techniques are returned to again and again with ever increasing detail and depth to match and extend the child's development.

A network

Drama consists of an interconnecting web of elements, forms and processes set within a socio-cultural context. These connections can be made with other areas of the creative arts, across the curriculum, and with key resources (e.g. people, places, materials) within and outside the school community.

These underlying metaphors provide insight into how drama has been perceived by others. By considering these definitional and structural metaphors, drama mentors can more fully understand where they position themselves in the debate about what constitutes drama.

Also, being aware of the types of metaphor used by others will help a mentor understand how drama as a field of study has been perceived enabling him or her to make appropriate choices about which metaphors and drama methods to use to meet students' needs and the learning outcomes of the curriculum.

In addition to metaphors that reveal underlying beliefs about drama, educators have developed several different orientations towards drama that can help mentors make decisions about how to structure drama programs. The two types of orientation presented here focus on: (1) what the mentor's intentions for drama are and (2) what the child does during drama.

The first orientation in Drama Intentions (Concept Box 1.6) relates to how a mentor intends to use drama in the learning process (Bolton 1986, p. 213; 1979, p. 11). Each intention makes use of a recognised 'type of drama', namely, exercises, dramatic playing, and theatre.

Concept Box 1.6

Drama intentions

The intent is to isolate a skill.
'Exercises' isolate skills and these exercises can be grouped as those that are: 'directly experiential, dramatic skill practice, drama exercise, games, and using other art forms such as story, song, and dance.'

The intent is *to experience*.
'Dramatic playing' involves living through an experience in a make-believe setting that is 'fixed' by: place, situation, anticipation of conflict (e.g. gang-fighting), anticipation of elemental disaster (e.g. flood), storyline and character study.

The intent is to demonstrate experience.
Experience is demonstrated through 'theatre' skills and processes through which participants create a drama product to be shared with an audience.

O'Neill and Lambert (1982) use a similar framework, but refer to the 'types of drama' as 'modes of dramatic activity' (p. 22) suggesting that each mode will require different classroom organisation.

The second orientation in Drama Process (Concept Box 1.7) focuses on what the child does during drama. Two complementary approaches that emphasise drama process are presented.

Concept Box 1.7

Drama process

1   *Making, Performing and Appreciating* is the overview used in the syllabus, *Creative Arts K-6* (Board of Studies NSW 2000). Here the emphasis is on the child who uses the elements of dramatic interpretation (i.e. space, contrast, focus, mood, time, symbol, tension) and dramatic forms (e.g. mime, puppetry) to *make* his or her own drama and/or to *perform,* that is, to become an 'interpreter of dramatic art' (Nicholson 1995, p. 36). The child, in the role of spectator or audience member, learns to *appreciate* the drama that he or she makes and performs, and also the artistic work of others.

2   *Identification, Commitment, Engagement and Reflection* are stages of dramatic involvement aimed at deepening a child's participation and learning. Pioneered by Heathcote (1984) and developed by others (e.g. Bolton 1979), children's meaningful reflection on drama work is an ultimate goal.

Neelands's model for drama involvement (1990) is a complementary approach with the following phases:

– Phase 1 Building the Context—Getting Them Interested, which contains initial activities to build motivation and define the context.

– Phase 2 Developing the Narrative—Deepening the Commitment, which consists of a range of group activities.

– Phase 3 Introducing the Problem—Testing the Commitment and Getting Engagement.

– Phase 4 Reflecting and Reviewing—Relating Fiction to Reality.

Related to each phase is a range of drama 'conventions' (e.g. exercises, activities, group work, visualisations) that can be used to deepen the drama for participants at each stage of the model.

Mentors can make use of drama metaphors and orientations developed by others as a starting point for clarifying their own positions in relation to how they view drama. Thinking about drama and its structures lays the groundwork for the mentor to develop a more in-depth philosophy related to drama in education.

CONTEXTUAL CHARACTERISTICS

Children learn through drama as they solve problems by empathising and using their critical thinking skills (Cockett 1997). However, far from happening in a vacuum, this learning takes place in space. In drama this space consists of both an imaginary space and a physical, tangible space. To participate within the imaginary 'inner frame' of the drama (Courtney 1990, p. 73) requires that participants suspend disbelief and commit themselves to engaging in a make-believe experience that parallels and simulates the here-and-now experience. Learning becomes real within the situated context of the drama that has as its aim—'understanding human situations' (Fleming 2000, p. 39). Creating a positive make-believe space for group imagining is important because young people need to feel safe to participate in drama activities without criticism or outside interference. A non-judgmental environment, which recognises the value of each participant's contribution, is crucial, then, in bridging the imaginary and actual worlds of the drama.

The physical setting in which the drama takes place, known as the **contextual frame** (Courtney 1990, p. 75), is an important factor, too. Having an enclosed space that sets boundaries for the activity contributes to participant focus and wellbeing. The ways in which physical space is used can reinforce interpersonal and role relationships; for example, sitting participants in a circle makes them feel part of a group while arranging the drama space so there is no definite front or back encourages power sharing. Where the mentor is placed—in the centre or on the periphery—also can encourage or discourage the participants to take more or less responsibility for the drama.

Participant roles, drama structures and contextual characteristics shape drama interactions. When mentors understand the synergy that can result from interconnecting these factors in diverse ways, they are better able to develop and facilitate relevant and meaningful drama programs for their students.

Summary

Despite the fact that educators, researchers and educational authorities alike have identified drama as a beneficial way of learning, shifts in educational priorities, sometimes driven by economic imperatives, have buffeted drama between those who hail its centrality in the curriculum and those who would relegate it to the margins. Drama encounters the same challenges that other arts in education (e.g. music, dance, visual arts, media) face in having to justify their place within what is claimed to be an already overcrowded curriculum (Abbs 1989). As paradigms compete for acceptance in the educational environment, there is a continuing need for the case to be made for drama as a valid way of knowing. The aim of this chapter has been to provide such a justification by demonstrating that drama is a long-standing cultural tradition; explaining how drama can be described in the learning environment; outlining drama's benefits for learners and as a learning medium; discussing the important interconnections among participant role, structure and setting when implementing drama; and presenting an integrative approach towards drama grounded in a social constructivist perspective.

For further study

1. What is meant by drama as a process or a product? How can each concept be used as an approach to drama in educational settings?
2. Consider the definitional and structural metaphors given for drama. What are the advantages and disadvantages of modelling an approach to drama based on metaphors?
3. What strategies can be used to promote drama as a learning medium in an educational environment?

For reflection

Analyse and discuss your own views of drama. How are these influenced by your background and prior experience? What benefits do you believe drama has for students in learning environments?

Preview

Chapter 2: The Drama Mentor Prepares considers the basic knowledge and skills a teacher needs to function as a drama mentor.

The Drama Mentor Prepares

'[When you have] only one looking glass, you never discover that you are a prisoner of its refraction' (Bohannan & van der Elst 1998).

Introduction

This chapter is written especially for those who are new to drama as a means of introducing them to the key knowledge and skills a drama mentor needs in order to work effectively with young people in educational drama settings. Through self-reflection that aims to provide self-knowledge, drama mentors are made aware of how the knowledge, values and beliefs they hold shape their approaches to teaching, in general, and to drama as a learning medium, in particular. Because feelings and human relationships are central to drama learning, knowing about self and about others are crucial starting points for knowing about drama, whether one is a drama mentor or a drama participant. For this reason, the way in which this chapter is structured mirrors Section Two, Part Three of this book where the mentor begins drama work with children by introducing them to the drama building blocks of sense of self, sense of others and sense of drama.

Know yourself

Just as gaining a sense of self is important for young learners as a preparation for drama, so too mentors need to understand, as people, who they are and, as teachers, where they position themselves in relation to educational theory and practice (also known as **praxis**). To gain this deeper level of understanding about one's self requires a person to be both self-reflective and self-analytical.

One of the ways teachers can achieve self-awareness is to reflect on the **assumptions** that underlie what they do and to make these explicit. Understanding Assumptions (Concept Box 2.1) provides some key questions drama mentors can ask themselves to discover how they view the world and their relationship to it.

Concept Box 2.1

Understanding assumptions

An assumption is:

- Something that we take for granted;
- Something believed without proof.

Assumptions underlie everything we do, although we are not always aware of them.

As teachers and as drama mentors, it is important to recognise these assumptions and state them explicitly.

Ask yourself:

How do I view reality?	Ontological assumptions
Is there an outer, objective reality and an inner, subjective reality? Is one 'more real' than the other?	
How do I view the nature of knowledge?	Epistemological assumptions
Is all knowledge socially constructed or is there such a thing as universal knowledge?	
What is the relationship of learners to knowledge?	
What values and value judgments underlie what I do?	Axiological assumptions
Does everyone have the same values as I do? Why do we differ, if we do?	
What methods and procedures do I think are appropriate for doing things?	Methodological assumptions
Does everyone do things in the same way? Why do we differ, if we do?	

What do I think is artistic? Does everyone else agree? Why do we differ, if we do?	Aesthetic assumptions
What does 'beautiful' mean to me?	
Is the artistic process as important as the product?	

Once you have thought about these assumptions in relation to yourself and how you view things, revisit the Definitional Metaphors for Drama (Concept Box 1.4) in Chapter 1. These are: Drama as a grab-bag; a performance; a language; and a catalyst. What assumptions about reality, knowledge, values and value judgments, methods and procedures, and aesthetics do you think underlie each of these views of drama?

Assumptions affect how teachers teach and learners learn. This includes how knowledge is structured, the way content is selected, the strategies used to address educational issues and how teachers and students interact—in fact, everything about the ways in which teaching and learning occurs has assumptions attached to it. Worth considering also is the fact that while teachers may express an 'espoused' theory (i.e. how they say they teach); this may or may not be consistent with their 'theory in practice' (i.e. how they actually teach).

Clarifying assumptions and making these explicit can help teachers uncover any discrepancies between these two theories and make them more informed and consistent in their approaches, understanding what they are doing and why they are doing it and also recognising their educational orientations and potential biases. By becoming more self-aware and gaining a clearer idea of 'who they are', drama mentors take an important step in preparing themselves for meaningful interaction with participants in drama settings.

Underlying Assumptions (Concept Box 2.1) reinforced how assumptions affect everything we do, including how we teach and how we approach learning through drama. Educational paradigms are established views of teaching and learning that are built around a cluster of similar assumptions about reality, knowledge, values and value judgments, methods and procedures, and aesthetics. Pondering Paradigms (Concept Box 2.2) compares and contrasts two recognised educational paradigms, the teacher-centred and the learner-centred approaches.

Concept Box 2.2

Pondering paradigms

A **paradigm** is *a way of thinking that has a whole 'world view' associated with it.*

This way of thinking is evident in the vocabulary used, the ideas selected and how they are structured, and the underlying assumptions beneath thinking and action.

The following chart indicates some key phrases that have been associated with the two learning paradigms, teacher-centred and learner-centred.

	Teacher-centred	Learner-centred
Reality	The teacher controls and organises the learning environment, including planning and assessment. Teacher and student roles are clearly distinguished.	A socially constructed reality recognising that student needs and interests are central to learning.
Knowledge	The teacher 'knows' and shares this knowledge with students; the teacher is the gate-keeper to information.	Co-construction of knowledge, situated learning; student learning tasks are scaffolded by the teacher.
Values	The teacher evaluates student progress; control remains with the teacher; importance of listening to the teacher.	A decentred classroom with power sharing between the teacher and students; the productive noise of sharing and interacting.
Methods	Teacher-talk; explanations; testing	Student-talk, peer teaching, self-assessment, discovery learning.
Aesthetics	Teacher as arbiter of artistic taste; standards-based judgments.	Artistic sensibility develops through student experience in doing and viewing drama.

Paradigms can both limit and facilitate. As Grady (1996, p. 63) describes it, paradigms are 'filters with a potential to cloud or clarify our theoretical lenses'. At best, these constructs are 'useful as a way to examine more closely our motivating assumptions' (p. 63). Investigating educational paradigms, then, is a useful starting point for drama mentors as they consider where to position themselves and their drama programs in relation to educational theory. Contemporary drama theorists such as Bolton, Carroll, Neelands, O'Toole and Taylor, to name a few, have already considered the main assumptions that they believe underlie drama education. Some of these are presented in Assumptions Underlying Drama (Concept Box 2.3).

Concept Box 2.3

Assumptions underlying drama

Reality	Negotiated reality characterised by metaxis; shifting from the here-and-now to the 'as if' world and back again through a process of being **in role** and then **de-roling**.
Knowledge	Situated learning and co-constructed knowledge resulting in contextualised meaning.
Values/Value judgments	A social orientation that values inclusiveness and community building with feelings and human relationships as pivotal.
Methods/Procedures	Dialogic and reflective approaches using symbolisation and distancing to stimulate meaning-making within the group and for individuals.
Aesthetic	Artistic views and sensibilities developed through doing drama and sharing with others as well as appreciating the work of others.

In short, in drama there are multiple realities; knowledge is co-constructed and situated; social values are pivotal to the drama process; methods are interactive and reflective, and aesthetic appreciation is acquired through participation and experience of one's own and others' work. Learning through drama is essentially a 'reframing' in new ways of what students already know; feelings and human relationships, instead of facts, are central to the transformation that occurs (Bolton 1985). When drama's assumptions are compared with the two educational paradigms presented in Pondering Paradigms (Concept Box 2.2), it can be seen that drama education is consistent with the learner-centred paradigm. The teacher becomes a drama mentor who has the role of scaffolding students, being their guide and serving as a resource person rather than assuming the roles of expert, leader or authority figure that are usually associated with the teacher-centred approach. In drama, the mentor and students work together and share power as they co-construct knowledge.

Know others

All teachers, including drama mentors, need to recognise what children bring with them to the learning experience in the classroom. Groups in the same grade and at the same age differ markedly one from another. The diverse backgrounds and experiences of individual students contribute to an overall 'culture' in the classroom that, like a fingerprint, is unique. The drama mentor needs to embrace this diversity and to draw on it to enrich student learning through drama.

In most classrooms there will be students from a range of cultural backgrounds, some of whom may have lived in Australia for a long time, for a while, or be newly arrived. As the classroom 'culture' develops it needs to represent all its members so that 'difference' does not equate to 'less equal' and so that existing 'similarities' among children as human beings are emphasised. Cultural study terms, such as 'marginalised', 'the Other', and 'on the periphery' all suggest what happens when individuals are disenfranchised by 'mainstream' culture—a situation that is not acceptable in education or anywhere else for that matter.

Questions of **hegemony** in the classroom are critical to identify and address. The egalitarian medium of drama is an appropriate way to do this. Through its elements, forms and processes a classroom community can be built. Not dependent on only one form of literacy, such as reading or writing, drama enables students with languages other than English to participate at first through non-verbal means, including movement, mime, body percussion and soundscapes. As their language facility increases, so, too, the nature of their participation will change to include verbalisation through dialogue and discussion. The introductory exercises and activities in Chapter 6, Sense of Self, and Chapter 7, Sense of Others, can assist children to discover more about themselves and to help them get to know and appreciate others. Likewise, strategies in Chapter 5, Social Learning Through Drama, focus on encouraging group cohesion through developing self-concept, building community and learning how to get along with others.

Not only do students need to respect and value cultural diversity in the classroom, so, too, does the drama mentor. First, because active involvement with others characterises most drama activities, the mentor needs to anticipate whether there will be any students whose participation will be constrained by cultural and related social factors such as views about how close to stand to other people, whether direct eye contact with adults is viewed as appropriate, or how participation in mixed-gender groupings is regarded. Rather than being seen as problematical, these variations provide opportunities to find out more about others through drama work.

When stories and other resources are chosen as a stimulus for drama work, their selection needs to extend beyond monocultural choices. Because we are all most comfortable with our own values and perspectives, a drama mentor needs to be consciously inclusive when making decisions that affect drama. For example, if the tale of Cinderella is chosen for role play and improvisation with young children, consider that there are hundreds of versions worldwide from which to choose. In Cinderella Around the World (Concept Box 2.4) four of these are highlighted to demonstrate how the cultural background of a story shapes its characters, settings and events even though the plotlines may have some common elements.

Concept Box 2.4

Cinderella around the world

Egypt: *The Egyptian Cinderella* (Climo 1989)
A hawk drops a sandal of the slave girl, Rhodopis, into the window of the palace. The Pharoah vows to find out whose sandal it is.

Mexico: *Domitila* (Coburn 2000)
Domitila, 'sweeter than a cactus bloom in early spring', wins the hand of the governor by means of her inner qualities and her respect for family traditions.

Vietnam: *The Golden Slipper* (Lum 1994)
Ill-treated Tam is kind to the animals who help her attend the Autumn Festival, where she loses her brocade slipper and is discovered by the prince.

Zuni (Native American): *The Turkey Girl* (Pollock 1996)

The girl who tends the turkeys thinks she has no hope of going to the Dance of the Sacred Bird, until one day a turkey offers to help her.

The drama mentor makes choices in determining how, when, where and in what contexts to introduce drama. In making these choices, the backgrounds, interests and needs of the children need to be the prime considerations.

Within a class there will also be a mix of ability groupings as well as students with special needs. Drama as a learning medium can accommodate such variability when students are able to participate at their own levels. The drama mentor must carefully plan ways to structure drama so that it is both physically and psychologically safe for all participants. This may include modifying the drama activities themselves. Nature of the Drama Activity (Concept Box 2.5) provides parameters that are useful for helping mentors analyse potential drama activities for their suitability for specific groups.

Concept Box 2.5

Nature of the drama activity

Analyse the nature of a drama activity using these parameters.

Concrete ⟷ Abstract
Simple ⟷ Complex
Nonverbal ⟷ Verbal
Low Energy ⟷ High Energy
Directed ⟷ Self-regulated
Individual ⟷ Group

Being able to analyse the nature of a particular drama activity assists in determining whether it is appropriate for use when working with mixed ability groups or children with special needs.

There also need to be mechanisms for students to withdraw from activities (e.g. 'time out', 'take five') should the exercise become too tiring or, conversely, overstimulating. Sometimes a whole group will 'need a change'. This is when the mentor may choose to vary the nature of the drama activity (e.g. from a high to a low energy activity, from a directed to a self-regulated activity). The challenge for the mentor is to be able to 'tune in' to the group (and individuals within it) at any given time in order to determine the nature and extent of their participation. By learning about self and others the drama mentor is in a better position to engage in the relationship building that happens during drama—'a complex, subtle, dynamic process of navigating the boundaries between self and other … '(Lawrence-Lightfoot & Davis 1997, p. 158).

Know drama

In addition to gaining confidence with the elements of drama (see Chapters 6–8) and the forms of drama (see Chapters 9–13), there are other necessary skills that the novice drama mentor needs to develop that relate to talking and listening, questioning and responding, and to managing time, space and group interactions during drama. Each of these areas will be discussed in turn.

Talking and listening skills

In the drama environment, it is important to ask: Who shapes the acoustic space with their talk? Is it the teacher or is it the students? As a general guide, in drama there needs to be less teacher-talk and more student-talk. From both an educational and a motivational perspective, 'respecting and privileging students' voices' is of primary importance (McLean 1994, p. 57). Because drama is a social medium, children need opportunities to interact with each other in small groups from the outset; not only for companionship and support, but also because 'talk about the work is most essential for [its] development' (Heathcote 1984, p. 210).

With the emphasis in drama on student participation and reflection, the mentor needs to develop listening skills in order to understand and support students in what they 'do' and 'say'. Listening involves focusing on the student, hearing what is being said, and being able to understand and interpret what is meant. In relation to students and their 'talk', the mentor may serve as a sounding board, prompter, interpreter, supportive audience or catalyst for further thought.

Also, in relation to the amount of talk, the drama mentor needs to recognise the importance of the silence. Not every moment of a drama session needs to be filled with conversation, as productive as it can be. On the contrary, silent time provides mental space for internal reflection, aids focus and concentration, and facilitates imagination and visualisation. One way for the mentor to avoid excessive teacher-talk is to establish non-verbal patterns that the children recognise so that, at a signal, they know what is expected (e.g. sit down, move into a circle, close your eyes, freeze in position).

Because listening is critical both for the success of the mentor as a facilitator and for the students as they work in collaborative partnerships or groups in drama, it is worth taking time to address listening skills directly. To hear, to understand, and to interpret what is being said are the important goals of listening. 'The Six Thinking Hats' created by Edward de Bono (1999) provide a useful tool in helping people think about their thinking and for decision making, as well as for helping listeners understand the thinking behind what people say.

Each hat is a symbol for a particular type of thinking. As one person listens to another, do they primarily hear facts and figures (The White Hat); the sharing of emotions and feelings (The Red Hat); cautious and careful comments (The Black Hat); speculative-positive thinking that is forward looking and constructive (The Yellow Hat); creative thoughts that provide alternatives (The Green Hat); and/or a focused, organised and controlled approach that reveals a person is in control of all the other thought processes (The Blue Hat)? The way in which a person expresses thoughts provides an indication of 'where they are coming from'. When a listener is able to 'tune in' and get 'on the same wave length', interpersonal communication is enhanced and the groundwork for further dialogue, discussion and debate is laid.

Questioning and responding techniques

Knowing how to question is an essential tool for the drama mentor. Effective questioning is the means of drawing children out, making them think, and having them consider possibilities and consequences. For drama, one of the most important points about questioning is for the drama mentor to recognise the distinction between closed and open questions. A **closed question** (e.g. 'Are you hungry?') is one that requires a direct 'yes' or 'no' answer or a limited response. An **open question** (e.g. 'What can you do to make all students feel valued at school?') is one that provides scope for a more extended answer. In drama, open questions are most frequently used because they engage students' thinking and encourage their verbal interaction.

Another important type of question used in drama is the **hypothetical question**; for example, 'What if you were in the school library and your favourite book characters came to life and talked to you?' or 'What if you were in the city and there was a transport strike and you couldn't get home?' The 'what if ...' question followed by 'show me what happens next' can be a stimulus for drama propelling students into 'as if' roles and situations.

Other essential questions are the **prompt** and the **probe**. When a question prompts, it reminds students of something they know or have experienced (e.g. Do you remember the role play yesterday when you were the king who wept for joy? How is your role in today's improvisation similar or different?'). A prompt can also 'plant the seed' of an idea for further thinking (e.g.' How could adding the drama element of mood to your tableau change it?'). Like a prompt, the aim of a probing question is to trigger and deepen students' thoughts and dramatic responses. A probe encourages students to take a closer look (e.g. What more can you tell me about the story? Why do you think the character acted in that way?). Questions that prompt and probe are vehicles for helping students extend their own thinking to deeper levels.

Questioning can also be purposefully related to Bloom's Taxonomy of Educational Objectives (1956), a hierarchy of cognitive thinking levels. By asking questions at different levels, the mentor can help to develop a range of student thinking skills. Levels of Questions (Concept Box 2.6) identifies each of Bloom's cognitive categories with examples of question types for each.

Concept Box 2.6

Levels of questions

Bloom's cognitive categories	Sample questions
Knowledge (identifying and listing)	*Who* is Keith Johnstone? *What* is Theatresports? *When* did Theatresports begin? *Where* was the first Theatresports competition/performance?

Comprehension (showing understanding)	Why are vocal exercises important for actors?
	What is the main point of the story?
Application (using and transforming)	How can the moral of 'The Ant and The Grasshopper' be related to everyday life?
	If this character with its personality traits were an animal, what one would it be?
Analysis (separating into parts to discover underlying characteristics)	When you walk in slow motion, what are the elements of this movement?
	What is the role of each character in the puppet play script?
Synthesis (combining elements in new ways)	In what ways can you mix story, puppetry and role play to create a dramatic presentation?
	How can you add movement and sound to this tableau to bring it to life?
Evaluation (making judgments)	How would you rate this children's theatre performance compared with others you have seen?
	Which version of your play script do you think has more well-developed characters?

Although questioning is a strategy used at every stage of drama work, **hot seating** is one particular drama technique that specifically focuses on questioning as a mode of enquiry. As such, both mentor and students can develop and practise their questioning skills during a hot-seating session that involves a person who is in role being asked questions by other group members in order to discover the *who*, *what*, *where*, *when*, *how* and *why* of the character's background, interests and life story (e.g. Burke and Wills are quizzed about what happened on their last expedition; Fruit Fly Circus members are asked why they like performing). The questioners benefit because they have an opportunity to craft questions from a range of perspectives, while the hot-seated students benefit too, because by responding to questions in role, their thinking about the character is extended and deepened.

To ensure that when children express themselves during drama they are psychologically secure, a supportive and nurturing environment is required.

The mentor lays the groundwork for this 'safe space' by knowing how to respond appropriately to students' comments, suggestions and dramatic contributions. Question Time (Concept Box 2.7) provides some suggestions on the range of ways a mentor can respond to a question posed by a drama participant.

Concept Box 2.7

Question time

Answer a question with:

- A direct answer.
- An **analogy** comparing one thing with another.
- A story that provides a fictional frame for the answer.

Ask a question.

- A prompt that encourages students to continue speaking.
- A probe that inspires children to dig deeper.
- An open question that requires a more extended response.
- A hypothetical question that asks 'what if?'

Encourage reflection.

- Redirect the question to the group.
- Issue a challenge for the child or group to find out more and report back.

Mentor note

Human interaction involves both verbal and non-verbal cues (e.g. smiling, nodding, clapping). Be aware of how you use these cues when responding to children. In particular, ensure that your facial expressions and gestures match your words and verbal tones to minimise misinterpretations of what you mean.

Children need to view the drama mentor, not as an expert who has the answers, but as a facilitator who helps them discover for themselves both the questions and the answers. 'Why' or 'what if' questions, in particular, challenge children to draw on their own experience, knowledge and imagination in order to respond to and reflect on their actions. By this means the **locus of control** shifts from outside students to inside, as they are empowered through the realisation that they are responsible for their own learning.

Know how to manage the process of drama learning

As happens during any active learning experience, in drama children can sometimes become overexcited, lack focus or even lose control. For this reason, within a drama lesson strategies for maintaining an effective learning environment need to have high priority. There are a number of positive ways to do this. The first involves **metacognition**, making the children themselves aware of their thinking about the processes and the parameters by which their learning through drama will occur. Together both the mentor and students can set workable guidelines as student-teacher Kristy-lee did when she and her 5th grade students agreed on the phrase 'Keep it together' as a signal to indicate that more on-task behaviour was needed. Likewise, student-teacher Elisa and her class decided that she would raise her hand when she required their attention. The class practised the procedure until Elisa was satisfied that the children would respond immediately. Being able to gain attention instantly is essential for children's learning and their safety, however, the mentor should try not to raise his or her voice. Instead, one of the strategies mentioned, or a musical instrument such as a drum or tambourine as a signal, should be used. Mentors may also institute the 'time out' as a procedure for children to withdraw from drama for a while until they are ready to re-enter and participate sensibly again. Managing Drama (From the Classroom 2.1) provides insight into one student teacher's thoughts about managing the drama experience.

From the Classroom 2.1

Managing drama

Rochelle writes of her experience with a Year 1 class in preparing them to participate in a group-story sharing exercise where the students' role was to provide the animal sounds as a 'big book' was shared aloud.

'The students were new to the drama experience in the classroom and had little understanding of what it meant to be a good audience member. In general, they were attentive; however, listening and watching became an issue halfway through … the students became unfocused. Activities to enhance their focus and to teach them the proper etiquette of being an audience member (e.g. when it is appropriate to applaud or laugh) would greatly improve this area.'

Space constraints affect how a drama session is implemented. Work within the limitations of the classroom or, when possible, move to a larger space. Whatever the space, it is important that it have designated boundaries, particularly when doing drama in an open space such as a playground or a large school hall. Making Space for Drama (From the Classroom 2.2) demonstrates how even limited space can be modified to make it workable for drama.

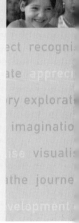

From the Classroom 2.2

Making space for drama

Student–teacher Meagan reports: 'The classroom with limited floor space made it difficult for students to move around and fill the space.' During a subsequent lesson Meagan rearranged the furniture. 'The lesson worked a lot better as more room was established. Tables were relocated to provide more floor space, enabling the group to sit in a circle to share ideas. Students were more inclined to get involved; students' interest and attention were more sustained.'

Managing the people in the space is also an important skill. One strategy is to ensure that the mentor does not establish a front to the room, but moves around continually interacting with individual students and with groups. Handling High Energy (From the Classroom 2.3) presents one student teacher's suggestions based on her experiences of doing drama with energetic primary school children.

From the Classroom 2.3

Handling high energy

Katrina, who did drama activities with eight- and nine-year-olds, writes, 'Nothing prepared me for the extremely high energy levels of these children. I was "blown away" by the enthusiasm and excitement shown by the majority of children.' On the basis of working in such an energy-charged situation, Katrina advises:

- 'Ensure that all students can see you as you talk to them and give directions. This will help them listen effectively and follow instructions accurately.'
- 'Make sure there is enough room for all students to have their own space where they are not squashed or having to touch other students in the class.'
- 'In some activities where partners are needed and there is an odd number of students, form a group of three or have the student be the teacher's partner for that activity.'

With the active involvement that drama can engender it is important to be open to the possibilities of developing situations and not to push for only one solution or for closure before the group is ready. Part of the power of drama to transform learners lies in its potential for opening up alternate ways of thinking and doing. This means that the mentor needs to be 'tolerant of temporary confusion' when it happens (Bolton 1996) and to be able to cope with the reasonably high level of energy and ambiguity that can accompany divergent thinking. Like the genre of science fiction, which often leaves the reader contemplating the future, so, too, open-ended drama activities keep the participant thinking about things long after the session has ended.

Know how to find out more

Novice drama mentors need a place to begin. In trying to find an entry point into drama it is worth considering the points in Knowing What to Do (Concept Box 2.8).

Concept Box 2.8

Knowing what to do

The drama mentor bases decisions about what to do on:

Experience

Insight into drama as a learning medium is quickly gained through actually working with children in drama. Expertise as a drama mentor increases with reflection about what happened during each session and how that can inform what happens next.

Intuition

Let your 'inner voice' kick in. If you have a 'gut feeling' about something, listen. Often it is well founded and can provide you with valuable insights. In drama, let children's interests, attitudes and responses guide you to an understanding of the nature and depth of their involvement.

Expert opinion

Find out what 'authorities in the field' say about drama education—their philosophies, the strategies they recommend and the specific activities they suggest. Use these to inform your own drama approaches. Read seminal works or consult directly in person, by phone or by email, with others who have expertise in mentoring drama.

Research

Research studies provide the latest findings on drama education. Journals such as: *NJ (NADIE Journal)*; *Research in Drama Education*; and *Youth Theatre Journal* are valuable sources of such research.

Drama associations and conferences

Sharing and exchanging ideas at conferences and becoming a member of a drama association are motivating ways to keep up to date in the field of drama. Two relevant associations are: The National Association of Drama in Education (NADIE) and the International Drama/Theatre in Education Association (IDEA), both of which publish journals and hold periodic conferences. There are also state educational drama associations.

Information sources such as libraries and the Internet

Libraries contain a multitude of books, journals and multimedia resources (e.g. videos, photographs, computer programs) that address drama philosophies and strategies, provide examples of drama workshops and performances, and include generic lesson plans and activities—all of which can be used as source material for developing an approach to drama with the children in your class.

The Internet, too, has innumerable websites of theoretical and practical importance for drama. Learn how to use the online abstracting and indexing services (with access available through most academic and public libraries) such as *Australian Education Index, ERIC* and *Academic Search Elite*, to name several essential resources. These services provide bibliographic details of journal articles, research studies and reports related to your chosen area of study. In addition, there is often the facility to retrieve the full text of an article or a study you find online. Avoid limiting your drama investigations to local resources only; instead, include worldwide references that provide varied perspectives.

Summary

The drama mentor needs to be a skilled facilitator who encourages students to engage actively in their own learning through drama. To develop the skills necessary takes time and patience, but is well worth the effort. Becoming self-reflective, learning about educational processes, finding out about drama and how to listen, question and respond to students are essential understandings for the drama mentor. Drama is not only about producing a polished performance, which is the perception of some school communities, but it is also about transforming learning through drama process as students generate ideas, explore issues and learn to respect differing perspectives.

For further study

1 Discuss possible strategies for involving a child with (a) special needs (identify these) or (b) a first language other than English (identify the language) in drama. Use the premise 'Work with what a child *can* do' as your guide.

2 Find children's resources that explore cultural identity and what the experience of being an emigrant or a refugee means. Use these resources as discussion starters and consider how they could be used as preparatory material for drama. Two examples are:

Grandpa's Journey by Allen Say (1993)

Synopsis: *As a young man, Grandpa emigrates from Japan to America. He grows to love each place equally recognising their similarities and differences and the strong points of each. Over his lifetime, he spends time in both countries.*

A True Person by Gabiann Marin (2007)

Synopsis: *A young girl in a detention centre searches for her own identity.*

3 The following **vignettes** are brief accounts of incidents that occurred in primary schools. Use them as the basis for reflection about drama and the learning process. Add your own examples to the list.

VIGNETTE 1

A storyteller was seeking approval from the educational authority to be officially recognised as a storyteller in schools. This teller shared a 50-minute program of stories with a group of 250 students in the auditorium of a large inner-city school. At the end of the program, the assessors refused the accreditation because they said the program was not 'multicultural' enough.

VIGNETTE 2

A primary school in a major city invited a children's theatre group composed of student teachers to perform a children's play for K-3 students. The troupe did an adaptation of the classic E.B. White children's book, *Charlotte's Web* (1952), which tells the adventures of a pig named Wilbur and his friend, a spider named Charlotte. After the performance the deputy principal met with the student teachers. She shared with them the fact that in this particular school references to 'pigs' were inappropriate because of the religious beliefs of some children.

VIGNETTE 3

A student-teacher puppeteer brought some marionettes to a school for a workshop with children. In one of the upper primary classes a student was so frightened of the puppets that they would not touch them or even look at them—let alone take part in the workshop.

VIGNETTE 4

A student teacher wanted to use the theme 'The Circus', with a lower primary class. As soon as she asked the students what they wanted to be in the circus, they all demonstrated at once—tightrope walking on tables, turning over chairs to escape lions and becoming slapstick clowns. For safety reasons, the activity had to be immediately curtailed.

VIGNETTE 5

When visiting a school, a student teacher asked what multicultural resources were being used in the class. The teacher answered that there was not a cultural mix of students in the class, so there was no need to share stories from different cultures.

For reflection

Consider your own background, current skills and experience. What can you bring to your role as a drama mentor? What areas will you work to develop?

Review of Part One

Part One: Introducing Drama: Parameters and Possibilities focused on drama's contribution to society and to education, with particular emphasis on drama's benefits for students. There was also focus on what a teacher needs to know to function effectively as a drama mentor.

Preview

Part Two is entitled, Maximising Learning: Drama in the Curriculum and consists of Chapters 3, 4 and 5.

Chapter 3: Systematic Planning for Drama considers the levels at which planning for drama occurs within the curriculum development and evaluation process with attention given to subject syllabi, scope and sequence documents, and drama programming in the classroom. Evaluation strategies for drama are also highlighted.

Maximising Learning: Drama in the Curriculum

PART TWO

Objectives

By the end of this section you should be able to:

- Understand the planning process for implementing drama within the school context and the classroom;
- Relate drama to a range of learning models, from those which focus on learning within individual subjects to full subject integration; and
- Identify the role that drama can play in students' social learning.

Part One of this book introduced drama and set it within its historical, cultural and contemporary contexts as well as providing drama mentors with key concepts and strategies. Part Two examines in more depth the role that drama can play in learning in the classroom. Chapter 3 presents a planning process for drama, taking into consideration the broader educational and school contexts and the specific classroom. Evaluation strategies from the perspective of drama as both a process and a product are considered. Chapter 4 shows how drama can be the means for integrating learning within a key learning area and across the curriculum, while Chapter 5 examines the role that drama can play in social learning.

Systematic Planning
for Drama

'Much of the work generated in the drama classroom is fragile and by its very nature, somewhat ephemeral' (Dunn 2005).

Introduction

In this chapter the planning process for implementing drama within the school context and in the classroom is examined. A discussion of the role of subject syllabi and the importance of scope and sequence planning precedes a framework for use in developing a specific drama lesson. Finally, evaluation methods are examined with particular emphasis on ways to collect evidence about student participation and lesson impact and how to provide constructive feedback to students.

Drama: The planning process

Planning involves taking into consideration the student learning needs, the specific school situation, and curriculum subject outcomes in order to create an overview of the content and skills to be addressed during schooling. Learning continua may be within a particular grade, grade range or extend beyond primary school grade groupings to provide a whole-school perspective. Planning for classroom drama implementation, then, must be viewed within the broader perspective of curriculum planning within the school context.

Educational authorities within Australian states and territories have developed curricula for various subjects or clusters of subjects, also called **key learning areas**. Policy statements, syllabi and support documents that provide units of work are produced for use in schools. In practice, these are applied and adapted to meet the educational learning needs of students in individual schools.

Within such documents drama is described as one of the 'creative arts' (New South Wales) or 'arts' (Queensland), along with music, dance, visual arts and media. The different states and territories in Australia have developed guidelines (i.e. policy statements, syllabi and support documents) that provide assistance for teachers in integrating drama into learning at primary, middle and secondary school levels. In New South Wales (*Creative Arts K-6 Syllabus*) and Queensland (*The Arts: Years 1–10 Syllabus*), for example, there are outcomes-based approaches to drama, presented as 'Making, Performing and Appreciating' in New South Wales and 'Forming, Presenting, and Responding' in Queensland. These **outcomes-based** syllabi provide a 'developmental framework' that indicates what students are to 'know' and 'do' at different stages (i.e. levels) (Stinson 2000). These syllabi are part of an ongoing planning and evaluation process in which achievement is based on students demonstrating an outcome at a particular stage/level before they move on to the next one.

An outcomes-based syllabus enables teachers to select specific outcomes and develop lessons that help students meet these outcomes. Stinson (2000) points out that to do this effectively teachers first must know their students and what 'prior knowledge' they have, then 'understand where in the total continuum of learning the outcome lies'. Assessment must relate to the whole outcome and at what level the student meets this outcome must be assessed in different contexts (Dunn 2005). The overall philosophy of an outcomes-based approach, then, is that 'all students can achieve given sufficient time, access and resources' (Stinson 2000, p. 15). Curriculum documents, such as these, are essential source materials in systematic planning for drama within schools.

Systematic planning for drama

Within the school context, planning for drama may occur at several levels: whole-school, at grade (or stage) level, and at the individual classroom level.

Drama's role and emphasis in learning may vary depending on whether it is perceived as a skill or process, a learning method, or as an area of study in its own right. When drama is a subject of study it may be viewed independently or as a strand in an integrated creative arts approach along with visual arts, music, dance and media arts. As a subject, drama's elements and forms receive specific focus in stand-alone sessions or in a series of sequenced lessons. When whole-school or grade/stage planning for drama is undertaken it is usually part of a total-school curriculum development process. Together, teachers collaboratively plan the scope and sequence of the learning program for their school year keeping both the learning needs of students and curriculum outcomes in mind.

Understanding scope and sequence

A **scope and sequence document** is an educational tool developed in a school to identify what is to be taught, in what order, and at what level. This planning map assists in the organisation of learning at a local level within and across subjects by showing where specific subject knowledge and skills fit into the overall learning program. In creating a scope and sequence document, teachers draw on their knowledge of student needs, interests and development levels, content knowledge, and existing policy and curriculum documents (e.g. outcomes based syllabi).

Scope and sequence documents (sometimes called 'charts') are advantageous because teachers can see at a glance what areas are to be covered, in what sequence and at what level. This means that the overall learning program can be designed to avoid overlap and repetition and to achieve balance within and among subjects. Designing the scope and sequence document around the **spiral principle** enables knowledge and skills in a particular area to be revisited at different times during a student's learning career at school with increasing levels of complexity as students' understandings increase.

At its most fully developed, the scope and sequence document maps the territory of student learning with an ongoing flow of carefully planned experiences based on a graduated sequence of ideas and skills extending from preschool through primary school and into the middle school and secondary school years. School Planning for Drama: A Scope and Sequence Document (Concept Box 3.1) discusses the steps to be taken in whole-school planning for drama.

Concept Box 3.1

School planning for drama: A scope and sequence document

Taking steps

Within a whole-school or grade/stage context:

1   Conduct a review of the current drama program at each grade level to identify what is currently being covered.
2   Review the outcomes from syllabus documents that relate to drama.
3   Reassess the local school learning environment in relation to student needs and other relevant factors.
    With (1), (2) and (3) in mind:
4   Determine concept categories or activity areas that relate to the subject or subject cluster (e.g. drama and/or the creative arts).
5   Identify or develop possible units and learning experiences that will help students achieve the outcomes in these concept categories or activity areas.
6   Within each chosen category list all the possible units of study; then arrange them by relevance and/or level of difficulty. When several experiences meet the same outcome but cannot be included due to lack of time, choose one of the possibilities.
7   Create scope charts for each grade using the categories and units/learning experiences chosen.
8   Put learning into a sequence that moves from basic to more complex knowledge and skills. At each stage consider and document students' prior knowledge and the outcomes to be met.
9   Identify and document the resources available within the school and the wider community to support learning for each component.

Drama Forms: Scope and Sequence (Concept Box 3.2) provides one abridged example of a planning chart developed around selected drama forms for a hypothetical primary school. Although limited in its scope, this chart, nonetheless, shows how four selected drama forms could be developed sequentially across the primary grades. In addition to the categories listed, the learning outcomes to be met and the specific activities to be implemented need consideration.

Concept Box 3.2

Drama forms: Scope and sequence

Scenario

SITUATION

Teachers at Glen Cove Primary School developed a scope and sequence chart for drama to overcome the perceived overlap and repetition in how drama forms were approached at the various grade levels in their school.

SEQUENCE

At each grade level, the coverage of the drama forms builds on what students have previously learned in earlier grades, thus taking into consideration their prior knowledge.

SCOPE

The drama forms were selected from a wider range of options. Reading across the scope shows at a glance the drama learning areas for each grade level. Teachers can treat these individually or group them together when appropriate; for example, in Kindergarten, students could make finger puppets to represent characters in the told story or, in Year 5, students could use life-size puppets to tell individual stories.

FURTHER ACTION

A range of units of study or learning experiences can be developed to meet each of these grade level drama areas. Teachers select those that are most relevant to the needs and interests of their students and appropriate to learning outcomes.

NOTES

Sample units of work are provided in curriculum support documents in conjunction with subject syllabi from state and territory education authorities. These can be examined for their relevance and adapted to the local situation, when appropriate.

For demonstration purposes in this example, the learning outcomes for drama are taken from *Creative Arts K-6 Syllabus* (Board of Studies NSW 2000). In 'actual' situations, drama outcomes in the relevant state syllabi would be used; also, special local needs would be identified and catered for during the development of the scope and sequence chart.

Years 5 and 6

LEARNING OUTCOMES

1   Develops a range of in-depth and sustained roles.
2   Interprets and conveys dramatic meaning by using the elements of drama and a range of movement and voice skills in a variety of drama forms.
3   Devises, acts and rehearses drama for performance to an audience.
4   Responds critically to a range of drama works and performance styles.

		Improvisation and role play	Story making, telling and dramatising	Puppet making and operating	Readers' theatre
Sequence ↑	Year 6	Participates in talk back, play back and Theatresports forms; prepares a character monologue for performance; provides feedback to others on their performances	Participates in a storytelling festival; tells individual stories to a larger group; provides feedback to others on their stories	Makes basic marionettes and performs with them, focusing on meaningful movement; provides feedback to others on their puppet plays	Writes an original readers' theatre script; with a group stages and presents it for an audience; provides feedback to others on their presentations
↓	Year 5	Takes part in issue-based improvisations and role plays; with particular focus on drama elements of symbol and time	Tells individual stories in small groups; with emphasis on vocal variety, pacing and storytelling skills	Makes and performs with life-size puppets; focuses on developing the puppet character's voice and movement	Explores options for staging readers' theatre scripts; takes part in a readers' theatre presentation for an audience

← ————————————————— Scope ————————————————— →

Years 3 and 4

LEARNING OUTCOMES

1 Takes on and sustains roles in a variety of drama forms to express meaning in a wide range of imagined situations.
2 Builds the action of the drama by using the elements of drama, movement and voice skills.
3 Sequences the action of the drama to create meaning for an audience.
4 Responds to, and interprets drama experiences and performances.

		Improvisation and role play	Story making, telling and dramatising	Puppet making and operating	Readers' theatre
Sequence	Year 4	Role plays using mantle of expert and improvisations with teacher in role	Dramatises stories with focus on drama elements, particularly use of space, focus, contrast, tension, mood	Makes and uses shadow puppets in performance for an audience	Combines short scripts into one longer program for presentation in readers' theatre form
	Year 3	Role plays as characters from a story; focus on character motivations and feelings	Explores a range of options for making and telling stories	Makes and uses rod puppets; develops puppet characterisations using voice and movement	Develops a script from an original story; presents story in readers' theatre form

←——————————————— Scope ———————————————→

Years 1 and 2

LEARNING OUTCOMES

1 Takes on roles in drama to explore familiar and imagined situations.
2 Conveys story, depicts events and expresses feelings by using the elements of drama and the expressive skills of movement and voice.
3 Interacts collaboratively to communicate the action of drama with others.
4 Appreciates drama work during the making of their own drama and the drama of others.

	Improvisation and role play	Story making, telling and dramatising	Puppet making and operating	Readers' theatre
Year 2	Improvises stories in role	Creates circle stories about actual events; with other group members contributes a line of the story	Makes and uses sock puppets; focuses on puppet personalities and feelings	With others in a group, presents picture book texts as readers' theatre scripts; learns about vocal expressiveness and projection
Year 1	Role plays in 'actual' and 'as if' worlds	Creates group sound stories with others using voice and movement	Makes and uses paper bag puppets and in groups creates a simple puppet play	Participates in group presentations with some students using scripts and others miming

Sequence →

← ———————————————— Scope ————————————————→

Kindergarten or entry level at school

LEARNING OUTCOMES:

1 Uses imagination and the elements of drama in imaginative play and dramatic situations.
2 Dramatises personal experiences using movement, space and objects.
3 Responds to dramatic performances.

	Improvisation and role play	Story making, telling and dramatisting	Puppet making and operating	Readers' theatre
	Engages in free play and role plays from life experiences, using different types of space (e.g. common, personal, shared)	Participates as the mentor tells stories; provides sound and action for told stories	Makes and uses finger puppets to create dialogue with others and share poems and songs	Mimes story action as mentor reads script

Sequence

← ———————————————— Scope ————————————————→

Consistency and coherency in the scope and sequence document are the product of collaborative school planning that works through ideas in the process of developing shared philosophies, beliefs and understandings towards the arts and their role in learning. This in-depth collaboration among staff may also result in the desire to develop a 'school creative arts policy' to assist in future planning and development.

Because scope and sequence documents are most frequently developed within the local school context, teachers use these documents to guide the planning and development of their individual classroom programs. A scope and sequence document helps teachers to balance the content within drama and, when scope and sequence charts exist for other subjects, it also enables the teacher to determine priorities and inter-relationships between drama and other key learning areas.

Understanding programming

Programming is 'the process of selecting and sequencing learning experiences for a class, groups, and individuals to develop understanding and skills and achieve outcomes' (Board of Studies NSW 2000). The individual planning document that a classroom teacher develops and follows on a day-to-day basis in the classroom is called a teacher's program. When programming, the teacher draws on knowledge of the students, their needs and prior learning; curriculum policies, syllabi and support documents, and relates these to the school scope and sequence document (once one has been developed).

Within the classroom, learning experiences are usually developed around units of work that can be short or longer in duration. In drama these units can focus on drama elements and their applications (e.g. How drama elements are used in staging plays), forms of drama (e.g. improvisation, readers' theatre) or a theme that integrates other art forms (e.g. 'making silent films'). In short, classroom programs are a record of intention for what content and skills will be covered during a specified period (e.g. term, school year) to meet outcomes, and how these areas will be evaluated and assessed. In creating programs, teachers need to make opportunities for links to other subject areas and to make these programs relevant to the diversity of student interests, backgrounds and ability levels within the class.

Developing a drama lesson

Drama uses interactive, improvisational approaches, but this does not mean that lessons are unplanned. The Lesson Plan Template (Concept Box 3.3) is a guide for developing and documenting a drama session under the sections: session name, outcomes, student prior knowledge, structure and content, resources required and evaluation strategies.

Concept Box **3.3**

Lesson plan template

1   Session name—(What is the title or theme?)
2   Outcomes –(What specific outcomes at what stage?)
    – *Drama*
    – *Subject* (If drama is being used in conjunction with other key learning areas, what are they and what are the outcomes?)
    – *Learner* (What are the levels of involvement or expected attitudes and behaviours?)
3   Student prior knowledge
4   Structure and content
    – *Warm-up*—This section provides the introduction and orientation to the lesson.
    – *Body of lesson*—This section gives the drama (and other subject) activities showing their sequence and inter-relationships.
    – *Cool down period*—This section provides the mental and/or physical debriefing for students.
5   Resources required—These are the materials needed for the lesson.
6   Evaluation strategies—These are the ways the mentor/students will judge the lesson.

Identifying outcomes

Carefully considering appropriate outcomes and how a lesson can be struc-tured to help children achieve these is important, whether the lesson is part of a larger series of sequenced drama episodes or an individual 'stand alone' session. To make decisions about what content is appropriate, Stinson (2000, p. 17) points out that it is essential to 'unpack' the outcome by understanding how it fits into the level below it and above it in the syllabus. Once this is done, all the ways in which this outcome can be demonstrated are considered with the most appropriate activities being arranged into a meaningful learning order. In addition to focusing on specific creative-arts outcomes related to drama elements and forms, drama may be used as a medium to support learning outcomes in other key learning areas.

Student prior knowledge

When a mentor takes into consideration students' prior knowledge in planning a lesson, it demonstrates for learners that their past experiences and previous learning are valued. Such acknowledgment builds rapport between the mentor and students and, also, helps the group find common ground. Shared experiences provide a relevant, motivating entry point into drama. That is why it is important to consider student prior knowledge as an essential part of lesson planning for drama.

STRUCTURE AND CONTENT

Once the appropriate outcomes are selected, a workable lesson structure for the content is designed. In general, this involves: (1) the **warm-up**, (2) the body of the lesson, and (3) the **cool down period**, each of which will be discussed in turn.

The warm-up phase has the function of preparing students for the body of the lesson to follow. Warm-ups may include physical movement, vocal exercises, cooperative group interaction activities, or mental preparation through visualisation or setting the scene. (Refer to exercises in Chapters 6–8). When these initial activities relate in content or process to the body of the lesson that follows, a smooth transition and coherence between the two stages can be achieved.

The body of the lesson benefits from a 'spine' or what Heathcote (1984) calls the 'central idea' out of which the activities develop. This central core needs to be 'contextualised' with regard to students' interests and abilities as well as the intended learning outcomes. As a 'coherent through line' (McLean 1994, p. 44), this pivotal idea can be an issue (e.g. using time wisely), a subject or cross-curricular study (e.g. simple machines), a drama element (e.g. understanding focus) or a drama form (e.g. communicating through mime). Once the idea is chosen, drama tasks relating to it need to be planned and sequenced in meaningful order (Bolton & Heathcote 1999, p. 22). Consider how the ways presented in Organisational Patterns for a Drama Lesson (Concept Box 3.4) can be used to organise the body of a lesson and the learning tasks within it.

Concept Box 3.4

Organisational patterns for a drama lesson

Pattern	Explanation
Chronological, time order	Follow in order the steps needed to complete a process: step 1, step 2, step 3 (e.g. folding a paper puppet).
Nature of participation	Work from individual, to partner, to entire group tasks (e.g. mime building a wall alone, with a partner, all together).
Order of importance	Start with the main idea, then work on ideas that lead into it or follow from it. In tableau, students depict an achievement (e.g. climbing Mt. Everest). Then they create the still photo that comes before this central photo and the one that comes after it. This series of photos can be run in order, in reverse order, or be changed to show a different outcome.
Spatial	Assign different tasks to different spaces. For example, the warm-up and cool down occur in one part of the room; the body of the lesson in another. Movement between the spaces literally signals a change in direction for the lesson.
Energy level	Recognise tasks that require low, medium and high energy levels. Arrange the tasks appropriately for the lesson. (e.g. end the lesson with a low-energy activity, a 'cool down').
Control	Consider who controls each task, the teacher or the student? Gradually move from teacher-controlled to student-controlled activities.

Ultimately, the way lesson segments are organised may be influenced by a range of factors, including the prior experience of students with drama, the nature of the subject matter and the level of the outcome to be met.

The cool down period (Moore 1988, p. 40) is the time when children shift mentally from the 'as if' world back to the 'actual' world leaving behind the roles they played with their associated attitudes, moods and behaviours. This process, called de-roling, helps students make the transition from 'role playing someone else' to 'being oneself'. This shift may be achieved by means of discussion about what happened when they were in role (e.g. When you played the part of the policeman, how did you feel when you arrived at the scene of the accident?). Relaxation and breathing exercises are another way to help them make the transition (e.g. Close your eyes. We are leaving the space station and slowly returning to earth). Physical activity (e.g. drama games) can also change the focus, shift the mood, or alter the energy level of the group. In short, during this essential phase of the lesson, students debrief on both a mental and physical level.

Resources required

The range of resources used during a drama lesson varies considerably depending on which activities are chosen to support the central core of the lesson. Music, puppets, readers' theatre scripts, drawings, hats, masks and props are all possibilities. On the other hand, the attraction of drama is that, in many cases, no resources are needed at all except the imaginations of the students and a workable space.

Evaluation strategies

Strategies for evaluation are usually employed throughout a drama lesson. In addition to assessing student learning outcomes, a teacher may want to judge how well the drama process worked, asking such questions as: How well did the lesson flow? Were the transitions between activities managed effectively? How actively did the students participate? What is the quality of the drama products students created? Has student participation improved from the last drama session? To make such judgments teachers will need to decide on appropriate criteria and then apply methods for collecting and recording the evidence on which to base their evaluations (Stinson 2000,

p. 17). An overview of the terms, concepts and methods used to evaluate drama are discussed more fully in the following section, Drama evaluation.

Drama evaluation

An overview

This section provides a more in-depth treatment of evaluation as it relates to the drama planning process. First, a number of interrelated terms need explanation. The broad term **evaluation** implies that a judgment is to be made. When evaluating a drama lesson, this appraisal can occur at any stage. If evaluations happen throughout the lesson, the evaluation is known as **formative**. The advantage with this approach is that participants have the opportunity to adjust and make changes, if necessary. If an evaluation occurs at the end of a process, it is called **summative**; for example, when a mentor waits until a drama session finishes to evaluate how well students participated. A mentor can combine both formative and summative approaches to evaluation into an overall evaluation strategy.

Feedback can be in the form of either a **description** or an evaluation that provides observations, statements or a running commentary on what is happening. Mentors can provide feedback to individual students or the group during or after a drama activity. However, the teacher is usually not the only, nor even the main, source of feedback. Students themselves become an essential part of the feedback cycle as they de-role, debrief and reflect on their own work, whether it is an improvisational role play or a staged performance.

When the term **assessment** is used in education it usually refers to a teacher's formal evaluation of student progress. This result (e.g. grade, mark, comment) can be used to motivate a student, to diagnose a learning difficulty, to inform parents of their child's progress, to predict future student achievement, to select particular students for certain responsibilities or awards, to assign a rank or grade on a formal report, or to make the student and the school known in the wider community. Specifically, in an outcomes-based approach to the curriculum, assessment relates to whether an individual student meets target outcomes at the designated levels across the key learning areas.

The process of evaluation

In drama the debate about what to evaluate, how to evaluate it, or whether to evaluate at all is ongoing. The controversy intensifies when drama is perceived as *only* a 'process' or *only* a 'product' instead of as a continuum along which a range of perspectives lie with evaluation possible at any given point. The following sections cut across this debate viewing evaluation as a progression of steps involving collecting and recording evidence, analysing evidence and reporting findings based on the evidence.

COLLECTING AND RECORDING EVIDENCE

Keeping an ongoing record or 'evidence gathering' (Dunn 2005) is essential to the evaluation process. Teachers as 'evaluators' have a number of options open to them both for observing and recording evidence of student involvement and for approaching the evaluation of drama products systematically.

Observing student participation

When drama process is the focus, a central component of evaluation is an analysis of student participation. Overall, evaluators ask: How does the group function as a whole? Sharing tasks, a willingness to work together towards **conspectus**, the ability to problem solve and to overcome potential conflicts are all characteristics of a group that evidences communality. Self respect and respect for others are judged by the ways in which the members of the group support one another in working to achieve a common goal through the drama process.

How each individual contributes to the group is also an important feature to consider when evaluating student participation. Evaluators ask: Is each student participating and at what level? How do individual students interact within the group; for example, are they 'talkers, processors, participant observers, or listeners/outsiders' (Warner 1997)? With regard to the 'quality' (i.e. nature) of student involvement, McKone (1997) suggests three levels: action, personal relevance and meaning making.

When a student participates, yet seems unaware of the purpose for doing so, he or she is functioning at a basic action level. A student who engages in a drama activity because of its perceived relevance to personal interests and a concept of self-worth is operating at a personal-relevance level. When a student shows 'high-level initiative' through being aware of how the drama impacts on self and others and takes a leadership role in the interaction helping others gain more from the experience, the highest level, meaning making has been reached.

If evaluators decide to use student participation as an evaluation approach, they develop criteria by which to assess the participation. They then observe students. When the criteria relate to identifiable outcomes, the evaluators observe the students in a range of contexts in order to 'gather as wide an array' of evidence as possible to use in determining whether a student has met a given outcome (Dunn 2005, pp 3–4).

Using checklists and rating scales

Checklists and rating scales are an efficient means for collecting information about the nature and extent of student participation. A checklist asks observers to record for each item whether a criterion has been met (e.g. a tick or an X), whereas a rating scale requires observers to give an indication of the level at which the criterion for each item has been met based on specified indicators. Rating Student Interaction (Concept Box 3.5) is an example of a rating scale.

Concept Box 3.5

Rating student interaction

One approach is for observers to rate a student's level of interaction in an arts activity according to indicators such as the ones developed by Schiller and Veale (1989, p. 9).

Circle the level at which the student interacts:

1   a single trial attempt
2   more extended but personal involvement
3   social cooperation with at least one other child
4   cooperative project planned and executed by children

Depending on the focus for the evaluation, other rating scales can be developed.

Monitoring these checklists or rating scales over time helps teachers identify how individual children participate, including any gaps or changes in their involvement. However, as Dunn (2005, p. 3) points out, it is not possible to monitor all participants at the same time, so teachers will need to choose particular children for 'focussed observation' in any given drama session.

Using technology

Audio, video and photographic images taken during drama interactions can be kept as a record of what happened and how children responded to it (Dunn 2005, p. 4; Schiller & Veale 1989, p. 7). Over time, teachers may want to keep a 'digital portfolio' of such episodes as an aid to reflection about student and group progress in drama. As useful as these records can be in reconstructing classroom drama activities, making and archiving digital records need to be done in conjunction with the school policy on student confidentiality.

Keeping a journal

Teachers themselves can keep a daily journal in which they record events and reflections about children's changing interests and their develop-mental progress. (Schiller & Veale 1989, p. 7). Within this journal they can also record anecdotal evidence of what is happening to the class as a whole or to individual students. Teachers may choose to feature students whose drama work 'stood out' for some reason. This may take the form of 'thoughts and responses in relation to the work they have just witnessed' or a vignette that serves to provide detailed insight into a situation (Dunn 2005, p. 3).

Gathering student responses

In addition to teacher observation, it is important to find out from the participants themselves what they experienced and their evaluations of it. Worth remembering here is that '[t]he meanings that students attach to experiences are not necessarily the meanings that their teachers would ascribe' (Innes, Moss & Smigiel 2001, p. 212) For this reason, student responses, in combination with teacher observation and insights, enable the development of a more 'authentic' evaluation of a drama interaction than either teacher or student evaluation alone could claim.

Individual self-evaluation

During or following a drama activity, teachers can survey students about what they learned, including their knowledge, attitudes and feelings. Written feedback can be collected by means of a questionnaire. When gathering written responses, older children can be given a questionnaire based on a **Likert scale** that requires them to rate their views on each question under value categories (e.g. from 1 least favourable to 5 most favourable). Questions about a drama activity can relate to their level of interest, enjoyment, comfort and depth of perceived learning. Older children can also be encouraged to keep a learning log of their drama experiences. For younger children, a simplified visual feedback form can be used consisting of three different faces: one smiling, one neutral and one frowning. Young students are asked to colour in or circle the face that best describes how they feel about the session.

Feedback from children can also be verbal, gathered by means of a conversational interview. When using this approach, the evaluator must listen closely to determine what a child means by what he or she says. Asking for explanations and carefully probing for further detail can help the mentor understand the ways that individual children express themselves and their drama learning. Listening to student talk also helps teachers evaluate **aesthetic engagement**, a state characterised by 'animation, connection and heightened awareness' (Bundy 2005). To be 'animated' is to be 'alive', 'alert', with a feeling of 'invigoration' in response to an artistic work or, in the case of process drama, to the dramatic engagement. To be 'connected' is to relate to an idea or ideas stimulated by an art work or process, but not directly contained within it. To have 'heightened awareness' is to experience a connection beyond the immediate drama encounter, leaving participants thinking about new things or having fresh insights. Listening to the language students use to describe their experiences and watching their level of enthusiasm as evidenced in vocal tone and physical response can help the mentor evaluate the extent to which students have been 'aesthetically engaged' with an artistic work or drama process.

Another way for children to respond to a drama experience is by using another creative arts medium to synthesise their understandings, attitudes and feelings. Writing a poem or song, drawing a picture or making a clay sculpture, or developing a mime or dance drama, enables them to apply understanding gained in one situation to another. Teachers gain insight into a student's perspective by talking with him or her about the artistic work. A general probe, such as, 'Can you tell me about what you've made?', initiates the dialogue. From these interactions, teachers come to understand the personal meaning that a student attaches both to the art work and to the drama that inspired it. Student Self-Evaluation (From the Classroom 3.1) provides an example of how one student teacher used self-evaluation with her class.

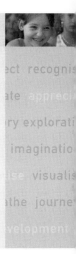

From the Classroom 3.1

Student self-evaluation

Tina wanted to find out from her second grade students what they had learned from a drama lesson using the student self-evaluation approach. She says she chose self-evaluation because: '[It] is a useful tool in the teaching and learning process. It helps students reflect on what they learn which encourages high-order thinking. Also, the teacher can learn from students' comments by finding out areas of strength and weakness and things to improve for future lessons.'

Group feedback

The drama session itself is often punctuated by student responses to the ongoing action. This occurs during debriefing from a specific activity or at any other point in the drama where the students stop for in-depth reflection involving clarification, prediction, questioning, problem solving and hypothesising. Such in-drama discussion and debate enables students to demonstrate cognitively that they 'know and comprehend', and that they can 'apply, analyse, synthesis and evaluate ideas' (Bloom 1956).

As a more formal evaluation tool, the teacher may form small **focus groups** of six to eight children to reflect back on a drama session together. Pre-arranged or spontaneously developed topics (e.g. What did you think of … ; How well do you think … ; What would you have done differently?) are presented and children contribute their views to the group discussion with one person's ideas building on another's. Focus-group discussions are generally fast-paced with many ideas presented. For this reason the teacher, who usually asks the questions, may choose to audio record the session in order to remember the range of ideas. The aim of gathering student responses, whether they are in written or oral form, is to get at the 'experiences, knowledge and understandings of students' (Innes, Moss & Smigiel 2001, p. 212). Group Reflection on Drama Learning (From the Classroom 3.2) shows the way Jodie, a student teacher, used group reflection with her upper primary class to gain insight into a series of drama exercises.

From the Classroom 3.2

Group reflection on drama learning

Jodie discusses how she used group reflection to evaluate drama learning in a session she conducted with Year 6 students entitled, 'Sense of Self through Imagination' that used Imaginary Object Pass, Balloon Trip, and Monet's Garden (Activity Boxes 6.4, 6.5, 6.7).

> After everyone had a go [at Imaginary Object Pass], we stayed where we were on the floor and had a class discussion on what the students had learnt so far about drama and what the activities meant to them. This was meant to encourage the students to self-reflect. They each wrote down their favourite and least favourite activities with reasons why. In this final reflection stage the students were very positive about their drama experience and what they had learnt. To my surprise their explanations of the term 'imagination' were very detailed and thoughtful. In general, their favourite activity was Imaginary Object Pass because they could choose an object they really liked and they enjoyed trying to guess what each other's objects were ... The next day I also conducted a few general conversations with students about the lesson to gain some [additional] feedback.

In summary, there is a range of evaluation strategies that can be implemented as part of a process drama approach to learning. Mentors need to consider carefully the purpose for evaluation, at what point evaluation can be most effectively introduced and how best to collect the evidence on which to make their judgments.

ANALYSING EVIDENCE

Once the evidence is collected and recorded, an evaluation needs to be made. The data that will form the basis for this evaluation can be numerical (e.g. number of ticks) or narrative (e.g. vignette) form. Somehow, all of it must be consolidated into an appraisal. Two data verification approaches known to researchers, namely **triangulation** and **crystallisation,** are helpful to the evaluator who is faced with compiling and analysing evidence in order to make a judgment (Taylor 1996; Denzin & Lincoln 1994). When evidence is triangulated, it means that different data-collection methods or sources of information are examined to determine what they reveal. For example, a teacher may look at a rating scale and comments kept about a student's level of participation in a drama session, review audio-taped reflections from the same student about how he or she regarded the participation in that session, and refer to videotape footage that documented this lesson. The aim of triangulating the evidence is to find the points at which these sources intersect (e.g. are similar, complementary, have things in common) as the basis for developing a composite view of how this student participated; a view that can be supported with reference to more than one source of evidence.

Crystallisation, instead of aiming to discover the common points at which the data intersect, instead has the goal of illuminating the evidence as a whole with all its potential discrepancies (i.e. 'warts and all'). Because how we see things depends on our 'angle of repose' (Taylor 1996, p. 45), it is important that observations are made from a range of perspectives. The evidence gathered in this way is used to construct a multifaceted evaluation indicating the child's areas of strength in drama and those that need development. For example, a child may excel in individual expression, but have difficulty relating to others during group work; or the student may participate well in improvisation but not in a staged performance. The purpose of the evaluation, ranging from the mentor trying to confirm an intuitive feeling about the group on the one hand to the writing of official reports for each student on the other, will determine the amount, level and type of evidence required and how it is compiled.

REPORTING EVIDENCE

How the evidence is reported again depends on the purpose for which it will be used. Some teachers keep digital records for their own future use in planning. In other cases, evidence is accumulated as part of the assessment process for a student's school report. Students themselves may keep records of their work in personal portfolios, or to share in a classroom or school-based display. Teachers may choose to share selected records with parents during parent-teacher conferences, or include a report on drama in the curriculum in a newsletter sent to parents and other school stakeholders (Schiller & Veale 1989, pp. 7–8).

In summary, developing a systematic approach to evaluating drama lessons can contribute to a mentor's increased understanding of how students participate in the drama process and of the impact that these sessions have on student learning. The results of such evaluation can demonstrate for teachers, parents and others the benefits of using drama in the classroom.

Drama product evaluation

A drama product is a tangible creation made during or at the culmination of a drama process. This artistic product can take a range of forms including a written script, dance drama, verbal monologue, playbuilt performance, puppet play, storytelling session or readers' theatre presentation, to name a few. When the creation of a drama product is the main focus, teachers may feel pressured (or even be required) to provide an evaluation of its 'quality' to include as part of a student's formal assessment.

The incongruity here is that most drama theorists and practitioners emphasise student development over product development. Nonetheless, drama, when conceptualised as a continuum, has many legitimate points along its span for engagement from the interaction of process drama to the design of an artistic product. When a student is perceived as a 'creative artist', his or her 'productions' become part of the work of the broader artistic community. Like other 'creators', a student dramatic 'artist' benefits from evaluative feedback (e.g. How do others receive their work? How does the standard of their work compare with other creative output in the same genre?). In many cases, the main difference between a student and a practising dramatic artist (e.g. actor, director, designer, puppeteer, storyteller, choreographer) is not what they do, but the amount of experience each has. When students are not made aware of the quality of their products and where there is room for improvement, they are being denied the opportunity to grow as dramatic artists.

When assessment of the drama product is the aim, criteria are developed against which to judge its quality, or where there are already pre-existing standards (e.g. speech associations, eisteddfod guidelines) the drama product can be judged against these. Having applied the criteria, teachers may choose to write a critique for the student's own benefit or as part of the formal assessment record. Buchanan (n.d.) suggests that such a critique can be prescriptive, descriptive or developmental. A **prescriptive critique** is teacher-centred and focuses on what the 'critic' sees as the strengths and weaknesses of the work from his or her perspective.

Descriptive and developmental critiques invite more student engagement with the product evaluation process. In a **descriptive critique** the observer presents what they have received from the work—not what they think they should have received. In this way students are able to decide whether what they intended is actually conveyed by their work to those viewing it. Non-judgmental, this critique provokes thought within the student and is not a means for comparing one person's work with another's (Buchanan, n.d.).

A **developmental critique** involves an appraisal of a student's drama product at various stages. The 'improvement' from one stage to the next is what is judged, whether this product consists of the subsequent drafts of a script or the videotaped records of a dance drama's development. In this approach, student 'dramatists' may also be given the opportunity to assist the assessor in developing the criteria by which their product will be judged. Improvement rather than final product 'quality' is the key feature of this approach (Buchanan, n.d.).

When judging a performance, such as a children's play, puppet play or a dance drama, Whitmore's concept of theatrical systems (1994) is a useful framework. Although originally intended for theatre directors, the systems and signs identified are also useful for those evaluating productions. Each system provides a lens or framework through which a performance can be viewed such as 'the performers', the 'visual' and 'aural' systems, and 'the audience', to name those of particular relevance.

When focusing on the performer system, the evaluator can judge how effectively the actor plays a part using voice, facial expression, gesture and movement, as well as employing personal charisma. The visual aspects of a production can be evaluated in relation to how space, setting, costumes, properties (i.e. props), lighting and colour are used, while the aural systems can be judged in relation to how effectively music and sound are used. Although the audience system has a number of signs attached to it, audience communication, which consists of applause, talking, movement, gestures, sounds and laughter, is of particular use (Whitmore 1994, pp. 61–62). Watching for these signs during a performance can help an evaluator determine whether an audience is engaged or disengaged, an appraisal that can contribute to the overall evaluation of the production.

Peer Evaluation (From the Classroom 3.3) provides examples of questions that were asked during a peer evaluation session with an upper primary class.

From the Classroom 3.3

Peer evaluation

Kristy-lee discusses how she used peer evaluation with an **opportunity class** of 5th graders (i.e. class of students identified as gifted and talented) to provide feedback on a readers' theatre performance. Each class member filled out a written evaluation of the performance answering the following questions:

- How well were the students able to be heard in the audience?
- Were students talking into the script or did they refer to it only when required?
- What did you enjoy most about this adaptation?
- What could this group do to improve on their performance?

This feedback was given directly to the group after the performance. There was positive interaction and discussion of the responses as they were read aloud. Kristy-lee believes the feedback provided was 'successful in its evaluation outcomes'.

In summary, dramatic products take a range of forms from scripts to performances. Product evaluation, when it occurs, can be the role of the teacher or it can be shared with the individual or the group responsible for the creation. The purpose for the evaluation (e.g. motivational, formal assessment) usually determines who performs the evaluation and how it is conducted.

Summary

This chapter introduced systematic planning for drama and examined a range of ways to approach drama evaluation in an educational setting. Of course, no single way of evaluating is appropriate in all circumstances. Nonetheless, if drama is not to be marginalised within the curriculum there needs to be ways to assess its effectiveness in the learning environment through an examination of its processes and products. When curriculum outcomes are used as the basis for student assessment in drama it is important to view these in a wide range of contexts in order to make an informed judgment about whether an outcome has been reached. In all of the approaches to drama evaluation the students and their learning are central.

For further study

1 Examine several different scope and sequence plans for drama and/or the creative arts. What are their similarities and differences?
2 Develop a drama lesson using the Lesson Plan Template (Concept Box 3.3). With a group of young people in a school or community setting, implement this plan and evaluate the session using strategies suggested in this chapter.
3 Discuss the advantages and disadvantages of the following evaluation approaches: observation of children, checklists and rating scales, written questionnaires, conversational interviews with individual children and group feedback sessions with young people.

For reflection

Debate the statement: 'Every drama session should be evaluated.' What are the arguments for and against this position? Where do you stand on this issue and why?

Preview

Chapter 4: Integrated Learning through Drama considers the role that drama can play in a range of learning approaches from no or limited subject integration to a fully integrated approach.

Integrated Learning Through Drama

'Drama affords students the opportunities to develop understandings that move beyond subject-specific, skills-based outcomes' (Innes, Moss & Smigiel 2001).

Introduction

The reality of life in the 21st century is that it is fast-paced, information and change-oriented, technologically driven and global in its outlook. On a daily basis people face complex issues and confront contradictory ways of doing things. In order for young people to cope with the complexities of modern life and find their own personal meanings they need to understand how what they learn in school integrates with their own lives. Breaking down the barriers among traditional subjects and developing ways of making learning relevant in authentic contexts are two of the means that educators have used to bridge perceived gaps between learning within the classroom and outside it. This chapter focuses on approaches to integrating learning and, in particular, the role that drama can play.

Introducing integrated learning

Integrated learning implies a 'connection' between previously separated content or skills areas (Kysilka 1998, p. 198). Commonly held views suggest that integrative learning involves an 'interdependence of knowledge and processes' that results in a 'holistic context' for learning where a person 'reflects on the complexities of life' (Walker 1995). More specifically, an integrated curriculum is

> Education that is organized in such a way that it cuts across subject-matter lines, bringing together various aspects of the curriculum into meaningful association to focus upon broad areas of study. It views learning and teaching in a holistic way and reflects the real world, which is interactive (Shoemaker 1989, p. 5).

Curriculum integration can occur at various points along a continuum where each point represents a different 'degree or depth of integration' (Relan & Kimpston 1993, p. 36). Fogarty (1991) identifies integration models that range from no integration at one end, where subject areas are separate (i.e. 'fragmented'), to the approach at the other end where learners take responsibility for integrating their own learning by selecting a relevant network of experts and resources to consult (i.e. 'networked'). A continuum view of curriculum integration provides educators with options, enabling them to implement those models that are 'the best fit' for the content, concepts and skills to be learned; the outcomes to be achieved; and the curricular context in which this learning will occur, whether it be within one subject, across subjects, or as part of a whole school curriculum integration approach (de Vries & Poston-Anderson 2001, p. 25).

Drama can serve as a pivotal strategy for integrating learning because its underlying premises are consistent with holistic and authentic learning in situated contexts (Andersen 2004). Social construction of knowledge through group interaction and reflection using role play, decision making and problem solving is at the core of meaningful drama experience. For this reason, drama can provide the 'adhesive' to link content, concepts and skills; the 'catalyst' to stimulate learners' active participation and critical thinking responses; and the 'linchpin' around which to construct an interactive, integrated curriculum.

Drama in integrated learning

How drama elements, forms and strategies can be used to support learning will be demonstrated in the sections that follow using the key learning area, science and technology. Developing scientific literacy, the central aim of a 'science for all' approach to science education, will be the specific focus (Commonwealth of Australia 2005b; Kemp 2002; Millar & Osborne 1998). Becoming scientifically literate involves acquiring knowledge and understandings about science (i.e. conceptual); learning about scientific processes and developing the related skills and abilities (i.e. procedural); and identifying feelings, attitudes, and values related to science (i.e. affective) (Kemp 2002). Scientifically literate children see the 'relevance' of science to their lives and have developed skills that enable them to 'engage in the discourses of science and evaluate scientific evidence and arguments' (Commonwealth of Australia 2005b). They also are better prepared to face the attitudinal and ethical issues posed by scientific and technological advances (Kemp 2002).

An active hands-on approach, reported as the most common way primary teachers introduce science into the curriculum (Commonwealth of Australia 2005b), is consistent with drama's interactive strategies. In learning about science, drama can illuminate concepts and understandings (e.g. electric currents), processes (e.g. evaporation), natural phenomena (e.g. the solar system), discoveries (e.g. polio vaccine) and issues (biodiversity versus extinction). Reframing science's concepts and procedures through role play, improvisation, mime and other drama techniques also contributes to a positive attitude towards science.

Drama, science and the curriculum integration continuum

How a combined drama and science approach can facilitate learning will be explored at five different points along the curriculum integration continuum. The first point is a **separate subject** approach in science where active drama involvement brings to life the scientific concept of evaporation. The second point is a **nested** approach where drama enhances the development of social, thinking, and content skills related to what scientists do. The third point is a **shared** approach to curriculum where the outcomes in both science and drama are met through use of puppetry to demonstrate the life cycle of a butterfly and through the development of **readers' theatre** scripts (see Chapter 12). The fourth point on the continuum is a **webbed** approach based on the theme Wonderful Water, which is treated in various ways within a range of subjects simultaneously. The final point is an **integrated** approach to learning about caring for the environment where subject boundaries blur and the arts (i.e. drama, dance, music, media, and the visual arts) are used to contribute to a central core of learning activities that serves to deepen student understanding and commitment to environmental issues.

Concept Box 4.1

The curriculum integration continuum

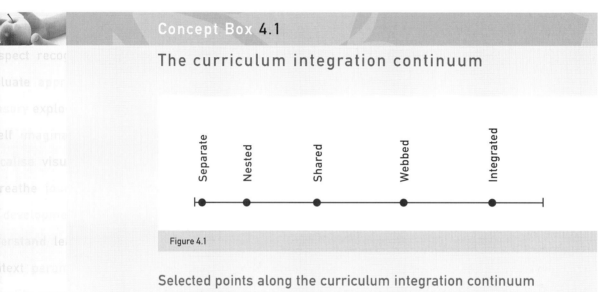

Figure 4.1

Selected points along the curriculum integration continuum

Five selected points along the continuum have been chosen to demonstrate how integration across subjects can develop. The range shown moves from those approaches that use no (or limited) integration (towards the left) to those that are more integrated and, as a result, more holistic (towards the right).

Each of these points on the curriculum integration continuum will be discussed in turn.

A separate subject approach

In this approach, science is viewed as a separate subject and drama becomes one of several teaching methods used, in this case to explain the process of evaporation. In Scientific Concepts and Processes: Evaporation (Activity Box 4.1), the process is first broken into its basic components and then children, in groups, re-enact what happens.

Activity Box 4.1

Scientific concepts and processes: Evaporation

Description

OBJECTIVES

- To introduce the concept of matter and its substances.
- To understand how the substance water can change.
- To understand the evaporation process.

Procedures

1 Make certain children have the basic understandings about matter.
   - Matter has mass, occupies space, and can be converted to energy. Matter is composed of three substances: solid, liquid and gas.
   - Ask children: What is a solid, a liquid and a gas? List examples of each.
     - A solid retains its shape.
     - A liquid takes the shape of the container into which it is poured.
     - A gas has no definite shape.
   - Many substances may exist in all three states at different temperatures.
   - Water is found in different states: solid (i.e. ice), liquid and gas (i.e. steam). To transform one state to another, change the temperature.
   - Have students mime the transformation of water from one state to another. As the mentor gives the signal, children become solid (i.e. sturdy, immovable body position), then change to liquid (i.e. fluid body position), then gas (light, floating body position). Discuss with children how they made each state with their bodies. Ask: how did each state make you feel?

2 Make certain children have the basic understandings about atoms and molecules.
   - Ask: What is an atom? (I.e. the smallest part of an element that takes part in a chemical change, such as evaporation; for example, an atom of oxygen or an atom of hydrogen.) What is a molecule? (I.e. a combined group of atoms; for example, a molecule of water that has two atoms of hydrogen joined with one atom of oxygen.)

3   Experientially demonstrate how water evaporates.

– Each child becomes an atom of either hydrogen or oxygen. Each hydrogen atom takes a label and writes H on it; each oxygen molecule takes a label and writes O on it. Children attach the labels to their shirts. (There should be twice as many Hs as Os.)

4   Say: Here is the formula for water, H_2O. Ask: What do you think this means? (Two parts hydrogen to one part oxygen.) Ask children to combine with others to make a water molecule that has two parts hydrogen and one part oxygen. (Two hydrogens join hands. One oxygen puts his or her hand on top of the two hands that are already joined. Then each water molecule stands next to other water molecules in a designated space called 'the water container'.)

5   Prediction

– Using a pre-made prop of a thermometer on which temperatures are indicated, raise the temperature gradually from the freezing point (0 degrees Celsius) to the boiling point (100 degrees Celsius). (Note that these temperatures indicate freezing and boiling points under normal atmospheric conditions.)

– What happens to the water molecules as the temperature changes? (With increased temperature, the water molecules become more agitated, that is, acquire more kinetic energy, and escape from the other molecules out of the 'water container'. As the molecules become steam, they break apart reverting to atoms of their original elements (i.e. hydrogen and oxygen).

Mentor note

As children demonstrate what happens through movement, have them keep these points in mind:

1   The molecules in a liquid are in continual motion. The temperature determines how vigorous this motion is (i.e. the hotter the temperature, the more the activity).

2   Although evaporation in a liquid is ongoing, the number of molecules evaporating increases as the temperature increases.

In a similar hands-on experience, Carlsson (2003) engaged upper-primary students in the transformation of matter in photosynthesis. She found that this experiential process enabled students to understand concepts that are usually taught at much later points in their schooling.

A nested approach within a single subject

A nested approach to curriculum occurs within a designated subject area or within an individual lesson where social and thinking skills, as well as content, are targeted. In this context, drama is one of a number of strategies used to enhance learning.

Being a Scientist: What's it all About? (Activity Box 4.2) focuses on what scientists do, including how they find and use information and technology. One of the keys to **authentic learning** in a **situated context** is to have participants understand not only the concepts, skills and procedures of the discipline, but also the attitudes (i.e. the habits of mind) of those whom they role play. Curiosity and scepticism about evidence are thought to be two predominant mindsets of scientists. In the following example, students function as a community of enquirers who use the learning process of investigation to find out about scientists and their fields of study. In this way they develop content knowledge as well as social and thinking skills.

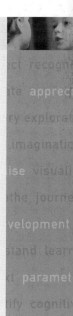

Activity Box **4.2**

Being a scientist:
What's it all about?

Description

AIM
The aim is to answer the following questions:

- What do scientists do?
- What characteristics do you think they have?
- What is systematic enquiry?
- How do scientists use technology to assist them in their investigations?
- What benefit does scientific investigation have for society?

Procedures

1   Scientific mindset

Explain that scientists are curious people who try to find out about things in systematic ways. Develop students' own curiosity by asking them to put themselves in the role of a scientist.

Say: 'You are a scientist. What would you most like to study?' For example:

- people
- solar system
- plants
- sea life
- rocks and fossils
- animals

2   What's in a name?

Challenge students to discover the specific name for each scientist in (1). Provide them with clues: first, definitions, then word derivations, and finally the actual name for the scientist. Match the name of the scientist to what they study.

CLUE 1: DEFINITIONS

- A scientist who studies the origin, development and varieties of humans
- A scientific observer of the celestial bodies (e.g. sun, planets, asteroids)
- A scientist who studies plants
- A scientist who studies life or living matter in the sea (e.g. origin, growth, structure)
- A scientist who studies life forms that existed in former geological periods, as found in fossil animals and plants
- A scientist who studies animals

CLUE 2: WORD DERIVATIONS

- (Greek, *anthropo* meaning 'human being' + *logist*)
- (Greek, *astro* meaning 'star' + *nomy*)
- (Greek, *botan*+y)
- (Latin, *marine* meaning '*of the sea*' and *bio* meaning 'life' + *logy*)
- (Greek, *palae* meaning 'old' or 'ancient' + *ontology*)
- (Greek, *zoo* meaning 'animal' + *logy*)

CLUE 3: SCIENTIFIC NAMES

- anthropologist
- astronomer
- botanist
- marine biologist
- palaeontologist
- zoologist

Mentor note

Indicate to students that, like scientists, they have engaged in a systematic enquiry to find out something.

You may wish to expand the list of specific types of scientist.

Once students have successfully matched the name of the scientist with the description of what they study, encourage them to use an **etymological dictionary** (e.g. Skeat's *An Etymological Dictionary of the English Language, 2004*) to find out more about how the name for their scientist developed.

3   What scientists study

Consider what each type of scientist studies and create a tableau. Two examples:

- *Botanist*. Each student chooses a plant. Create a plant tableau keeping in mind those that grow closer to the ground and those that grow taller. When signalled by the mentor, each plant explains why they think the botanist would be interested in them.
- *Palaeontologist*. Each student becomes a type of rock. Create a rock tableau showing the different levels of rock on top and below the earth's surface. When signalled by the mentor, each rock explains its special qualities and why it might be of interest to a palaeontologist.

Creating these tableaux may lead students to do further research as they develop reasonable arguments for their placement within each still sculpture.

4   How scientists work

- Ask children: What does it mean to be sceptical? Why are scientists described as being sceptical of evidence? What is the scientific method? (I.e. systematic enquiry to test hypotheses.)
- As a scientist, how would you study people? The solar system? Plants? Rocks? Sea life? Fossils? or Animals?

Discuss:

– How and when would each of the following strategies be relevant: observation, measurement, testing, interviewing, experimenting and describing, comparing, contrasting, categorising, and evaluating. Are there other procedures that could be used?

– How and when would the following technologies be useful: telephones, photographic cameras, videotape recorders, computers, other?

Using mime, each student shows what his or her scientist does. The other class members guess what type of scientist is represented.

5 Scientific discoveries

Use 'Bower Bird' (Activity Box 9.5) as the basis for having each 'scientist' organise his or her three greatest scientific finds or discoveries. Students move from one 'scientist' to another hearing what each has to say. In reflection, ask students how it made them feel to talk about their work in the role of scientists.

6 Science and society

Create a science talk show where each student is an 'expert' scientist and discusses his or her job, how it is done, and how this work advances scientific knowledge and/or is beneficial to society. Students base their remarks on research they have done into a type of scientist. Videotape the program and play it back for discussion and reflection on science's role in society. In particular, consider any ethical or social issues raised by the scientists or ones that, on reflection, seem relevant.

When working with drama and science it is important to 'build student belief in the context and their expert role'. By taking on a role, students work in a situated context where they engage with ideas 'as if' they were scientists. This strategy is based on the premise that 'the closer the instructional activities resemble that of a professional scientist, the more authentic and scientifically meaningful the learning will be' (Andersen 2004).

A shared approach between subjects

In a shared approach to integrated curriculum, two or more subject areas are brought together in such a way that the outcomes of each are met. This is reflected in the term **science drama** that is sometimes used to describe it. Metamorphosis: The Life Cycle of a Butterfly (Activity Box 4.3) uses a Stage 1 (i.e. Years 1–2) science outcome 'to identify and describe the ways in which living things grow and change' (Board of Studies NSW 1999) and a drama outcome for Stage 1 related to 'making meaning through the forms of drama' (Board of Studies NSW 2000). The life cycle under investigation is that of a butterfly. In conjunction with science-learning activities–such as: observing an egg, a caterpillar (i.e. larva), a chrysalis (i.e. pupa) and a butter-fly; drawing the life cycle; and reading and discussion—a drama strategy that involves making puppets to demonstrate the metamorphosis (i.e. process of transformation) is used. This drama experience reframes and personalises learning as children explain the life cycle to others using puppets they have created.

Activity Box 4.3

Metamorphosis: The life cycle of a butterfly

Description

AIMS
Each child is able to:

- Explain and demonstrate the life cycle of a butterfly; and
- Design, make, and use a puppet.

Procedures
1 Children learn about the life cycle of a butterfly;
2 Children make puppets to represent this cycle.
- Egg
  Children make a fist on the opposite hand to the one on which they hold the puppet. This is the egg.
- Caterpillar (i.e. larva)
  Make a hand puppet using a long sock. Decorate it with pipe cleaners for antennae and buttons for eyes.

- Chyrsalis (i.e. pupa)
  Pull the bottom edge of the sock back over the head of the puppet to form the chrysalis.
- Butterfly
  Design a colourful paper butterfly. Cut it out and attach it to a Paddle Pop stick to make a rod puppet that is placed inside the sock on the top of the hand. When the sock is pulled off the hand, hold the butterfly by the Paddle Pop stick and make it fly away.

Demonstration

Before the demonstration begins, place the butterfly on the top of the hand with the Paddle Pop stick towards the wrist and arm. Then gently pull the sock puppet over the butterfly.

Begin the demonstration by showing the egg that hatches into a caterpillar (i.e. fist), with the sock puppet on the other hand behind your back. Then have the egg disappear as the caterpillar crawls out and begins to eat imaginary leaves and grass until it makes its chrysalis (i.e. pull sock over top of hand). After a pause to show the passage of time, gently pull the sock puppet off the hand to reveal a butterfly that flies away.

In small groups, children demonstrate the process using their puppets. Then play music as the whole group has their puppets transform together from egg to butterfly.

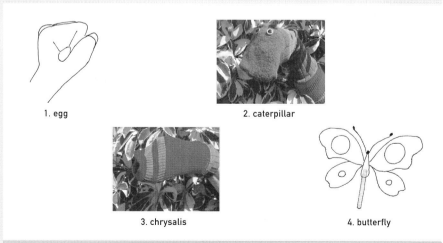

1. egg
2. caterpillar
3. chrysalis
4. butterfly

Figure 4.2 Demonstrating the life cycle of a butterfly

Variations

Have children mime the life cycle, becoming the egg, caterpillar, chrysalis and butterfly.

Champlin and Renfro (1985) suggest using a caterpillar puppet to share Eric Carle's classic picture book, *The Very Hungry Caterpillar* (1970).

Although the term science drama can refer to the full range of drama elements, forms and strategies as they are used in conjunction with science, when teachers use this term, they sometimes mean the presentation of short skits to demonstrate scientific principles or concepts (Smith 2006). Students can be scaffolded to write these skits themselves or prepared **playlets** can be used, such as those developed for readers' theatre by the Science WOW Factory (http://www.gvc03c32.virtualclassroom.org). These scenes take a range of forms, such as involving students in the re-enactment of a science experiment or putting them in the role of a scientist being interviewed by a media commentator. Once prepared or selected, students can readily stage these scripts in readers' theatre style (see Chapter 12). In this way, selected outcomes in both science and drama are identified and reinforced during reflection by asking such questions as: Were the science principles correct and clearly presented? and Was the readers' theatre script well written and performed?

A webbed approach using the theme Wonderful Water

A webbed approach to curriculum integration uses a theme as the basis for teaching and learning within a number of subjects. When meaningful and relevant themes are selected, students can be motivated to see new connections between ideas (Fogarty 1991). In this approach drama is viewed as one of a number of separate subject areas, each with its own outcomes that incorporate the chosen theme.

Wonderful Water is the theme chosen for the extended example that is discussed in *The Giant Frog* (Story and Script Box 4.1) and A Learning Web for the Theme Wonderful Water (Activity Box 4.4). The Aboriginal story of the giant frog, Tiddalik, known across Australia in various versions (e.g. Ellis 1991; Troughton 1977), is used to introduce the theme that is then revisited in different subjects in diverse ways.

Story and Script Box 4.1

The Giant Frog

Story summary

The Giant Frog

In the Dreamtime there lived a frog. Some called him Tiddalik. Every day he hopped down to the billabong to drink water with the other animals. One day he decided to take all the water for himself. He drank and drank and drank until it was all gone. He drank so much that he grew from a small frog into a giant frog. With all that water inside him, he couldn't hop far so he settled himself on top of the hill overlooking the billabong.

When the other animals came to drink, there was no water left.

'Where is it?' they cried. 'We need water or we will die.'

Then the animals saw Tiddalik on top of the hill—no longer a small frog, but a giant frog indeed! They realised what had happened. All the animals cried, 'Tiddalik! Give us back the water!'

At this point the story diverges. Some versions say the animals speared Tiddalik so that all the water came running down the hillside into the billabong. Others have each animal tell a joke or do something funny until Tiddalik laughs uncontrollably and the water spills out his mouth. Whatever the means, the water is returned and with it the animals and landscape recover.

MENTOR NOTE

This Aboriginal story can be read on different levels. While it is a **pourquoi story** explaining why frogs act the way they do, it is also a **cautionary tale**. What lessons does this story teach? (E.g. water is necessary for life; the need to share scarce resources.)

Student response to *The Giant Frog* (From the Classroom 4.1) shows how children responded to the story of Tiddalik through artwork.

From the Classroom 4.1

Student response to *The Giant Frog*

Kindergarten children who heard the story of Tiddalik drew the main character and interpreted the story's message through their illustrations.

(a) Tiddalick at the billabong (Ronan)

(b) Tiddalick gives back the water (Leilani)

(c) Sunshine and a rainbow after Tiddalik gives back the water (Kyle)

Figure 4.3

A Learning Web for the Theme Wonderful Water (Activity Box 4.4) provides a range of activities within different subjects or key learning areas that can be used to explore the theme.

Activity Box 4.4

A learning web for the theme Wonderful Water

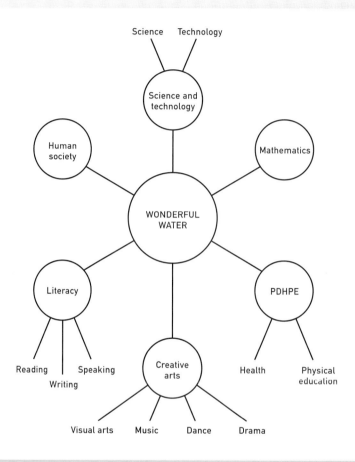

Figure 4.4 Learning web

Subjects and/or key learning areas

CREATIVE ARTS

- Dance
  Use dance movement to explore different types of water: a still pool as the breeze ripples across it, a waterfall, a tidal wave, a whirlpool. Begin with individual movement and then combine with others to create a larger movement piece.

- Drama

  Improvise in a group the story of *The Giant Frog*. Decide in your version how the animals will make the frog give back the water.

- Music

  Create a xylophone using glass bottles with different levels of water in them. Explain why each bottle makes a different sound when it is lightly struck. Create a tune using your musical instrument.

- Visual arts

  Create from clay a receptacle to hold water (e.g. bowl, cup, pitcher, vase). Use colours and designs to suggest how important water is to all of us.

  Create with poster paints and poster board a poster to promote water conservation.

  Design the plan for a public fountain that recycles water. Consider integrating into its structure symbols that remind people of water (e.g. water pattern motifs, dolphins, seagulls, boats, sails).

HUMAN SOCIETY

Investigate the relationship that Aboriginal peoples have traditionally had with the land and the commitment they have towards sustaining it.

Brainstorm what we can do to conserve water. Make a series of still photographs to show these solutions.

LITERACY

- Reading

  Read *The Wonder Thing,* a picture book written by Libby Hathorn and illustrated by Peter Gouldthorpe (1995). In this artistic and poetic treatment, children are given hints about what 'the wonder thing' is. They discover at the end that it is 'a miracle thing' called water.

- Speaking

  Debate the following issue:

  When there is a water shortage, water restrictions should apply in the same way to everyone everywhere.

- Writing

  Write a letter based on this scenario:

  Over the years, many people have settled along the river. Upriver a farmer decides to dam the river for irrigation. This stops the flow of the river to the people downstream. You are either a person who lives upstream or downstream.

Write a letter to the town council outlining the problem from your perspective. Include any possible solutions you would like to have considered by the council. Share your letter aloud. Reflect with others on the points made in the letters.

MATHEMATICS

Learn about the concept of volume. Pour water into different sized containers to see how much each will hold. Record the results in millilitres (ml).

PDHPE (PERSONAL DEVELOPMENT, HEALTH AND PHYSICAL EDUCATION)

- Personal health
  Learn about the role of water in a healthy lifestyle (e.g. drinking water, washing hands and bathing).
- Physical education
  Research and report on a sport that is played in, on or above water (e.g. water polo, scuba diving, water ballet, swimming, surfing, diving, rowing, sailing, waterskiing, paragliding).

SCIENCE AND TECHNOLOGY

- Science
  How does a plant get water? Learn about osmosis.
    Learn about the water cycle (see Activity Box 4.1 Scientific Concepts and Processes: Evaporation).
- Technology
  Learn about the following machines that use water to make them work: water-wheel, steam engine, hydroelectric plant, car radiator, water clock.

Using the same identified theme in different ways within a range of subjects and key learning areas helps children bridge the gap that they often perceive among the subjects they are taught within the curriculum. The webbed approach acknowledges the uniqueness of these subjects, yet at the same time explores the possibilities for building common ground by means of the selected theme.

An integrated arts approach to 'caring for the environment'

Today the **sustainability** of the environment is of major concern. Sustainability can be regarded as a 'frame of mind' that leads to the development of personal values, attitudes and actions that relate to maintaining the balance of nature or an ecosystem (Bonnett 1999, p. 317). As part of learning about and taking responsibility for caring for the environment, it is important for children to acquire 'empathy and compassion' for others and the world around them (Scott & Oulton 1998, p. 213). An integrated arts approach using drama, music, dance, visual arts and media, regarded as the five strands of the arts, provides an interactive way to help children investigate the meaning and relevance of sustainability for their own lives. In this approach the boundaries between separate subject areas disappear. What is important is the central core to which the various subject areas contribute as depicted in Integrated Learning: The Central Core (Concept Box 4.2).

Concept Box 4.2

Integrated learning: The central core

Story sharing

Digital media production

Play writing

Dance drama

Singing and composing

Docudrama

Caring for the environment

Figure 4.5 An integrated arts approach

This model represents an integrated arts approach. Within the central core, 'caring for the environment', there are no distinct subject boundaries; instead the learning tasks are integrated when appropriate.

Story sharing and playbuilding

The approach in *Sense and Sustainability*: Story Sharing and Playbuilding (Story and Script Box 4.2) uses a story as the basis for story sharing and **playbuilding** about environmental issues.

Sense and Sustainability: Story sharing and playbuilding

Story background

This modern retelling was inspired by a Native American legend. In the Comanche traditional tale, a girl gives her doll to the Great Spirit as a gift so that he will bring rain to the drought-stricken people. Tomie de Paola has recreated this story as a pourquoi tale about the origin of the flower called the bluebonnet in his picture book, *The Legend of the Bluebonnet* (1983).

Story

Sense and Sustainability: A Timely Tale

(Adapted and extended by Barbara Poston-Anderson)

Once not long ago or far away, there lived a child who was all alone except for her doll. With no mother or father or sister or brother for company, she loved her special doll more than anything else in the whole world. One day she and her doll came upon a group of farmers near the bank of a quick flowing river.

The farmers said, 'Welcome, little girl. You and your doll may stay with us—as long as you work.'

So she did. Every day the little girl helped them plant their crops. She enjoyed being in sunshine with her doll and with something useful to do. For a while, everything was fine. There was plenty to eat. There were even enough plants left over to send them down the river to the market.

But one day the chief planter held up a plant for all to see. 'Look! How will we ever get rich with such small plants as these? What shall we do?' Everyone thought for awhile until one of the planters said, 'I know! I'll dam the river and dig irrigation trenches!'

Another cried, 'I'll fertilise the soil and spray the fields with insecticides!'

So they did. For awhile everything was fine—but then the fertiliser ran off into the ditches. Chemicals poured unchecked into the stream. Slowly blue-green algae formed. Sludge clogged the waterways sinking back into the soil to poison the land. The once quick flowing river slowed to a trickle.

'The plants are wilting,' cried the little girl.

'The land is dying,' replied the planters.

'I don't hear a sound,' sighed the little girl hugging her doll.

There was nothing to hear—not a bird sang, not a frog croaked. All the animals that once roamed freely across the land and drank at the stream were gone. The planters began to worry about themselves.

'There's not enough to eat now. You must go.'

So the little girl, with only her doll for company, sadly walked away. She followed the stream down to the sea where she saw a ship ready to sail with passengers onboard.

'Hello,' she cried. 'Where are you going?'

'To see the world,' they replied. 'We'll go ever so far. See many wondrous sights! Whales, penguins, polar bears!'

'Take me with you! I want to see them, too!'

But the little girl's dreams of marvels were not to be. The ship left port trailing behind it a dark ribbon that grew and grew until it seemed to blacken the whole sea.

'Look! Look!' cried the girl.

No one wanted to know that the huge oil slick stretched in all directions, driving the whales deeper to sea, polluting the lands of the penguin and polar bear and everything else it touched.

'You bring bad luck!' cried the travellers. 'If you hadn't noticed the oil spill, we'd be far away from here by now. Leave us!'

With tears in her eyes the little girl clung to her doll and wandered for a long time until she found a busy place where tall chimneys belched smoke into the sky. All around her were factories packed with people using the latest technologies to produce more, more, faster, faster, faster!

Exhausted and frantic workers collapsed with stress and overwork.

'No time to relax!' they cried quickly gobbling their fast-food snacks, dropping their rubbish without thought or care.

'There's no place for me here,' thought the little girl, sadly.

The work foreman called, 'You, little girl! Clean up this mess!'

The little girl carefully picked up every lolly wrapper, chip packet, and soft drink can placing them in the bins. Then she hugged her doll, closed her eyes and wept, dreaming of a better world. 'I'm so alone.'

Suddenly in front of her stood an old lady.

'Who are you?' asked the little girl.

'I am Mother Earth,' the old lady replied. 'I have always been with you since the day you were born.'

'Oh, Mother Earth, if things go on the way they are, you will sicken and die. No one seems to care. Why?'

Mother Earth replied, 'My child, people look but don't see. They deplete but don't renew. They take my gifts but don't give in return.'

The little girl thought about what Mother Earth said. She made a decision, 'Mother Earth, I love this doll more than anything else, but I want you to have it. I give this gift to you. Now I'll have plenty of time to help you. I'll do whatever I can. Where should I start?'

'Where you are, my child,' answered Mother Earth, smiling.

The planters, travellers and factory workers all watched as the little girl gave her doll to Mother Earth. Her gift warmed their hearts. They realised what she had done. She had given everything she had.

'We want to help, too,' they cried.

So the planters cleaned up the stream and grew organic crops. Sludge no longer had a place in their fields.

The travellers cleared up the oil spill. Slick was no longer seen.

The factory workers purified the air and took time to relax and breathe it. Smog disappeared without a puff.

Figure 4.6 Student teacher in the role of Mother Earth

With everyone working together, Sludge, Slick and Smog were contained at last.

Mother Earth kept the doll always with her to remind her of how one little girl gave up what she loved most to help save the earth.

Mentor note

As the mentor tells the story children mime the parts of the planters and growers, travellers and workers. Another alternative is to use this story as the basis for playbuilding a script (see Chapter 9). When playbuilding, use movement, mime, improvisation and **soundscapes** to bring the various locations in the story to life. Juxtapose the people (e.g. little girl, planters, travellers, workers) against the pollutants, Smog, Sludge, Slick. How does each group feel in the different story situations?

If the mentor and children decide to adapt the story into a **children's theatre** script (see Chapter 13), consider whether you will use dialogue only, narrative only with the actions mimed, or a **narrator** with some dialogue. If you choose to use a narrator, who will it be—The Little Girl, The Doll, one of the pollutants (e.g. Sludge, Slick, Smog), or a representative from the various groups of people? Will the narrator remain constant throughout the play or will it change for the different segments?

As children discuss how to best resolve the drama, recycling is one reasonable response. Discuss the concept of recycling, then have students explore what this means by creating a giant recycling machine (see Activity Box 7.10: Great Gizmo!); for example, show how the machine transforms polluted air into fresh air and compresses waste.

Creating with digital media and computers

Digital cameras, videos and computers have made it possible for every student to create media art. *Sense and Sustainability*: Creating Media Art (Activity Box 4.5) encourages students to create their own projected visual backdrops for their playbuilt performance of *Sense and Sustainability* (Story and Script Box 4.2) and to design and produce the play program and tickets.

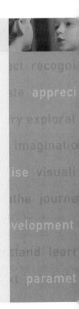

Activity Box **4.5**

Sense and Sustainability: Creating media art

Description

BACKGROUND VISUALS
For the playbuilt show based on the story *Sense and Sustainability*, use a digital camera to take actual photographs of different places in the environment, both positive (e.g. blue sky, open field) and negative (e.g. smoke stacks belching smoke, overflowing storm water drains). Sequence and/or combine photos through computer graphics to create a projected background for the show. Link the background to the script and project it during the performance.

TICKETS AND PROGRAM

Use the computer (e.g. word-processing and visual-design programs) to create the tickets and program for the playbuilt script based on the story of *Sense and Sustainability*. Develop a title and a logo that represent the show. Then create the tickets and the program using this information.

TICKETS

Include title, logo, date, time and place.

To judge the effectiveness of the ticket, use the criteria: Is the information accurate? Complete? Clearly written? Attention-getting?

PROGRAM

The program cover includes the title of the show, logo, date, time and place.

The inside of the program includes something about the play (i.e. overall synopsis and scenes), the playwright(s), the director, cast and crew.

Choreographing a dance drama

A **dance drama** is a story with a beginning, middle and end told through movement and mime. The 'dancers' can represent people, animals, forces of nature, physical features of the landscape, emotions or colours based on the requirements of the storyline. Although it is more usual for the performance to be developed around informal improvised dance akin to drama movement, more formalised dance techniques (e.g. ballet, folkdance, modern, jazz) may be **choreographed** depending on the skills of the mentor-choreographer and the students. In preparation for developing the movement piece in *Save the Environment!*: Dance Drama (Activity Box 4.6), explore the different types of movement (see Activity Box 6.8: Movement Essentials, and Activity Box 6.10: Exploring Movement).

Activity Box 4.6

Save the environment!: Dance drama

Use this photo of Smog, Sludge and Slick (top to bottom) as a stimulus for the dance drama. Have students explore how they think each one of these three

Figure 4.7 The villans (from the top) Smog, Sludge and Slick

pollutants would move, interact with one another, and interact with people. Encourage them to use different levels (e.g. high, medium, low), directions (e.g. forward, back, to the side), speeds (e.g. quick time, slow motion) and movement energies (e.g. lyrical, vibratory, percussive, suspended, collapsed).

Decide what roles the 'dancers' will play (e.g. pollutants, planters, travellers, workers), then create the dance drama. One possible structure is: (1) At the beginning, show how the pollution developed; (2) In the middle, show what each pollutant did alone and together; and (3) to conclude, show how the pollutants were or were not changed by what people did in response to them.

Singing and composing a song

Often songs carry strong messages in their lyrics. The lyrics in Sing-a-long (Activity Box 4.7) provide a rallying cry to 'renew, recycle, regenerate as we cooperate' and also emphasise the responsibility everyone has to care for the earth. The tune for this song is in Appendix 1.

Activity Box 4.7

Sing-a-long

Sense and Sustainability (lyrics and music by Barbara Poston-Anderson)

Sense and sustainability,
We've all got responsibility
To make this world a better place.
Join in the global chorus
And accept every task before us
As we make this world a better place.

The land and the sky and the sea
Are there for us to care for.
Taking it seriously,
We all must do our share.
Renew, recycle, regenerate
As we all cooperate
To make this world a better place to live in.
Sense and sustainability,
We've all got responsibility
To make this world a better place.
Join in the global chorus
And accept every task before us
As we make this world a better place.
A better place!

Mentor note

Children compose their own songs about the environment and perform them for others. They may make up their own lyrics and music or set their lyrics to a familiar tune.

Extension

As **pre-text** for composing environmental songs, share with children *Where the Forest Meets the Sea* by Jeannie Baker (1987), set in the tropical rain forest of North Queensland. This visually textured picture book is a celebration of the environment that makes the reader think about the forest and wonder how long it will last.

Making a docudrama

A **docudrama**, also called a 'drama-doc' or a 'fact-fiction drama', is a reality-based story that is dramatised (usually for television). The script is based on fact (i.e. known people, events and important issues), even though actors recreate the events through invented dialogue. Rosenthal (1995) claims that 'reality-based stories' are one of the most popular television genres (p. 9). Environmental Investigations: Creating a Docudrama (Activity Box 4.8) gives students the opportunity to develop their own docudrama based on environmental problems.

Activity Box 4.8

Environmental investigations:
Creating a docudrama

Description

Have students research environmental problems (e.g. global warming, overpopulation, salination of rivers). Create a video docudrama that addresses these problems with students in role. Some examples:

- A news reporter interviews school students about their views on the environment. The students share poems and songs they have written as part of the program.
- Media coverage of a conference at which eminent scientists report the results of their research into various environmental problems and their proposed solutions. Following their statements, members of the press interview them.
- A special news report about a group of people who return to society after having lived for the past twenty-five years in the desert without contact with the 'outside world'. These individuals are asked to comment on what changes they see in the world today and what their views of these changes are.

Implementation

For the chosen idea, create a **storyboard** (i.e. a sequential plan of camera shots). Consider camera techniques of: extreme close up, close up, medium shot, long shot, extreme long shot, low angle shot (from below), high angle shot (from above), bird's-eye view (i.e. from directly overhead). Design the title and credits.

Videotape the segments. Edit them together on a computer movie program (e.g. iMovie). Consider inserting transition shots between segments as appropriate (e.g. dissolve, that is, one shot fades out as another shot fades in).

Hold a premiere for your docudrama with invited guests.

Reflective evaluation

Watch the docudrama and discuss the following questions as a group. Encourage children to give specific examples to back up their views.

- How well do you think the ideas you selected are covered?
- How well have you used the docudrama strategy?
- How well have you used camera angles and sound to convey the ideas?
- What things would you do differently if you made the docudrama again? (I.e. add, delete, change.)

The integrated approach to learning draws on the subject content and skills that are necessary to enhance student learning in relation to a chosen core theme, issue or problem. Because there are no artificial boundaries or limits, the range of ideas and resources used to support learning can be extensive.

Summary

Scientific literacy served as the vehicle in this chapter for demonstrating how drama can be used at various points along the integrated curriculum continuum, namely, within an individual subject (i.e. separate, nested), between subjects (i.e. shared) or across the curriculum using a theme (i.e. webbed) or a core around which learning centres (i.e. integrated). Not only is drama motivating, but it also helps students reframe what they learn in personally meaningful ways. Drama's interactive approaches enable students to delve beyond the surface of a learning experience to explore in more depth what lies within it. Although in reality few primary schools in Australia integrate their entire curriculum (and a total school commitment is what a fully integrated curriculum requires), it is useful for teachers to realise that there are degrees of integration that can be successfully used within their programs and that drama can be a catalyst for such integration.

For further study

1 Develop a case for and against the proposition: 'All primary school learning should be done through drama.' Explain the strengths and weaknesses of each position.
2 Consider the statement: 'Posing science problems in motivating ways is the key to increasing the interest of primary school students in science.' In what ways can drama help to do this? Support your statements with examples.
3 Select one of the following points on the curriculum integration continuum: separate subjects, nested, shared, webbed or integrated. Choose a drama element (e.g. space, focus) or form of drama (e.g. improvisation, puppetry). (See Chapters 8–13 for information on particular drama elements and forms.) Construct a learning sequence using this drama element or form that reflects

your understanding of what curriculum integration means at the point you have chosen on the continuum.

For reflection

Reflect on your own experience of learning during primary, middle and/or secondary school. What specific learning events do you remember? Analyse why you think these memories are still salient. In what ways can the points you make about your own learning help to inform your approach to helping children learn through drama?

Preview

Chapter 5: Social Learning through Drama considers how drama can be used to build community in the classroom through helping students understand themselves and others. Particular attention is given to positive strategies for preventing conflict and dealing with it appropriately if it occurs.

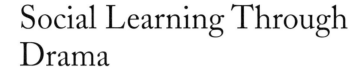

CHAPTER 5

Social Learning Through Drama

'The concepts we deal with in drama are more fundamental to living than subject classification will allow' (Bolton 1986).

Introduction

This chapter examines the role that drama can play as a catalyst for social learning. Strategies for supporting social learning within the classroom aim to help students recognise similarities and respect differences that exist among individuals within the group. Working with others to make group decisions and solve problems, exploring means to achieve collective outcomes, and modelling socially acceptable behaviour are all components of this process that taps into 'human awareness, aspirations, attitudes and values' (Jacobs & Cleveland 1999). In order to become a productive group member, individual students need to develop their own self-concepts and build their confidence about their capacity to contribute to the total group effort.

The Australian Government recognised how significant both the group and the individual's contribution are to social life when developing the key values that are regarded as part of 'Australia's common democratic way of life' (Commonwealth of Australia 2005a). These are: 'care and compassion, doing your best, fair go, freedom, honesty and trustworthiness, integrity, respect, responsibility, and understanding, tolerance and inclusion.' Exploring these values as they relate to social learning in the classroom underlies the drama interaction strategies presented in this chapter. To facilitate this, children interact with hypothetical situations presented in the form of reflective exercises, stories followed by discussion, and talk back theatre sessions involving improvisation, reflection and prediction in order to unpack the scenarios and develop ways of handling similar situations should they arise in their own lives.

In addition to drawing on the improvisational form of role play (discussed in Chapter 9), recognised **sociodrama** techniques are emphasised. These include: **doubling** (e.g. **thought tracking** where one person does the action while a second says what the person is thinking); **role reversal** (i.e. participants change places to see things from other viewpoints); **sculpting** (i.e. some group members use the rest of the group to create a human sculpture); and **mirroring** (i.e. the group's ideas are reflected back to them through talk back and play back theatre techniques).

Essentially this chapter uses drama strategies to help the group learn more about itself. In addition to the actual drama activities, briefings and debriefings by the mentor are central in helping students deepen their social learning. In the in-depth discussions and reflections that form part of this process, the mentor needs to understand how children morally reason in order to prompt, support, confront and challenge their thinking as appropriate.

Kohlberg's theory of **moral development** (1963) is one well-established means for describing these stages. His theory, consistent with Piaget's developmental stage theory, holds that children progress through stages as they develop their moral judgment. According to this theory developed from research into young people's development, young children are motivated by reward and punishment, believing that if you follow the rules you will escape punishment (i.e. Stage 1, Obedience/Punishment Orientation). Later they begin to see that there is more than one right view with several sides to any issue (i.e. Stage 2, Individualism and Exchange). As their social skills develop they enter a stage where they believe that people should live up to others' expectations and behave in 'good' ways (i.e. Stage 3, Good Interpersonal Relationships).

Next is the stage where there is a belief that people should be concerned with society and obey its laws, respecting authority and performing one's duty with moral decisions based on a societal perspective (i.e. Stage 4, Maintaining the Social Order). Young people begin to realise that different groups have different values, yet they believe that all people should work together to preserve the rights of all (i.e. Stage 5, Social Contract and Individual Rights);

and finally, when people reach the stage where they are concerned for justice and how to achieve it, they are able to see things from others' perspectives (i.e. Stage 6, Universal Principles) (Crain 1985; Graham 1972). Moral development occurs over a person's lifetime and the final stage, if reached, may not always be the level at which an individual operates. How a person morally reasons may depend on the situation and circumstances.

The mentor's role is to identify how different children make moral judgments and to push their reasoning through the use of questioning, presentation of hypothetical moral dilemmas, and the implementation of a range of interactive drama techniques that promote reflective thinking. Such building blocks can be used to help individuals link their own self-concepts to how they see their positions within the collective group as well as in society. Freire's concept of conscientisation is the ultimate aim, where an individual's consciousness is 'transformed' and he or she 'achieves a deepening awareness of both the sociocultural reality that shapes their lives and of their capacity to transform that reality' (1993, 1970, p. 27). This process begins with the social learning understandings gained in childhood and extends well into the adult years.

When developing social understandings and dealing with the potential issues that can arise, a classroom environment in which students feel safe and can trust one another is a necessary prerequisite. Although this is essential in any drama experience, it is especially important when examining self-concept and the process of community building that involves delving into attitudes, values and social behaviour. At all times, respect for oneself and others is paramount. Achieving gains at a deeper level over a longer period is more important than dealing superficially with issues. To achieve this depth, ideas are worked on incrementally and are revisited at ever increasing levels of complexity and intensity. As experienced playback theatre director, Sarah Halley (2006), who explores issues of social change in her drama work, confirms, 'It takes time to go deep'.

Sociodramatic strategies

Particular sociodramatic strategies are useful when working with groups to achieve depth of understanding about the social learning process. The first, This Door Swings Both Ways (Activity Box 5.1), reinforces for students that the space in which social ideas are explored is the 'as if' world. When students open the door, they enter an imaginary space. Later they return back through it to reflect and discuss the experience they have had beyond the door. During the debriefing stage, 'real life' applications for the hypothetical experiences may become apparent.

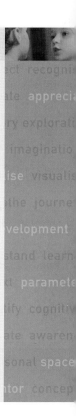

Activity Box 5.1

This door swings both ways

Description
Each child imagines and draws a door that can be decorated and coloured in any way that the student visualises it. Cut around three sides of the door so that it can open and shut.

When going into the 'as if' world, children open the door and use their imaginations to walk through it. Leave the door open.

When they have completed their role play, they come back through the door and shut it. In this way the door becomes a symbolic boundary that separates the actual world from the 'as if' world of the drama.

Mentor note
Use this strategy as a means of signalling that students are entering a hypothetical world, not their own. Although the issues may be the same type as the ones they face, they are distanced from them because they occur in another 'as if' world.

The second strategy, called a **locogram** or an 'opinion map' (Zachariah & Moreno 2006), is a technique that facilitates group decision making. First, locations in the classroom are labelled to represent the anticipated or real responses of the group (e.g. one side 'yes', the other side 'no'). The children are then asked to go physically to the spot that best represents their response. By this means, everyone can literally see what the overall class response is to a given question. Discussion can develop as different individuals indicate why they made a particular decision.

When the intensity of feelings towards an issue is required the technique is known as a **spectogram.** A line is drawn in the classroom with either end of it being the opposite extreme (e.g. strongly agree to strongly disagree, happy to sad, easy to difficult). A series of questions is asked and children place themselves along the line according to how strongly they feel about each issue. As the children stand at their chosen spot, the mentor asks each to explain the reasons why they have chosen a particular place on the line. At the conclusion of the discussion, children are asked to reconsider the question. They may stay in their initial positions or, if they have changed their minds, move to a new place. Another discussion may then occur.

A **decision walk** is a technique for objectifying a decision and identifying the reasoning that lies behind it. A child volunteers or is chosen to be in the role of a person making a decision that will have consequences (e.g. whether to report a misdemeanour they have witnessed on the playground, whether to share toys with their sibling, whether to audition for a part in the school play). The other children make two lines facing each other forming a pathway down which the child in role walks. As the student passes between the lines, one side gives all the positive reasons for a course of action, while the other side gives all the negative reasons against it. As the person walks down the pathway, the two lines alternate their responses. At the end of the walk, the child in role makes a decision and explains the reasons behind this choice. The group can then debrief by means of a general discussion that explores the consequences that can result from certain choices.

In this chapter, these sociodramatic strategies, called deep 'action methods' (Amatruda 2006, Moreno 1978), are used in combination with improvisation, thought tracking, role reversal, sculpting and mirroring to focus on social learning as students develop their self-concepts and together work to build a classroom community. The aim in the sections that follow is to extend children's thinking beyond surface interactions with situations to deeper understandings of the complexity of the issues involved. To achieve this, initial stimulus activities are extended through discussion and reflection. (The exercises and activities in Chapter 6, Sense of Self, and Chapter 7, Sense of Others, are recommended as preparatory work for the sections in this chapter on Building Self-concept, Building Community and Getting Along with Others.)

Building self-concept

Self-image, self-control and self-reliance are all aspects of a positive self-concept. For children to work effectively as group members they require a strong self-image. This section, Building Self-concept, extends and deepens introductory ideas in Chapter 6, Sense of Self.

Self-image

A person's feelings, attitudes, beliefs and values form an important part of an individual's identity. The active step of making one's feelings and attitudes conscious through self-reflection helps children shed light on why they feel and act the way they do. Sharing positive discoveries with others reinforces a person's self-concept. What Makes Me Happy? (Activity Box 5.2) provides students with opportunities to share positive thoughts and experiences.

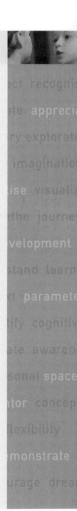

Activity Box 5.2

What makes me happy?

Description

- Write down or draw something that makes you happy.
- Mime what makes you happy for others. Have them guess what it is.
- Join with others who mimed the same kind of happy things.
- Discuss why these things make you happy.

Extension

- Have each group sculpt the rest of the class into a 'happy' group.

Mentor note

- Focus on the positive. The aim is to make children aware that they do have things that make them happy and also that they may have these things in common with others.
- Have each child write a list of things that make them happy and put it in a place they can look at when they need encouragement.

Variation

- This activity builds on How do You Feel? (Activity Box 6.18) and Sculptor's studio (Activity Box 8.3).

Children may not recognise or be able to deal with the ambiguity they sometimes feel about things. What Do I Think? (Activity Box 5.3) invites participants to see a given situation from at least two different viewpoints. As a participant shifts location from one chair to another, the student is also required to shift mental position in order to address the situation, problem or issue from another perspective.

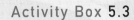

Activity Box 5.3

What do I think?

Description

1   Think of something about which you have mixed feelings. Here are some examples:

I like my sister, but sometimes she can get on my nerves;

I like school, but sometimes I think I have to work too hard.

2   There are two chairs in front of you. Sit on the first chair and say everything you can about one way of looking at things; now sit on the other chair and say everything you can about another way of looking at things.

  Discuss: How does it make you feel when you talk about something in different ways?

Mentor note

This exercise reinforces the idea that our feelings and attitudes towards things can be complex. The value of the exercise is that it 'legitimizes emotional shifts' and being able to have 'different feelings about the same thing' (Amatruda 2006, p. 174).

Variation

Amatruda (2006): One person identifies something about which they have different feelings, then *another* person models these feelings for the person.

Self-control

Developing children's competence in monitoring and controlling their own feelings and behaviour is an important component of social learning. What do I Know? (Activity Box 5.4) requires children to take on the mantle of the expert (see Chapter 9) as they become spokespersons for children of their age. This distancing technique enables them to deal with ideas that, in a personal context, might be confronting.

Activity Box **5.4**

What do I know?

Description
You are invited to participate on a panel concerned with 'what children think'. You will be asked your opinion about what you think most upsets children of your age.

Mentor note
Instead of asking directly what upsets individual children, phrase the question hypothetically. Say: On one half of the paper write (or draw) one thing that you think upsets children of your age. On the second half of the paper, write one thing you think children can do about it. Children write or draw the answer anonymously. Then the mentor (with the group's permission) reads or shows the pictures. Similar answers are grouped together. For each grouping, examine the strategies provided by the children. Have the group brainstorm even more ideas. Improvise a scenario that tests each of the strategies. Have the group decide which things they think would be most effective.

Exercises (Chapters 6 and 7) that focus on how to express and manage emotions are also useful starting points for helping children learn self-control.

Self-reliance

How a person handles challenges can provide insight into how self-reliant a person is. **Fables** can give children vicarious experience in facing such tests. These short stories with a moral attached present animal characters with human traits who must confront the consequences of their actions; for example, Aesop's fable *The Ant and the Grasshopper* is a classic tale of industry versus idleness and provides insight into what it means to be self-reliant. This story and some follow-up drama activities to aid in reflection are found in Who is Responsible?: *The Ant and the Grasshopper* (Story and Script Box 5.1).

Story and Script Box 5.1

Who is responsible?:
The Ant and the Grasshopper

Overview
Share the following adaptation of one of Aesop's well-known fables with the children.

The Ant and the Grasshopper (retelling by Barbara Poston-Anderson)

One day near the middle of summer, a grasshopper jumped for joy at the fine weather. 'What a beautiful day!' he cried as he hopped and chirped without a care in the world. As he did, he saw a little ant crawling through the dirt towards his nest carrying a big lump of damper on his back.

'What are you doing, little ant?' asked the grasshopper.

'I am busy putting away food for the cold times to come.'

'You work too hard. Come, dance with me in the sunshine.'

'I can't!' said the ant. 'I am too busy. The cold times will come soon.'

'You worry too much,' chided the grasshopper.

'I advise you to do the same or you will be hungry soon enough.'

'I can't!' said the grasshopper. 'I have too much singing and dancing to do to think about tomorrow. Today I want to play in the sunshine.'

'Suit yourself,' said the ant, 'but don't say I didn't warn you.'

All through the bright days of summer the grasshopper danced. 'I'm not worried,' he chirped as he watched the little ant struggle back and forth to its nest always carrying something for the cold days ahead. 'I still have plenty of time to gather my food!' Instead of preparing, he continued to play in the sunshine.

One day the sun didn't shine. The sky turned dark, the clouds rolled in, and the rain poured down. The cold times had come.

'I can't believe it!' shivered Grasshopper. 'I'm so hungry!' He gave a long, sad chirp, 'Ant has lots of food to see him through the cold, but I have none. How I wish I'd listened and done something for myself.'

Grasshopper had learned this lesson too late. *Be self-reliant; be prepared.*

Mentor note

1   Introduce the concept of a fable (i.e. a story with a moral or message) before sharing the tale. Stop the story before the end and ask the children to provide their own moral(s).

2   Role play
   – Have children improvise the story using the doubling technique:
     One child is the grasshopper, another is the grasshopper's thoughts.
     One child is the ant, another is the ant's thoughts.
   – Stop the improvisation at several points to have the characters' thoughts shared.

3   Decision walk
   – Have children line up in two lines through which the grasshopper will walk. One line is A; the other B. As the grasshopper walks down the passage formed by the two lines the As and Bs alternate giving the grasshopper advice. The As give all the reasons why the grasshopper should work hard; the Bs give all the reasons why he shouldn't.
   – At the end of the walk, the grasshopper indicates which decision to make.

4   Tableau: Consequences of actions
   – Based on the decision made in (3) Decision Walk, create the next scene in the story. For example, if grasshopper decides not to prepare for the cold weather, show a tableau of the inside of the ant nest with ants happy with lots of food and a tableau of grasshoppers shivering in the cold with nothing to eat.

5   Debriefing
   – Children de-role and discuss their own reflections about the moral of the fable and how it can apply in familiar situations they know.

Student Response: *The Ant and the Grasshopper* (From the Classroom 5.1) shows how two primary students depicted the central idea of the fable.

From the Classroom 5.1

Student response to *The Ant and the Grasshopper*

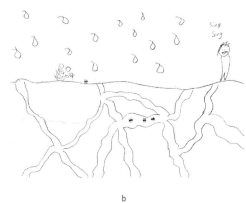

a   b

Figure 5.1   The Ant and the Grasshopper

As part of a storytelling workshop with Year 3 and 4 students, this fable was shared. Students were asked to capture the main lesson of the story (i.e moral) in a picture. Here are the artistic responses of two of the students.

In (a) Benjamin depicts Ant carrying damper while Grasshopper sings. In (b) Serene shows Ant still working and Grasshopper singing as the rain begins to fall.

This fable demonstrates that when people make choices, there are consequences. Being able to anticipate the outcomes of their actions is a positive growth step for children.

In summary, an important way that students learn about themselves is by clarifying what they think and feel about the moral dilemmas they face in the social world around them. **Self-reflexivity** helps them sort out their thinking, which in turn assists them to identify and develop their own attitudes and beliefs. Stating an opinion and being able to provide reasons for it; engaging in spirited discussion and debate about an issue; and developing listening and reasoning skills are all powerful means of building self-identity and projecting a positive self-image to others.

Building community

A cohesive group is composed of self-aware individuals who work together in positive ways for the mutual benefit of the group. Because drama is 'a collective activity' that 'involves people working together with a more or less single purpose' (Neelands 1984), drama's elements, forms and strategies are useful tools for building community within the classroom. Exercises and activities in Chapter 7, Sense of Others, can be used as preparation for the ideas in this section, Building Community.

Developing cohesion

Developing group cohesion begins with knowledge of and respect for others. In order to grow from tolerance towards acceptance and mutual respect, children must first get to know each other beyond a superficial level. Social Circles (Activity Box 5.5) provides an informal structure for gaining more in-depth knowledge about others and their preferences, opinions and beliefs.

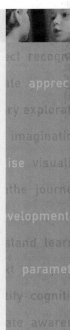

Activity Box 5.5

Social circles

Description

SHARING CIRCLE

1 Children sit in a circle and share something positive about themselves.
   - One way to do this is to have a phrase, such as: 'I like to …', or, 'What I do best is … ' Go around the circle with each child adding something. For example, Tom says, 'I like to play cricket'. The second child in the circle says, 'Tom likes to play cricket, I like to go to the movies'. The third child says, 'Tom likes to play cricket, Ann likes to go to the movies, and I like to eat pizza'.
2 Have children stand with others who have a similar 'like'. Create a tableau showing this activity.

Mentor note (sharing circle)

The main benefit of the 'sharing circle' is that children can introduce themselves and their 'interests, feelings, talents, or special qualities' and be provided with recognition by the group (Zachariah & Moreno 2006).

Concentric circles

Two circles—an inner and an outer—are formed facing each other. Each person identifies the person sitting opposite him or her in the opposite circle. At the mentor's signal, the partners begin discussing a topic such as: my favourite game, my pet peeve, or my happiest memory. At the next signal, the outer circle moves one position clockwise, while the inner circle stays still. Each person should be with a new partner. At the signal, the discussion begins again until the next signal, when the outer circle moves one position clockwise and so on.

Mentor note (concentric circles)

Encourage children to keep the pace moving in their interactions.
- Another name for 'concentric circles' is the 'doughnut' (Brady 2006).
- The main aim of 'circle' activities is to give children the opportunity to socialise with others in the class and to learn something positive about them.

Variations

Other types of circles are: Name Circle (Activity Box 7.1) and Circle Story (Activity Box 10.2).

Listening to what others say is an important first step in the process of developing meaningful dialogue within a group. Getting to know others by focusing on what links the group, rather than what divides it, also helps to foster cohesion and build empathy among group members.

Acquiring empathy

Acquiring **empathy** has as its prerequisite knowledge, understanding that people may see things in different ways and 'that's OK'. Helping children understand what a point of view is and how others can have differing, yet acceptable, views from themselves can be achieved by colouring what they see through a pair of glasses as in What a Spectacle! (Activity Box 5.6).

Activity Box 5.6

What a spectacle!

Description

PREPARATION
Make a pair of glasses out of cardboard. Choose from different colours of cellophane to make the lenses for your spectacles.

Involvement
Put on your glasses. Sit in a circle. There are a number of objects in the centre. Look at these objects. Describe what you see. Listen to what others say.

Discussion
Ask the listeners to report what was the same and what was different. Of course, the colour of the objects will differ depending on the tint of their lenses. There may also be some variation based on where the respondents were sitting in relation to the objects (see Activity Box 6.2, What do You See?).

Relate this experience to 'real' life. We may all experience the same event, but each person may perceive it differently.

Application
What factors cause individuals to perceive things differently (e.g. educational or cultural background, personal experience, age, gender)? As a basis for discussion, select and show different objects that some of the children may recognise and others may not; for example, a particular type of pasta, a specialised gardening tool, a cooking implement. Ask children who knew what the object was and why they were able to recognise it.

Variation

Share the Hindu fable of *The Blind Men and the Elephant* in which each man touches a different part of the elephant and describes the animal differently. To the first, the elephant's side felt like a wall; to the second, its tusk a spear; to the third, its trunk a snake; to the fourth, its knee a tree; to the fifth, its ear a fan; and to the sixth, its tail a rope. The fable ends: 'And so these men of Indostan disputed loud and long!' … 'Each of them was partly in the right, and all of them were wrong.'(From the poem version of the story composed by John Godfrey Saxe (1816–1887), Paul Galdone created a picture book [1963].)

Extension

Have children draw a composite picture of the elephant as the six different men perceived it.

Once students appreciate that how they perceive things is not always how others do, stretch their understandings by putting them in someone else's shoes as in Whose Shoes? (Activity Box 5.7), an exercise that uses **role play** (described in more detail in Chapter 9).

Activity Box **5.7**

Whose shoes?

Description

Draw a picture of a pair of shoes that could belong to anyone (i.e. a jogger, a princess, a ballet dancer, a cowboy, an astronaut, a superhero, the prime minister).

Sit in a circle and place your shoe picture with others in the centre. Now take a pair of shoes (not the ones you drew) and decide to whom they could belong. Share your ideas about who might own the shoes. Listen to what others say about who they think owns their shoes.

Take on the role of the person you think owns the shoes. Provide a brief in-role monologue in which you become the person who owns the shoes and tell the others about yourself (e.g. Who are you? What are you like as a person? Why do you own this pair of shoes? What activities do you do in these shoes?).

Still in role, find a partner. With your partner solve a range of problems together, taking into consideration how you think your characters would approach them.

Activities	Issues
Changing a tyre on a car	Pollution
Going shopping	Using report cards in primary schools
Putting up a tent	Talking on a mobile phone while driving
Baking a cake	The high cost of living today

Debriefing

How did the way you approached the problems differ based on the role you were playing?

Variations

Children practise seeing things from different perspectives with such exercises as:

- Choose a story character and retell the story from this point of view.
- Develop a courtroom scene in which children take on different roles (e.g. defendants, judge, jury, witnesses, prosecuting attorney, defence attorney) in relation to a 'crime' (e.g. theft: Jack who has taken the golden goose in *Jack and the Beanstalk*; the nursery rhyme character, the 'Knave of Hearts who stole the tarts'; child abuse: the father and stepmother in *Hansel and Gretel*; and murder: Jack the Giantkiller for killing 'seven at one blow' [flies]).

Sharing responsibility

For a community to work effectively, responsibility is shared. To be part of a group means that an individual takes on a commitment to help the group achieve its overall goals. Stories that emphasise the key theme of sharing or the consequences of not working together responsibly can be used as springboards for discussion as in Fair is Fair: *The Little Red Hen* (Story and Script Box 5.2).

Story and Script Box 5.2

Fair is fair: *The Little Red Hen*

Description

BRIEFING

Listeners are divided into four groups (i.e. Little Red Hen, Dog, Cat, Mouse). As the mentor tells the story, each group responds through voice (e.g. 'Not I' or 'Then I will') and mime (e.g. animals sleep in the sunshine; Little Red Hen plants wheat, prepares cake).

Figure 5.2 Little Red Hen

Story

The Little Red Hen

Once upon a time a Little Red Hen lived in a cottage in the countryside with her three friends: Dog (*barks*), Cat (*meows*) and Mouse (*squeaks*).* They were very happy until one day Little Red Hen woke up early and thought, 'I would like to bake a cake. First, I will have to plant the wheat.' 'Who will help me plant the wheat?' she asked.

'Not I,' said the Dog (*barks*).

'Not I,' said the Cat (*meows*).

'Not I,' said the Mouse (*squeaks*).

'Then I will!' said the Little Red Hen as the other three slept in the sunshine.*

Little Red Hen worked hard, preparing the ground, and planting the wheat.

Then she said, 'Who will help me water the wheat?'

'Not I,' said the Dog (*barks*).

'Not I,' said the Cat (*meows*).

'Not I,' said the Mouse (*squeaks*).

'Then I will!' said the Little Red Hen as the other three slept in the sunshine.*

She found her watering can, filled it with water and watered the wheat. Soon it began to grow.

It was not long until it was time to cut the wheat and take it to be ground into flour.

'Who will cut this wheat and take it to the mill to be ground into flour?'

'Not I,' said the Dog (*barks*).

'Not I,' said the Cat (*meows*).

'Not I,' said the Mouse (*squeaks*).

'Then I will!' said the Little Red Hen as the other three slept in the sunshine.*

She cut the wheat, took it to the mill, and watched as it was ground into flour. Then home she came.

'Who will help me bake a cake from this flour?' asked the Little Red Hen.

'Not I,' said the Dog (*barks*).

'Not I,' said the Cat (*meows*).

'Not I,' said the Mouse (*squeaks*).

'Then I will!' said the Little Red Hen as the other three slept in the sunshine.*

She mixed the batter and baked the cake. It smelled delicious.

'Now, who will help me eat this cake?' she asked as she took it from the oven.

'I will!' said the Dog (*barks*).

'I will!' said the Cat (*meows*).

'I will!' said the Mouse (*squeaks*).*

'Oh, no!' said the Little Red Hen. 'All by myself I planted the wheat, watered it and watched it grow. All by myself I took it to the mill to be ground into flour. All by myself I baked this cake. Now all by myself I am going to eat it!'*

So she did—down to the very last crumb!*

Follow-up

Tell the story again. This time stop at the points marked *. Ask children who are in the role of animals and/or the Little Red Hen, how they are feeling; what choices they have; or how the Little Red Hen might deal with each animal's behaviour.

Debriefing

At the end of the story, children de-role and consider whether they think the Little Red Hen did the 'right' thing in eating the cake herself. What other options did she have?

Including others

Group affiliation and being recognised as a valued member of the group are human needs identified in Maslow's hierarchy of needs (1970). Inclusion and acceptance are consistent with the Australian Government's initiative into values education (2005a). On Task (Activity Box 5.8) provides opportunities for students to see how important it is to feel included in a group and to work together to achieve goals.

Activity Box 5.8

On task

Description

1 Task: Group affiliation
   - You receive a card on which there is a number.
   - If you have an odd number, you are IN. If your number is odd (e.g. 1, 3, 5) go to the centre of the room, hold hands with others, and form an inner circle with others who have odd numbers. Face inward towards each other.
   - If you have an even number, you are OUT. If your number is even (i.e. 2, 4, 6), find a spot alone as far as you can away from the group in the centre and from others with even numbers.
   - Circle a face to show how you feel about where you are placed and how you are labelled (i.e. IN or OUT). On the line under the face you have chosen, write a word for how you feel and why you feel that way.

_____   _____   _____

Figure 5.3

Circle how you feel.
Write a word for how you feel.
Explain why:

2 Task: Role reversal
   – Do the task again with a role reversal (i.e. odds and evens change places).
     Again circle the face that shows how you feel now. Write a word for how you
     feel and why you feel that way.

Mentor note for tasks 1 and 2

- As a discussion starter, ask students to share what they have written on their
  cards.
- What was the best thing about being an IN/OUT? What was the worst thing
  about being an IN/OUT?
- Which did you prefer, being IN or being OUT? Why?
- What effect did labelling (i.e. calling you IN or OUT) have on how you felt?
- How could everyone feel positive about this situation? (e.g. Having a choice in
  where they go).
- Consider appointing several observers who watch the responses of children as
  they are placed in the groups and report back during the discussion on what
  they saw.

3 Task: Group task
   You are in a group with six to eight others. You will be given a task. Your job
   in the group is to divide the task up so that everyone has a job. To do this,
   you will need to break each task down into steps and then assign a person(s)
   to each step. Once you have decided how your group will undertake the task,
   mime the entire task together.

Mentor note for task 3

- Some suggested tasks: putting up a tent, giving the dog a bath, making a
  salad.
- Discuss how the group made its decisions on what the steps in the task were
  and how they divided the task so that everyone had a role.

In summary, it is important for individuals to feel included. Being
excluded, besides being detrimental to the person, is also counterproductive
to the group. Students need to recognise that in the classroom community
everyone should have the opportunity to make a contribution.

Getting along with others

Developing strategies for living in harmony with others is a crucial part of living in today's world. Drama is a useful means for achieving this because it 'teaches many life skills including teamwork, the ability to give and receive feedback, and the confidence to explore one's ideas in groups' (Norris 1999).

Understanding role behaviour

Knowing about the principles of **role theory** helps children understand how the roles people play affect their behaviour. Role theory holds that in everyday life each person plays roles governed by certain rules or norms that serve as a blueprint for behaviour; for instance, a child simultaneously enacts the roles of a sibling, a friend, and a student. Each of these roles puts demands and pressures on him or her to 'perform' in certain socially recognised and acceptable ways. At various times, the child may also play the role of: troublemaker or peacemaker, whinger or enthusiast, bully or the one who is bullied. Associated with each role are stated or unspoken goals, tasks, and characteristic ways of interacting.

Over time children build up patterns of behaviours associated with each role that they play. In order to change behaviour, then, role theory holds that modification must occur to the way the person plays any given role. The improvisational technique of role play, accompanied by in-depth **reflection** and discussion, is one of the main strategies for examining the roles people play. Exploring Role Behaviour (Activity Box 5.9) provides students with the opportunity to examine the roles they and others play.

Activity Box 5.9

Exploring role behaviour

Description

BRIEFING

1   What is a role? What roles do you play at school? At home? How does the role you play affect what you do?

2   What roles do people play at your school? (Some examples: student, teacher, principal, crossing guard, school bus driver, tuck shop personnel, school cleaner.)

   – Are people in these roles expected to act in a certain way? Explain.
   – For each role: What are the tasks? How do these tasks contribute to the school?
   – What would happen if these tasks were not performed?

Role play

1   Take on one of these roles. Who are you? In common space, walk until you hear the signal. Introduce yourself in role to the nearest person, telling them who you are, what your job is, and why this job is important to the overall working of the school.

2   Find a partner. Conduct an in-depth interview with your partner in role. At the signal from the mentor, partner A introduces partner B to the group, then partner B introduces partner A.

Mentor note

In a large class, divide the class into two large groups for the role play exercise and have partners present within each of the smaller groups.

Debriefing

During discussion create a network of the people who work in the school and how they are interconnected with each other. Draw it first on paper and then see if small groups can create the network with people standing in role and linking arms to show the relationships.

Variations

Consider the roles that people play in a group discussion (e.g. the person who contributes new ideas, gets the discussion off-course). Assign group members roles but do not let them know who is in which role. Improvise a short discussion. Then see if the group can guess by the role behaviour of each person who was playing what role.

Consider the roles that people play in families.

Dealing with stereotypes

Stereotyping involves classifying objects, events, and people without regard for their individual qualities or situations. Stereotyping can be insidious when it leads to unfounded prejudices. Breaking Down Stereotypes (Activity Box 5.10) explores the idea that grouping is based on selected characteristics resulting in group commonality for those characteristics, but not necessarily for others.

Activity Box 5.10

Breaking down stereotypes

Description

TASKS

1   Sit in a circle. Look at the pile of coins in the centre. What do they have in common? How are they different? (In the pile are Australian coins for different amounts 5, 10, 20, 50; also some coins from other countries; they are made from different metals.)
   –   These are all coins, but they are not all the same.

2   In front of you on a table is a range of items. Place these objects into groups based on a characteristic you think they have in common. Once you have completed this task, discuss with others how you decided what item to put in which group.
   –   Now examine the same items again. Can you group them again in a different way based on another characteristic?
   –   We group things by characteristics. The same things can be grouped in different ways.

3   As the mentor describes different categories, place yourself in the category that you think describes you.
   –   People in the same group are not all the same.
   –   Stereotyping is when we make judgments based on using only selected characteristics.

Mentor note

1   In the first task, make sure there is a mixture of coins.

2   In the second task, use a range of small items, such as pencil, cup, plant, plate, toys, etc. Some of the ways by which items can be grouped include colour, size, surface texture (e.g. soft, hard), function and use.

Extension

3   In the third task, name characteristics and have children form groups according to these, such as:

- all children wearing the colour blue in one group, red in another, yellow in another;
- all children with birthdays in the first half of the year in one group; in the
- second half of the year in another group.
- all children with surnames starting A-L in one group; all M-Z in another.

(Be sensitive about the groupings you suggest so as not to reinforce unintentionally any stereotypical behaviours the children might already have [e.g. gender, race].)

Reflection

Reflect with the children:

- Why are groups necessary in school and in society?
- Are all objects/people in the same group exactly the same?
- What is a stereotype?
- How can stereotyping be avoided?

The main point of this exercise is to introduce children to the idea that, although things are grouped by various characteristics for convenience, not all items in a group have exactly the same characteristics. Although this is a motivational way to introduce the concept of stereotyping, to have a lasting impact, this game needs meaningful follow-up through reflection, in-depth discussion, and other drama involvement. *A Tale of Two Soldiers* (Story and Script Box 5.3), based on a true story that happened during World War I, provides a discussion starter about how people's stereotypes provide a biased and limited view.

A Tale of Two Soldiers

Stereotypes never reflect the total reality of a person, group or situation. This story breaks down the stereotypical view of a soldier.

Story

During an intense battle of World War I fought on Turkish soil, soldiers from both sides fought ferociously against each other. There were many casualties. Finally, a short truce was held long enough for each side to enter the battlefield and reclaim their dead and wounded.

However, one British soldier was trapped in what was called 'no-man's land'. He had fallen beyond the line of the truce. He was sure to be killed when the fighting began again if no one rescued him. Although he called and called, no one from his side heard him. He was beyond their reach. He was given up for lost.

Then across the battlefield came a man with a white flag tied to his rifle and carrying this wounded soldier. He wasn't British—he was the enemy. He placed the wounded soldier near the British lines, then disappeared again back across the battlefield. This brave, Turkish soldier had risked his own life to bring his wounded enemy out of danger.

The British soldier later became the Governor General of Australia, Lord Casey. The name of the Turkish soldier is unknown.

Reflection

How does the unknown rescuer differ from the stereotypical view of a 'soldier'?

Mentor note

Compare this story with another true story from World War I, when Allied and German troops sang carols from the trenches on Christmas Eve much to the annoyance of the commanding officers on both sides. Have children discuss why they think the soldiers were singing carols in a war zone, why the officers might have been upset, and what they would have done if they were in the position of the soldiers or the officers.

Extension

A picture book version of this story is Norman Jorgensen and Brian Harrison-Lever's *In Flanders Fields* (2002).

A Tale of Two Soldiers (Story and Script Box 5.3) demonstrates how simplistic and one-dimensional the stereotypes that people hold can be. Just as a stereotypical view of a soldier in battle does not reflect the total picture of how soldiers behave, so, too, stereotypes held about other people, places and events, which are based on a limited perspective, do not reflect the full story.

Coping with conflict

Within any social group, such as the classroom, there is always the potential for conflict. The intent of social learning through drama in the classroom is to explore potential problems before they develop into major issues. Managing conflict begins with learning how to listen and how to respect the views of others. Within most discussions there will be a range of points expressed. When a group arrives at consensus after a long discussion it can give the impression that there is total agreement within the group when, in fact, the quest for finding common ground may have marginalised competing arguments that are valid, but not generally held by the majority of the group. How does one forward the discussion yet at the same time recognise such divergence? Neelands (1984, p. 40) suggests that the use of drama can achieve what he calls 'conspectus', or 'a commonality of expression' that presents a collective viewpoint but at the same time recognises and is able to show individual differences. Stopping at points in the discussion to portray the positions that different children hold towards the ideas under discussion through role plays, tableaux or spectograms reminds the group that not everyone sees things in the same way.

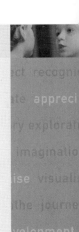

Activity Box **5.11**

That's debatable!

Description
Choose a topic, such as:
- Everyone should be banned from using mobile phones at school.
- The school canteen should sell only low fat, 'healthy' food.
- There should be no homework for students in primary school.
- All students should have a 'say' in how they learn in the classroom.

Mentor note

Open up the discussion. After a short time ask students to identify their positions along a spectogram from 'strongly agree' to 'strongly disagree'.

After further discussion, use role reversal. Ask students to identify the opposite point of view from the one they hold and present the arguments against their own position.

- Conduct another spectogram.
- In the discussion, chart the various opinions that were expressed.
- How do you think your view would have changed if you had been the principal, a teacher or a parent?

That's Debatable! (Activity Box 5.11) uses a process called crystallisation (i.e. illuminating a problem from different angles) to see the full range of possible opinions. The aim is not to gain consensus, but rather, after careful consideration, to arrive at conspectus, a 'synopsis' of the range of opinions. Often this involves trying to find a way to identify overall patterns and 'mesh' competing ideas.

Flower Power (Activity Box 5.12) aims to help children understand what is gained and what is lost when a group is asked to reach a consensus. In trying to reach an agreed upon outcome negotiation and compromise are strategies that are used, implying that at least some (if not all) individuals must modify their original ideas. Depending on the situation this may or may not be beneficial. Sometimes the outcome from the group's deliberations is stronger than any of the original ideas, at other times the outcome is less satisfactory.

Activity Box 5.12

Flower power

Description

1   Design your own flower. Make a picture of it and discuss its outstanding qualities. For example: How does it smell? Under what conditions does it grow? What are its characteristics?

Figure 5.4 An example of two individual flowers

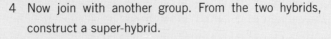

2   Join with another person who has also designed a flower. Now develop a hybrid that combines the best features of both flowers. Draw a picture and describe this hybrid's outstanding characteristics.

3   In this process, what characteristics of your original flower did you keep? Which did you discard or modify?

4   Now join with another group. From the two hybrids, construct a super-hybrid.

Mentor note

After children work on constructing the super-hybrid for some time, stop them and ask whether they are having any difficulties in reaching a decision on what they will keep and what they will not. Consider approaches for how to make the decisions (e.g. everyone in the group gets to include one idea, or they put all the possibilities in a hat and draw them out).

Figure 5.5 An example of what the hybrid looks like when the two individual flowers are combined

Reflection

- How did you feel about the process of constructing a super-hybrid?
- Are you satisfied with your group's results?
- When a group needs to reach agreement, what is lost? What is gained?
- What are some workable strategies for making decisions?

Flower Power (Activity Box 5.12) is meant to help children understand how conflict can develop (i.e. its nature and causes) and how important it is to have strategies to resolve such conflict. Exercises such as this one form part of what has come to be known as 'conflict literacy', a process for providing students with the tools to manage their own conflicts rather than relying unnecessarily on outside intervention (O'Toole & Burton 2005, p. 270).

According to the Brisbane DRACON project, a long-term study of drama's role in assisting conflict management in schools, the optimum way to learn conflict literacy is outside actual conflict situations with peers, teachers or siblings. Instead, hypothetical situations and moral dilemmas, which aim to develop 'empathy' yet at the same time provide 'intellectual distance', are used to engage students (O'Toole & Burton 2005, p. 271).

How Unbearable!: *Goldilocks and the Three Bears* (Story and Script Box 5.4), a traditional children's story, and Talking Back (Story and Script Box 5.5), a talk back theatre technique, are strategies used to generate discussion about resolving conflict.

Story and Script Box 5.4

How unbearable!:
Goldilocks and the Three Bears

Story

Read or tell this well-known story aloud.

Goldilocks and the Three Bears

In the forest lived the three bears—Mama Bear, Papa Bear, and little Baby Bear. One day they decided to go for a walk while their porridge cooled. While they were away, a girl named Goldilocks came through the forest. She saw the cottage of the three bears. No one was home. She stepped inside the front door and saw the three bowls of porridge cooling. She tasted them all. Papa Bear's porridge was too hot. Mama Bear's porridge was too cold. Baby Bear's porridge was just right, so she ate it all.

Then she saw three chairs. She tried them all. Papa Bear's chair was too big. Mama Bear's chair was too big, too. Baby Bear's chair was just right so she sat down. When she did, the chair cracked and broke.

Goldilocks was feeling tired so she climbed the stairs. At the top she saw three beds. She tried them all. Papa Bear's bed was too hard. Mama Bear's bed was too soft. Baby Bear's bed was just right so she fell asleep.

Then the three bears came home. Papa Bear said,

Figure 5.6

'Someone's been eating my porridge.' Mama Bear said, 'Someone's been eating my porridge.' Baby Bear said, 'Someone's been eating my porridge and it's all gone!'

Next Papa Bear said, 'Someone's been sitting in my chair.' Mama Bear said, 'Someone's been sitting in my chair.' Baby Bear said, 'Someone's been sitting in my chair and broke it to pieces!'

The three bears went upstairs. Papa Bear said, 'Someone's been sleeping in my bed.' Mama Bear said, 'Someone's been sleeping in my bed.' Baby Bear said, 'Someone's been sleeping in my bed and she's still here.'

Just then Goldilocks woke up and saw the three bears.

What do you think the three bears should do?

When the three bears come home early and confront Goldilocks in their house, how might they respond? Consider these choices: they could be aggressive (e.g. 'be mean'); or assertive (e.g. 'be strong'); or submissive (e.g. 'give in'). Which choice would you choose? Why? What other choices could the three bears make?

Mentor note

Terminology is based on 'Two lessons for grades 3–5: Be strong, be mean, or give in?' (http://www.teachablemoment.org/elementary/strong_mean_giving_in.html).

Extension

Robert Southey, a poet, wrote the story about the three bears and published it in 1837. Originally, there was no Goldilocks, only a prying old woman who the bears chased away from their cottage. In later versions, the old woman became a girl. The names for the intruder ranged from the earliest, Silver-Hair to Silverlocks, Golden Hair and finally Goldilocks (Ashley 1997, pp. 619–20). Ask children why the evolving name is an example of stereotyping? (I.e. focus on hair colour to the exclusion of other attributes).

Talk back theatre is a useful technique for children who are able and willing to reflect thoughtfully on issues. Talk back theatre involves presenting scenarios with a problem or issue focus that serve as discussion starters for the group. This sociodrama strategy aims to help children explore social issues using a hypothetical context. After sharing Talking Back: *Recess on the Playground* (Story and Script Box 5.5), children brainstorm ways to de-escalate the growing conflict.

Story and Script Box 5.5

Talking back: *Recess on the Playground*

Script
Present this talk back script.

Recess on the Playground

Jack   Come and play tag with us, Tim.

Tim   That would be good.

Mary   May I play, too?

Tim   No.

Mary   Why not?

Jack   You're not our friend.

Tim   Go away!

Mary   I'd like to be your friend. Won't you let me play tag with you, please?

Jack   No way!

Mentor note

1 Ask for student volunteers to enact the parts of the three children. Read the script aloud once. Then have them read the parts aloud again.
2 At the conclusion of the second reading, have the other students ask questions of the three who are still in role (e.g. How are you feeling?; Why did you say what you did?).
3 Replay the script using thought tracking. Have one person read the dialogue and a second person after each line say what they think the character is thinking or feeling.
4 The three students de-role. Have a general discussion.

Extensions

1 After this talk back scenario, select three volunteers. Have the class sculpt these volunteers into the scene showing their body positions and emotional responses to the incident.

- Examining the sculpture, discuss what could be said or done to make this situation better?
- Remake the sculpture to show the changed situation.
- Ask the children to create the next scene: What happens next?
- What could be said or done to de-escalate the situation?

2   Develop other talk back scripts based on 'authentic' school situations, such as a choice between healthy/unhealthy food at the canteen; sharing playground equipment; not listening to instructions given by a teacher.

3   Another form of feedback theatre is **forum theatre**. First, participants watch a scene, then, when it is played a second time, audience members can stop the scene at any point and take the place of those enacting it. This approach is useful for exploring different pathways through the action and can be used as an extension of talk back theatre.

There is an emphasis in schools on teaching children to understand and deal with conflict. Programs, such as the Brisbane DRACON Project (O'Toole & Burton 2005) and the 'Cooling Conflicts' program (NSW Department of Education and Training 2003), aim to improve children's ability to manage themselves and the conflicts they may encounter.

Confronting bullying behaviour

Bullying is a type of conflict in which there is a recognised power imbalance. When someone is bullied there are usually three parties: the bully, the person bullied, and the bystander, each of whom has 'the power and responsibility to de-escalate the conflict' (O'Toole & Burton 2005, p. 274). Ways to do this include: 'acknowledging and confronting the bullying, avoiding the situation, mediating or appealing to others for assistance' (O'Toole & Burton 2005, p. 274).

Choices and Consequences: *The Three Billy Goats Gruff* (Story and Script Box 5.6) involves reflecting on the characters and action in this adaptation of a well-known Scandinavian folktale. Using a traditional story as the focus provides students with the opportunity to distance themselves from any actual bullying situation, yet at the same time confront some of the issues involved.

Story and Script Box 5.6

Choices and consequences:
The Three Billy Goats Gruff

Story

Share this folktale. Use it as a springboard for discussions about bullying.

The Three Billy Goats Gruff

Once a bridge linked one hillside to the next. Below the bridge there lived a troll who would not let anyone cross over the bridge. When anyone tried, he cried, 'Who is that crossing my bridge?' When the townspeople in the nearby village heard his fierce voice, they avoided the bridge and never tried to cross it.

On one of the hillsides lived the Three Billy Goats Gruff. One day they decided that they would cross over the bridge because the grass on the other hillside looked greener.

First came the Little Billy Goat. As soon as the troll heard the pitter-patter of his hooves on the bridge he cried, 'Who is that crossing my bridge?'

'It is I, Little Billy Goat. I'm going over to the other hillside to eat some sweet grass.'

'NO, you're not! If you take one more step across my bridge, I'll bump you, thump you, and gobble you up!'

'Oh, please don't do that. My middle brother is tastier than I am. He'll be along soon.'

'All right then!' cried the troll. 'Cross my bridge before I change my mind.'

The Little Billy Goat hurried across the bridge.

A few minutes later onto the bridge came the Middle Billy Goat.

'Who is that crossing my bridge?' demanded the troll as he heard the louder pitter-patter of hooves on the bridge.

It is I, the Middle Billy Goat. I'm going over to the other hillside to eat some sweet grass.'

'NO, you're not! If you take one more step across my bridge, I'll bump you, thump you, and gobble you up!'

'Oh, please don't do that. My big brother is tastier than I am. He'll be along soon.'

'All right then!' cried the troll. 'Cross my bridge before I change my mind.'

The Middle Billy Goat hurried across the bridge.

A few minutes later onto the bridge came the Big Billy Goat.

'Who is that crossing my bridge?" demanded the troll as he heard the LOUDEST PITTER-PATTER of hooves on the bridge he had ever heard.

'IT IS I!' answered the Big Billy Goat in his Big Billy Goat voice. 'I'm going over to the other hillside to eat some sweet grass.'

'NO, you're not! If you take one more step across my bridge, I'll bump you. thump you, and gobble you up!'

'Come and get me then,' cried the Big Billy Goat. 'I'm crossing this bridge NOW.'

The troll jumped onto the bridge. The Big Billy Goat stood his ground. He stared into the troll's big, yellow eyes, then lowered his horns and charged.

BIM! BAM! BONG! The fight wasn't long. Over the bridge flew the troll. Down into the water below he sank, never to be seen again.

The Big Billy Goat continued across the bridge. He reached the opposite side where he joined his other two brothers.

As far as anyone knows, they're still there on that hillside eating sweet grass to this day.

Reflection

In this story of *The Three Billy Goats Gruff*:

- Who is the bully? (Is there more than one?)
- Who is being bullied? (Is there more than one?)
- Why didn't the troll want the billy goats to cross the bridge?
- What could the troll have done differently?
- What could each of the billy goats have done differently?

Extension

Re-enact the story showing the different ways in which each character could respond. Show the various positions through mime; for example, an aggressive response in which the character physically grows in size; an assertive response in which the character keeps direct eye contact and an upright position; or a submissive response in which the character physically shrinks. Relate these positions to the words: 'confront', 'be strong', 'escape' and help children recognise there are different ways in which they can respond to confrontation (Cossa 2006). Discuss the advantages and disadvantages of each strategy.

This story demonstrates that there are choices that can be made in relation to bullying behaviour and that each one has its consequences. The Brisbane DRACON Project stresses that 'anybody can be a bully, bullied or a complicit bystander depending on the context, and that all have a responsibility and a potency in escalating or de-escalating bullying situations' (O'Toole & Burton 2005, p. 281).

In summary, primary school students need to learn strategies for dealing with conflict and resolving it and for responding to bullying behaviour. Students need to be able to assess different situations as they arise and interact appropriately, being aware of the range of options (from direct intervention to calling for assistance) and being able to apply these in accordance with the individual school's policy on bullying. A child's ability to respond to conflict situations is enhanced through relevant drama activities that provide experience of coping through role play with situations analogous to the ones that could be encountered.

Children as peacemakers

Popular song lyrics are a vehicle for helping children learn about 'keeping the peace' because they often contain compelling social messages. Such is the case with *One Tin Soldier* (Lambert-Potter n.d.), a protest song from the 1970s with a strong anti-violence message. The ballad's verses gradually reveal the tragic story summarised in *One Tin Soldier* (Story and Script Box 5.7).

Story and Script Box 5.7

One Tin Soldier

Story

The Mountain People possess a treasure that the Valley People desire more than anything else, even though they have no idea what it really is. They send a message to the mountain that the people must give up their treasure or suffer the consequences. The Mountain People reply that they will share the treasure of the mountain. The Valley People refuse the offer and storm the mountain. After much loss of life, the Valley People defeat the Mountain People and gain the prize. At last, the victors turn over the stone on the mountaintop to reveal the treasure. Underneath the stone they find the message 'Peace on Earth'.

Mentor note

This **allegory** introduces children to a poignant scenario where everyone loses and no one wins (i.e. a Lose/Lose situation). Have children think about the story and then rework it searching for a scenario where everyone wins (i.e. a Win/Win situation). Have them enact and then discuss the different versions.

Extension

Introduce children to Covey's Six Paradigms of Human Interaction (1990, 1989), namely: I Win/You Win; I Win/You Lose; I Lose/You Win; I Lose/You Lose; I Win/---; No Deal (we agree to disagree). Discuss when each one of these could be appropriate.

A picture book with a similar theme is Nikolai Popov's *Why?* (1998).

Everyone a Winner (Activity Box 5.13) gives children additional practice in working towards resolutions that aim to meet everyone's needs, when possible.

Activity Box **5.13**

Everyone a winner

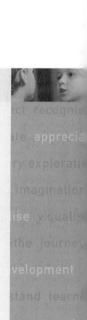

Description

BRIEFING

Explain that there can be a range of different outcomes for a situation where there is conflict. Three of these outcomes can be: Everyone loses (e.g. Lose/Lose); some win, some lose (e.g. Win/Lose); and everyone wins (Win/Win).

Here are some scenarios that each have the potential for conflict. Brainstorm each one, trying to find solutions where both parties will win. Role play these solutions.

Scenarios

- Both Sam and Karen want to work on the computer at the same time.
- At recess Jane and Kathy always play together, but today Jane wants to jump rope, while Kathy wants to play hopscotch.
- Mother wants Tom to eat his green vegetables. Tom only wants to eat his dessert.
- You want to do your homework, but your brother wants you to play tag with him.
- Someone at school teases you.
- At lunchtime at school your friend wants to swap sandwiches with you, but you're happy with what you have and don't want to do this.

Extension

Can you think of other situations where you can change a Win/Lose situation into a Win/Win situation?

Debriefing

After each role play, reflect on the situation through questions, such as:

- What happened?
- What did each person want?
- What feelings did you see?

Try out different solutions to the conflict.

- In each solution, did both persons get what they wanted?
- Which solutions were most effective in getting everyone what they wanted?

Mentor note

An alternative to role play is to have children use puppets to present the scenarios. This has the advantage of providing a 'safe' vantage point for the children in confronting challenging behaviour or situations.

Making a personal commitment to peace is an important part of a child's development, whether that peace relates to an internal sense of well being or a concern for local and global harmony. Peace Offering (Activity Box 5.14) provides children with the opportunity to reflect on what peace means to them and to share this view with others.

Activity Box 5.14

Peace offering

Description

Figure 5.7 A symbol of peace

Briefing

- Discuss the importance of peace both at the personal, local and global levels.
- Brainstorm the **symbols** that have been used for peace; for example, the peace pipe for the Native Americans, the dove with the olive branch, the vision of the lion and lamb lying side by side.
- Ask children why they think these symbols are used to represent peace. Can they suggest any other ideas for appropriate symbols?

Activity

- Design your own peace stamp that has your vision of peace on it.
- Glue the stamp to an envelope.
- On the inside of the envelope put a peace offering. This can be a poem, a picture you draw, a song you compose, an idea for a dance, a story you write, or words that tell why you think peace is important for the world.

Sharing

In a sharing circle (see Activity Box 5.5 Social Circles), each child presents the peace offering.

Mentor note

Combine these peace offerings into a drama presentation that the students perform for others in the school.

Extensions

Introduce children to the true story of Sadako and the peace cranes. Versions of the story are: Elizabeth Coerr's junior novel, *Sadako and the Thousand Paper Cranes* (1981) and *Sadako* (1995, 1993). Sheila Hamanaka has written a picture book poem, *Peace Crane* (1995) relating to the same story. Make children aware of the Peace Memorial in Hiroshima, Japan, where children each year send thousands of paper cranes.

When children take on the role of peacemaker they contribute to their own well-being and to that of others. Although there is always the potential for conflict in social situations, they learn that there are constructive ways to approach it.

Summary

This chapter has examined how drama can contribute to the social learning of the group, including developing both individual self-knowledge and building group community. Working together towards harmony in the classroom, in the wider community and in the world is a crucial goal of education now and into the future.

For further study

1   Investigate programs that have been developed to study or address conflict management in schools (e.g. Brisbane DRACON Project, 'Cooling Conflicts' [NSW]). Discuss how these programs use drama as a strategy. If the program you have selected does not use drama, make suggestions regarding how drama could be integrated as part of this program's approach.
2   Collect song lyrics from popular music or children's songs that address getting along, helping others or living in harmony. Choose a song(s) upon which to base a lesson for children. Into this session incorporate some drama (e.g. role play, talk back theatre, playbuilding, puppetry). If possible, share the lesson with children and reflect on their responses.
3   Read more about talk back theatre and forum theatre. (If possible, see some of these techniques in action.) Consider the potential of each technique for helping children develop social learning skills.

For reflection

In your view, what knowledge, skills and strategies does a drama mentor need in order to use drama as a catalyst for social learning in the classroom? Which of these do you already have? Which do you need to develop? How will you do this?

Review of Part Two

Part Two: Maximising Learning: Drama in the Curriculum focused on the planning processes for using drama as a 'stand alone' subject within the curriculum or as part of an integrated arts approach. In addition, drama was discussed as a method for assisting subject integration and as a catalyst for social learning.

Drama Building
Blocks for Learning

Section Two, consisting of Parts Three, Four, and Five of this book, uses the concept of construction as an analogy for developing participant engagement with drama. The underlying assumption is that once participants understand and experience the building blocks of drama, they will be able to assemble this knowledge in a multiplicity of meaningful ways.

In Part Three (Chapters 6, 7 and 8) the building blocks of drama are discussed with each one analysed in turn. First, the participants' knowledge of themselves as gained through the senses and self-reflection provides the groundwork. Making connections with others follows, culminating in a detailed introduction to the elements of drama.

In Part Four (Chapters 9, 10 and 11) participants use these building blocks to shape their understandings of some established drama forms, namely improvisation, role play, playbuilding, storytelling and puppetry.

In Part Five (Chapters 12, 13, and 14) participants draw on their developing understandings and skills to present drama as performance and to appreciate the ways in which diverse traditions and cultures contribute to drama work.

The overall aim of Section Two is to demonstrate through explanation, analysis and example the range of drama strategies and techniques available for use with students in educational settings. These range from process-based activities and exercises that focus on drama elements to student-generated products in a variety of drama forms.

Preview

Section Two: Drama Building Blocks for Learning consists of Parts Three, Four and Five.

Part Three: Realising Drama: Developing the Senses consists of Chapters 6, 7 and 8.

Chapter 6: Sense of Self considers knowing about how to use one's imagination, express oneself vocally and physically, and share feelings as a key building block of drama.

Realising Drama: Developing the Senses

Chapter 6: Sense of Self
Chapter 7: Sense of Others
Chapter 8: Sense of Drama

Objectives

By the end of this part students should be able to:

- Understand the role that drama plays in helping children learn about themselves;
- Recognise how drama fosters cooperation and team work; and
- Apply the elements of drama when working with children in learning environments.

When participants are introduced to drama, they benefit from an initial familiarisation and adjustment period, a motivational time for mentor and participants to get to know each other and to lay the groundwork for further drama work together. Part Three focuses on this introductory period, regarding it as a time to concentrate on the 'senses': Sense of Self (Chapter 6), Sense of Others (Chapter 7), and Sense of Drama (Chapter 8). Through participating in these sense-making activities students learn the physical and social limits of drama, including self-control and the care needed for others within the bounded space of the drama action. They also discover the developmental nature of drama. Time is necessary to develop skills, to build relationships with others, and to learn to respond appropriately to drama's shared power relationships.

Sense of Self

'At the centre of any drama experience is the child' (Way 1967).

Introduction

Children first learn about their world by exploring it through their senses. Piaget (1966) in his **cognitive development** theory recognised this and named the earliest years of a person's life as the **sensorimotor stage**, a period when young children put all their senses into the service of investigating the wonder of what they find around them. As young children grow and develop, they continue to use sensory experiences and play to understand their world. In the initial stages of drama, building on the young child's propensity for learning through sensory exploration and for acting out situations in order to understand them provides a seamless transition from the child's world of play to the 'as if' world of drama. Likewise, when using drama with children in the later years of primary school, revisiting the sensory mode of learning can develop self-awareness and helps to centre learners in space and time, useful starting points for more in-depth drama involvement.

This chapter focuses on the self, emphasising direct sensory experience, visualisation using sense memory, and imaginative response to external stimuli. In addition, the importance of vocal and bodily self-awareness and the expression of feelings are highlighted. The aim for students, whether they are in the lower or upper primary years, is to understand and value how they individually respond to the world outside themselves.

Experience

Children first learn about the world through their sensory perception; however, children need to understand that how they perceive and make sense of the world is not necessarily how others do. Experience Your World (Activity Box 6.1) encourages children to note their individual responses and to consider how these compare with those of others. Recognising, appreciating and respecting similarities and differences are important aims.

Activity Box 6.1

Experience your world

Description

See, touch, hear and smell different objects. How are they alike? Different?

- Close your eyes. Touch each object again. See each one in your 'mind's eye' as you touch it.
- Listen to songs in different styles of music, for example: rock, classical, country. Do you enjoy any song more than the others? Explain.
- Listen to each piece again. As you hear each one, draw with a coloured pencil a picture of how it makes you feel.
- Show your drawings to others. Tell them how you respond to each song. Do they feel the same way? Find out why or why not.

Mentor note

Stress that there is no right or wrong answer. Everyone's opinion is valued.

Note that taste is not included in this exercise, although students need to be aware that it is one of the senses.

Variation

'Enter the Picture': As children listen to a description of a scene or view an artwork, they visualise themselves in the situation. Then they enter this 'as if' world using actual voice and movement to recreate it. In this exercise, ensure that children have their own **personal space** and that there is sufficient room for everyone to move comfortably (Schotz 1998, p. 108).

Extension

Picture storybooks that simultaneously portray two different worlds can serve as pre-text for 'Enter the Picture'. Examples for younger students include: Venn's picture storybooks featuring Roy and Matilda, two mice who live in the National Gallery of Victoria and venture into the paintings on the Gallery walls (e.g. *The Gallery Mice* [1992] and *The Golden Locket* [1994]); and Mayhew's *Katie Meets the Impressionists* (1997) where a little girl goes inside five different impressionist paintings to find flowers for her Grandma on her birthday.

In addition, paintings, such as Bruegel's *The Village Fair* (Craft 1975), depicting villagers engaged in a range of activities at a medieval fair, can provide the stimulus for older students to choose a character and bring the scene to life.

What Do You See? (Activity Box 6.2) helps students learn that even something that seems as straightforward as describing familiar objects is open to interpretation.

Activity Box 6.2

What do you see?

Description

Take a seat around a table on which are placed a few small items. Write down or draw what you see. Now find another place around the table. Again write down or draw what you see. How did where you sat change what you saw?

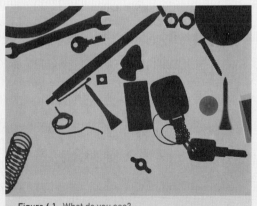

Figure 6.1 *What do you see?*

Mentor note

Encourage children to take places at different levels and distances from the table. Give them enough time to write or draw at each location before they are asked to move.

At the end of the exercise have children share what they saw from different positions. How did distance, level and their knowledge of what the objects were affect what they saw? Have children discuss why they think their descriptions vary.

Variation
'Observation Exercises' (Janesick 1998, pp. 14–18) inspired this activity.

Thinking back on this exercise helps students understand that they cannot assume that everyone sees things in the same way. As McLuhan (1967) once put it—we all see life through our own pair of coloured glasses. Understanding that people's views may differ—and that that's OK—is an important underlying concept for drama.

Visualise

In drama, children move back and forth between two worlds, the actual and the 'imaginary'. Bolton (1984) and Boal (1995) use the term 'metaxis' to describe this state of belonging to more than one world simultaneously. According to Warren (1993), not all children, particularly the youngest, find this concept an easy one at first. For this reason, strategies are needed to bridge these worlds for them. One suggestion is to have children handle real objects before asking them to visualise imaginary ones. Now I Remember (Activity Box 6.3) provides an exercise for doing this.

Activity Box 6.3

Now I remember

Description
Pick up a small object, like a pencil. As you hold it, notice its weight, length, colour and texture. Also, note whether it smells and what sound it makes when tapped against the desk.

Demonstrate how to use this object (e.g. pencil), starting with its most obvious functional uses (e.g. writing, erasing) to its more imaginative uses (e.g. conducting an orchestra or twirling it as a baton).

Now put the object down. Close your eyes and visualise it.

Use your sense memory to imagine the object and take it in your hand. Use it to write, erase, conduct an orchestra, twirl as a baton—and any other use you can make of it.

Try this same exercise with several different objects—moving from the actual object to the imaginary one.

Mentor note
Choose objects that are readily available to each child (e.g. crayon, book).

In Now I Remember (Activity Box 6.3), a child has the experience of touching an actual object before having to recreate that object in his or her imagination. Schotz (1998) affirms the importance of such an approach: 'our imagination can only flourish when it is firmly rooted in reality' (p. 53).

Once children comfortably transform actual objects into imaginary ones, Imaginary Object Pass (Activity Box 6.4), in which a make-believe object changes as it is passed from person to person around the circle, challenges them to draw on their sense memories to make items 'real'.

Activity Box 6.4

Imaginary object pass

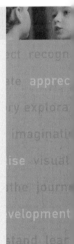

Description
- Sit in a circle with others. Imagine you are holding an object. Demonstrate its use through your actions.
- Pass this object to the next person in the circle. This person takes the object, uses it as you have shown and then makes it into something else, which in turn is demonstrated and passed on to the next person in the circle. For example, change an umbrella to a broom, change the broom to a hat. This process continues until everyone in the circle has had a chance to participate.

Mentor note

Make the circle a manageable size (i.e. 6–8 is workable). If there are more children than this, make several circles so that all the children can participate at the same time.

Variations

Changing the Object (Johnstone 1999, p. 304) and Pass it On (Schotz 1998, pp. 99–100) are similar exercises.

For older students

A more complex variation of Imaginary Object Pass is 'What are you doing?' Divide students into pairs, A and B. A mimes an action (e.g. combing hair) and when B asks, 'What are you doing?', A answers with something other than what he or she is doing, such as 'I'm reading a book'.

B then mimes this action (e.g. reading a book) and when A asks, 'What are you doing?', B says something else, such as 'eating an apple', which A mimes and so forth. This exercise requires flexibility of thought and quick thinking. The challenge for older students is to keep the pace moving (Moore 1988, p. 10).

In addition to encouraging fluency and flow of ideas, Imaginary Object Pass (Activity Box 6.4) enables children to make individual choices that draw on their knowledge and experience, what O'Neill and Lambert (1982, p. 11) say children do to create a 'make-believe' world.

Imagine

Imagining parallel worlds, what Henry (2000, p. 53) calls 'world creation', requires children to have the capacity to make-believe, to ask 'What if?' and to have the skills to explore ideas using their mental, emotional, and physical powers. Moving between actual and imagined space is helped by using 'triggering mechanisms' to 'mark the passage' (Harrison-Pepper in Wolford 1996, p. 36). A **triggering device** can be as simple as flashing or dimming the lights, signalling with a musical instrument, or having participants don special 'gear' for the journey. In Balloon Trip (Activity Box 6.5), a large floor mat helps children make the transition. Before the journey, the mentor establishes with children that when they move onto the mat, they leave the here-and-now and venture into an imagined world.

Activity Box 6.5

Balloon trip

Figure 6.2 Up we go in our beautiful balloon

Description

(Children stand around the perimeter of the mat.)

It's a beautiful day—not a cloud in the sky. What a great day for a hot air balloon ride! Show me you are ready by facing the mat and putting on your sunglasses. Now dab on some sunscreen. *(pause)*

Now that we're all ready, it's time to climb into the gondola, the basket of the balloon. Grab the side of the gondola and pull yourself up and over into the basket. In you go! *(wait for children)*

Good! You're all inside. There are a number of compartments in this gondola. You are sitting in one of them all by yourself. Get yourself settled. *(pause)* Now, close your eyes ready for the trip. *(pause)*

Hold on! The pilot is giving a burst of hot air under the balloon. It begins to lift from the ground. Feel it sway ever so gently.

Now as you look over the side of the gondola—watch the ground getting smaller and smaller as we go higher and higher in the balloon.

It's so quiet up here—not a sound. *(pause)*

Smell the air. It's fresh and crisp and cool. *(pause)*

Look down to the right. That's where we left the ground—so far below us now. *(pause)*

Look to the left—way to the horizon. *(pause)* What do you see? Trees? A waterfall? Mountains? Is that a skyscraper in the distance? Maybe it's a city— what do you think?

Take a closer look—what is the best thing you see? Really look at it—try to remember every detail so you can tell us later. *(pause)*

No rush—no hurry. Enjoy the warm sun and the feeling that you can see forever.

(pause)

The pilot touches the controls. The balloon starts to descend. Slowly, gently we float back towards the ground. Down, down, down. Now the pilot needs a place to land. Oh! There is a safe spot. Hold on to the edges of the gondola. Look back the way you've come—towards the sky. Prepare to land. A gentle thump—we've come back to earth. What a wonderful balloon ride!

Keep sitting in the gondola with your eyes closed. Breathe deeply. Relax. *(pause)*

When you're ready, open your eyes and sit quietly. *(wait for children)*

Now get up and carefully climb back out of the gondola. Stand quietly at the edge of the mat until everyone is there with you.

Mentor note

- Keeping eyes closed during the balloon ride encourages children to concentrate; this keeps distractions to a minimum. Maintain a calm and relaxed vocal tone as you guide them through the journey. This will help children feel safe in the imagined space. (This exercise is not the time to introduce unexpected catastrophes!)
- Pause frequently to provide the opportunity for individual visualisation.
- At the journey's end, avoid rushing. Let children relax with their eyes still closed before asking them to open them and disembark from the basket. If they have identified with the experience, they may be reluctant to leave the balloon behind. That is why it is important to give them time to make the transition mentally back to the here-and-now.
- Reflect on the experience by asking children to share the 'best' thing they saw during the balloon journey.

Variations

Soothing Environments: This is a relaxation exercise in which mentally relaxing situations (e.g. floating) are described that the participants visualise, usually with their eyes closed and sometimes accompanied by soft music (Cassady 1993, p. 16).

For older students

Guided Dream in Character: This visualisation is similar to 'Balloon Trip' in that the scene is imagined by participants as it is narrated by the mentor; it differs in that participants visualise the scene as characters they have chosen (Izzo 1998, pp. 45–46).

Imaginative Journeys: Evolving problems in imagined settings are described; for example, at the beach the shark alarm sounds. Lifeguards urge swimmers quickly, but without panic, to make their way to shore. As a group, children imagine and act out without words the solutions. The aim is active group involvement and cooperation, rather than individual visualisation as in Balloon Trip (Novelly 1985, pp. 32–34).

What student teachers said

- 'Balloon Trip stretched my imagination' (Rochelle).
- 'I have never been in a balloon before. It was almost like I was there!' (Kim)
- 'I could really feel the experience and actually see in my mind's eye the sights below me' (Tracey).
- 'I felt completely involved; I forgot where I was. I wasn't thinking about anything else. I used all my senses' (Carly).
- 'It made me relax, focus on my breathing, and calm down. I think this exercise would work well for students, especially after lunch' (Robyn).
- 'It is a great idea to get children settled' (Jodie).
- 'I have led similar relaxing scenarios with children prior to creative writing lessons and have seen how such a simple activity can provide stimulus for many writing topics' (Meagan).

Taking a Balloon Trip (From the Classroom 6.1) shows how one student teacher implemented a visualised journey with Year 2 students.

From the Classroom 6.1

Taking a balloon trip

Julie records her observations about how Balloon Trip (Activity 6.5) worked with a Year 2 class consisting of twenty-three students.

> There was a little bit of restlessness during the initial stages of the journey as students changed their positions to get comfortable and occasionally a student would sneak a peek to check that everyone else had their eyes shut.
>
> By the time the story reached the students climbing into the balloon basket, the class was impressively settled. As I described climbing up one at a time into the basket I was caught by surprise (along with the other two teachers) as the majority of the class actually started moving their arms and legs as though they were climbing up and over the basket.
>
> As the story progressed, these actions continued to occur as the balloon swayed from side to side. Students even peered over the side of the basket to see how far away the ground was. At this point, one student buried his head in his hands as though he was scared but very slowly started looking over the side again.
>
> After the balloon returned to the ground, a couple of students, ready earlier than the rest, had to be reminded to sit and wait quietly. When students were asked what they saw from the balloon their responses ranged from waterfalls with fairies dancing around them to weddings and jungles. The depth of description that students could communicate was astounding. As the class got up and stretched, students impressed me with how sensible they were.

The aim of Balloon Trip (Activity Box 6.5) is to strengthen a child's ability to visualise and imaginatively respond to a make-believe situation. The mentor provides sensory rich descriptions to help children 'materialise' the experience, emphasising details in such a way that each 'traveller' can find the events personally relevant (Cremin 1998, p. 212; Izzo 1998, p. 46).

Guided Dream in Character (From the Classroom 6.2) demonstrates how one student teacher used a visualisation exercise with Year 4 students in conjunction with a unit of curriculum study.

From the Classroom 6.2

Guided dream in character

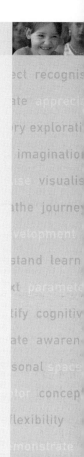

Kimberley adapted the 'guided dream in character' strategy and applied it to a unit about the arrival in Australia of the First Fleet. The thirty-six Year 4 students were asked to think of the 'different types of people on the First Fleet, such as convict, captain, cook, first mate'. As children closed their eyes, the teacher described the passengers boarding the ship and farewelling their families, the conditions aboard ship, and the long trip from England to Australia. Students were encouraged to think about how their characters would feel at various stages of the journey (e.g. hungry, cold, scared, excited, relieved). Following the journey, characters were 'hot seated' by the other students who remained in character.

Kimberley says of the lesson, 'Students really loved the guided dream in character. I think they liked it because they were able to apply knowledge they had learnt (i.e. in studying the First Fleet) to the activity. The students were quiet the whole way through this activity and listened really well … The 'hot seat' activity did not go quite as well. It may have been too much to ask of students to come to the front of the class and answer questions on the spot in character during their first drama lesson. Next time I would give them more support by discussing the types of questions they could ask and how different characters might respond to different questions.'

In imaginative play children freely express their ideas and emotions, often in role—changing from one role to another at will (Warren 1993, p. 3). What If I Were … (Activity Box 6.6) builds on the role-playing elements characteristic of dramatic play as children put themselves into 'someone else's shoes', changing roles in quick succession while focusing on various senses.

Activity Box 6.6

What if I were …

Description
Put yourself into the following roles. Use your sense memory. Imagine and show what you think each person would do.

See   *What if I were ...*

- An astronomer who finds a new star through a telescope.
- A sailor who sights land after being lost at sea.
- A miser who discovers a pot of gold.

Hear   *What if I were ...*

- A spy who overhears a whispered conversation.
- An audience who listens to a boring speech.
- A musician who hears a beautiful song.

Smell *What if I were ...*

- A fire fighter who smells smoke.
- A gardener who gets a whiff of fertiliser intended for the garden.
- A hungry person who sniffs biscuits baking in the oven.

Touch *What if I were ...*

- A pastry cook who kneads sticky dough.
- A potter who makes a pot from messy clay.
- A seamstress who sews with velvet cloth.

Taste   *What if I were ...*

- A judge who is a cake taster at a baking competition.
- A sick person who swallows bitter medicine.
- A child who licks a chocolate ice cream cone.

Mentor note

Encourage children to use their imaginations to visualise each character, the objects they use, and what this character would do in the given situation. Try each role several times. Build on the sensory elements of each situation. Have all children explore roles at the same time. Start with a still pose, move, add sounds, then finish with a still pose.

For older students

Using these roles as examples, students develop additional roles under each sensory category.

Can You Imagine? (From the Classroom 6.3) shows how one student teacher adapted the What If I Were … framework (Activity Box 6.6) to literacy work with upper primary students, using a popular children's book.

From the Classroom 6.3

Can you imagine?

Kristy-lee worked with Year 5 students with the aim of sharing Roald Dahl's 'revolting rhyme', *Cinderella*, as an in-class readers' theatre presentation. In preparation, she adapted the What If I Were … exercise to help students explore the riotous characters and situations. Her list, based on story characters and situations, included:

See The sight of …
- A lonely cleaner with a mean stepmother.
- An arrogant prince who chops off heads.

Hear The sound of …
- An excited stepsister who thinks she has tricked the prince into marrying her.
- Mice 'nibbling' on Cinderella's toes.

Smell The odour of …
- The missing shoe belonging to the stepsister.
- The food at the disco ball.

Touch The feeling of …
- The prince struggling to put the slipper on a stepsister's foot.
- Cinderella 'pressed against the prince's manly chest'.

Taste The taste of …
- The 'home-made marmalade' that Cinderella's new husband makes.
- The taste of success the magic fairy feels, knowing Cinderella is happily married.

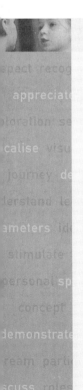

Kristy-lee says of the activity: 'Students enjoyed the humour of the *Revolting Rhymes*, which ignited their curiosity in all of the activities. In the What If I Were ... exercise, I first modelled the *see* examples, then let students interpret the situations in their own style. Next we completed *hear, smell, touch* and *taste*. Some students did become over excited, but I reminded them to "keep it together", a phrase I had introduced in a previous drama lesson to use if things needed to get back on track. This was an effective way of redirecting their attention to the job at hand.'

What If I Were ... (Activity Box 6.6), in which the senses provide a focus for each brief re-enactment, encourages children to think and respond from a perspective that is not their own. Monet's Garden (Activity Box 6.7) takes this approach one step further as it stimulates students to respond from different perspectives within the same environment.

Activity Box 6.7

In the garden

Description
Look at this photo of flowers in a garden. Close your eyes. Visualise the garden.

As yourself:

- Smell the fragrance.
- Touch the smooth, shiny flower petals.
- See the rich colour.
- Hear the birds singing in the garden.
- Open your eyes.
- Find a space of your own in the room.

Figure 6.3 Flowers in a garden

As the gardener:

- Plant a seed, water it, and watch it grow from a seedling into a colourful flower.

As the seed:

- Feel the drops of rain that make you unfold and start to grow.
- Feel the sun on your petals as you open them one by one.
- Grow until you are finished. You have become a remarkable flower.

As the famous painter, Monet, who had a beautiful garden in France:

- Paint a picture of the most remarkable flower in your garden.
- Find a space to display your painting. Tell others about it. (This may be an actual or an imaginary picture.)

Mentor note

Avoid rushing this exercise; try each part several times, breaking in between for discussion and sharing of ideas.

Encourage the group by asking them questions that extend their thinking. (What can a gardener do to ensure plants remain healthy? How does a seed know which direction to grow in when it first starts to sprout? How does an artist mix the colours needed for a painting?)

The many ideas shared provide children with options for developing their own individual responses as the exercise is repeated.

What student teachers said

- 'This exercise helped me visualise beautiful things. My imagination ran wild looking at all these wonderful flowers and breathing in their scents. It's always calming to be filled with a sense of beauty and feeling close to nature. I felt content' (Nickola).
- 'It was effective on a number of levels: examining perspective, taking different roles, using the body for actions and also role playing the artist' (Benjamin).

Reflection, or what Heathcote (1975, p. 96) calls 'stopping to consider', is an important learning tool for children as they explore the same environment from different perspectives. Relevant here are Schön's concepts of **reflection-in-action**, where participants pause to consider what is happening as it happens and, as a result, confirm or reconsider their responses, and **reflection-on-action** where individuals look back on what they have done to reinforce, consolidate, challenge and evaluate their learning (Schön 1983). In Monet's Garden (Activity Box 6.7), reflective discussion occurs both during the exercise and afterwards as children, in the role of artist, share their imaginary paintings with others. When reflection follows action in drama, learning occurs and drama becomes more than just another 'fun' or 'fill-in' activity (Heathcote 1975).

In summary, to each drama experience children bring themselves—their prior experiences, current values and attitudes, and existing knowledge and skills. In the process of doing drama, something happens—they grow, developing more fully the sense of who they are and the potential of what they can become.

Self-awareness

A child's awareness of self can be enhanced through increased communication competence. Developing communication skills through drama, in which voice, facial expression, gesture and body movement are used, increases children's confidence as they establish their own identities in relation to others.

Employing movement and gesture

From their work, dance teachers have found that movement holds memory (Butt 1999). What this means is that recreating a once-learned movement can recapture the learning that was originally associated with it. A research project involving older people who were asked to recreate string figures (i.e. cat's cradles) that they knew as children demonstrates this. Although many at first denied they remembered any string games, once the string was on their fingers, memory returned and many of the figures came back to them (Poston-Anderson & Bathgate 1997).

This physical way of knowing is called **embodiment** and the drama researcher, Grotowski, describes the knowledge gained through 'doing' as **somatic knowledge** (Wolford 1996, p. 32). Movement Essentials (Activity Box 6.8) uses the concept of embodiment to reinforce the essential movements that children use to write their names.

Activity Box 6.8

Movement essentials

Description

- Write your name. Notice what movements are necessary to do this, then write your name in the air in front of you without using the pencil.
- Have you discovered the essential movements needed to write your name?
- Once you feel confident try writing your name in the air with different parts of your body, such as your nose, elbow, big toe.
- Experiment with making the letters first with normal sized movements, then with large and small ones.

Mentor note

Apply the above approach to learning something new; for example, when studying volcanic eruptions let children experience the building pressure through embodiment until the volcano finally erupts. Ensure each child has enough space to avoid bumping into others.

Variation

Start using only the arms to show the entire action; gradually transfer the 'essence' of these movements to the entire body.

For older students

An alternative is to have students write a haiku, that is, a Japanese poem with seventeen syllables in three unrhymed lines of five, seven and five syllables. Have students determine what the essence of the poem is and then capture this in movement.

For example:

Fierce bushfire raging
Racing through the underbrush
Like a speeding train

The bushfire's comparison to the speeding train suggests that its essence is one of force, speed and focused direction

What student teachers said

- 'I think this exercise would help children develop gross [i.e. large] and fine motor movement. They can learn to gain better control of their body parts, which is important for their physical development' (Tina).
- 'I loved the exercise of being a volcano and trying to visualise and reflect it through movement' (Kim)

At the start of a drama session, particularly one that requires children to move vigorously, participants need to warm up their bodies to avoid injuring themselves (Schotz 1998, p. 25). Warm-ups may include stretches, jumping or hopping in place, skipping or running in the space provided, or active group activities, including games such as: tag, which at a signal can change to 'Slow Motion Tag' (Schotz 1998, p. 26), or following the leader (e.g. 'Follow Me'— Schotz 1998, p. 34). Movement warm-ups serve to focus attention, relax the body, and prepare participants physically for the drama activities that follow. Warm-ups may also include visualisation and vocal warm-ups. O'Neill (Taylor 1995) refers to this introductory stage of a drama session and what happens within it as the pre-text (i.e. the preparatory work for the drama action to follow).

Physical Warm-Ups 1 (From the Classroom 6.4) provides insight into how one student teacher used warm-ups to prepare students for further movement activities in drama.

From the Classroom 6.4

Physical warm-ups 1

Tina worked with a Year 2 class whom she described as 'enthusiastic and eager to do drama'.

She writes of the experience: 'The students were very creative and involved in the process. I explained to them that before actors start doing physical movements they need to warm up their bodies, like before you play sport. I asked the students to shake their arms up and down, then their hands, legs, followed by rolling their feet and then their neck slowly. They did everything sensibly and especially loved drawing numbers with their knees and names with their elbows. Some students even suggested that they write the teacher's name with their foot.'

When using movement and gesture, children need to learn how to make and control their own actions. Awareness and Control (Activity Box 6.9) introduces these concepts.

Activity Box 6.9

Awareness and control

Description
- Shake your head from side to side to say 'no'; then nod to say 'yes'.
- Smile, frown, smile again.
- Raise and lower your shoulders.
- Shake your right hand; left hand; both hands.
- Bend from the waist towards your right side, up; towards your left side, up; towards the front, up; gently towards the back, up.
- Shake your right leg; shake your left leg; jump in place.
- Tap your right foot, left foot, walk on the spot.
- Turn all of your body from side to side.

Mentor note
Have students slow down then speed up each movement focusing on how each is made. Encourage children to keep movements under control even when they are moving at a faster pace.

Extension
Use and control movements when singing the children's song *Hokey Pokey* by Roland Lawrence LaPrise. (The lyrics and the tune are available at website www. niehs.nih.gov/kids/lyrics/hokey.htm.)

For older students
An alternative is to mime an action such as: throwing a cricket ball, disco dancing or running a race. Once students have done the action at normal speed, have them repeat it in slow motion with focus on how each part of the body moves. Repeat the process several times going from normal speed to slow motion and back to normal speed again until students feel they are in total control of the action.

Self-control of bodily movement is an important prerequisite for further drama work. Participants must know where they are in space and how to adjust their actions in order to accommodate others in the same space.

Physical Warm-Ups 2 (From the Classroom 6.5) shows the importance of physical warm-ups as a precursor to drama activity.

From the Classroom 6.5

Physical warm-ups 2

Meagan describes how she used bodily movement warm-ups with her composite Year 1–2 class. Meagan writes: 'As the focus of my lessons was movement and non-verbal communication, I began the teaching and learning sequence with simple body warm-up movements. Awareness and Control [Activity Box 6.9] was used in order for students to gain an understanding of the movements possible for the body as well as to relax their bodies and minds. As the students became comfortable with moving in particular ways, they were asked to base their movements on particular animals or characters; for example, move your hands like a penguin's flippers; hold your heads, necks, and backs like an old man; walk like an elephant. As their bodily awareness increased, I asked them to use their bodies to portray everyday activities.'

Exploring Movement (Activity Box 6.10) focuses on the nature of movement: directions, levels, speeds and energies (also called 'energy qualities' [Sabatine 1995]), providing examples to help students learn about the range of movement possibilities.

Activity Box 6.10

Exploring movement

Description

DIRECTIONS
- Find your own spot. Respond to the directions you are given.
- *Look, reach*—in front of you, behind you, to each side of you, up, down.

- *Walk, skip, hop*—forward, backward, to the right, to the left.
- *Take a Turn!* Demonstrate and practise the following: quarter turn; half turn; full turn.
- An element of challenge will be added when everyone is asked to turn in different ways (e.g. 'All those wearing something red—turn quarter turn left; those with something yellow—turn quarter turn right'). Complete this exercise standing on your own spot.

LEVELS

- You are a photographer always looking for an unusual shot.
- With your fingers, make a camera lens and look through it. Examine objects in the room from different levels looking through the camera lens you have made.

> Crawl along the floor.
>> Tiptoe around the room.
>>> Hunch over and walk forward.

- How do objects change when you see them from different levels?

SPEEDS

- You are an astronaut who explores different planets.
- Walk to the spaceship on earth.
- Walk to the spaceship on the moon—where there is no gravity and you will float.
- Walk to your spaceship on a planet where gravity is much heavier than earth.

ENERGIES

- *Lyrical*   like the smooth, even flow of a ballet dancer.
- *Percussive* like a robot jerking with a strong beat.
- *Vibratory*   like milk shaking in a milkshake machine.
- *Suspended* like a bat hanging on a branch.
- *Collapsed*   like a balloon after it's popped.
- *Swinging*   like gorilla arms swaying.

Capture in movement each of the above energy qualities.
Can you think of other examples for each type of energy?
Move back and forth among the different energies.

Mentor note

The Energies are based on Sabatine's movement training work for actors (1995).

For older students

Introduce the concepts of movement, then have students in groups develop a short movement piece on a theme of their choice integrating different levels, directions, speeds and energies as introduced in this Activity Box.

Engaging in various types of movement can enhance and extend learning. Photo Shoot (From the Classroom 6.6) gives one example of how students in a curriculum-related activity used movement to make their roles as photo journalists realistic.

From the Classroom 6.6

Photo shoot

Katrina developed a movement lesson for use with her Year 3 class. In one of the exercises, students became photographers who travelled to different countries to take photos of places, people and objects. She encouraged them to crawl, tiptoe, hunch over, squat—whatever was the best position to take the photo.

Katrina reported: 'The children really got into character and moved around the room. We were fortunate to have a large space for this activity, so that helped a lot. I watched for how the children were moving around, their facial and body expressions and how they were holding their "cameras". I could see that they were taking some terrific "photos".

'In the discussion afterwards, the children commented on how "cool" it was pretending to be in another country and placing yourself in any situation that you wanted. In the future I think this activity would benefit from a few tables, chairs and other obstacles around the room that would enable children to move in different ways (e.g. over and under), although this can still be achieved by reminding children to use different levels.'

Meaningful Moves (From the Classroom 6.7) demonstrates how using and extending the exercise Exploring Movement (6.10) helped students add depth to an improvisational **skit** in a Year 4 classroom.

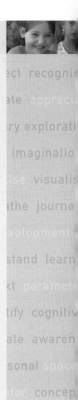

From the Classroom 6.7

Meaningful moves

Kirsty-Ann's aim was for her Year 4 students to create a short skit on any theme, such as 'on the way to school', 'in the supermarket' or 'in the classroom'. After an initial attempt in groups at improvising a scenario, Exploring Movement (Activity Box 6.10) was one of the exercises used to help students extend their drama skills.

Kirsty-Ann reported that she worked through the directions, levels, and speeds of the Exploring Movement exercise with the children. 'Once we got down to energies I allowed them to form a follow-the-leader line. They had to use each of the energies while everyone followed behind. It had a Mexican wave effect as one after the other they would change to the next energy.' She reported that 'the students absolutely loved moving their bodies and wanted to contribute to everything.' As the result of movement and vocal exercises, 'when the students repeated their improvised script, they extended its length with content that made it much more meaningful than it was in the initial attempt.'

Once children know how to make and control a range of different movements, **mime**, which involves 'communicating through gesture and action—usually without words' (Moore 1988, p. 45), can be introduced to help them fine-tune these movement skills. Talented performers, such as Marcel Marceau, have elevated mime into a sophisticated art form; however, participants do not need a performer's high level of expertise to be successful in expressing themselves non-verbally through mime.

Whether mime or **pantomime** is the more appropriate term to use to indicate movement without words is a contested point. Some sources use pantomime (e.g. Novelly 1985; McCaslin 1974); others use mime (Board of Studies NSW 2000; Moore 1988). The distinction between the two is not clear-cut; depending on the source, both can refer to similar processes. This author uses the term mime to describe purposeful movement that conveys an idea without words, that is, 'movement with meaning' (Moore 1988, p. 45), and the term pantomime to refer to a drama form where a story is enacted with exaggerated and often comic movement (e.g. the English pantomime, a melodramatic stage show where the audience is encouraged to cheer or boo the characters).

Use Mime Activities (Activity Box 6.11) as a stimulus for children to develop their own movement ideas.

Activity Box 6.11

Mime activities

Description

- Tie your shoelaces. Test the knots to make sure each is tightly tied.
- Walk a tightrope. Concentrate on keeping your balance.
- Thread some needles. The eye of the first needle is large—easy to thread; the second is smaller—a little more difficult to thread; the third is tiny—very difficult to thread.
- Roll an imaginary ball.

Mentor note

In the final example, roll an imaginary ball, encouraging children to establish the size and weight of the ball.

- Sit in a circle. Roll the ball to each child; each rolls it back to you.
- Make the ball smaller and lighter or larger and heavier.
- Now try smaller and heavier or larger and lighter.
- Repeat the process encouraging the children to visualise the different sized balls, rolling each to reflect its size and weight.

Variations

Snowball: In personal space each person rolls (not throws!) a snowball, combines this snowball with another person's and so on. The snowball gets bigger and bigger until the whole group is rolling one massive snowball. Ask the children what snow structure they would like to make from this huge snowball. Have them work as a team to make it. Ask individual participants to describe what part they built. (Note: because some students may not have experienced snow, spend time describing it and having children imagine the sensations associated with it: cold, wet, sticks together). As an introduction to this activity, refer to actual ice sculpture festivals and competitions around the world (e.g. in Finland, Sweden, Japan, Canada, USA, China, Russia) where sculptures (and even buildings like hotels) are made completely from ice.

Energy Ball: Participants toss energy from tingling fingers to one another (Bany-Winters 1997, p. 15).

For older students,

Explore mime activities associated with the circus, for example, putting up the 'big top' tent. In a large group have the children differentiate and assign tasks for setting up the 'big top' (e.g. Who is in charge of the poles, the tent, the guide ropes, the decorative flags, the advertising posters?). Play circus music and together construct the 'big top' using mime. Once finished, discuss what could have worked more smoothly, then repeat the process.

This exercise can lead to further mime work with students taking on the role of clowns, each one developing an individual routine. A typical clown routine (i.e. act) consists of:

1 the clown's entrance and acknowledgment of the audience,
2 the clown's **stage business** (e.g. mimed action such as: peeling and eating a sour orange, finding an unusual object and offering it to members of the audience with mixed results; pulling an imaginary flower from a buttonhole, sniffing it and sneezing);
3 and the clown's bow and exit in character. (See examples in Jamieson 1981.)

Once each clown has developed a personal routine, group different clowns together and challenge them with the task of combining their individual scenarios into a joint act.

What student teachers said

ROLLING/THROWING AN IMAGINARY BALL
• 'This activity would be useful in the classroom with students of all ages. It engages you, makes you focus on the task at hand, and develops concentration because you don't know when the ball is going to come to you' (Elisa).

- 'This activity requires everyone to be attentive. Every student has a turn at catching and throwing the ball. It encourages teamwork with all students participating actively. This "pretend" game is great for students in Years 1 and 2 because it requires them to use their imaginations' (Katrina).
- 'This movement activity encourages the use of the imagination (i.e. What kind of ball? How big? What does it weigh? How would it move?), whole body movement and concentration (i.e. students need to use eye contact to indicate to whom they are throwing the ball). I would definitely use this exercise with my students' (Tina).
- 'Students learn to communicate through eye contact' (Rochelle).
- 'Students don't have to think too hard about what movements are required. It enables students who may struggle with ball skills to experience success' (Julie).

MAKING A SNOWBALL

- 'This activity is helpful in "breaking the ice" and warming up the group' (Kirsty).
- 'Not only was I thinking more about my own movements but also about how everyone's movements worked together. This activity encourages kids to think about specific movements and how the movements of others affect their own' (Carly).
- 'Snow isn't something that I am used to seeing and feeling so I wasn't quite sure how to mime handling it. I think this exercise would be good to use after a Year 6 camp [i.e. to the snowfields] where children have had the firsthand experience of snow' (Jodie).

When movements are clearly made, the effectiveness of non-verbal communication increases. Mime Time (From the Classroom 6.8) shows how Year 2 students used mime to communicate non-verbally and to create a story.

From the Classroom 6.8

Mime time

Julie describes how she placed ideas for mime in a hat and had her Year 2 students draw out an idea and mime it for others.

I picked up the hat and looked for a volunteer to choose a piece of paper. Lucy came out and chose the action 'using a hairbrush'. Her demonstration was fantastic. She picked it up from a table, brushed her hair a few times, and then put it back down while she used an imaginary hairtie to put her hair into a ponytail. Students then had their own turns to stand in their own personal space and use a hairbrush. This process was repeated with Rob who put on a pair of shoes, John who used an umbrella, and Alex who put on a jumper.

The class moved smoothly into a game of 'Simon Says' using these actions as well as a few new ones. By the end of the activity, students were brushing hair, putting on shoes, putting on jumpers, walking outside and putting up their umbrellas. I was really excited to see the actions we had attempted separately starting to come together to form a short story. I was also astonished by the detail some of the students [used]. For instance, Cathy held onto her long sleeve as she placed her arms into the jumper, while Rob wriggled around in his jumper to make it feel right.

(Note: 'Simon Says' is a game where a leader tells the others to do things using the phrase 'Simon says'; for example, 'Simon says touch your toes'. Participants follow instructions. However, if the leader does not use the phrase 'Simon says', they are not to do the actions [e.g. Touch your nose]. The ones who do the action when the phrase is not said are out. The game continues until only one person remains who is not out.)

In summary, an individual's movements and gestures help identify who they are in their own space and in relation to others. Focusing on expressive movement through warm-ups and body awareness activities; through exercises that familiarise children with the range of movement; and through mime, where participants move purposefully to convey meaning, extends children's somatic knowledge. Facial expression, which is also important in communication, will be discussed under the heading Expressing Feelings later in this chapter.

Exploring vocal expression

The ability to vocalise and make meaningful sounds is important for a child's social development, both at school and at home. Encouraging children to make a variety of sounds, as in Exploring Sound (Activity Box 6.12), helps them discover their own vocal potential.

Activity Box 6.12

Exploring sound

Description

Create a sound poem together. Create the sounds using vocal noises and **body percussion** (i.e. using your hands or feet to make claps, snaps, taps).

Here is the beginning of a sound poem to which you can add more sounds.

Song of the Bush

Snakes slithering

Dry leaves rustling

Kangaroos hopping

Noisy kookaburras calling

Wind whistling

Mentor note

After a sound is selected for the poem, create a graphic sign (i.e. line, circle, dot) to represent it. When you, or a student you choose, point to each sign, children make the sounds—forward in order, then in reverse order.

Variations

Have some children start at the beginning and others at the end. Everyone shares the poem at the same time creating a symphony of sound.

Think of subjects for other sound poems and create them.

For older students

Mystery sounds: Encourage older children to explore sound by sampling sounds in the environment using a tape recorder, playing them back and having other children guess what these sounds are. Young people may then mix the sounds to create their own 'actual' sound poem.

As well as developing an awareness of sounds and how to produce them, children need to realise the importance of breath control for vocal production. AHHH *Breathing Exercises* AHHH (Activity Box 6.13) and Vocal Wake-up (Activity Box 6.14) encourage participants to centre on their breathing.

Activity Box 6.13

AHHH *breathing exercises* AHHH

Description

- Close your eyes. Concentrate on your breathing. Let the breath come from the diaphragm. Breathe in, out, in, out.
- As you breathe out, let an open relaxed AHHH happen. Avoid any strain in your throat. Relax, breathe deeply, and again … AHHH.
- Breathe deeply again and project the AHHH to various points of the room (e.g. close to you, the floor, the ceiling, halfway across the room, the sides of the room, the back wall). Keep the sound relaxed.

Mentor note

It may take children a while to get used to closing their eyes and concentrating on their breathing. Keep encouraging them.

What student teachers said

- 'This breathing activity in which you make a noise as you exhale gets students to relax and let go. It may be useful when students need to feel comfortable as a group, perhaps before an emotional or creative activity where barriers and inhibitions could get in the way' (Nickola).
- 'This activity gives you practice in controlling your voice. It is useful for teachers because they need to know how to project their voices in the classroom appropriately. Also, when using this exercise with children, they get to experiment with getting louder, but not shouting' (Tracy).
- 'Having taken singing lessons and being involved in drama for many years, I was often told I needed to project my voice but was not shown how to do this. This exercise, choosing different parts in the room at which to "aim" your voice, would have been beneficial to me because it gave examples of different spots to which to project your voice rather than just "normal" voice and "projected" voice which, before I did this exercise, meant "shouting" to me' (Robyn).

In Vocal Wake-Up (Activity Box 6.14) control is needed to support and sustain vowel sounds. Because proper breath control is a prerequisite for effective vocal production, making breathing exercises a regular part of the vocal warm-up for drama is recommended.

Activity Box 6.14

Vocal wake-up

Description

Wake up your mouth and throat—yawn, chew vigorously, lick your lips, say 'ooo-ahhh' dropping your jaw as you say it. Add consonants, such as: m, n, t, s, f ... to the following vowel sounds: *ee, ah, oh, oo*. Repeat each phrase several times before moving on to adding the next consonant. Example: *mee, mah, moh, moo.*

Mentor note

- For each set of sounds, have children notice how their lips move and where their tongue is placed inside the mouth in relation to their teeth.
- Have children repeat each phrase until they need to take another breath.

Exercising the mouth, lips, and tongue is another worthwhile vocal warm-up. **Tongue twisters** are effective in doing this because they challenge children to produce a series of similar sounds distinctly. Tantalising Tongue Twisters (Activity Box 6.15) can be used to inspire children to create their own phrases.

Activity Box 6.15

Tantalising tongue twisters

Description

Say each of the following phrases three times in rapid succession.

- Angry ants always attack.
- Boggy billabongs bring bright birds.
- Crazy koalas climb carelessly.
- Daring dingoes dislike dirty dens.
- Enquiring echidnas explore everything.
- Flying foxes find fine fruit.
- Go, goanna, go!

Make up your own tongue twisters to complete the alphabet.

Mentor note

As children say each tongue twister, have them enunciate each phrase clearly. Have them overdo it, exaggerating the sounds that come out of their mouths and noticing the placement of the tongue and shape of the lips as each sound is made. For a challenge, have them close their mouths completely and try to say the same phrases again working to be heard.

Now explore pitch and volume as each tongue twister is said.

- Whisper each phrase.
- Call out each phrase as though you are speaking to the back of the room.
- Start softly. As you say each word build the volume.
- Start loudly. As you say each word decrease the volume.
- Start with a soft low voice and on each word raise the pitch and grow louder.
- Start with a loud high voice and on each word lower the pitch and grow softer.

Variations

Bany-Winters (1997, p. 12) and Novelly (1985, pp. 65–66) provide other examples of tongue twisters.

What student teachers said

- 'This exercise warms up the voice and gets the whole mouth and face moving' (Tina) and 'is useful because you must pronounce the words properly and concentrate on how your mouth and tongue are moving' (Kimberly).
- 'Tongue twisters are fun because you get to say silly things. Children enjoy this sort of nonsense game. Tongue twisters enable children to concentrate on what they are saying as they try not to slip up. It almost becomes a competition with themselves' (Elisa).
- 'This exercise is great for getting kids to practice articulation. Other good activities are getting them to say things like "How now brown cow?" to practise saying blends. Children could then go and write a list of other words with an "ow" sound. This is especially helpful for **ESL** students and students in the lower primary years' (Jodie).

As tongue twisters are said, tongue and lip movements need to be exaggerated so that sounds can be clearly produced and heard. Clarity of vocal sound production is important if communication is to occur.

Once children are heard and understood, vocal variety can be used to add expressiveness to what they say. The voice, a unique dramatic instrument, can soothe as in the cooing of a lullaby or command as in the giving of an order. Expressiveness is the result of effective use of vocal characteristics including pitch, volume, pace, inflection, tone and vocal quality. In Express Yourself Vocally (Activity Box 6.16), children have the opportunity to practise each of these vocal elements.

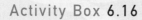

Activity Box 6.16

Express yourself vocally

Vocal warm-ups before a performance

Description

Figure 6.4 Vocal warm-ups before a performance

- **Pitch**: where a tone is located within the range of vocal sound from the lowest to the highest note you can make.
  Say—AAAHHH.
  Make your voice go from the lowest sound that you can comfortably make to the highest and back again. How can you do this without straining your voice?

- **Volume**: the loudness or softness of your voice.
  Say—'very softly', softly; loudly, 'very loudly'.
  What are you doing?
  What do you have to do to change the volume of your voice?

- **Pace**: the rate or speed at which you speak.
  Say—'very slowly', slowly; quickly, 'very quickly'.
  I have to go home right now.
  Is this sentence more difficult to say when you speak faster? Explain.

- **Inflection**: voice modulation accomplished by a change in tone or pitch.
  - Ask a question: Who are you?
  - Make a statement: I am happy.
  - Make a demand: Give me that.
  - Ask for help: Help me, please!

    Listen to your voice. How does it differ each time?

- **Tone**: the way you say things to show the intent behind what you say.

  Say each phrase in different ways:
  - *Who are you?* (afraid, kindly)
  - *I am happy.* (excited; trying to convince someone)
  - *Give me that.* (angrily, begging)

    Can you hear the differences in the way you say the phrases?

- **Vocal quality**: the nature of the sound made when a person speaks.

  Make the following sounds:
  - A lion roaring
  - A king commanding
  - A rock star singing
  - A rooster crowing
  - A parent scolding

    How does your voice change? How do you make each sound differently?

- **All together now**

  Say—using different vocal characteristics to change the meaning.

  Wait for me.

  Please, let me go

  I like that.

  Will you be back soon?

    How does the meaning change when you express a phrase differently?

Mentor note

Use the examples under each heading as starting points. Encourage students to extend the lists with their own ideas.

Vocalisation exercises are useful as part of the warm-up for a drama session. Vocal Exercises (From the Classroom 6.9) shows how one student teacher implemented these verbal workouts with a combined class of upper grade students.

From the Classroom 6.9

Vocal exercises

Kristy-lee used vocal exercises with a composite Year 5–6 class as a warm-up. With Express Yourself Vocally (Activity Box 6.16) as a basis, students were asked to repeat what she said at the same volume and in the same style, starting with 'la la la la' going up and down in pitch. When this was repeated, students were asked to open their mouths to the widest and smallest size and listen to what happened to the sound. Next students made the loudest noise, then the softest noise they could and finished by using their tone of voice asking angry and sad questions with the opposite tone in answer (i.e. an angry question received a sad response).

Kristy-lee reported that 'students enjoyed warming up their voices and many asked to take my job of stating what everyone else must reply. [When several students did this], they approached the task with seriousness.'

Diction, which involves enunciating each word clearly, and **projection**, which involves saying the words loudly enough to be heard in the given situation, are important factors in a young person's overall communication success. As part of oral-skill development through drama, both need emphasis. Vocal Reflections (Activity Box 6.17) provides the opportunity for children to practise these skills.

Activity Box 6.17

Vocal reflections

Description
- Stand with a partner. Say a sentence clearly and carefully.
- Your partner will try to say exactly what you are saying as you say it.
- Change so that your partner becomes the speaker and you the person who is vocally mirroring.

Mentor note

Johnstone (1999) developed the vocal mirror technique for use with storytellers. This exercise requires partners to watch each other closely in order to say the words at the same time.

For older students

Once partners have mastered how to mirror each other vocally, gradually expand the size of the group doing the mirroring until one student speaks and the whole drama group vocally mirrors what this person says.

What student teachers said

- 'This involved close observation of the mouth. Half the secret was mimicking the mouth shape before knowing what the word would be. It helps to focus on how mouth shape and word enunciation are related and to see that the way we pronounce words means different mouth formations' (Ben).
- 'This exercise helps to warm up all areas of the mouth; exaggeration shows the [normally] small movements of the mouth and tongue. It helps with individual awareness' (Rochelle).
- 'I was thinking more closely about my mouth movements as I spoke and examining the other person's movements as they spoke' (Carly).

Vocal Reflections (Activity Box 6.17), in which participants speak distinctly as another person mirrors what they say, reinforces the observation and concentration skills that are needed to project a clear vocal sound.

Exercises such as the ones provided in this section, Exploring Vocal Expression, aim to help children become more aware of their own voices, to assist them in learning how to produce and control the sounds that they make, and to encourage them to add vocal variety as they express themselves aloud. Knowing how to use the voice effectively is not only an important skill for drama, but it is also useful in other classroom learning situations and at home with family and friends.

Expressing feelings

In How Do You Feel? (Activity Box 6.18), children explore how they can express feelings using facial expression and body action.

Activity Box 6.18

How do you feel?

Description

Express the following feelings using only your face:

Happy	Angry	Surprised	Sad	Bored

Figure 6.5 Using the face to express feelings

Mentor note

After children show the first feeling, have them use their hands to hide their faces while their expressions change to the next feeling. Drop the hands to show the feeling; then raise them again to change to the next feeling. Follow the same procedure until all feelings have been revealed.

Variations

After suggesting feelings on the face alone, add gestures to the facial expression for each feeling; then add full body movement.

Mime an emotion: Passing hands across the face to hide the change of expression is called a 'face wipe' (Moore 1988, p. 55).

Picture feelings: Make a picture of a feeling, then change from one feeling to another one in slow motion as the mentor counts to six. Using slow motion as a transition between feelings actively demonstrates how bodies change to express different emotions. Have children observe this and reflect on it.

Weather as mood barometer: Ask the children, 'What weather are you today?' (e.g. bright with sunshine, cloudy, a thunderstorm). Help them understand that weather can be an analogy for their feelings. Also, that, like weather, feelings can change quickly (Amatruda 2006).

For older students

Doubling: Given a situation, students work in pairs to present both the inner feelings and the outer expression of these emotions; for example, in a situation where a student receives an award at a school assembly, one person mimes the outer expression of the emotion as felt by the student, while the second person expresses these feelings in words. Doubling different situations can serve as a discussion starter; for example, does every student who receives an award feel the same way about it?

Doubling can include thought tracking (Neelands in Carey 1995) where one person speaks and the second person reveals the first person's inner thoughts (e.g. (1) speech: 'I'm lost. I don't know how to get out of here'; (2) thought: *I really don't want to be found. It feels good to be on my own for once*).

What student teachers said

FACE WIPES

- 'Students can create each expression as well as feel the slight changes and movements between the different feelings. It also shows how different people show emotions slightly differently' (Rochelle).

WHOLE BODY EXPRESSION OF FEELINGS

- 'This exercise is particularly useful in helping children to learn to express their emotions, not just with their faces but with their whole body movement. Potentially this could help children understand what other people feel from their body language' (Tina).
- 'It was good to be able to think separately about what to do with different body parts before putting them together to make a more complete picture [of the feeling]'(Julie).

CHANGING FEELINGS IN SLOW MOTION

- 'Exploring how to move from one emotion to another without stopping was quite challenging' (Kim).
- 'This exercise provided a chance to consider physical changes, such as body language and stance, and how they differ from one extreme emotion to another' (Meagan).
- 'This exercise really made me think about the degrees of a feeling and how the whole body is used to portray them' (Carly).

How people express their feelings may vary greatly from person to person, or not much at all. Personality traits, cultural backgrounds, values or even where a person was at a particular time may help to explain these variations.

Of interest as well is the fact that people relate particular feelings to certain events. To recapture a particular feeling at a later date, think back to how that feeling was experienced in a given situation. This is called using **emotional memory** (Cassady 1993, p. 36). I'm Feeling (Activity Box 6.19) asks participants to remember how they felt in familiar situations that most of them will have experienced.

Activity Box 6.19

I'm feeling

Description
- Happy
  - Because I received a special present.
  - Because the holidays start today.
  - Because ...
- Upset
  - Because I can't go out to play.
  - Because someone made a face at me.
  - Because ...
- Sad
  - Because I'm alone.
  - Because I misplaced my favourite toy.
  - Because ...

Mentor note
For each feeling have children consider how their actions change to reflect the differing circumstance. Have them think of other situations in which they have experienced each of these or other feelings and demonstrate how they reacted.

I'm Feeling (Activity Box 6.19) reinforces the idea that emotions and feelings are affected by people's perceptions of what happens to them. Exactly how the same feeling is expressed, such as being happy, will vary with the circumstance. In addition, not everyone will have the same emotional response to the same event, for example, a sunrise, a scolding, or a surprise party. Through participating with others in drama experiences, children learn to recognise and appreciate these differences, valuing their own feelings while, at the same time, respecting those of others.

Applications for middle school students

Psychologists (e.g. Erikson 1959, 1950; Havighurst 1952), suggest that adolescence brings with it special needs and concerns. Erikson, who regards each stage of life as having its own psychosocial crisis, sees adolescence as a time when young people confront the issue of 'identity versus role confusion'. Questions such as 'Who am I? Where am I headed in life?' are accentuated because of the physical and cognitive changes that happen to young people at this time.

During this dynamic transition period from childhood to adulthood, drama exercises that focus on self and relationships with others can provide a means for supporting adolescents in developing their individual self-concepts and in building relationship skills. However, these exercises need to be approached with care in order to ensure that they do not accentuate any embarrassment or awkwardness that students may already feel about the changes they are undergoing.

Students at this stage are often sensitive to others' perceptions and do not want to do or say anything that might make them look 'silly'. Stressing the importance of working in one's own personal space, doing exercises together rather than singling out an individual student to demonstrate them, and giving young people plenty of choice in how they participate can help to reduce any feelings that they may have that they are 'on show'.

In approaching drama with young people of any age, but particularly adolescents, the drama mentor is well advised to find out what students already know and start where they are in terms of prior knowledge, attitudes and behaviours. A learner-centred approach makes drama meaningful for students because it builds on their own interests and ideas. To involve adolescents in meaningful ways, then, the mentor must consult students at all stages of the drama planning, implementation, and evaluation process.

When working with adolescents, it is particularly important for them to understand the relevance and purpose of the exercises they undertake. For example: visualisation exercises serve to strengthen the imagination that, in turn, enables them to make the transition more easily from the here-and-now into the 'as if' world of drama; breathing exercises relax them and provide support for the voice; stretches and other physical exercises warm up muscles and prepare them for safe movement. Giving students time to reflect on what they are doing, thinking and feeling also deepens the experience and enables them to contribute their own ideas.

Professional actors use a range of exercises to help them warm-up, get into character, and control stage fright; so, too, can student actors benefit from an established rehearsal routine. Placing students in 'authentic' roles (i.e. as actors) makes the drama process meaningful and relevant for them. If possible, have them attend a rehearsal for a local theatre company to see how actors use exercises as part of their training, or have a practising actor visit the class to conduct a drama-skills workshop with them. In this way, adolescents come to accept warm-up and cool-down exercises as an essential part of drama work.

Summary

Having a sense of self involves knowing 'who you are'. In drama, this means understanding how to use your voice, move your body, and express your feelings in ways that represent you, but are also appropriate for the context. Drama exercises that focus on verbal and movement skills make individuals aware of how they express themselves and enable them to extend their vocal and physical repertoires. Helping students become aware of their own feelings and how to express them is an important step in the process of learning how to manage and control one's emotions.

For further study

1   Provide three reasons why a positive 'sense of self' is an important starting point for drama.
2   Drama educator Dorothy Heathcote (1975) said that: 'Emotion is at the heart of drama' and that 'talking about emotion is no substitute for feeling it.' In what ways is this statement relevant to drama work with children?

3 Consider the role that students play in learner-centred education. How can developing the awareness of self through drama prepare them to fulfil this role?

For reflection

Work through the exercises in this chapter, recording your thoughts on the potential of each for use with younger and/or older children? How can these activities be combined in meaningful ways to help students learn more about themselves?

Preview

Chapter 7: Sense of Others considers getting to knowing others, responding to their feelings and working with others as a team as essential groundwork for drama.

Sense of Others

'Drama is about filling the space between people with meaningful experiences' (Heathcote 1975).

Introduction

Drama is an effective means for learning about others because it is a medium that involves social interaction. During drama, participants engage in a 'dialogic' process of making meaning that enables them to grow and change (O'Neill & Lambert 1982) as they continuously 'give and take'—sharing viewpoints, insights and understandings with each another. Drama's transformative journey requires that the mentor be patient, tolerant and provide a supportive environment. For this reason, taking time to build a positive group dynamic at the start of drama work with children is well worth the effort. The activities in this chapter aim to achieve the goal of helping children get to know each other.

Getting acquainted

Being able to call a person by name values them as an individual. All group members, including the mentor, benefit from knowing each other by name. Name Circle (Activity Box 7.1) presents different ways of learning everyone's name.

Activity Box 7.1

Name circle

Description

You are with a group in a circle. One child is picked to say his/her name. It's YOU! You add an adjective that matches the first letter of your name. If your name is Chris—you could be Clever Chris or Calm Chris. If your name is Beatrice, you could be Brave Beatrice or Bouncing Beatrice.

Once you have said the adjective with your name, the person next to you repeats it, then adds his or her name—adding an adjective to match the first letter (e.g. Dynamic David or Terrific Tanya). Each child in the circle in turn repeats all the names so far and then adds his or her name with a matching adjective.

The exercise is over when everyone in the circle has said the names and it is your turn again.

Mentor note

Children choose the descriptions to go along with their names. If the group is too large, divide it into smaller circles. Run the exercise several times mixing up the children each time so they are not always in the same circle.

Variations

- Animal names: Children use animal names to match the first initials of their names, such as Andrew Ant, Carla Cat, Drewe Dingo, and Brad Bear.
- Cue names: Children give a sign or make a movement as they say their name (e.g. clap, touch chin) (Schotz 1998, p. 14).

For older students

- Country names: Students add the name of a city or country to their names (e.g. Barbara from Barcelona, Karen from Kiama) (Murray 2006).
- Name games: Go around the circle several times repeating students' names. Each time the pace gets faster (Amatruda 2006).

Drama games are fast-paced, involving and fun for children as they get to know and feel comfortable with one another. Educators suggest that these motivational activities have a range of benefits, including: fine-tuning observation, memory and listening skills; improving concentration;

developing cooperation; encouraging spontaneity and the imagination; and helping children relax (Schotz 1998, p. 5). In playing drama games, children integrate their physical and mental capacities as they attempt to reach a goal or meet a challenge. The game, Over There! (Activity Box 7.2), has a focus on observation skills and challenges participants to be alert in order to respond quickly to the directions given.

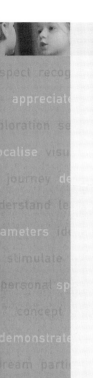

Activity Box **7.2**

Over there!

Description

The mentor will direct you to put a body part on a colour. For example: Knees on brown or fingers on yellow. As you hear these directions, look around the drama space and find objects with these colours. Place the body part indicated on the object with the colour described.

Mentor note

Colours must be on objects that are within reach in the room and are not part of a person's clothing or possessions.

Variation

Search and Touch is a similar exercise (Moore 1988, p. 8), as is the commercially produced game, Twister, which requires participants to touch different coloured circles on a playing mat in response to directions.

Because motivational activities, such as Over There! (Activity Box 7.2), 'establish relationships' and 'help develop group cohesion' (Moore 1988, pp. 1–2), they are frequently used at the start of drama sessions to warm up the group and prepare them for further drama participation.

Sharing feelings with others

Key tenets of Coleman's theory of **emotional intelligence** (1995) are knowing one's emotions, managing them, recognising emotions in others, and empathising with them. An underlying purpose in drama, too, is the concern for feelings and emotions, related both to self and others. Participants learn to express their feelings and control them in socially acceptable ways while at the same time developing respect for others and being able to empathise with their feelings.

Making children aware of how people other than themselves express a range of feelings can help them understand the link between emotions and actions. Actors make use of this connection in order to reveal a character's feelings to the audience through facial expressions and movements. As Feelings and Emotions (Activity Box 7.3) demonstrates, what people show 'on the outside' often (although not always) reflects how they feel 'on the inside'. Once an awareness of how emotions can be expressed is raised, learning how to convey feelings in ways that enable others to interpret them is important.

Activity Box **7.3**

Feelings and emotions

Figure 7.1 Bottom (left) and Titania from *A Midsummer Night's Dream*

Description

Here is a photograph of two student actors in Shakespeare's play, *A Midsummer Night's Dream*. One plays the part of Bottom as a donkey; the other plays the role of Titania, the Fairy Queen. Look at the picture closely. What clues are there to how these characters feel? How do facial expressions and gestures help you decide?

Find other photos of people. What clues are there to how people in these photos feel?

Mentor note

Remind children that these clues may or may not correspond to how people in the photos *really* feel. The only way to know that is to ask them, which is not always possible. Sometimes educated guesses are used to make judgments about how others feel, based on their expressions and actions.

Far Out! (Activity Box 7.4) provides a starting point for the process of expressing emotions so others can interpret them as children are asked to project feelings to others.

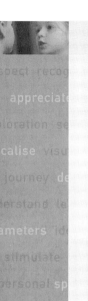

Activity Box **7.4**

Far out!

Description
As the mentor whispers the name of a feeling to you, demonstrate it for others in your group.

Mentor note
At first have the child 'demonstrator' and the group stand close together. After everyone has a turn, move the group half way across the room. Repeat the exercise giving each child a different feeling. Finally, repeat the exercise a third time, moving the group as far from the demonstrator as possible. Have children consider what can be done to project feelings across a larger distance as actors must do when they perform on the stage.

In Pass It On! (Activity Box 7.5), participants express feelings and then pass them on to others.

Activity Box **7.5**

Pass it on!

Description
Participants form two lines facing each other at opposite ends of the room. One line is called A, the other B. Both lines approach each other. The A line approaches the B line expressing an emotion. The B line approaches the A line with a neutral expression. As the A line passes through the B line, the Bs take on the A emotion

and the As become neutral. Both lines continue until they reach the opposite end of the room and turn to face each other again.

Then change so that the B line approaches the A line with an emotion, which is passed on to the neutral A line as they pass through and go to the other side of the room.

Mentor note

All of the A line may have the same emotion (e.g. anger, happiness) or each person may choose a different emotion. It is important that each member in the A line has a corresponding partner in the B line. For this reason, you may wish to have students find partners first, and then split the students into two lines with partners opposite each other.

The point of the exercise is to learn how to let go of an emotion.

For older students

Reflection: Think of situations where people are likely to take on the emotions or moods of the people around them (e.g. cricket game, religious service, rock concert). Discuss the positive and negative aspects of shared emotions.

What student teachers said

- 'I think children would enjoy passing on a feeling as they get to "overact" a specific feeling ... [Doing this] enables children to think about their body and voice' (Elisa).
- 'It was interesting to create in myself a feeling so I could portray it and then in an instant pass it on, wiping it all away. I think this would help students understand how they feel, control it, and then let it go. It would be a good anger management practise for people' (Tracy).

In addition to facial expression, gesture and body movement, vocal tone is often used to convey how someone feels, whether or not the actual words are understood. Salt and Pepper (Activity Box 7.6) demonstrates that meaning can be conferred by tone alone or in combination with movement, even when the words themselves do not make sense in the context.

Activity Box 7.6

Salt and pepper

Description

- Find a partner. Using only the words 'salt and pepper', show each other that you are pleased, afraid, excited, upset.
- Now add gestures, facial expression, and body movement to the tone of your voice. Using the same words, 'salt and pepper', take turns showing your partner that:
  - You are pleased when you open the present.
  - You are afraid because a lion has escaped from its cage.
  - You are excited because you are getting a new computer.
  - You are upset because your bicycle has a flat tire.

Mentor note

Have each group share, while the other groups listen. Then reflect on the following:

- How did the tone of voice convey each feeling?
- Was it easier to understand what was meant when facial expressions and gestures were added to the vocal tone?
- What have you learned about communication from this exercise?

Variations

- Gibberish: Children use nonsense talk to show how to do something (Bany-Winters 1997, p. 95).
- Start with nonsense words on cards before having participants create their own nonsense words (Johnstone 1999, pp. 214–16).

For older students

- Gobbledyegook: Use nonsense language to say a nursery rhyme or a familiar folktale (Schotz 1998, p. 80).
- The storyteller starts with recognisable words. At a signal from the mentor, the teller changes to nonsense words and continues the story. At a second signal, the teller changes back to actual words to complete the story (Cassady 1993, p. 71).

What student teachers said

- 'At first the "Salt and Pepper" activity was funny. It was hard not to laugh. Then came the challenge of trying to change the tone of voice you had [as the situation changed]. This activity would be helpful for children to practice changing their tones of voices as they ask questions, state something, or just talk in general. It would be fun for children to make up their own words' (Kirsty).
- 'Talking about a certain topic using only the words salt and pepper requires kids to think about "how" they say things and the tone they use. Also, have them discuss why "tone" is important. This would be great with middle and upper primary kids' (Katrina).
- 'A variation would be to have each small group of children plan a conversation in a *particular situation* (e.g. buying something in a shop, putting on a parachute for a sky dive, baking a cake) using only the words "salt and pepper". Have children in the other groups "see if they can guess the situation from the tone alone" (Meagan).
- 'Students may struggle [with this exercise] if they haven't previously been made aware of tone and the different ways we speak. A solution to this would be to do "Salt and Pepper" and then encourage students to listen to the tone of conversations throughout the rest of the school day. Have them make a list of possible ways of having a conversation. Trial these in class. [Then do "Salt and Pepper" again to see what they have learned about tone]' (Julie).

This section focused on feelings, those emotions that motivate action in drama as well as in life. The exercises aimed to enhance children's emotional intelligence, making them more aware of their own feelings and how to use body action and vocal tone to express them. The exercises also demonstrated that, while everyone has feelings, each person can express them in different ways. Educators claim that knowing about feelings, how different people express them and put them into action, is one of the unique contributions that drama can make to children's learning (Heathcote 1975, p. 102).

Working together as a team

At the core of the drama experience is the ability to cooperate with one another. To cooperate with other people, a person must take notice of them and respond in supportive and constructive ways. Mirror, Mirror (Activity Box 7.7) is a well-known means for children, in pairs, to focus their attention on each other and respond. First, one person becomes the mirror and the other the reflection. Then the partners change places. Mirroring in partners or in larger groups fosters rapport as participants alternatively initiate actions and respond. The goal is ultimately to have the leadership flow between partners or among members of the group without specific directions from the mentor.

Activity Box 7.7

Mirror, mirror

Description
- Stand facing a partner. You are A; your partner is B.
- Stand in place moving the fingers of your right hand slowly. Your partner (B) mirrors your actions. When your partner is mirroring you exactly, slowly add your right arm, fingers of the left hand, left arm, shoulder, facial expression. Don't rush—make sure your partner mirrors you exactly.

Mentor note
The aim is not to trick the partner, but to have the partners mirror each other exactly. Encourage A to move slowly so B can follow and vice versa.
- Have A and B switch roles, so that B initiates the action.
- Have partners look each other in the eyes. This helps them to coordinate their movements.

Variations
- From the exercise as described above, change to mirroring basic activities (e.g. eating soup, washing one's face) (Schotz 1998, p. 41).
- Build from mirroring in partners to mirroring with an entire group (Krupar 1973, p. 3).

For older students
- Guess who's the mirror: No signal is given as the leadership passes between the two partners. A third person tries to guess who is initiating the action and who is following (Bany-Winters 1997, p. 16).

- Mirror move and groove: In groups of four or more, participants stand in two dance lines, one line directly behind the other one. When the music starts, one person provides movements in time with the music until a signal sounds; then the next person takes over the dance and so forth around the group moving clockwise. When the responsibility for movement reaches the back line, it is helpful for the back line to move to the front; or for the entire group to turn around facing the opposite way (i.e. so the back line becomes the front line).

What student teachers said

- 'Mirror, Mirror was silent; I found it calming. It required thought and creativity on the part of the person being mirrored, and concentration on the part of the person doing the mirroring. This activity would be useful to help students to focus before a lesson' (Nickola).
- 'This exercise highlights that communication isn't always done through words' (Kristy-lee).
- 'I used this with Kindy classes to help them concentrate and look closely and carefully at different movements' (Tracy).

Mirror Image (From the Classroom 7.1) demonstrates how exercises, such as Mirror, Mirror (Activity Box 7.7), can be adapted and used in performance.

From the Classroom 7.1

Mirror image

Figure 7.2 Mirror, mirror on the wall ...

Mirror, Mirror (Activity Box 7.7) shaped the interaction between the vain mother and her mirror image in *Bella Venezia*, an Italian variation of the Snow White story presented for upper primary children (Poston-Anderson 1999a). With the hoop as the mirror frame, the student actors (who were student teachers) began with matching movements that they choreographed into a dance sequence with music.

Extend the awareness children gain from doing mirror exercises to other types of collaborative group activities that involve people making connections with others. Connect: Over, Under, Around and Through (Activity Box 7.8) gives children the opportunity to interact with others to create a group tableau.

Activity Box 7.8

Connect: Over, under, around and through

Description
You and your group will make a tableau. One person begins by taking a pose. Each person joins the tableau and must choose whether to connect with it by going over, under, around or through the existing shapes made by the poses others have taken.

Mentor note
The aim is to cooperate to make a group tableau with participants at different levels and facing different directions. As you, the mentor, walk around it, the tableau should look filled out in all directions and at all levels. Once the tableau is made, have the participants remove themselves from the structure one at a time in reverse order, when possible.

Do this exercise several times encouraging them to use different levels and directions for their body positions. Vary how they enter (e.g. spies on a mission, explorers caught in quicksand). Any pose they assume must be sustainable until the tableau is complete.

Variations
Start with 'pick-up' sticks, toothpicks, or straws. Have each child place one on the pack. Then have the children as a group decide in which order the sticks or straws should come back out of the pack in order to cause the least disruption to the others. Have them use this experience as the basis for determining how to develop and then dismantle the group tableau.

For older students
Staveley (2000), a music educator, plays different styles of music as students do this exercise. Match the musical piece to the students' roles as spies

seeking information, explorers getting caught in quicksand, or spaghetti tangling in a pot.

What student teachers said

- 'In this whole-body exercise, students conceptualised what over, under, around, and through meant in relation to other students. This interactive body sculpture involved teamwork, particularly in figuring out who leaves when' (Ben).
- 'We were all considering ways to fill the gaps in the different directions and levels' (Meagan).
- 'The focus on over, under, around and through is beneficial for those who need suggestions to get them started' (Robyn).

Cooperation involves responding to others in constructive ways. In Feathered Friends (Activity Box 7.9), inspired by Heathcote's idea of 'stillness and movement' (1975, p. 103), only one person moves at a time; the rest remain stationary. For this to succeed, children must be in tune with others, taking the opportunity to move when it arises, and stopping when another person begins to move.

Activity Box 7.9

Feathered friends

Figure 7.3 Students choose a role from pictures on the wall

Description

Examine pictures of birds that have been placed around the room on the wall. Choose one of these birds. Become that bird using sound and movement. With others, fill the space with birds. Everyone moves, but does not interact with anyone

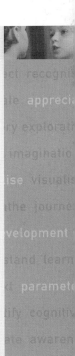

else. At the signal, stop, be as still as you can, being aware of the other birds. One bird, maybe it is you, starts to move. Move making the bird sound until another bird starts to move, then you stop.

Mentor note

- When pictures provide the stimulus for the child's invention of a bird, this is a variation of the drama technique **role on the wall** (Neelands in Carey, 1995).
- Make it clear that only one bird moves at a time.
- Signal the first several changes. After that, rely on individuals in the group to sense when it is time to stop and start.

For older students

Use specific curriculum tie-ins (e.g. goldminers panning for gold) or areas of student interest (e.g. mini-bike riders or fashion models on a catwalk) as alternative starting points for this exercise.

Mentor note

This exercise builds group awareness and cohesion, as well as concentration skills. Make the point that movement captures attention, a useful concept when staging a play.

In Feathered Friends (Activity Box 7.9), each child created a unique bird using movement and sound. In Great Gizmo! (Activity Box 7.10), children work together as designers to invent a giant machine.

Activity Box **7.10**

Great gizmo!

Description

Together in one large group create a giant gizmo with all its various buttons, switches and gears. Which part of this machine are you? How does your part move? What sound does it make as it moves?

Mentor note

One child begins by making the movement and sound of a machine part. Gradually, one at a time, everyone else joins in to make the gizmo until it is fully operational. The mentor sets up the situation and intervenes as a coach when necessary to facilitate the action. Encourage children to connect with the gizmo at different levels and from all angles. Experiment with pace, speeding up or slowing down the movement of the machine.

Variations

- Living patterns and live machines: Working in groups, participants create the 'latest machine from science fiction', a 'mood machine' (e.g. happiness, sadness); or a 'clown machine'(Novelly 1985, pp. 35–56).
- Machines: Options for machines include a pizza machine, laughing machine, computer, music machine—among others (Bany-Winter 1997, p. 32).

For older students

Building a machine: Students take turns as the operator and suggest the nature of the machine (e.g. fragile, sturdy, erratic). The operator presses the imaginary control button indicating whether the machine is to slow down, speed up, or stop (Schotz 1998, pp. 75–77).

Extension

Share with children *Everyday Machines* by John Kelly (1995), a visually appealing non-fiction book that explains through drawings and text the workings of many modern devices, such as a microwave oven, smoke alarm, television, camera, digital watch, telephone, personal stereo, video cassette recorder and computer.

Great Gizmo! (Activity Box 7.10) and its variations encourage children to work together as a group, making them aware of how to cooperate and build on each other's ideas. After experiencing the basic exercise, children can be encouraged to work in small groups to create their own special-purpose machines (e.g. doughnut maker, washing machine). This requires them to visualise the process involved and animate it through their actions.

Group activities that involve decision-making give children the experience of learning how to state a point of view and negotiate with others. Building a sandcastle on the beach, planting a vegetable garden or cooking a banquet for the king's table all require children to use their communication skills. Vary the approach by sometimes having the group work with action only (no words) in order to focus on nonverbal skills.

In Bush Emergency! (Activity Box 7.11), children work as a group to extinguish a fire in the bush.

Activity Box 7.11

Bush emergency!

Description

You and your friends are camped along a river in the bush. You see smoke. You grab the one bucket you brought with you to carry your supplies. Empty it. Stand in a line stretching from the river to the bushfire. The person near the river fills the bucket with water and passes it down the line until it reaches the fire. The last person pours the water on the fire and sends the bucket back down the line for more water. As the fire gets worse increase the pace of the bucket going up and down the line.

Someone remembers there is a second bucket and runs back to camp for it. Now the buckets are going back and forth up and down the line. Remember which is full and which is empty. Pass the bucket of water from hand to hand until the last person pours it on the fire. The empty bucket is then passed back down the line to the person who fills it, then back down the line again to the fire.

Mentor note
- Have children visualise a camping trip in the bush; create the situation as it is before the fire begins.
- The buckets are imaginary. Have children demonstrate how they would hold a bucket that was empty or one that was full.
- As the fire begins, increase pace and intensity by calling out 'The fire is worse' or 'Look! Another spot has erupted' or 'Water! Quickly!'

Variation

Fire!: In this version the last person to receive the bucket throws the water on the fire and then races back to the start with the bucket, fills it and takes a place at the beginning of the line as the bucket is passed again (Schotz 1998, pp. 55–56).

Setting the context through visualisation and heightening the urgency as the situation evolves both help to create a feeling of authenticity; the imagined situation takes on a reality as the children commit themselves to dealing with the crisis. As with any drama activity, be sensitive to children's prior experience and adapt exercises to suit their needs.

Applications for middle school students

A basic human need is for group affiliation and to be recognised as a valued group member (Maslow 1970). During adolescence this need becomes particularly salient as a person's peer group gains increasing importance, a factor that has implications for drama work. First, involvement in drama can help students widen their group affiliation. Students in one five-day drama workshop confirmed that the activities had enabled them to work with others with whom they would not ordinarily have come into contact (Murray 2006).

Group identification, although a recognised aspect of social development, has the potential for presenting challenges within a drama context. On occasion, some students may resist working with others who are not part of their immediate circle of friends. For this reason, it is essential to spend time establishing a sense of community within the drama group. Activities aimed at doing this are not time wasters, rather they provide the adhesive that helps the group make connections with each other.

The mentor can also facilitate an individual's participation in a range of groups by varying the ways in which small group membership is determined. In addition to letting students form their own small groups, the mentor may assign students to groups, have students 'count off' to form groups (e.g. all ones together, all twos together, etc.), or use some other non-traditional means (i.e. everyone wearing red in one group, green in another; or by asking students to form a group with others with whom they have not already worked).

Addressing the concepts of 'peer pressure' and 'pack mentality' through appropriate drama activities is a useful strategy for raising student awareness of these potential issues. One constructive activity is Decision Walk (a sociodramatic strategy described in Chapter 5), an exercise that provides individuals with the opportunity to experience decision making when there is pressure both 'for' and 'against' a course of action within the group.

Also, gaining perspective on an issue by distancing it through the use of relevant examples from literature is an effective strategy. Here are several powerful, yet accessible sources appropriate for adolescents as a basis for improvisation and reflection about group behaviour. Although these stories appear in picture book and junior novel formats, it is older students who can most meaningfully understand and apply the ideas presented in these prize-winning books.

- *The Great Bear* by Libby Gleeson (1999), illustrated by Armin Greder, depicts group bullying behaviour towards a bear before the tormented animal escapes into the sky to become a well-known constellation. Gleeson (n.d.) writes, 'I wanted the reader to feel the bear's anguish and to understand the desire to break free.'
- *The Rabbits* by John Marsden (1998), illustrated by Shaun Tan, is a thought-provoking allegory about the consequences of colonisation and one group's subjugation of another.
- *The Lemming Condition* by actor-author Alan Arkin (1976) relates the story of Bubber, a non-conformist lemming who questions life and refuses to follow the other lemmings in their destructive leap into the sea.

Literature and media tie-ins (e.g. film, video clips, pop songs) with content relevant to issues of belonging and group affiliation provide motivating starting points for adolescents as they discuss and reflect on their own experiences relating to groups and group attachment. Of course, such exploration needs sensitive treatment and a mentor who intuitively knows when to probe and when to change direction or curtail discussion. The drama group itself can be encouraged to set its own parameters about what is and is not appropriate for discussion and/or exploration through drama.

Literary and experiential sources, then, can be successfully used as springboards for older students to recast their ideas and insights into dramatic form (e.g. improvisations, playbuilt scripts, film treatments). Through this means, reflective exercises develop into meaningful scenarios that have relevance for the students who created them.

Summary

Through exercises that focus on personal and interpersonal skills, participants learn to develop and value their own sense of self, while at the same time building positive relationships with others. Abbs (1982) indicates that this fulfils two important needs for the child: 'to be' and 'to belong'. Since drama, by its nature, is a social medium, developing group rapport and the ability to work together are crucial.

If early in the process, group work in drama appears to be disconnected and 'not going anywhere', or even worse, 'out of control', it is helpful to remember that drama skills develop gradually. As children's confidence and skills grow over time, their concentration levels, commitment and depth of involvement increase. As trust among group members develops and they begin to work in more collaborative ways, everyone's learning is reinforced. The patience and persistence of the mentor and the students at the start bring rewards later.

For further study

1 Provide a rationale for using drama games in the classroom.
2 What strategies can a teacher use to encourage children to participate within group drama situations enthusiastically, yet sensibly?
3 Consider what impact you think the following factors could have on how a teacher uses drama in the classroom:
   – children who have never done drama before
   – the nature of the group (e.g. gender, perceived ability, behaviour patterns)
   – the time available
   – the allocated space
   – the teacher's prior experience with drama and/or a particular group of students.

What other factors might be relevant? Where you have indicated potential problems, what could a teacher do to overcome these?

For reflection

Reflect on the following scenario:

A teacher wants to use small group drama activities to help young people learn to cooperate with others. Consider the following factors:

1 In the class there are several students who usually hold back from joining in small group work of any kind.
2 Previously, a particular student has engaged in disruptive behaviour when placed in small group situations.
3 Some students are always motivated and self-directed; others have demonstrated in the past that they need more scaffolding.
4 There are several students who have minimal English-language skills in the class.

Provide suggestions for the teacher about how to take into consideration the needs of specific students, the class as a whole, and the aim of enhancing cooperation with others through drama. Suggest specific approaches and drama activities. (It may be useful to set the context within one of the following: (a) lower primary; (b) upper primary; or (c) middle school.)

Preview

Chapter 8: Sense of Drama considers the elements of drama, namely space, contrast, focus, mood, time, symbol and tension, providing explanations and examples of each.

CHAPTER 8

Sense of Drama

'Drama is a language with its own symbol system for communicating ideas and feelings and for making meaning' (Pascoe 1999).

Introduction

Drama's 'language' system consists of identifiable components that can be combined in countless ways. As with any language, time needs to be taken to understand the various parts and how they can work together to make meaning for the participants.

Drama's underlying components are named in different ways depending on the source. This book uses the 'elements of drama interpretation' as found in the *Creative Arts K-6 Syllabus* (Board of Studies NSW 2000). These elements are: space, contrast, focus, mood, time, symbol, and tension. The goal in this section is to discuss each element individually, providing examples of exercises that can be used to build children's skills in each area as a prelude to making in-depth connections across the elements. The underlying assumption is that when participants are able to identify drama components and understand how they function, they are in a better position to make informed creative choices when synthesising these elements into a holistic drama form. In addition, analytical treatment of drama through the examination of its elements provides students with the basis for appreciating and, ultimately, making informed judgments about their own creative work and that of others. The overall aim of the exercises in this chapter, then, is to assist students in their ability to recognise, understand, apply, analyse, synthesise and evaluate drama elements, a developmental process that parallels Bloom's Taxonomy of Educational Objectives (Bloom 1956).

Before drawing on these elements, alone or in combination, it is useful for children to understand the terms found in Basic Concepts (Concept Box 8.1).

Concept Box 8.1

Basic concepts

Freeze

Participants stand still like statues—not moving, not speaking. On cue, children practise freezing where they stand, moving, then freezing again. The strategy of freezing is an important control device for the mentor if the drama needs to be stopped for any reason. The opposite concept—**melt**—is a convenient way to start the action. Have a frozen statue melt bringing it to life in movement, sound, or both.

Still photograph

This is also known as 'making a picture' or a 'tableau' and can be done individually (e,g, make a picture of yourself waking up) or as a group (e.g. make a tableau of your family at the football game). Like a photo in an album, the still photograph is silent and does not move. Before group work begins it is useful to establish the 'front' of the photograph. Although this is not always essential, it is important if the group photograph is to be viewed by others.

On the spot

Children engage in movement standing or sitting where they are, that is, in place.

Fill the space

Children spread out and use all the space provided. The mentor sets the limits of the space before the activity begins.

Children need to know what these directions mean. If and when the mentor uses them, participants must respond immediately. Sometimes there may be a safety issue, at other times the mentor may need to give further directions. For this reason, practising each of these directions is well worth the time spent.

The next sub-sections discuss each of the drama elements in turn. Although treated separately, it is important to note that these components do not function in isolation; instead, drama participants combine them in various ways to make drama experiences meaningful.

Space

Drama takes place in **space**—space that 'can be moulded just like clay' (Cassady 1993, p. 83). When we move through space, it changes. Drama practitioners have described different types of space and how to make use of them (Cassady 1993; Moore 1988).

Physical space can be regarded in different ways. First, individual space is a person's own space. In drama, it is important that children develop a sense of their own personal space. As part of a drama experience, the mentor may direct participants to 'find your own space.' In On the Spot (Activity Box 8.1), children explore the boundaries of this space.

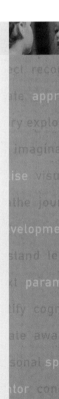

Activity Box **8.1**

On the spot

Description

- Stand on the spot. Make sure you can reach all around yourself without touching another person.
- Explore your individual space as far as you can in all directions without leaving your chosen spot.
- Grow from the smallest shape you can make at the lowest position in your space to the largest shape you can make in the highest position.
- Pretend you are inside a box into which you fit comfortably. Explore this box— above you, below you, all around you. You see a window in this box. It is open. Climb through this window.
- Now you are in a bigger box. Explore this box. Climb through another window.
- Now you are in the biggest box. Explore this one, too. Once you are finished, climb through the last window to the outside.

Mentor note
Remind children to stay in their own space and to remain on the spot.

Variations

The Box (Cassady 1993, p. 95): Vary the texture inside each box (i.e. sticky, rough, smooth) or change the window to a zipper, a set of buttons, or a long piece of adhesive.

What student teachers said

- 'This exercise helps children recognise their personal space, which is especially important for younger children' (Kirsty).
- 'Having different textures was a good idea for exploring imaginary tactile surfaces. Encourage not only the use of hands but also the whole body to show the limits of the box' (Ben).

Second, group space is the area shared with others. Of critical importance here is the awareness of and responsibility for others that everyone shares when they are in group space. Participants need to learn to adjust the nature and pace of their movements to take this into account.

Moore (1988, pp. 37–38) suggests there are two types of group space. One is the **common space** that everyone shares even though they do not directly interact. Drum Beat (Activity Box 8.2) gives students the chance to explore common space.

Activity Box 8.2

Drum beat

Description

- In 'common' space, walk forward; backward. With your group fill the space.
- Vary the speed as you hear the drum beat change. Step to the beat of a drum as it varies—a step for each beat.
- Without the beat of the drum, step around the space. On each step say: the months in order, names of animals, flower names, count by twos.
- Move like a robot, dancer, rabbit, space person, blob.

Mentor note

For each tempo, keep the beat steady. Use a variety of tempos.

In common space, unless instructed to do otherwise, children move independently without touching each other. Awareness of others in the same space is necessary to avoid bumping into them or unintentionally interfering with their movement.

The second type of group space, called **shared space** (Moore 1988, p. 37), is when participants interact directly with others. Sculptor's Studio (Activity Box 8.3) and A, B, C—1, 2, 3 (Activity Box 8.4) provide children with practice in sharing space with others.

Activity Box 8.3

Sculptor's studio

Figure 8.1 The Monster Gallery: Sculpting human forms gives children practice in sharing space

Description

In a pair, with one person named A and another B, do some sculpting!

- A, the sculptor, shapes B into a: reader, body builder, and ice skater.
- Then B becomes the sculptor, shaping A into a: rock star, tennis player, and soldier.

Mentor note

Change often between who is A and who is B. Also, encourage the group to generate more ideas about what sculptures to make next.

Variations

- UTS Youth Theatre Company (CREA) 'Scenic Statues': Decide on a scene (e.g. the sports carnival). Several children become the sculptors who shape the rest of the group into this scene; for example, the young people in the photo chose The Monster Gallery and were sculpted together into the scene.

For older students

Statue Maker: Children freeze as statues that the statue maker shows to a shopper, who switches each one on. Each statue melts and demonstrates what it is, before being switched off. The shopper chooses one who becomes the next statue maker; the former statue maker becomes the next shopper (Bany-Winters 1997, p. 112).

What student teachers said

- 'This exercise helps students to understand the idea of shared space. To do this, they would have to be quite comfortable with each other' (Jodie).
- '[As a sculptor] it helped to stand back and look at the sculpture [you were creating] to see what was right, what was wrong, and what needed to be changed' (Julie).
- 'The "Statue Maker" exercise was challenging because you had to think of something to mime, and entertaining when each sculpture was tapped [on the shoulder] and came to life without making a sound' (Nickola).
- 'When each statue was switched on, everyone only mimed the action [of what they were]. I would have added voice as well [to help the shopper figure out who I was]' (Robyn).

A, B, C—1, 2, 3 (Activity Box 8.4), an exercise undertaken in shared space, requires children to use their bodies to make letters and numbers. Once this is completed, they combine the letters to form words and the numbers to solve problems. This use of embodiment can be directly linked to language and mathematics learning.

Activity Box 8.4

A, B, C—1, 2, 3

Description

LETTERS

- With your body, make the following letters: T, C, R.
- Combine with two or three others, see if you can make the following letters together using your bodies: A, E, F, W.
- Join with two other small groups to form simple words of three letters: CAT, DOG, HOT, SIT, BOY, SUN.

NUMBERS
- With your body, make the following numbers: 1, 7, 9.
- Combine with two or three others; together make the following numbers: 4, 8, 10.
- Join with two other small groups. As your mentor calls out the problem, see if you can solve it. Write out the problem and the answer using your bodies (e.g. 8 + 2 = 10).

Mentor note
- Children may stand up or lie down to make the letters and numbers, whatever is easier for them.
- Remind them that the words and the problems need to be created from the performers' right to left to be understood by an audience.
- When doing the problems, select certain children to make the signs (i.e. +, -, X, =) to link the numbers.

What student teachers said
- 'You really have to think about how each letter is formed to make sure it is not back to front [to the viewers]' (Carly).
- 'It was lots of fun working collaboratively with peers and learning at the same time. [This is] great for use in Years 1–4 as a warm-up or cool down (i.e. a finishing activity) for maths or spelling' (Katrina).
- 'This exercise encourages children to be imaginative in how they can use their bodies to make letters and numbers. It is interactive and visual so it helps children learn and remember. It can easily be extended to spelling and maths lessons' (Tina).
- 'After children learn to make letters of the alphabet, you could have them make the words in the class spelling list' (Kimberly).
- 'This activity is a good way to get children to think about their own personal space and how they can share space with others' (Elisa).

When using different types of space, the concepts of near or far, open or closed, and crowded or empty are helpful. Near or far refers to the distance among the bodies in the space; open or closed refers to whether bodies are extended outwardly or turned inwardly; while crowded or empty refers to how many people are in the same common or shared space. Although each set of terms is linked with 'or', it should be remembered that there may be degrees of near/far; open/closed; and crowded/empty.

Setting the Scene (Activity Box 8.5) provides examples of how the description of a particular psychological or physical space can provide the initial situation from which a drama episode can develop.

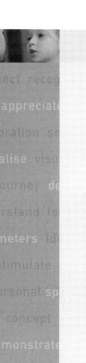

Activity Box 8.5

Setting the scene

Description

1   You need time to think. Find a place as far as you can from other people.
2   The caravan left you behind! You're lonely—you curl yourself into a tiny ball.
3   It's summertime! The beach is crowded. Can you find a place to sit?
4   It's sunrise—like the petals of a flower you open yourself to the new day.
5   The snow blows and the wind howls as you and the other Antarctic explorers huddle close together for warmth.

Mentor note

- Once the initial scene is established either alone, in small groups, or as one large group, reflect on how space was used.
- Brainstorm with students what follows next in each scene. Choose ideas to try out encouraging students to be aware of how they use space.

Space is an essential building block of drama. Once the physical boundaries for drama interaction are set, participants explore the limits of this space and 'mould' it to suit their purposes.

Contrast

To understand **contrast**, children must be able to distinguish between sameness and difference. Since contrast is most dramatically seen in terms of opposites, an appropriate starting place for working with this concept is ⇑Opposites⇓ (Activity Box 8.6).

Activity Box 8.6

⇑ Opposites ⇓

Description

Use gesture and body movements to explore these opposites:

- up—down
- slow—fast
- big—little
- open—shut
- heavy—light
- hot—cold
- light—dark

Mentor note

With the children, think of and demonstrate other opposites. Examples of variations could include:

- For each set of opposites, have half the group do one (e.g. up) and half the other (e.g. down).
- For each set of opposites, have each child do both parts in succession. Then start with one (e.g. big) and at a count of six change in slow motion to the other (e.g. little).

For older students

Expand the complexity of the verbal contrasts; for example:

- defiance—compliance;
- millisecond—light year;
- understated—exaggerated;
- trash—treasure;
- sophisticated—naive; and
- hovel—mansion.

Have students contribute their own contrasting terms to this list, then represent them as contrasting still photographs.

What student teachers said

- '[I liked] the more abstract opposites; for example, dark (e.g. enclosed and retreating) versus light (e.g. open and advancing)' (Ben).
- 'You had to really think about how you could appear that way [i.e. as one of the opposites]. This task encourages creative thinking' (Elisa).
- 'You could also do this activity by saying one action and having the students work out and mime the opposite' (Kimberly).

A pair of opposites is an example of a **dichotomy**, that is, where two concepts are set at opposite poles in what is called binary opposition (e.g. either a door is open or it is shut). However, when contrast is only thought of in 'either-or' terms, the levels of meaning that are in between are missed (e.g. What if a door is partially open?). Up-Down In-the-Middle (Activity Box 8.7) demonstrates that contrast can be based on more than opposites. In this example, children position themselves at one of three levels: up, down or in-the-middle.

Activity Box **8.7**

Up-down in-the-middle

Description

- You and two other children are given the following situations to 'act out', using your voice and body movement.
- As you begin each, one of you is up, one is down, and the third is in the middle. When the mentor says 'change', you must change positions in such a way that there is still one person who is up, one down, and one in the middle.

AT THE BEACH

Start positions:

Student one lies down sun baking

Student two stands up surfboarding

Student three sits under a beach umbrella.

PICKING PEACHES

Start positions:

Student one gathers peaches from the ground

Student two is on a ladder picking from the tree top
Student three picks peaches from the middle branches.

AT THE GARAGE
Start positions:
Student one works under the car
Student two cleans the roof
Student three looks under the bonnet.

Mentor note

At the signal, 'change', each child takes up a new position, so that a different child is low, high, or in the middle. At first it may be helpful to have one group demonstrate the process involved for the rest; later, have various groups of three working in their own space at the same time. Use the still photograph technique or build a moving sequence.

What student teachers said

- 'This exercise helps children understand the difference between movements at different levels' (Kirsty).
- 'A good way to develop team work'(Carly).
- 'You had to think fast and be creative within the group. I think children of every age could do this with more challenging scenes for those in upper primary' (Tracy).
- 'This is a similar exercise to "Sitting, Standing, and Lying", which I have used in schools. In the classroom we acted out a moving scene [using these concepts]. I think the movement worked because we had done a lot of still photographs beforehand' (Robyn).
- 'This trio game encourages children to use all the space and challenges them to think of all kinds of different activities in a particular scenario rather than just the obvious choices' (Nickola).
- 'Working with three people is a different dynamic than working with two' (Kristy-lee).

Taking Shape (Activity Box 8.8) further expands the meaning of contrast as difference, using the concepts **symmetrical** and **asymmetrical**. When symmetrical, one side of a picture matches the other; however, when asymmetrical, the sides are unmatched and contrast.

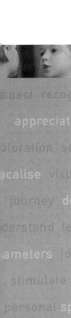

Activity Box 8.8

Taking shape

Description

- Make shapes with these two words as a guide: symmetrical and asymmetrical.
  - *Symmetrical* means that everything matches; both sides are the same.
  - *Asymmetrical* means that the sides differ and are unmatched; there is contrast.
- In a group of three, make a picture with your bodies that is symmetrical.
- Then make a picture with your bodies that is asymmetrical.
- Try the same thing in a group of four, then in a group of five.

Mentor note

The key to this exercise is establishing where the centre line of the picture is. Then children will know what they have to do to match the sides or to make them different.

For older students

Have one group make a symmetrical or asymmetrical shape with their bodies and the other groups try to copy it exactly.

What student teachers said

- 'This exercise works well. Students need to think about their positioning, not only in space but also in relation to others' (Rochelle).
- 'This interactive group exercise encouraged students to work together through talking, problem solving, and negotiating. It would also help children learn about symmetrical and asymmetrical shapes and how to differentiate between the two' (Tina).
- 'This is a team-building activity that uses discussion and compromise, suitable for Years 3 and 4' (Katrina).
- 'Children would have to know the meaning of symmetrical and asymmetrical before doing this exercise. This drama activity could be integrated into a maths lesson on symmetry' (Jodie).
- 'This exercise could provide a lead-in activity for lessons in other KLAs [key learning areas] where children need to work in groups because it's not easy' (Julie).

Contrast can be used in many ways to enhance drama work, including changing the pace of an episode, differentiating characters, or shifting intensity within the action, to name a few. Using contrast helps participants to distinguish among differing ideas, value positions, and decision-making options. It also stimulates participant interest and involvement because when things contrast they differ, potentially heightening areas of tension or conflict that need resolution. For these many reasons, contrast is regarded as an important drama element.

Focus

Focus means pointing the attention of observers to what is important. Within a drama interaction, what takes the focus is what is emphasised. A change in movement and positioning can be used to shift attention. At the Race (Activity Box 8.9) introduces participants to the concept of focus.

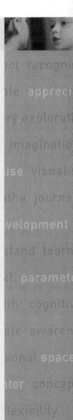

Activity Box **8.9**

At the race

Description
You are part of the crowd at a foot face. Watch the runners advance from left to right across your vision. Build your response through action and sound until you see the winner cross the finish line. Show how you feel about the result.

Mentor note
Set the starting line and the finish for the race. Describe the race as it is run following it with your own eyes. Stand with the group so you are all facing the same way.

Variations
- Do this exercise a few times; each time participants concentrate on moving their focus together and on responding to the events in front of them.
- Use this strategy to follow the progress of other events, such as a fashion show, a royal procession, a parade, or a horse race. How will the reactions of the crowd differ depending on the event?

What student teachers said

- 'A fun activity to practise focus skills in a group environment where you don't feel watched' (Katrina).
- 'The activity develops imagination and helps the group work cooperatively with others' (Carly).
- 'You have to gauge what the rest of the group is doing. Actually seeing a picture in your mind and believing that you see it directly in front of you really draws on your imagination skills. I would combine this drama activity with an art lesson (i.e. drawing what they see) and an English lesson (i.e. writing an account of what they saw and what happened)' (Kim).
- 'I was at the front so it was hard to tell where the group was looking so I had to pay particular attention to what was said behind me' (Tracy).
- 'This activity is useful for teaching students to work together as a group' (Kimberly).
- 'The crowd activity enables students to improvise and express their emotions as well as release some energy. The scene used could relate to something they are currently learning about in class or could relate to an excursion they have recently taken' (Nickola).
- 'Initially, there was reliance on the [mentor's] voice narrating the events unfolding. Imagination was required to picture the events. When there was no narration, and we as a group determined the focus and the pace without a leader, it was more difficult' (Meagan).
- 'I used this particular exercise with children who were of different ages and backgrounds. They didn't go to school together, so they didn't know each other well. The exercise was a success because the children developed an awareness and understanding of each other in the group' (Tina).

As children focus on the unfolding scene, they become involved and react with their voices and movements. The atmosphere intensifies and the experience becomes believable and authentic for them.

Playground (Activity Box 8.10) places children within a familiar context in which they explore ways to give and take focus as it shifts from group to group.

Activity Box 8.10

Playground

Description

- It's after lunch on the playground on a bright spring day. Children skip ropes, play ball and have fun playing other games. Some chat with the teacher on duty.
  - – Who are you?
  - – What are you doing?
  - – Where are you in the playground?
- The mentor asks the group to make a picture of the playground.
  - – Put yourself inside the picture.
- When the mentor asks you, tell the others what you are doing.
- Join others who are doing the same or related things and remake the playground picture to reflect these groupings.
- As the mentor asks your group, tell the others what you are doing.
- At a signal, the mentor directs you to shift the focus to particular groups using eye contact, facial expression, gesture and body position.

Mentor note

- Using the groups identified by the children, ask them to shift the focus from group to group; for example, to children jumping ropes, playing ball, talking to the teacher.
- Have selected children stay outside the picture. Let them determine whether the focus has shifted. Have them give suggestions for what the groups might do to shift the focus. Change children in this role after each shift.
- Have children reflect on what they did to change the focus. This might include: pointing with arms, legs, feet, head; turning the body into an open or closed, extended or contracted position; or using eye contact.

What student teachers said

- 'Playground was something to which primary students would really relate. It was good to start with an individual activity, moving from a group to the whole class' (Julie).

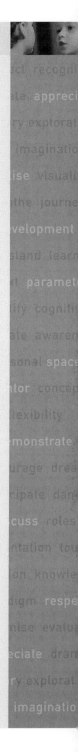

- 'This was a great activity to practise all different ways to pass focus to others. Body language and dialogue make you aware of how people do it in real life situations. This is relevant in the classroom to show how teachers/students know when they are being acknowledged and affirmed' (Robyn).

When a drama experience develops into a presentation that is shared with others, the element of focus becomes particularly crucial. This concept, when put into practice, helps observers determine where they should look at any given moment. For this reason, learning how to attract attention through effective use of focus is beneficial for helping convey the intended meaning of an episode.

Mood

Mood reflects a person's internal emotional state that can be composed of a range of feelings. An individual's mood can usually be detected through his or her speech and actions. Just as people have particular moods, so, too, do moments of drama. Eerie, light-hearted, sombre—whatever the mood is, it will affect the overall emotional impact of the drama for the participants and the observers (if there is an audience present).

In drama, sounds and sound effects can help establish a particular mood or atmosphere. Mood Makers (Activity Box 8.11) uses soundscapes. These are compositions made from vocal sounds and body percussion used to create the mood of an environment.

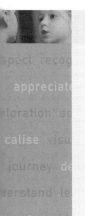

Activity Box **8.11**

Mood makers

Description
In a small group, work together to create one short soundscape. Use your voice (limit identifiable words) and noise from body percussion to make the sounds you could hear in your chosen environment; for example:

- Loneliness of the cold, forsaken sea;
- Noisiness of the rainforest brimming with life;

- Rejoicing at the hero's homecoming;
- Spookiness of the haunted house; or
- Chaos at the busy traffic intersection.

Mentor note

Everyone sits in small groups of four or five students. Number each small group so they know the order in which they will present their soundscapes. After they have been given several minutes to create their soundscapes, group one begins. When they finish, the next group begins without any talking between the soundscapes. This enables a smooth transition from one group to the next. When not sharing, the other groups close their eyes as they listen.

After hearing them all in sequence, have children guess what the soundscapes represented and reflect on the concept of mood and how it changed with each soundscape.

Variation

Bringing an environment to life: Imaginatively explore different locations (e.g. circus, airport, seashore) and visualise the sights, sounds, tastes and smells you would find there (Berghammer et al, n.d., p. 52).

What student teachers said

- 'This exercise made us think about how we can use our voices and body percussion to create moods and the sense of a place. It also made me think about developing a logical beginning, middle and end to the soundscape' (Carly).
- 'It worked on our prior knowledge of the situations. I really like the idea of guessing what each group had portrayed' (Tracy).
- 'This activity enables students to create scenes without visual aids' (Rochelle).
- 'It encourages children to be creative with what they can do with their voices and body percussion. It also teaches the power of group work as the participants work together to create a soundscape' (Tina).
- 'Turning the lights off meant we focused on listening' (Julie).
- 'We visualised the sounds in our own minds' (Elisa).
- '[A variation would be to] have all groups do the same soundscape to show how the same scenario can be interpreted differently' (Robyn).

In drama, the mood of an episode can change when something unexpected happens. In What's Inside? (Activity Box 8.12), participants open envelopes that contain different messages. Each message is intended to engender a different mood.

Activity Box 8.12

What's inside?

Description
You receive an envelope in the mail. In it is:

- a letter from your best friend inviting you to a party;
- an unexpected bill for $1000;
- a cheque for $1,000,000; or
- a ransom demand.

The envelope is the same but, in each case, the contents are quite different. How did you reflect your mood when you found out what was inside?

Mentor note
Have children 'make a picture' to reflect the different moods. Discover if children express themselves in different ways for each situation. Use your observations as the basis for reflection (e.g. Can they think of reasons why someone who receives a cheque for $1,000,000 might be in an angry mood?).

Variation
Change the envelope to a box and think of things that could be shipped in it.

Extension
Create a group improvisation based on the theme of the picture storybook, *The Red Parcel* by Linda and Gino Alberti (1987), in which a wise woman wraps up an empty box and gives it to her neighbour saying, 'Here's a surprise present, but don't open it, otherwise you'll lose what's inside.' This neighbour gratefully receives the present and enjoys imagining what is inside before passing it on to

another neighbour with the same instructions. Finally, after the package has gone around the whole village, it comes back to the wise woman who explains to her granddaughter, 'The red parcel doesn't need to have anything inside it in order to bring happiness. It's the giving that's important.'

Suddenlies are unexpected events that change the direction of what is happening or, as Wood (1999) who coined the term puts it, suddenlies 'shift gear with a logical jolt' (p. 38). Within a drama scene, suddenlies can be used to change the mood immediately. First, try the examples in Guess What Happened Then! (Activity Box 8.13), then have children make and use their own.

Activity Box 8.13

Guess what happened then!

Description
A meeting is in progress *when suddenly* there's a fire in the building!
Children are bored *when suddenly* a rock star arrives!
The family swims *when suddenly* a shark is sighted!

Variation
The picture book, *Suddenly*! by Colin McNaughton (1994), provides a humorous introduction to the concept of 'suddenlies'. A clumsy wolf stalks Preston, the pig, unsuccessfully on his way home from school.

For older students
In small groups, use the concept of the 'suddenly' to create an action-packed, suspenseful story that is then told and/or re-enacted for the other groups.

Far from being emotion-free, drama actively seeks to engage participants' emotions and feelings as they interact with others in situations aimed to increase their empathy and understanding. Exploring the concept of mood and how it can impact on actions is part of the process of making drama emotionally relevant for children.

Time

Drama activity 'takes time' and takes place 'in time'. The passage of **time** is an important concept for children to grasp. Such expressions as 'time waits for no one', 'time to move on', 'time flies' and a 'waste of time' only gain meaning when the passage of time is understood. In Time Sense (From the Classroom 8.1) a student teacher uses a simple exercise to make students aware of how time passes.

From the Classroom 8.1

Time sense

As an introductory drama activity for Year 3 and 4 students, Elisa used an exercise she called 'time sense'. In this activity, students tried to estimate how long a minute was. With eyes closed, students raised their hands when they believed a minute had passed.

Elisa indicated that 'the children focused well as they wanted to get the closest time to a minute! This activity was done twice because the children enjoyed it and asked to repeat it. ... [Before lunch] the children asked to repeat "time sense" [again] and the closest student to a minute received an early mark to lunch.'

As a concept, time can be considered from different perspectives. Two that will be highlighted are: sequential time, in which events follow one after another, and cyclical time, where events repeat using the same pattern (e.g. military parade, a religious service, a graduation ceremony).

In sequential time, also called chronological time, events occur one after another. The advantage of drama over 'real' life is that in drama a sequence can run forward, but also be reversed. This gives children the opportunity to reflect on action and even to return to events and change them to achieve a different outcome. Time Sequence (Activity Box 8.14) helps children explore sequential time in pairs and small groups as they develop a sequence of events.

Activity Box 8.14

Time sequence

Description
Create still photographs in pairs:

- A batsman and a bowler;
- A lion tamer and a lion in the centre ring; and
- A puppeteer and a puppet performing.

In a group of three or four:

- A family in the car on an outing;
- Mountain climbers nearly at the top of Mt. Everest; and
- Prisoners making an escape.

Mentor note
The above still photos become the middle shots in a sequence of three. For the first photo created, have children make the photo that comes *after* it. Show these two photos in sequence.

Following this, make the photo that comes *first* in the sequence of three. Show the three still photos in sequence.

Variation
Each group of children shows the others their sequence. The mentor says to those watching 'Close your eyes'; when the group is ready with their first still photo, the mentor says 'Open your eyes'; then 'Close your eyes' as the groups prepare their second photo, then 'Open your eyes' and so forth for each photo. In this way, the sequence appears to those watching as a 'still frame' movie.

Once children show the three photos in sequence, have them 'melt' the photos, animating them with movement and sound. Blend the three together into a moving sequence. Have them begin the melt from the first still photograph and return to the 'freeze' after bringing the final picture to life. First try doing the melt in slow motion.

What student teachers said
- 'This is a good idea for sequencing, coming up with alternate endings, or introducing events that could change the overall outcome of the story' (Meagan).

- 'This exercise made me think about how we can use our bodies to show the passing of time and the development of a scene' (Carly).
- 'I hadn't thought before about using the sequence of events as a learning experience, for example, avoiding a car accident by running the sequence backwards to show what could have been done differently so that it doesn't happen' (Robyn).
- 'Children can take the snap shots and turn them into a short performance through the process of melting them together' (Tina).
- 'This develops well into a scene and is useful for playbuilding and scriptwriting' (Rochelle).

Enabling children to experience events in sequence, considering the consequences, and then modifying the approach to achieve another result is one of drama's benefits. By this means, children can have authentic experiences within the safe boundaries of a drama setting.

Time also can be cyclical, that is, events occur as part of a repeating pattern, as in the yearly return of the seasons. Celebrations, too, are an example of this because they have attached to them certain repetitive elements; for instance, a birthday is an annual event that may include a party, a special cake, blowing out candles, and singing 'Happy Birthday'. In some families, this pattern recurs almost unchanged every year. Create a Ceremony (Activity Box 8.15) helps children understand how cyclical time works by having them develop their own personal ceremonies.

Activity Box **8.15**

Create a ceremony

Description
A ceremony is a special series of events or activities usually done in the same way; in other words, it does not basically change over time.

Create your own special ceremony for each of these everyday events:

- Washing your hands;
- Packing your haversack for school;
- Walking the dog;
- Planting a flower garden; and
- Cleaning your teeth.

In pairs:

- Teach your partner your ceremony.
- Make sure they do it exactly as you do.
- Then your partner teaches you his/her ceremony.
- Repeat it exactly the way you are taught to do it.

Mentor note

- Have children develop their own ideas for ceremonies. (Note that the term 'ceremony' is used in this exercise in preference to the term 'ritual'; although both words can have similar meanings.)
- Choose one ceremony to teach the entire group. Make sure every child repeats it in the same way.
- To emphasise the concept of cyclical time, choose one ceremony. Have it start with one group who teaches it to the next, and so on through the groups. When each group's 'time' comes, they repeat the ceremony as the group before has taught them. At the end of the process, ask the first group who originated the ceremony: Were there any differences? If so, why might these have occurred?
- Reflect on this exercise asking the question: Why is a special ceremony an example of cyclical time?

What student teachers said

- 'This activity enabled you to see how different people interpret things' (Elisa).
- 'I love how we passed on one group's tradition' (Tracy).

The terms sequential and cyclical refer to the different ways people perceive that events occur in relation to the passage of time. However, there is another way in which the concept of time is used within drama, namely, to refer to beat, tempo or pulse. Body percussion and voice are used in Keep the Beat (Activity Box 8.16) to explore this meaning for time.

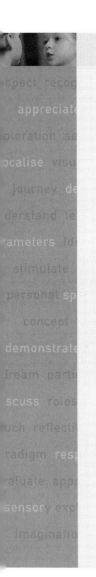

Activity Box 8.16

Keep the beat

Description

Sit with others in a circle. One person begins keeping a steady beat using body percussion. Each person around the circle, in turn, adds a vocal sound or body rhythm (e.g. clap, snap, tap) to accentuate or complement the beat. The rhythm piece builds until it reaches the person keeping the beat, then it reverses back around the circle, with each person, in turn, stopping until the only one left is the person keeping the beat.

Mentor note

It is important that the beat is kept steady so other sounds can fit around it. Assign one person in the group to maintain the beat while the others improvise around it.

Variations

- Have participants use vocal sounds only.
- Rhythm Kings I & II are similar exercises (Schotz 1998, p. 74).

What student teachers said

- 'This activity helps children think about how to keep the beat or pattern' (Kirsty).
- 'This exercise helped to develop a sense of timing and to work with the main beat. It was helpful for looking at finding gaps in the rhythm to fill' (Ben).
- 'This encourages students' creativity and concentration' (Nickola).

Within a drama activity, the use of time also may involve controlling the pace of the action, or what is called timing. In Skipping Rope (Activity Box 8.17), timing is critical.

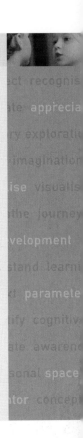

Activity Box 8.17

Skipping rope

Description

Take your turn at skipping over the rope! Watch the rope carefully because those who are turning it for you may speed up or slow down without warning.

Mentor note

Using an imaginary rope, two children turn it for the others as they jump. At your signal, have the children who are turning slow down or speed up the rope turning.

It may be useful to begin with an actual rope. When children are comfortable, change the rope to an imaginary one.

Variations

- Use two ropes—one swinging each way.
- Let's Skip Rope is a similar exercise suggested as a warm-up (Schotz 1998, p. 56).

In Skipping Rope (Activity Box 8.17), children needed to be aware of the exact timing of the turn of the skipping rope in order to know when to jump. In other drama situations, timing is useful as a device for speeding up or slowing down the action. Within a drama episode, the mentor may introduce a change in timing to increase the urgency or to slow the pace so children have the chance to reflect on what is happening.

There are many ways to use the element of time effectively in drama. Awareness of how events pass through time, knowing how to vary the beat or pulse of an action and using pace to speed up or slow down events are a few important ones.

Symbol

A symbol is an object, person, event, action, or place that can stand for something else. A symbol, by definition, 'holds many levels of meaning simultaneously' (Bolton 1979, pp. 76–78). Consider how people make meanings from each of the following: a flag, an object that can stand for national identity; a policeman, a person who can symbolise authority; the first day of school, an event that can mean independence; or curtseying, an action that indicates respect.

To view something as a symbol is to see beyond its mere function. The photograph in Symbolic Sight (Activity Box 8.18) can be viewed on several levels. First, the viewer sees a body of water. However, the plaque identifies this spot as Anzac Cove. For those who know about and identify with the World War I Gallipoli campaign, this place takes on another meaning and, for some, becomes a symbol of Australian national identity.

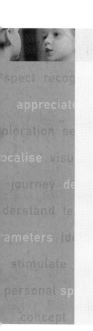

Activity Box 8.18

Symbolic sight

Description
- Look closely at this picture. What do you see?
- Do you see a wall, letters and water *or* a symbol of national identity?

Mentor note
What you see may depend on your age, level of education or experience, cultural background or interest.

Figure 8.2 Anzac Cove

Of course, symbols are not fixed in their meanings. People, depending on who they are and their country of origin, may have different views and understandings. For Australians and New Zealanders, this place has become a national symbol, but for others, not familiar with the battles of World War I or sharing the same perspective, it is only a body of water. An object becomes a symbol when like-minded people share a common view of it.

To understand how a symbol works, a child must first understand that the same object can be used to represent different things. In It's material!

(Activity Box 8.19), groups transform a piece of material into a range of items, demonstrating the point that meaning resides in people not in the objects themselves.

Activity Box 8.19

It's material!

Description

- In a small group, take a square piece of cloth. Together decide what your piece of cloth represents. Use the material in such a way that the other groups understand what it has become for your group.
- Reflect on the range of uses the groups found for the cloth.

Mentor note

- Some possible uses include a:
  - table cloth
  - scarf
  - screen
  - shawl
  - skirt
  - cleaning rag
  - flag
  - bullfighter's cape
  - sail
  - blanket.

Variation

- For older students, have each individual first establish what the cloth is, then combine with others into a small group of five or six students and create a story that includes all the items. Enact the story for the other groups.

When children recognise that it is people who give meaning to objects, they can begin to understand how an object becomes a symbol. What Do You Mean? (Activity Box 8.20) shows some objects that most people regard as having symbolic meaning.

Activity Box 8.20

What do you mean?

Description

- Look at the following drawings. Discuss what you think each might represent.

Figure 8.3 Objects or symbols?

- Once you have discussed the above items, find other examples of things that people might regard as symbols. Discuss them together, talking about possible meanings.

Mentor note

On a descriptive (denotative) level these images are: scales, a type of hat, a sign and a torch.

On a symbolic (connotative) level these objects may take on multiple meanings. Commonly recognised meanings for each item are: the scales of justice, a graduation cap, a no-fires sign, and the Olympic torch.

However, there is no one *right* answer. An object is symbolic when a person recognises that it means something more than its mere description.

Be supportive, encouraging children to explain their views. Their levels of experience, knowledge and backgrounds may account for any differences that are present.

Now that children understand what a symbol is, in small groups have them turn objects into symbols within a drama episode in Symbol Scenes (Activity Box 8.21).

Activity Box 8.21

Symbol scenes

Description

In a small group, put yourselves in the following situations. Think how you could show that the object suggested in each is a symbol for you.

A *torch* that represents *survival*: Your group is exploring a cave. The torch must be protected at all costs. Without it you will not be able to find your way out.

A *crown* that represents *power*: Within your group are several claimants to the throne. Each presents a case for why they should be the ruler. You must be convincing because securing the crown means that you will have absolute power.

A *butterfly* that represents *freedom*: You are a group of prisoners. A butterfly flits into your cell through the small barred window. You watch it thinking of freedom.

Mentor note

- Have the children think of other scenarios in which an object can become a symbol. Act them out.
- Consider how the same object can symbolise different things (e.g. a butterfly —freedom or fragility).

Variations

Find examples of how product advertising uses symbols. Create a television ad using symbols to advertise your own product that you design.

For older students

Use literary and media examples as pre-text for drama work with the concept of symbol; for example, *Memorial,* by Gary Crew (1999), a picture book for all ages, uses a tree planted on the return of soldiers in 1918 to symbolise the message 'Lest we forget'; the classic film, *The Gods Must Be Crazy* (Uys 1980), uses a Coke bottle to symbolise the modern world and how disruptive it can be for those people who live a simple lifestyle.

When doing drama with children, the use of symbols can motivate, focus and deepen the action. For example, a cell door key can represent freedom, motivating prisoners to attain it in order to escape; a bag of gold can represent a king's extravagance, sparking a revolt among his subjects; or the sound of rain on the roof can represent the drought breaking, causing farmers to rejoice. A symbol is a powerful tool that communicates ideas instantly among those who agree on its meaning.

Tension

Tension, also called 'dramatic tension' and sometimes referred to as 'conflict', is regarded as one of the linchpins of drama (Morgan & Saxton 1994; O'Toole 1992; Bolton 1979; Heathcote 1975). Tension results when participants in a problem-solving situation strive to reach a goal, but are blocked in some way. These impediments can be caused by character differences (e.g. one pulls against the rest for power and control), disasters (e.g. torrential rain) or changes of fortune (e.g. going bankrupt). In other words, tension results when there is a disparity between what people have and what they want to possess or to achieve.

In Imaginary Tension Tug (Activity Box 8.22), the concept of tension is demonstrated in physical terms when two teams pull on an imaginary rope in opposite ways.

Activity Box **8.22**

Imaginary tension tug

Description

You are part of a team. With them, grab one end of an imaginary rope. Your goal is to pull the other team, who are tugging at the opposite end of the rope, across the line.

Mentor note

As safety is of the utmost importance, be wary of using a 'real' rope because unless students are fully in control of their actions there is the potential for an accident to occur.

Begin by establishing the size and length of the imaginary rope. Consider what happens to a rope when it is pulled in two different directions at the same time. In what ways is the rope like a person when he or she is pulled in different ways (e.g. stretched, taut, evidencing bodily tension)?

Have students imagine the tension in their bodies and in the imaginary rope as they pull it.

This exercise requires concentration, control and sensitivity to what other people are doing. It may be useful to begin in partners (A and B). First suggest that A pulls B across the line using the imaginary rope, then change so that B pulls A. Gradually build up the sides and encourage children to work together to show their side pulling the rope.

Variation

Tug o' War: In this version, emphasis is on working together, not winning or losing (Johnstone 1999, pp. 57–58).

Imaginary Tension Tug (Activity Box 8.22) shows that tension is brought about when people pull in opposite ways (i.e. as the tension in the imaginary rope tightens, the bodies as extensions of the rope also become taut). Caught in the Middle (From the Classroom 8.2) shows student actors building on Imaginary Tension Tug during a performance.

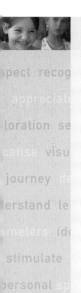

From the Classroom 8.2

Caught in the middle

Student actors use the concepts in Imaginary Tension Tug to develop a scene in which Peter Piper is pulled back and forth between the Doctor and the Owl in *The Peter Piper Pickled Pepper Mystery* (de Vries & Poston-Anderson 2000), an interactive children's theatre production for pre-schoolers.

Figure 8.4 Peter Piper being pulled between the Doctor (left) and the Owl

Extend students' understandings of tension by engaging in the exercise in Tense Times (Activity Box 8.23), where physical and mental tensions occur and things are not what they at first seem.

Activity Box 8.23

Tense times

Description
Make a still photograph:

You find a length of rope in the cupboard.	It's really a snake.
Your friend comes for a visit.	He's on the run from the police.
You find a mushroom. You eat it.	It's a poisoned mushroom.
You put on a wristwatch.	You can't remove it again.
You walk down the pathway.	It's wet cement.
You start printing a page from your computer.	You run out of ink.
You chew a stick of gum.	It gets caught in your 'false' teeth.

Mentor note

After children make a still photograph, introduce the element of tension. The pictures will change in response. 'Melt' the still photographs into an action sequence using movement and voice. Challenge children to create their own Tense Times examples.

The added element of tension means that children modify their responses to take into consideration the changed circumstance. This shift is evident in their reactions.

During a drama experience, the mentor may intentionally constrain a situation in such a way as to create a sense of urgency, limit the alternatives or force participants to reconsider their options. Heathcote (1975) suggests that an effective way to introduce tension to drama 'is to leave something to chance, but only one thing' (p. 100): for example, the participants never know exactly when they will be interrupted, when the alarm will sound, when the electricity will be cut off. The resulting tension heightens the drama, making the situation relevant and impelling participants to work together to make decisions. In Rescue! (Activity Box 8.24), children, who take on different roles during the course of the action, must work together to decide how they will handle stressful situations.

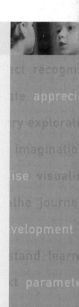

Activity Box **8.24**

Rescue!

Description
You are with a group of people who one afternoon go for a hike in the bush.

THE WALKERS
- You—a primary school student who likes sport
- Your mother, who competes in a marathon race every year
- A pensioner with a heart problem
- A retired military officer
- A couple who are overseas tourists with their three-year-old child; they speak only a little English.
- Two teenage friends; one of them wore sandals and now has blisters

ITEMS THE GROUP HAS WITH THEM:

- Everyone has a hat
- Two tubes of sunscreen
- Four large bottles of water
- A rope
- Box of matches
- A torch
- Five chocolate bars
- Four packets of instant soup
- Three mugs
- Small first-aid kit
- A flare.

What happens

Towards evening, it unexpectedly rains. When the storm is over, the track is covered in mud. In fact, in front of you and behind you there have been mud slides that completely block the path. There appears to be no way out. Together as a group decide what you will do. How will you survive until you are rescued? (Working as a group, try out some of your ideas—you must hurry because night is coming and you cannot be sure that you will be rescued before morning.)

What happens next

In the morning a helicopter flies overhead looking for your group. You signal them with your flare. They see you. One of the rescuers is lowered down a rope to bring you up one by one to the helicopter.

Role reversal

The group now becomes the team of rescuers aboard the helicopter. You must decide in what order the group is to be rescued. If there is disagreement, work out a plan to resolve these differences.

Mentor note

Not knowing when the group will be rescued increases the tension and provides an urgency to decision-making. Problem solving, acting out possible solutions and reflecting on whether the decisions taken are satisfactory for the entire group provide opportunities to explore the nature of the dramatic element, tension.

When working with the concept of tension, as with any other drama element, knowing the group (their backgrounds, needs and interests) is essential for the mentor. Such knowledge will assist the mentor in determining how the group is responding and will enable him or her to judge when to shift between action and reflection or to facilitate the group in a change of direction.

Applications for middle school students

Helping adolescents understand that elements of dramatic interpretation and elements used to interpret other art forms are similar reinforces for them in tangible ways how much the arts have in common. Drama, dance, music, visual arts and multimedia forms all use space, contrast, focus, mood, time, symbol and tension, even though how creative artists apply these concepts may vary depending on the medium in which they work. Consider as an example the Australian musical drama in film form, *One Night The Moon* (Romeril & Perkins 2001), the sad tale of a child who climbs out her bedroom window to follow the moon and is lost in the night. The moon, a mesmerising symbol of her quest, marks the passing days and nights, until the final tragedy unfolds. Notice how the filmmaker shifts focus among the characters, contrasts the outlooks of the parents and Aboriginal tracker, establishes a deepening mood of foreboding, and shows time passing through the juxtaposition of music, dramatic action, and visual images.

Compare how this film achieves a synthesis of artistic elements with how McCubbin in two of his well-known Australian paintings, both entitled 'Lost' (1907, 1886, in Pierce 1999, pp. 56–57), treats the same theme. In both artworks there is a stark contrast between the diminutive figure of the lost child and the dense, towering bush. The viewers' eyes are drawn to focus on the lone children in each canvas by the way in which the figure is positioned in the space. Any viewer who has ever been lost, particularly in a bush setting, cannot help but empathise with the lonely isolation of the child caught in a potentially deadly situation. This empathy builds an internal tension within the viewer and a desire to overcome the unresolved suspense by knowing what will happen next.

A musical example using the same theme of 'lost in the bush' is the Australian hit song of the 1960s, *Little Boy Lost* (Ashcroft 1960), based on the true story of Steven Walls who wandered away from his father's ute on a property near Guyra in north-west New South Wales. Listen to a recording of this song as it is sung for musical appreciation and also to identify how the artistic elements are used; for example, observe how the lyrics and melody combine to establish the mood and how the stanzas build the tension and reinforce the poignancy of the situation until the happy resolution.

Cross-media comparisons of creative works based on the same theme demonstrate for older students how important the artistic elements (i.e. known as elements of drama in this book) are as building blocks for all creative work. Although a play, song, dance, painting and film differ in outer form, the playwright, composer, choreographer, painter and filmmaker draw on many of the same artistic elements to construct their works. The commonality of building blocks across the art forms is one of the key justifications for an integrated arts approach.

Summary

Being able to recognise and use drama elements enriches a person's ability to participate in, appreciate and evaluate drama experiences, whether these are informal as in improvisation and role play or more formal as in a performance. However, it is important to remember that knowing how to use these elements in isolation is not an 'end in itself'. Instead, the aim is to know these elements in order to combine them in meaningful ways through drama. Makers of drama—no matter if they are children, young adults, teachers, professional actors, playwrights, directors, puppeteers— all use these building blocks, alone or in combination, to shape drama. Just as a language is composed of words and phrases that join to form sentences, so, too, drama elements combine to shape drama into different forms. Some of the most important of these forms are discussed in Part Four Activating Alternatives: Shaping Drama Experiences.

For further study

1 List and share with others three new insights you have gained from learning about the elements of drama as discussed in this chapter.
2 Consider how these elements of drama could be used: by a teacher when assisting children to develop a short, improvised scene; by a director working with actors to put on a play, or by a theatre critic when reviewing a stage production.
3 Develop a half-hour drama activity session that introduces children to the elements of drama as described in this chapter. Design the session for either a group of (1) younger children or (2) older children. Within the session incorporate strategies for giving children choice. In addition to the outline of the session, provide a rationale for the way in which you developed it taking into consideration such factors as child interest and relevance, content appropriateness for outcomes, and overall coherence of ideas.

For reflection

Respond to the statement, 'There is a danger that children will not see drama holistically if they only experience drama skills in isolation.' How can this 'danger' be minimised, while at the same time ensuring that students understand and are able to apply the elements of drama?

Review of Part Three

Part Three: Realising Drama: Developing the Senses focused on making sense of the senses, including sense of self, sense of others, and sense of drama. In doing drama, participants connect with others through the process of making imagined worlds 'real'. As children develop their own self-concepts, they learn to relate in positive ways to others. Gaining knowledge of the elements of drama and increasing their communication competence enables children to share ideas effectively, respect others and reflect on their own learning.

Preview

Part Four: Activating Alternatives: Shaping Drama Experiences consists of Chapters 9, 10 and 11.

Chapter 9: Improvising, Role Playing and Playbuilding considers each of these improvisational forms of drama in detail, providing explanations and examples.

Activating Alternatives: Shaping Drama Experiences

Chapter 9: Improvising, Role Playing and Playbuilding

Chapter 10: Story Making, Telling and Dramatising

Chapter 11: Puppet Making, Operating and Presenting

Objectives

By the end of this section you should be able to:

- Improvise, role play and playbuild a script;
- Understand and apply processes for creating, telling and dramatising a story; and
- Recognise puppet types and their distinctive characteristics as a prelude to developing a puppet play and performance.

Part Four examines drama's shapes and forms, building on the understandings and skills learned about self, others, and drama elements in Part Three. Although drama's shapes and forms are limited only by the imagination, focus will be on improvising, role playing and playbuilding (Chapter 9); story making, telling and dramatising (Chapter 10); and puppet making, operating and presenting (Chapter 11). Each form will be discussed in turn, with an explanation, rationale and selected strategies and activities for use with young people provided. Emphasis will be on making, presenting and reflecting on the processes involved.

Improvising,
Role Playing and
Playbuilding

'[In drama] just like in the sport of diving, the essential occurs in the air—between the jumping board and the water surface' (Krusic 1999).

Introduction

Improvisation involves spontaneous interaction in an imagined situation, while role play is a type of improvising in which children make-believe they are someone else (Moore 1988, p. 109). Playbuilding, as the name suggests, uses improvisation and role play as the basis for developing a structured presentation. Improvisational and role-playing activities range from quick-paced interactions, which Heathcote (1984, p. 46) describes as 'short/sharp/ shock', to more complex decision-making and problem-solving dilemmas in which children identify with and commit to situations and characters. Both of these approaches build on previous preparation work done in confidence building, group interaction and drama skills development. Time spent on developing improvisational and role playing skills is done for the children's own benefit with no expectation that there will be spectators present. On the other hand, playbuilding can develop into a more formalised presentation for an audience.

Improvising and role playing

Getting started

Improvising can be as straightforward as having participants actively and imaginatively engage with each or all of the following questions: *who?* (e.g. a child, a clown, a group of tourists); *what?* (e.g. climbing a mountain, eating a sandwich, sweeping the floor); *where?* (e.g. at a football match, in a fairytale, in the outback); *when?* (e.g. in the past, in the here-and-now, in the future); *why?* (e.g. driven by emotions such as anger or love; by motivation to succeed, to be happy, to meet a challenge; by circumstance, such as confinement, power, poverty); and *how?* (e.g. strategies for achieving the goal, such as alone, in pairs, or in a group or using a range of techniques, such as cooperating, bargaining, and compromising).

When focus starts with and emphasises the *who* of the improvisation, participants are said to be improvising in role. The following exercises introduce and extend this concept for children. In Class Photo (Activity Box 9.1) participants establish a role through facial expression and bodily position and then change to new roles in quick succession. The aim is for the children to respond spontaneously.

Activity Box **9.1**

Class photo

Description
Pose with others for a class photo. After the first photo, the photographer will call for a different type of class to pose. Change your position and attitude to reflect this new type of class.

Mentor note
Select a different student to be the photographer for each photo. Have the group members who are posing for the picture totally change places after each shot. Some possible classes are:

* A school class that is happy, sad, cute, hungry, tired, anxious, naughty.
* A class of cricket players, spies, rodeo stunt riders, opera singers, disco dancers, fishing experts, acrobats, trackers, window washers, filmmakers, dog trainers.

Consider using an actual digital camera to take the photos and then view or print them for the groups to see.

Variations

- Families: Different types of families pose for photographs (Bany-Winters 1997, p. 66).
- Photographs: A photographer arranges children in small groups to show relationships between those being photographed (e.g. mother and children; tour leader and tourists) (Moore 1988, p. 69).

Class Photo (Activity Box 9.1) is a useful starting point for improvisation in role because it acquaints children with the idea of taking on different characters and then discarding them to assume new roles. Children remain silent, showing these roles through still photographs. This encourages them to focus on using their body positions, gestures and facial expressions to communicate their roles.

Family Photograph (From the Classroom 9.1) provides insight into how one student teacher adapted the group photograph with students in her class.

From the Classroom 9.1

Family photograph

Robyn adapted the concept of the Class Photo to her drama work with children in a composite Kindergarten -Year 1 class where family identities was the unit under study. As part of this study, children created family photographs in groups.

Robyn says of the exercise:

The students worked well in their groups, interacting effectively in negotiating and creating their group tableau. Each group represented a different family arrangement that included:

- One parent, two children and two dogs,
- Two parents, two children,

- One parent, one aunt, one child and one cat, and
- One grandparent, one parent, one child and one baby.

  Students eagerly participated in a discussion on the similarities and differences of family identities.

At the Bus Stop (Activity Box 9.2) and Catch a Cab (Activity Box 9.3) are role play activities that encourage spontaneous participation and make children aware of others as they improvise. Not only do participants need to share space, but they also need to engage vocally with others.

Activity Box **9.2**

At the bus stop

Description

Decide the role you will play (e.g. child, police officer, person walking a dog) and sit down on a bench at the bus stop. Another person, who plays a different role (e.g. kite flyer, swaggie, bird watcher), sits down beside you. Talk together. Find out about the other person and where they are taking the bus today.

During your chat, a third person approaches. Your bus arrives and you leave. Now the second and third person converse until a fourth person arrives. Then the second person leaves and the other two speak—and so forth.

Mentor note

At first, assist the children to think of roles. Control the pace of the action by signalling each new person when to approach the bench. After the children get the idea, let them monitor the action making their own decisions about when to enter the scene. Role playing can proceed for as long as the children are motivated.

Variation

Park Bench: Children play the roles of famous people who meet on a park bench (Bany-Winters 1997, p. 86).

At the Bus Stop (Activity Box 9.2) encourages children to interact spontaneously as they create a scene without prior planning. The chat develops in any direction the participants choose to take it until the next person arrives and the focus shifts.

Catch a Cab (Activity Box 9.3) adds an additional level of complexity because participants no longer respond to each other only in pairs, but also in groups of three and four.

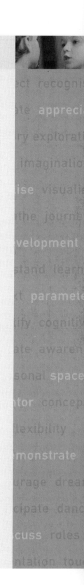

Activity Box 9.3

Catch a cab

Description

You are someone going somewhere (e.g. musician to the Opera House, politician to Parliament House, fan to the Melbourne Cricket Ground).

Signal a cab. The driver pulls up—you get inside.

Tell the cab driver where you want to go.

In this improvisation, more than one person may hire the cab at the same time. Talk to the driver until another person signals for the cab.

Move to the back left seat as the new passenger gets in next to the driver. The three of you talk. Get to know the new passenger and where this person is going.

A third passenger signals the cab. The other passenger and you move anti-clockwise to let the new one sit next to the driver. Get to know the new passenger.

When the next passenger signals, it is time for you to leave the cab through the back right door. Watch out for the traffic!

Mentor note

Place two chairs in front of two others to form the inside of the cab. The cabbie sits in the front right seat and remains there until you indicate it is time to change drivers. Each new passenger enters from the front left door and moves anti-clockwise in the seats until the cab is full. Passengers leave by the rear right door.

At first, control the pace by signalling when each new passenger is to enter; later, children will get the idea and choose when to enter at their own pace.

Remind participants that as each new person enters the cab, the focus needs to shift to that person.

Caution them to always be careful and watch out for traffic, particularly when they step out of the cab.

Variation

Each passenger enters the taxi in a different mood (e.g. happy, sad, agitated, angry, calm). All the passengers take on this emotion as they interact until a new passenger enters and changes the feeling.

Catch a Cab (Activity Box 9.3) builds listening and cooperation skills as children shift focus to interact with each new person who enters the cab. Participants gain the most from this exercise if they listen closely to each other and interact in ways that forward the group conversation. Maintaining momentum relies on having a new passenger join the cab when conversation begins to lag. Also, if necessary, stopping the action for a brief period of group reflection can help potential passengers understand the importance of listening and contributing to each conversation in a constructive manner. Once the conventions of this exercise are established, children become comfortable with the continuous shifts in conversation and mood and an atmosphere of excitement and cooperative participation develops.

Time Travel (Activity Box 9.4) engages children both vocally and physically as they adapt their roles and actions to suit changing situations.

Activity Box 9.4

Time travel

Description

Enter the space provided. Decide who you are and what you are doing (e.g. you are a tennis player serving the ball). Begin the action. When the mentor calls 'Time in!', freeze the action.

A second person joins you and begins with your last action, changing it into something else (e.g. you are serving a ball, when the second person takes your actions and changes them into putting up a tent). Join the second person in doing this action, carrying on a conversation related to what you both are doing (e.g. 'This tent is easy to put up!') until you hear 'Time in!'

You both freeze and a third person joins you, takes your last action, and transforms it into something else. More people join you one-by-one until the mentor calls 'Time out!'

At this point, the process reverses as each person comes back out of the time slip in the reverse order of how they went in, one at a time as the mentor calls 'Time out!' Actions are repeated in the reverse order until the first person who began the improvisation is the last one out.

Mentor note

A **bounded space**, one that has definite boundaries, is designated as the area in which the improvisation will take place. The mentor (or a designated student) is responsible for saying 'Time in!' when another player is to be added and the scene is to change, and 'Time out!' as the process reverses. During this activity, encourage each child to join with the new person immediately in building the next idea.

Add players to the improvisation until there are six; then have each player come back out of the scene in the reverse order of how they went in.

Encourage dialogue between participants throughout that does not directly describe what they are doing, but gives clues from what is said (e.g. 'This ice is great for skating, isn't it?' 'How many pieces of pizza do you want?')

Use Imaginary Object Pass (Activity Box 6.4) as a warm-up for Time Travel because both involve transforming one thing into another.

Variation

Time Travel is derived from the popular Theatresports game, Space Jump. Another version is Freeze/Switch where two players engage in activity until the leader calls 'Freeze'. The players remain motionless until the leader calls 'Switch' at which point an audience member exchanges places with one of the characters, changing the situation. The action begins again (Dodd 1998).

Short improvisational exercises, such as the four described (Activity Boxes 9.1 to 9.4) have as their main purpose 'the experience itself' (Heathcote

1984, p. 44). These motivational activities help children think on their feet, encourage their active participation, and foster group cooperation. In the last three exercises (Activity Boxes 9.2–9.4), leadership shifts frequently, enabling children to both lead and follow.

Spontaneous improvisation can be directly linked to learning in a subject content area. When finding out about community helpers, for example, children in the role of a police officer and a postal employee can compare what they do in their jobs. As part of a study about the natural environment, children can improvise a bushfire that develops in intensity through movement and sound until it is brought under control by fire fighters or a downpour of rain. When learning about the goldrush days, children, in the role of miners, can set up camp and pan for gold. These short segments of active participation are useful reinforcements for other forms of learning.

When developing these improvisational interactions, Heathcote (1975, p. 96) advises that the focus needs to be on ideas rather than the shape or form of the drama. The main aim of improvisation is to make the activity meaningful and relevant for the child rather than coherent and unified for an audience. For this reason, meaningful moments rather than sequential storylines need to be the emphasis. Although some improvisations may eventually be developed and performed for others, this is not the primary purpose of improvisation.

Delving deeper

Improvisation and role play may be explored at different levels. Although exercises, like those in the previous section, can introduce improvisation and role play to students, Heathcote (1975) points out that when exercises are the only way in which drama is experienced, 'the natural discoveries that come from emotional involvement cannot arise' (p. 104). In-depth work in improvisation and role play goes beyond exercises to focus on 'pupils' active identification with imagined roles and situations' through which they 'can learn to explore issues, events and relationships' (O'Neill & Lambert 1982, p. 11).

Particularly when in-depth improvisation is a new experience for the participants, the mentor assumes responsibility for the overall structure. Students participate within this structure by giving suggestions, adding details, making decisions and choosing alternatives. Three possible approaches for structuring improvisation—simulation, analogy and role—(Bolton & Heathcote 1999; Heathcote 1984, 1975) are introduced in Improvisation Starting Points (Concept Box 9.1).

Concept Box 9.1

Improvisation starting points

Simulation

This approach involves putting participants into situations that approximate real-life ones; for example, improvise how you would respond during a fire drill. Following the improvisation, discuss what happened and repeat the process again based on what you have learned from this virtual experience.

Analogy

This way begins with an example that parallels real-life; for example, improvise the story of Chicken Little who thought the sky was falling and started a rumour (Bishop 1984). Reflect on the experience drawing out the real-life implications of what happens when rumours spread.

Role

Improvisations can start with participants in role. The advantage of this approach is that emotions are often associated with particular roles. To illustrate, roles such as a bully, a sports hero or a thief prompt reactions from others, sympathetic or otherwise. In addition, because in improvisation it is usual for characters to want some goal and to face obstacles in reaching it (Novelly 1985, p. 90), beginning with roles immediately develops the improvisational tension (e.g. the principal confronts the bully; the umpire orders the football player from the field; the clumsy jewel thief accidentally sets off an alarm).

Whether the structure for an in-depth improvisation begins with simulation, analogy or role, gaining participant commitment and role identification are essential. Gaining commitment means that children agree to pretend (Heathcote 1975, p. 75), that is, to suspend disbelief in order to create together a 'believable' fictional world.

Role identification involves children empathising with an assigned or chosen character. Participants may acquire a role in a number of ways: imagining their own character; choosing from pictures that have been placed on the wall, known as role on the wall (Neelands 1990, p. 11); or drawing a card from a deck of character cards that provide background details about each character. Alternatively, the mentor may assign participants to a specific role or to a type of group where students are provided with background information about the characters and the situation.

Once a role is chosen or assigned, children investigate this role in order to 'build up a visual image of and a feeling for the character' (Moore 1988, p. 109). This may involve drawing pictures of the characters, creating verbal descriptions, or conducting research prior to the actual start of an improvisation to find out what a person in a role like this one might do or say. In addition, the group may 'hot seat' (Moore 1988, p. 110) students in role, asking them questions to which they provide improvised answers.

In addition to gaining commitment, role identification and reflection, Heathcote's 'stopping to consider' stage is an essential component that can occur at any point in the improvisation. This is the time where students think back on the previous action, how they felt, and what insights they have gained. Reflection is an essential component for learning through drama. This is because reflection 'permits the storing of knowledge, the recalling of power or feeling, and memory of past feelings' (Heathcote 1975, p. 102).

When taking responsibility for structuring an in-depth improvisation then, the mentor determines the starting point, chosen to reflect the interests and developmental levels of the children, and also keeps in mind the overall essentials of commitment, role identification and reflection. The next section discusses several special techniques used in improvisational drama.

Specific techniques

When role playing, there are different ways in which the participants and the mentor can interact. One approach is for the child to act as an authority on a subject, called 'mantle of the expert'; another is when the teacher plays a role in the drama, called 'teacher-in-role'. These drama strategies, pioneered by English drama educator Dorothy Heathcote, extend and deepen improvisation and role playing experiences.

Mantle of the expert

When a child's experiential and knowledge levels do not match the ideas being explored in drama, there is a danger that the overall experience will lack meaning for them. For this reason the technique of mantle of the expert is a useful one in helping children gain experience through making decisions (e.g. You are the ship's captain! What shall we do next?) or becoming an expert through study of an area related to the drama (e.g. What is the procedure for making a slab hut?). This research can also extend to finding out about certain characters and situations in order to provide authentic detail (e.g. a telegraph operator using Morse Code, a forensic scientist working with DNA evidence). By these means the learning that results takes on a personal relevance.

In Bower Bird (Activity 9.5), children become experts as they develop and explain their imaginary collections to others.

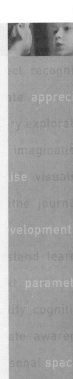

Activity Box 9.5

Bower bird

Description
Like a bowerbird, you collect things. You have one special collection that includes many items of the same sort; for example, plants, toy trucks, or teddy bears. Decide where your collection is in the space around you. Go to that place and stand near your collection. Somewhere in the room there are three special new items for your collection. Find the first item now. Look at it—see it in your mind's eye. Touch it—what is its colour, shape, texture, size and weight? Place the item in your collection. Now find the second item and do the same. Now find the third item. Arrange your collection and share it with the group showing and describing each piece.

Mentor note
The objects, of course, are imaginary. Make sure that children have enough space for their collections. Move the group from space to space as each child shares the items. When the child finishes talking, group members ask questions about the collection.

Variation
The Collection is a similar activity (Moore 1988, p. 60).

Bower Bird (Activity Box 9.5) uses hot-seating that involves each child being quizzed by other group members. Collectors draw item descriptions from their imaginations or past experience with similar objects.

Teacher-in-role

The teacher-in-role technique directly involves the mentor in the action of the improvisation. However, for ownership of the drama to remain with the children, the teacher usually plays a secondary or lower status role, not a main role (e.g. the apprentice, not the motor mechanic; one of the deck hands, not the captain). In this way the mentor can take part in the action, but at the same time monitor the responses of the participants by asking questions ('What shall we do next?'), providing prompts ('Perhaps the treasure is hidden in the cave. What do you think?') or making observations (e.g. 'The ship is filling with water, Captain!'). This leaves room for children in role to make the key decisions.

During the course of the improvisation, the mentor can play a number of different roles that enable the action. However, for this to be effective the child needs to know when the mentor is and is not in role. Sometimes mentors establish this by putting on or removing an item of clothing (e.g. hat, coat); by moving to a certain place (e.g. rug, chair); or changing vocal tone (e.g. character voice, teacher voice), or picking up a prop to represent each character (e.g. police whistle, reporter's notebook). These details need to be established with the children before the improvisation begins so they will know what to expect and how to respond.

When in role, mentors need to use voice and movement to make whatever part they play believable (Ackroyd-Pilkington 2001, p. 22; Moore 1988, p. 110). Commitment and role identification on the part of the mentor will strengthen the belief of the children in their roles. At the same time, the mentor needs to develop skill in slipping in and out of role in order to provide the necessary link back to the actual world when appropriate moments for reflection come within the drama.

Developing a skilful questioning technique is useful for the mentor. Both in role and out of role, the teacher can use questions effectively to forward the action. O'Neill and Lambert (1982) identify the many ways in which questions can be used to:

Establish atmosphere, feed in information, seek out the interests of the group, determine the direction of the drama, give status to the participants, challenge superficial thinking, control the class, draw the group together to confront specific problems, and guide reflection on the work (p. 142).

According to Heathcote (Wagner 1976, p. 65) questions help the mentor draw out the 'children's viewpoint and interpretation of ideas', the most important bases for the improvisation, in order to reveal their underlying feelings and beliefs and encourage their development of empathy with the characters and the situation.

Solve the Mystery: Teacher-in-Role (Activity Box 9.6) provides an example of a scenario where the teacher is in role.

Activity Box **9.6**

Solve the mystery: Teacher-in-role

Description
You are a group of detectives hired by the local council. A council worker arrives and asks for your assistance.

Mentor note
The mentor plays the role of the council worker and addresses the detectives. The mentor puts on a worker's hat and says:

> I am the council worker hired by you, the local council, to look after the picnic area. I asked for this meeting with you today to help me solve a puzzling mystery. Monday morning I came to the picnic area early on my rounds to find it was in a disgusting state. Papers, cans, rubbish everywhere! I decided I needed help so I headed back to base to get Joe to come with me. We got some bags and bins to clean up the mess. When we returned a little later to start the clean-up, all the rubbish was gone. It was nowhere in sight and the bin was missing! Joe and I can't understand what happened. We're hoping you might have some ideas to help us solve the mystery.
>
> Do any of you want to ask me any questions about what I saw and did?

You, the teacher, in the role of council worker, are hot-seated and quizzed by the children in their roles as detectives. Once this is finished, you remove the worker's hat, signalling that you are no longer playing the role of the council worker.

As the teacher, divide the children into small groups and have each group of detectives develop a solution to the mystery (e.g. aliens took the rubbish away to study it, thinking they had discovered a new life form; guilty midnight revellers returned the next day to pick up their mess; what looked like rubbish was really the set for a movie, the scene was shot after the council worker went for help and the movie crew picked up the rubbish and left before the council worker returned).

Improvise and use role play to bring each group's scenario to life in a small group or with the whole class.

In summary, these two specific techniques, mantle of the expert and teacher-in-role, are regarded as linchpins in the power-sharing relationship essential to in-depth improvisational work in drama.

Developing an improvisation

Whether the impetus for the improvisational drama comes directly from the children or is based on curricular areas, the children must find common ground, called 'defining the moment', so that everyone starts in the same 'exact spot' (Wagner 1976, p. 62). The mentor may use questions, pictures, group movement or discussion to focus the group. As the improvisation develops, the mentor interrupts the action at relevant points to question the children and help them reflect on what is happening. Rather than push for a resolution to the action, the mentor will often pose more questions to help the participants identify and empathise with the situation. Because feelings and ideas, rather than plot elements, drive the improvisation, the focus revolves around 'meaningful moments'. These moments gain relevance as children empathise with the situations or, as Heathcote (Wagner 1976, p. 59) puts it, they 'reach deeper insight about the significance of an act or situation'. Bolton and Heathcote (1999, p. 3) suggest that 'if children are to learn from role play, it is more likely to be effective if the treatment is indirect.' For example, avoid improvising a car accident. Instead have children play the role of witnesses who report the accident to others.

Little Lost Kitten (Activity Box 9.7) is an improvisational framework, intended for use with younger children. The framework uses a photo, questioning by the mentor and role play to help children realise the importance of caring for pets. The questioning helps to make the ensuing situation real as children think of their own pets, or ones they would like to have. Then children are introduced to a photo of Tommy's pet kitten. Through questioning, the children realise that they have something important in common with Tommy.

Activity Box 9.7

Little lost kitten

Description
Answer the following questions:

IDENTIFICATION

- Do you have (or have you ever wanted) a pet?
- What kind of pet? What is its name?
- What do you/would you do to take care of your pet (e.g. feed, wash, pat it)? Can you show us how you do that?
- How do you feel about your pet?

Figure 9.1 Tommy's kitten, Scooter

COMMITMENT
Here is a picture of Tommy's kitten, Scooter.

- Why do you think Tommy named him Scooter?
- What can you tell about Scooter by looking at this picture?
- What kinds of things might you have in common with Tommy?

BUILDING EMPATHY

One day when Tommy comes home from school, Scooter isn't there.

- How do you think Tommy feels?
- What can Tommy do to try to find his kitten (e.g. make a poster to hang in the shop; ask his parents, friends, neighbours; call the pound or local vet to see if someone has found Scooter)?

DIRECT ENGAGEMENT

- Do you think there is anything we can do (e.g. make posters; help him talk to the neighbours)?
- Which should we do first?

(If children say—Make a poster)

- Can you make a poster that we could put in shops?
- What could we put on the poster?
- Who will play the role of Tommy for us so we can find out what his phone number is and how to describe Scooter on the poster? (One child is hot seated and provides the information. Children make posters to put on the wall.)

(If children say—Talk to the neighbours)

- Who knows this neighbourhood? Can we all make a street plan of who lives where? (Draw the street and give it a name.)
- (To a child) Where do you live in this street? What's your name? Can you draw your house on this diagram? (Encourage children to draw in houses.)
- What questions should we ask the neighbours? (Develop the questions together.)

TEACHER-IN-ROLE

The phone rings:

- Should I get that? (Mentor answers phone and improvises a conversation with Cat Rescue, which has found the kitten.)

REFLECTION

- Why is it important to take care of our pets?
- What can we do to keep our pets safe?

The approach used in Little Lost Kitten (Activity Box 9.7) enables children to begin with their own knowledge, experience and feelings on which they draw to empathise with a character in a fictional situation. As they reflect on the insights they have gained from this experience, they deepen their understanding.

When preparing for an in-depth improvisation, the mentor needs to identify the aims of the drama taking into consideration not only curricular demands, but also the needs and interests of the participants. The guidelines that will be provided to the participants before and during the improvisation are also important to determine. Where the improvisation will begin also needs careful consideration: Will the stimulus be a real-life situation or a fictional one? Will simulation, analogy or role be the strategy used? Will the action start at the beginning, in the middle of things or at the end and then **flashback**? Will the children and the mentor take on roles in the developing drama? Finally, the possible routes through the improvisation need to be considered and strategies developed for handling each of the possible variations. This 'anything can happen' nature of improvisation makes it a dynamic learning medium for young people.

Playbuilding

Getting started

Playbuilding is a collaborative group 'meaning making' process through which ideas are developed, shaped and eventually refined into a more structured form for presentation. Initially a script is not written instead relevant ideas related to a chosen theme, issue or title are explored in-depth for their dramatic potential. Group decision-making processes are at the heart of playbuilding. The idea chosen to build a play must be important to the group and they 'make it their own' by having the main say in how the play develops.

The playbuilding process involves several stages. First, after brainstorming a range of ideas in the form of possible themes (e.g. maintaining a healthy lifestyle, finding happiness), issues (e.g. overcrowding, pollution of the environment), or title (Once in a Lifetime, Space Shuttle Adventure), the group selects one to explore in more depth. To arrive at this consensus, children use discussion and negotiation skills. Consensus Building (Activity

Box 9.8) helps children understand what reaching a **consensus** means. It provides an opportunity for them to learn how to resolve potential conflicts in order to reach an agreement.

Activity Box 9.8

Consensus building

Description

How can you be a 'good' friend? Write down three ways (e.g. be kind, share, help others). The mentor will collect what you and others have written and put the main categories on the board. As a group, you must decide which are the three most important things you can do to be a 'good' friend. This will involve discussion and debate. Finally the group will be asked to make the decision assigning (1) to the most important, then (2), then (3).

Mentor note

As part of the consensus building process, discuss with the children how they will make the final decision. Will it be by show of hands, secret ballot, compromise or some other means? When they have decided, help them follow it through to a satisfactory outcome. Reflect with the children on the consensus building process.

Extensions

- See Flower Power (Activity Box 5.12), which focuses on some of the potential problems associated with trying to reach a consensus.
- Compare consensus with conspectus, as discussed in That's Debatable! (Activity Box 5.11).

Once the idea (e.g. theme, issue, central question, title) is chosen, the aim is to explore it through a wide range of drama approaches in order to illuminate and deepen the children's understanding of the dramatic potential of each idea. Some possible ways of achieving this include: improvising dialogue; creating vignettes based on the theme; developing a mime and movement piece; vocalising and singing; working in role; constructing still photographs; and continually using group discussion and reflection. To enhance this investigation, the mentor uses questioning techniques and prompts that encourage, but do not dictate, the direction the development takes. The intent is to foster group ownership of the evolving ideas.

The group then discusses the outcomes of this 'trying out' phase and narrows the ideas by choosing the most workable segments. These parts are then sequenced to shape the 'play'. Among the possible forms this sequencing may take are: a unified plot with a beginning, middle and end; a series of linked episodes, each complete in itself; an issue about which a range of characters provide their views via **monologues** and vignettes; a **montage** of various creative art forms, such as poetry, dance, storytelling, which combine to reinforce the theme. Bridging episodes or montage items may be achieved by using music, lighting, projected visuals, a common setting to reflect the theme or mood, or a consistent character who appears in each scene to provide the narrative thread.

As the improvisations develop, decide on the order; do not rush to have the script written down. Have children pay special attention to both the opening scene and the concluding scene. A playbuilt show need not be written down at all—or if it is, not until much later, sometimes after-the-fact to preserve a record of what occurred.

Playbuilding in action

One way to playbuild is to provide the children with a stimulus (e.g. newspaper headline or article, poem, real-life situation) as a starting point as in Case of the Polka-Dot Rock (Activity Box 9.9). For example, identify from the source something that could serve as an inciting incident and then have participants take on and develop a role of someone who could be involved in that situation. The play can be built up from individual character monologues, improvised dialogue among characters and character interviews. Use the following newspaper article as a stimulus for playbuilding. Have young people choose characters who could have been at the scene. Let the play develop from the information provided and then extend its scope by integrating children's ideas.

Activity Box 9.9

Case of the polka-dot rock:
Playbuild from a stimulus

Description

Headline: Suburb rocked by vandals

Newspaper item:

> Overnight in the harbourside suburb of Mooney Beach, a well-known local landmark, a massive rock jutting out into the sea, was painted in bright red and white polka-dots. Some locals were amused; others were horrified. Some said the effect was awesome; others described it as being in poor taste. Environmental groups have called it yet another set back for the fragile environment. The mystery is: Who painted the rock? Why did they do it? Were they larrikins having fun, artists creating modern art, protestors making a statement or tourists leaving their mark? No one knows. The city council will meet Wednesday evening to decide what should be done. The local mayor hopes all interested parties will attend.

Starting points for play development

Map the scene on a large piece of paper (e.g. placement of rock, beach, shops, city council). Imaginatively transfer these places to the 'play space' available, a process called '**defining the space**' (Neelands in Carey 1995), so that the group knows where things are as the improvisation begins.

- Identify the types of people who could have been in the vicinity of the beach (e.g. joggers, dog walkers, surfers, sunbakers, shop owners, an exercise class, teacher and students on a day excursion to the beach). Choose a role.
- In role you are interviewed by a local newspaper reporter (i.e. teacher-in-role) about what you may have seen or what you know about the incident.
- In small groups, solve the mystery of who painted the rock and why they did it. Develop scenarios. Choose roles and re-enact them.
- Hold an improvised council meeting to collect views about what should be done about the painted rock.

- Based on the various exploration exercises, choose those you would like to use to build a play about this incident. Put them together.
- Decide how you will produce your play. Here are some questions to ask:
  - Will you use costumes, make-up, sound effects, or music?
  - Will you say all your lines or will you sing or dance some of them?
  - Will you use props or a set? How will you show the seaside and the rock?
- Rehearse your play and present it.

Mentor note

Encourage and extend the children in their thinking about the situation. Take time for ideas to develop and have the group frequently stop to discuss and reflect on what they are doing. Involve everyone in the improvisations. Some children may improvise while others watch and provide observations; some may even serve as scribes, writing down key ideas that need to be remembered for the next session. The mentor may collect these and save them in the group playbuildling folder.

Serve as a facilitator and guide, posing questions that enable the group to find their own solutions.

Another approach to the playbuilding process starts with actual events from personal experience (Weigler 2001). First, in relation to a common theme (e.g. The Best Birthday Party Ever, My Day at the Zoo), children recount stories of what personally happened to them. Starting the playbuilding process by focusing on children's own experiences values their knowledge and empowers them. These stories are then **deconstructed** (i.e. separated into components) to discover their basic elements. Plot structures, characters, settings and emotions embedded within the stories are compared and contrasted. With the idea of 'making a play', choices are made. The selected elements are then combined into a composite story to serve as the basis for play development. In this way, the final production is based on a collective group vision of what actually happens in 'real' situations. What Happened to Me (Activity Box 9.10) focuses on the experience-based approach to playbuilding.

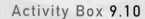

Activity Box 9.10

What happened to me: Playbuild from experience

Description

Think of one time when:

- You went somewhere special; or
- You argued with your parents; or
- You were surprised by something.

Tell what happened as a story. Tape record it or write it down.

Collect all the group stories related to one of these times. How are these stories alike? What do they have in common? How could you build a play using the common elements found in your stories?

Mentor role

Work through an example with the children. Ask them: think of a time when you were lost. Describe aloud what happened.

After a number of children have spoken, ask them to think of some of the common elements of 'being lost', which could include: first not realising it, starting to worry, looking around, trying to find landmarks, admitting you are lost, seeking help and finally finding your way. Children may also associate certain emotional states with being lost such as: on the one hand—fear, loneliness, worry; on the other hand— bravery, courage and self-sufficiency. Have children suggest how these elements could be worked into a play (e.g. What characters? What setting? What beginning? What events? What ending?).

Then have them improvise, select and order the scenes.

The final stage is producing the playbuilt work for an audience. To ensure that all children can be heard and seen as they perform, the mentor uses vocal and movement exercises during the rehearsal period to develop performance skills. Children are also taught how to portray the scenes in their play through aesthetic and meaningful **stage pictures**. The mentor assists children to use the elements of drama to shape and stage their play, always keeping in mind that the play belongs to the children and that it is their ideas and viewpoints that are of primary importance.

Students Have a Say (From the Classroom 9.2) demonstrates how drama exercises can be incorporated into a playbuilt performance.

From the Classroom 9.2

Students have a say

Ishbel, a PhD researcher, worked with older students in a school setting to create a playbuilt performance based on these students' views of schooling. Selected drama exercises were adapted to fit this theme and combined into a short performance. For example, Keep the Beat (Activity Box 8.16) was the basis for Teacher Talk that combined body percussion with phrases students had heard teachers say in the classroom (e.g. 'Good work!' or 'Try harder'). Connect: Over, Under, Around and Through (Activity Box 7.8) was the stimulus for creating a group sculpture to show the students' future aspirations after leaving school (e.g. 'I am a chef', 'I am a teacher'). Name Circle (Activity Box 7.1) was adapted for the curtain call that consisted of students saying their names preceded by a positive adjective (e.g. Hard-working Hilary) before exiting from the performance space. The unscripted performance built from improvisation was performed twice for the students' teachers and the principal, fulfilling the aim of having student voices heard by others, particularly the teachers. Ishbel and her team noticed a growth in student focus, concentration, teamwork and ownership of the drama work over the five days of the project (Murray 2006).

The result of the playbuilding process is a group presentation designed and created by young people, which has developed from casting the net wide for ideas and then gradually filtering these in order to choose ones that form part of the final work. Whatever approach is taken, playbuilding involves continuous group reflection on the development process from its initial improvisational stages to its final culmination in a performance. As children make decisions, they use their critical thinking skills and stretch their imaginations. They experience firsthand the difference between telling and showing and how to structure ideas into dramatic forms.

Applications for middle school students

One particular form of role play and improvisation that has proved popular with older students is **Theatresports,** an approach to improvisation that originator Keith Johnstone (1999) claims was inspired by observing audience involvement techniques used in pro-wrestling. Theatresports consists of two competing teams of 'improvisers' that challenge each other to role play and improvisational tasks that are completed in front of an audience of 'spectators', who often participate (e.g. providing suggestions, being volunteers, rating the improvisers). Two teams headed by captains, a commentator or facilitator, and the judges occupy the improvisation space. During a match of a specified length, teams present each other with challenges (e.g. the best: movie scene, rock-and-roll routine, re-enactment of a current event). Teams can add special requirements to the challenge, asking for these scenes to be done in 'mime, gibberish, verse, [or] song' (Johnstone 1999). Judges award points to the teams based on their performances. Some Theatresports terms include: 'issuing a challenge' (i.e. We challenge the opposite team to …); 'baulking' (i.e. a team refusing a challenge and giving grounds for this refusal, such as, 'The challenge isn't clear'); and 'warning for being boring' from the judges. This process aims to train participants in improvisational skills 'on the run' as well as to provide entertainment for an audience.

The Canadian Improv Games is one example of a Theatresports-based competition for young people. Five improvisational team events, namely: The Story Event, The Character Event, The Style Event (i.e. style of media, film or television), The Theme Event and The Life Event comprise this contest, where teams of high school students improvise scenarios of up to four minutes in length. These are adjudicated and scored according to a range of criteria, including: entertainment, narrative, technical stage usage and risk-taking (Young 2000, p. 81).

Johnstone's seminal works in the field of group improvisation, *Impro: Improvisation and the Theatre* (1979) and *Impro for Storytellers: Theatresports and the Art of Making Things Happen* (1999), are essential background reading for those implementing Theatresports or a version of this improvisational form with young people. These sources provide a detailed rationale for Theatresports in addition to scenarios, explanations and other improvisational activities.

Also, because Theatresports is a popular improvisational theatre technique worldwide, it is usually possible to see the technique in action at selected theatre venues. However, if the opportunity is not available to see Theatresports in person, the television programs, *Whose Line is it Anyway?* (an improvisational show that had its origins in a British radio program in 1988) and *Thank God You're Here* (a popular Australian show using professional actors who improvise) are ways for adolescents to see how Theatresports and other improvisational techniques work and how they have been adapted for the television medium.

Summary

This chapter examined improvisation, role play and playbuilding, providing explanations and examples of how these forms can be used to shape the drama experience with young people. Spontaneous, student-centred exploration of character, voice and movement are what makes these dramatic forms work, whether or not the discoveries made during the process result in a culminating performance.

For further study

1 Improvise 'as if' you were: caught in a lift, watching a football match, having a telephone conversation with an unwanted caller, watching a sad/funny/ frightening movie on television. Suggest additional situations for individual or group improvisations.

2 Role play a character who is concerned about an issue, such as: global warming, drugs and their effects on society, the care of the aged, or an issue of your choice. Present a monologue from this character's viewpoint about this concern.

3 Choose three newspaper articles, each one of which you think can provide an initial stimulus for playbuilding with children. Consider drama strategies for working with these accounts that encourage student input and ownership of the developing ideas.

For reflection

Reflect on your experiences in (1) and (2) in For Further Study. What have you learned from these exercises about improvisation and role play? How will these insights inform your approach to employing these techniques with children in drama?

Preview

Chapter 10: Story Making, Telling and Dramatising considers these three aspects of story collectively as a form of drama, providing explanations of each, as well as including several complete stories and story summaries for storytelling practice and dramatic development.

Story Making, Telling and Dramatising

'Our reality is made up of an interconnecting web of stories' (Cockett 1997).

Introducing story

People live 'storied lives' where life experiences are made meaningful by structuring and remembering them as stories (Poston-Anderson 2000a; Poston-Anderson & Redfern 1996; Connelly & Clandinin 1990; Reason & Hawkins 1988; Livo & Rietz 1986). Such reconfiguration, called 'storying', is beneficial because it 'helps us to better remember the event' (Livo & Rietz 1986, p. 5). Central to human existence, stories are also a meaningful way to shape the drama experience. This approach is consistent with drama because drama itself is identified as 'a way of making and telling stories' (Cockett 1997). As Taylor (1990) observes, 'in drama, we "story" most, if not all, the time' (p. 2). When stories are used to shape drama experiences, several key questions are relevant: What is a story? Where can stories be found? Whose story is it? How can a story be shared? Each question will be discussed in turn.

What is a story?

Traditionally, a **story** is defined as a narrative with a beginning, middle and end involving characters who overcome obstacles to reach a goal (Livo & Rietz 1986, p. 29). In addition to this time-honoured linear view of a story, however, is the recent less-structured, more open-ended view in **hypertext fiction** and computer games. Interactivity, multiple pathways and discontinuity characterise such stories, requiring participants to select options that determine the direction of the action or create the story themselves by writing it or contributing episodes (Poston-Anderson 1996).

Drama can benefit from both traditional and contemporary understandings of what a story is. Making stories may involve children interacting with others to choose options or to create alternative endings. Telling stories usually focuses on traditional storytelling methods that involve selecting and presenting a structured story to others. Dramatising stories may involve either a structured re-enactment of the entire story or presenting segments, not necessarily in sequential order, which highlight character, mood or action. This later process can be thought of as 'cracking open' a story to see what is inside.

Where do you find stories?

Stories surround us. Autobiographical material, family experiences, news-paper articles, media accounts, traditional folktales, children's books, and contemporary **urban legends** are all rich story sources. Whether the source is informal (e.g. conversations) or formal (e.g. written stories or media presentations), the challenge is to select and shape the accounts in ways that are appropriate for the group (i.e. interests, educational level) while, at the same time, preserving the integrity of the source material.

Whose story is it?

If as Winston (2002, p. 251) suggests, '[t]he spiritual beliefs of a culture are intertwined within its stories … ', then it is of critical importance when sharing a story to understand whose viewpoint is represented. Whether directly stated or embedded in underlying values, every story has a 'voice'. Clarifying this 'voice' deepens the appreciation and understanding of both the person telling the story and the audience.

Also, certain cultural materials, such as Australian Aboriginal stories, belong to recognised cultural owners and permission may be needed to share them. Likewise, published stories under copyright may need clearance to be shared aloud outside an educational setting. These points emphasise how important it is for the mentor to know the source and background of a story.

Sharing this information with those listening to the story also enriches their story listening experience.

How can a story be shared?

There are countless ways to share a story (Winch & Poston-Anderson 1993). The mentor may choose to tell it directly to children, perhaps as a prelude to further drama work. There may also be opportunities for the children, individually or as part of a group, to share a story with others. As stories are told, children listen and may sometimes be encouraged to take part actively in the story; for example, by miming actions or providing sound effects to accompany the story.

Sometimes stories are read rather than told. In this case, the person sharing the story makes the words come alive through vocal expression and, if the story is in picture book form, shows the illustrations to the children as the story progresses. When showing pictures is part of the story presentation it is important that the book is large enough to be seen by everyone in the group. A read story should be as dramatically shared as a **told story** with the sharer using different voices for the characters and using facial expressions, gestures and other movements as appropriate. The aim in both reading and telling stories is to have children visualise the setting, action and characters in their own minds (Poston-Anderson 1994).

In addition to telling or reading stories aloud, stories can be shared through other media, including: the visual arts (e.g. drawing, painting, sculpting); music (e.g. song, chant); dance (e.g. improvised dance drama, folk dance); and technology (e.g. video, photographs, interactive stories on line).

In summary, knowing the answers to these four basic questions helps the mentor and the students decide on the most appropriate approach to using stories as the basis for drama. The next sections focus on three general ways to use stories in drama: story making; storytelling; and story dramatising.

Story making

Through the **story making** process, children learn about the key elements used to shape a story; namely, setting, character, theme, action, complication and resolution; and how story characters interact and respond to their worlds.

From basic activities that identify and introduce these story elements, children proceed to more complex considerations, such as reflecting on a character's motivations or how the values expressed by a character compare with their own feelings, attitudes and beliefs.

The following two story making activities, Tangram Tale (Activity Box 10.1) and Circle Story (Activity Box 10.2), can be used as the basis for encouraging children to create their own stories in groups. At this initial stage, building participation, encouraging flexibility of thought and stimulating the flow of ideas are key aims. In other words, emphasis is more on idea generation, than on a structured storyline. Tangram Tale (Activity Box 10.1), a group approach to story making, starts with each child creating an image from a tangram. Then these **tangram pictures** are linked to create a brief story sequence.

Activity Box 10.1

Tangram tale

Description

You will be given a tangram that is made of seven pieces of paper that fit together in different ways. Make as many different things as you can with your tangram pieces (e.g. tree, ship, house). Use all the pieces in one object. Select your favourite object. With three others, combine your four different tangrams to make a mini-story. For example: One day a (1) *sailor* left his (2) *house* and went to sea in a (3) *sailing ship.* As he passed the (4) *buoy* in the harbour, he said, 'How lucky I am to sail to sea!'

Mentor note

Each child is provided with a tangram that is a square of paper cut into seven pieces as shown in the diagram. Cut

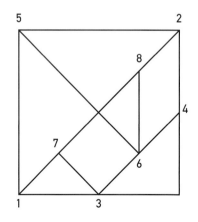

Figure 10.1 Tangram pattern

out the pieces and reform them to make different shapes joining the edges. Encourage children to use all the pieces for each image they make.

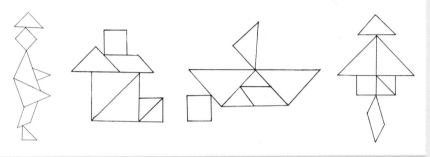

Figure 10.2 Tangram shapes

Variations

- Use Tangram Tale in a mathematics lesson to focus on shapes.
- William Cameron's picture book, entitled *A Tangram Tale* (1972), uses tangram shapes to make the illustrations for the story of two ill-fated lovers in old China. (This sad tale is also told on dinner plates that have the Blue Willow pattern).

The advantage of making a story from a tangram is that children have tangible visuals as a basis for shaping and structuring a story.

Circle Story (Activity Box 10.2) begins with children sitting in a circle, a recognised story setting sometimes referred to as the 'magic circle' or the 'golden ring' (Livo & Rietz 1986, p. 198). Someone in the circle (i.e. it can be the mentor or one of the students) provides the first line of the story. The story making continues around the circle with each person contributing a line until the story arrives back at the start of the circle again. At this point, the person who began the story can choose to provide the finishing line or keep the story going around the circle again.

If the story circle is too large (i.e. more than six to eight students), the group can be divided into several smaller circles. When this happens, a person in each group provides an opening story line while the mentor monitors the progress of each circle. When both groups have finished, they can compare notes on the different stories that they have developed.

Activity Box 10.2

Circle story

Description

Holding a **story stick**, one person begins the story, providing the opening that consists of the setting, main character and initial situation (e.g. One morning at Bundy Beach, Sally grabbed her board and headed for the surf). When this person decides it is time, she or he will pass the story stick to the next person in the circle, who adds to the story until deciding to pass on the story stick to the next person. At this point the next person continues the story and so forth around the circle. When the story reaches the person who started it, the story ends, or can continue again around the circle.

Mentor note

Emphasise that the only person who speaks is the one with the story stick (e.g. actual stick, dowel, pencil). The mentor may also use a **story rattle** (e.g. a sound instrument such as a tambourine) as a signal to pass the story stick. The mentor only shakes the rattle if passing the story stick around the circle takes too long and children start to get restless.

Variations

* Talking Ball: A ball is passed, thrown or rolled around the circle as each person tells a segment of the story (Bany-Winters 1997, p. 26).
* String Story uses a ball of string on which are wound different lengths of string. Each person continues the story while unravelling the string until it comes off the ball. Then the person passes the ball of string on to the next person in the circle.

The next approach to group storying, creating a **sound story**, introduces children to a cumulative tale structure in which one episode follows another in sequence. At each stage of the story, children contribute a sound and/or action to contribute to the plot development.

There are two main ways in which a sound story can develop. The first is by presenting a sequence of events that culminates in a resolution, such as reaching the end of a quest or solving a problem. The second way is to have a series of events end with a climax, then reverse the action so it rewinds back to the beginning of the story. In either pattern, the idea is for children to create sounds and actions to accompany the story as it is told making a group participation story.

Little Lost Dinosaur (Story and Script Box 10.1) is an example of the first type of sound story. The one-way action moves forward culminating in the little dinosaur finding its mother.

Story and Script Box 10.1

Little Lost Dinosaur

Figure 10.3 The young dinosaur looks for his mother

Little Lost Dinosaur

Once when the world was young a tiny dinosaur lost his mother. He stamped his feet (*stamp*). He shook his scales (*shake*). He cried (*sob*). Then he called, 'Mother!' (*repeat 'Mother!'*). In answer, came only the rumble of distant thunder (*rumble*).

He called once more, Mother! (*repeat 'Mother!'*). In answer, came only the gurgle of a simmering swamp (*gurgle*).

He called as loudly as he could 'MOTHER!' (*repeat 'MOTHER!'*) In answer, came only the buzz of an angry bee! (*Buzzzzzzz*) 'Sting! Sting! Sting!' it cried. (*repeat 'Sting! Sting! Sting!' Jab index finger to emphasise words.*)

Then came the roar of a dinosaur (*roar*). Away flew the bee as fast as could be (*buzz and make wings with hands*).

'Mother!' (*repeat 'Mother!'*)

Little Dinosaur was happy at last.

When sharing a sound story, the storyteller practises the sounds and actions with the children before the story begins so they understand the pre-arranged signals used to indicate when they are to participate.

Jo and the Coconut Crab (Story and Script Box 10.2) is an example of the second type of sound story in which the action is two-way. The main character, Jo, leaves and then returns back home again. As part of the introduction, the storyteller mentions the size of a coconut crab that enables it to crack open coconuts with its huge claws. In this way, children appreciate why Jo might want to escape its clutches.

Story and Script Box 10.2

Jo and the Coconut Crab

Jo and the Coconut Crab

One morning Jo, who lives on the island of Vanuatu, wakes up, yawns and stretches *(do this)*. He's hungry so he leaves his little hut and goes in search of food.

He looks to the right *(do this)*. He looks to the left *(do this)*. He looks straight ahead *(do this)*. There in the distance he sees what he seeks—a tall coconut palm with a large coconut ready to eat.

Figure 10.4 A tall coconut palm with a large coconut ready to eat

Down the road he trots *(sounds: dippity-doo, dippity-doo; actions: do body percussion on legs to reinforce words)*.

Soon he comes to a large river. He jumps in and swims across *(sounds: splish, splosh, splish, splosh; actions: swimming)*.

Then he wends his way through the tall grass *(sounds: swish, swash, swish, swash; actions: rub hands together)*.

He goes up a gravel hill and down the other side *(sounds: crinch, crunch, crinch, crunch; actions: grind one hand into the other)*.

There before him is the coconut palm. Like other clever children in Vanuatu, he knows how to climb it. Up he goes *(sounds: yibbidy, yibbidy, yibbidy, yibbidy; actions; climbing up a tree)*.

Now he's at the top. He reaches towards the coconut. Suddenly, the fronds on the coconut palm start to shiver *(sounds: shiver, shiver, shiver; actions: hands shake)* and to shake *(sounds: shake shake, shake; actions: hands shake again)*. There peering at him are two large eyes *(actions: make circles with thumb and index fingers on both hands and put around eyes)*. There grabbing for him are two huge claws *(sounds: pinch, pinch, pinch; actions: make fingers pinch)*. It's a giant coconut crab! It makes a horrible noise (*sounds: AAAARUUUGAHHH!; actions: throw arms back, fingers like claws*).

(Repeat sounds and actions in reverse.)

Down the coconut tree climbs Jo (*yibbidy, yibbidy, yibbidy*),

back up the gravel hill and down the other side (*crinch, crunch, crinch, crunch*),

back through the tall grass (*swish, swash, swish, swash*),

into the river and across it (*splish, splosh, splish, splosh*),

down the road (*dippity-doo, dippity-doo*),

until he reaches his own little hut.

At last he's safe. Jo wipes his brow (*do this*) and gives a huge sigh of relief (*sigh*).

Then he says, 'I don't think I'm hungry after all!' (*Repeat, 'I don't think I'm hungry after all!'*)

Mentor note

It is possible to tell this story and involve the children as you go without rehearsing the sounds and actions beforehand. Use prompts such as: Can you do this? and then demonstrate; or make a sound and action first and then say, 'Your turn'.

Variation

The picture book, *We're Going on a Bear Hunt*, written by Michael Rosen and illustrated by Helen Oxenbury (1989), is also based on a cumulative story pattern and can be shared as a chant, using voice and body percussion.

When children are engaged in making the sounds and actions for *Little Lost Dinosaur* (Story and Script Box 10.1) and *Jo and the Coconut Crab* (Story and Script Box 10.2), they feel part of the story sharing process. This involvement is even more evident when the listeners invent the stories themselves as outlined in Group Sound Story (Activity Box 10.3). In small groups of three or four, children choose a character who goes on an adventure or quest. The story ends when this goal is reached or when the character returns back home. Each group shares its story aloud with sound and action encouraging the listeners to join in at pre-arranged signals.

Activity Box 10.3

Group sound story

Description

Think of a character (e.g. child, spy, elf, astronaut). Create an adventure for this character in which there are sounds and actions. Each group tells the story to the rest, involving them with the sounds and actions.

Some examples are:

- A child wakes in the morning (*yawns, stretches*), gets ready for school (*changes from pyjamas to school clothes; eats breakfast*).
- A ship's captain prepares to sail (*tests the wind; puts up the sails*), sets sail (*pulls up the anchor; steers the boat*), encounters a storm (*feels the wind, rain, fixes sails*), and returns to port (*drops anchor*).
- A gourmet chef cooks a meal and everything goes wrong from when the chef makes the dish until it is put before guests on the table.

Mentor note

Encourage children to practise the stories aloud before presenting them, also have them consider how they will involve the others in making the actions and sounds to accompany the story.

For older students

Encourage older students to create written records of their stories that substitute graphic symbols for the oral sounds (e.g. X for a clap; # for a sigh). Include a key (i.e. **legend**) at the beginning of each recorded story to identify what the graphic symbols represent.

Branch out: Create a cumulative story that has branching options within it (i.e. the story could go this way or that, such as the horse could win the race or lose it); then develop each of these branches, sub-dividing them again when appropriate and developing each of these possibilities. Using this technique, the original story can end in a number of ways depending on the options chosen. When students are first learning how to use this technique, advise them to confine themselves to a few story branches only.

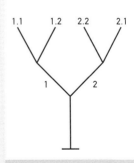

Figure 10.5 Story tree

As the creator reads or tells the story, the listeners choose from the alternatives which way they want the story to go, a concept similar to the popular Choose Your Own Adventure Series of books.

Action words: With the students generate a number of verbs, such as run, crawl, jump, turn, fall, roll, hop, stop, stand. Write these action words on the board. Each small group chooses an identity (e.g. spies, carpenters, gymnasts, a marching band) and creates a sound and movement story in which each group member does the movements in role, alone or synchronised with others (Berghammer, G. et. al. n.d., p. 53).

The sound story technique can be adapted for curriculum use, particularly in situations where a process is studied (i.e. The postal system: how a letter gets from A to B—writing, stamping, posting, picking up, sorting, sending, delivering, opening, and reading). At each stage, sounds and actions are made to reinforce the steps involved.

In summary, when children make stories together they learn how to work with others to structure ideas into a meaningful shape and, when sharing them aloud, how to communicate with listeners. Because students have developed the stories themselves, they also feel a sense of 'ownership' for the story that empowers them.

Storytelling

In **storytelling**, an individual and/or a group tell a story aloud to others bringing it to life through voice and movement. Storytelling is regarded as 'a negotiated oral language production' because during this process a 'relation-ship' develops between the person who tells the story and the listeners (Livo & Rietz 1986, p. 19). Philosopher Walter Benjamin (1968) describes how this happens: 'The storyteller takes what he tells from experience, his own or that reported by others. And he in turn makes it the experience of those who are listening to this tale' (p. 107).

Based on sharing stories in a range of settings, those who tell stories for a living have identified the reasons why they believe told story is important: stories make things real and are powerful; they contain messages and impart wisdom; and they create shared spaces (Poston-Anderson & Redfern 1996).

The storyteller uses memory (Scott 1985) to recall and present the story; organisational skills to sequence and structure the story; and communication skills that employ vocal expression and bodily movement to interest and hold the listeners.

Choosing a story to tell

It is important for tellers to choose stories they like and those that they think others will enjoy, too. The storyteller's enthusiasm for a story will help to inspire listeners and to make them appreciate the story's meaning. There are many types of story. Tellers may use their own stories (e.g. personal experience, family stories, made-up stories) or they may find their stories elsewhere (e.g. nursery rhymes, folk and fairy tales, newspaper accounts, written tales). Story Types (Concept Box 10.1) suggests ways to encourage children to develop or find their own stories to tell.

Concept Box 10.1

Story types

Description

Introduce these story types to children, then encourage them to make or find examples to fit into the different categories. Develop these stories to share during a storytelling session.

SESSION 1: PERSONAL INCIDENT STORIES

Everyone has stories to tell about funny, embarrassing, exciting or significant things that have happened to them. Think of something that has happened to you (e.g. What happened to me at the zoo; When I first flew in an aeroplane) that you could share aloud with others. Shape the story so that it has a beginning, middle and end.

SESSION 2: FAMILY STORIES

Families are a source of many stories. Interview your parents, grandparents, brothers and sisters to find out some of the stories that have been passed down in your family. Choose one that you could share aloud with others and shape it into a story.

SESSION 3: FOLKTALES

Folktales are a rich story source. When telling them it is important to let the listeners know as much about the story background as possible, including its country of origin. Also, identify and explain unfamiliar characters, terms and customs.

Learning a story

Learn a story by remembering the story structure, not memorising the story word-for-word, except for the opening and closing lines. Read the story through several times, trying to recall the main events in order, the central characters and what these characters do. If the story seems too complex, condense the number of characters and the storyline to the essentials. Use the theme or message as a guide to what to include.

When learning a story, there are several useful techniques. First, making a **story map** of the tale helps the teller recall the events in order. To create a story map, the storyteller lists or draws the story's events in order and links them in some way (e.g. arrows, lines, intersecting circles). Drawings may also include symbols for the characters and even suggest the setting. When complete, this chart depicts the story from its opening incident through the rising action to its conclusion. A Nursery Rhyme Story Map (Concept Box 10.2) provides a simple story map.

Concept Box 10.2

A nursery rhyme story map

Hickory, Dickory, Dock.
The mouse ran up the clock.
The clock struck one
Down he did run.
Hickory, Dickory, Dock.

Mentor note

Apply the story map idea to diagramming more complex narratives.

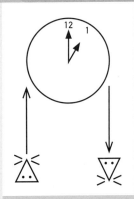

Figure 10.6 Story map

For older students

Encourage young people to create a story map of a short story or novel they have read and use this story map when sharing what they have read with others. Students may want to put their map into a PowerPoint presentation. Then as they share the story aloud, they can build the map on the screen by projecting relevant segments until the map is complete.

Another way to construct a story map is to use the shape of a mountain range seen from the side, complete with peaks and valleys, to represent the 'ups and downs' of the main character's journey or the points in the story where there is rising and falling tension (Moore 1991, p. 84).

The second technique involves creating a picture of the story in one's mind, called the **movie camera technique** (Moore 1991, p. 19). The teller visualises the story while learning it; then when telling the story aloud, replays the silent movie and adds words as the images appear in the mind. Each time the story is told the words will vary slightly because as Moore (1991) describes it: 'The language is not the story; the words are simply a way of getting to the real story that exists not in words but in the pictures in the mind' (p. 19).

Once the storyline is determined, create character dialogue. Make each character sound and speak in different ways so that listeners can identify them by means of voice and gesture. Practising the story aloud before sharing it with others is essential. Some storytellers practise by watching themselves in a full-length mirror; others tape or videotape themselves as they practise telling the story. As they play the recording back, they decide what changes they will make when telling the story for an audience.

Telling a story

The storyteller is the medium or instrument through which the story is shared. For this reason anything that detracts from the smooth passage of the story, such as a too-soft voice, shuffling feet or a lacklustre delivery, needs to be changed. Visualisation, concentration, voice and movement exercises (see Chapters 6 and 7) all assist in fine-tuning the storyteller's instruments (i.e. body and voice), preparing the storyteller mentally and physically to lead listeners into the landscape of the story.

Thinking about how to begin and end a story are important considerations. These parts of the story should be well planned and rehearsed. In Beginnings and Endings (Concept Box 10.3) a few examples of traditional openings and conclusions are given.

Concept Box 10.3

Beginnings and endings

Beginnings
Once upon a time ...
A long time ago when the world was young ...
Long, long ago ...

Endings
And they lived happily ever after.
All their troubles were over and they lived together in great joy.
Snip! Snap! Snout! My tale is told out.

Mentor note
Encourage children to brainstorm alternative ways to begin and end stories they know (e.g. for a creation myth, begin: 'Back before time began' and end: 'That's why things are the way they are today'). With the openings try to capture attention or set the scene; with the endings try to tie together the threads of the story in one final sentence.

As the teller begins, he or she uses different voices for the characters and movement (i.e. facial expression, gestures, bodily stance) to make the story come alive for the listeners. One pattern for sharing is to begin the story with narration; have characters and their dialogue in the middle of the story; and end again with narration. When presenting the story, combine a character's vocal traits with distinctive stance and movement. Also, project your voice so that everyone in the room can hear you. Voice and action enhance the listeners' ability to visualise the story and contribute to their understanding and enjoyment.

Often the story does not end for a child when the teller finishes or the picture book closes. Those who share stories often include follow-up activities to capitalise on student interest and enjoyment and to reinforce their learning. These can take a range of forms from discussion and reflection to dramatic interaction using still photographs, retellings, and other creative art extensions.

In summary, storytellers develop skill and confidence in telling stories through practice. Choosing a story is an important first step that is based on the storyteller's preferences and a consideration of the audience. The story is developed using voice and movement to bring it to life.

Story dramatising

Story dramatisation, **story drama** and **dramatic retelling** are all terms that have been used to refer to dramatising stories. When stories are dramatised, children can make up their own original tale and 'show' it through drama rather than 'telling' it; they can participate by providing sound effects or miming actions as someone else tells a story; they can re-enact a story after it has been told to them; or using improvisation, role play and other drama strategies, they can crack open a story to see what lies inside.

The first three approaches are **syntagmatic** because these activities rely on understanding the existing story sequence, that is, 'the particular relationship and progression of words and ideas' (Stephens & Waterhouse 1990, p. 274). However, the fourth approach, cracking open a story, is **paradigmatic** because focus is not on the story sequence itself, but rather on the story elements (e.g. characters, settings, moods, themes). These become separated from the story sequence and are explored in more depth using drama strategies. Ultimately this approach may lead students into avenues far removed from the original story.

Elements of story dramatisation can be used throughout the story sharing process. Approaches to Dramatising Stories (Concept Box 10.4) introduces ways to do this.

Concept Box 10.4

Approaches to dramatising stories

Before the story begins, engage the students.

- Ask them thoughtful questions or have them debate a key issue from the story.
- Have them create a soundtrack to accompany the story.
- Highlight characters or events through movement.

As a story is read or told, involve the students. Have them:

- Visualise the scenes.
- Provide sound effects.
- Become characters who provide pre-arranged lines of dialogue.
- Mime actions to accompany the story.

Once the story is shared, reinforce selected moments. Use:

- Still photographs and group sculptures as a review of the story line.
- Re-enactment in which children act out parts of the story, often in sequence, *with or without a narrator.*
- Retellings in which children recreate the story through different media (e.g. drawing, dance, song, video clips) or through different genre (e.g. melodrama, fairytale, poetry, newspaper article).
- Crack open the story so that the story becomes a springboard for exploring characters, settings, events, themes, issues and underlying ideas that may go beyond the scope of the original story.

How a tale can be enriched through the various forms of dramatisation is demonstrated in three extended examples: *Lazy Jack* (Story and Script Box 10.3), *A Gift for the Rajah* (Story and Script Box 10.4), and *The Three Little Pigs* (Story and Script Box 10.5). For each story, the background, a story summary and story dramatisation ideas are provided. These stories have been chosen for their child appeal and participation potential.

Story and Script Box 10.3

Lazy Jack

Background
This folktale is from Great Britain.

Story summary
Jack's mother tells him he must go to work, so he does. The first day he works for a farmer, who gives him a shiny penny at the end of the day. On the way home he drops the penny in the river. His mother is not pleased and tells him, 'Next time, put it in your pocket.' Jack answers: 'All right then!'

Figure 10.7 The home of the sad princess

The next day, Jack goes to work at a dairy. At the end of the day he is given a jug of milk. He remembers his mother's advice and pours the milk into his pocket. His mother is cross and says, 'Next time, put it on your head.' Jack answers, 'All right then!'

The next day Jack goes to work at a cheese factory. He is given a cheese. Remembering his mother's advice, he puts it on his head. The cheese melts. His mother is angry and says, 'Next time carry it in your arms.' Jack answers, 'All right then!'

The next day Jack goes to work in a factory. He is given a cat as payment. He remembers his mother's advice and carries the cat in his arms. He gets scratched and bitten. His mother is annoyed and says, 'Next time, gently tie a string around its neck and lead it home.' Jack answers, 'All right then!'

The next day Jack goes to work at a bakery. He is given a cake as payment. He remembers his mother's advice and ties a string around it and drags it home through the dust. His mother is cross and says, 'Next time, carry it on your back.' Jack answers, 'All right then!'

The next day he goes to work for the farmer again, who gives him a donkey as payment. He remembers his mother's advice and carries it on his back. He happens to pass the palace of the sad princess who never laughs (which causes her parents much concern). When she notices him from her tower, she thinks the sight of him carrying the donkey on his back is the funniest thing she has ever seen. For the first time, she laughs—and laughs—and laughs. Her parents are so pleased they offer Jack the permanent job of making the princess laugh. Lazy Jack finally finds a job he likes—one that suits him, too. That's why this story ends—happily ever after.

Mentor note

This story is also known as *Lazy John* (Corrin & Corrin 1964, pp. 33–35).

Dramatisation

Enhance dramatic involvement by having both the storyteller and the students in role. The storyteller both narrates the story and plays the role of the mother; the students each find their own space and all together play the role of Jack responding to all of the mother's directions with 'All right then!' As the storyteller narrates the various actions, each Jack simultaneously mimes them. In this way both the storyteller and the participants are fully engaged throughout the telling of the story.

Lazy Jack (Story and Script Box 10.3) integrates dramatic participation during the telling of the story. *A Gift for the Rajah* (Story and Script Box 10.4) also uses story participation but extends dramatic involvement by having children explore the different perspectives in the story through dramatic response.

Story and Script Box 10.4

A Gift for the Rajah

Background

This is a folktale from India. Before telling the story explain the terms: (1) rajah, an Indian ruler and (2) sage, a wise person. Suggest that the river could be the Ganges.

Figure 10.8 The Rajah's home

Story summary

The Rajah, who in days gone by ruled India, hated to bathe. One day when he does, he steps out onto the riverbank into some dust. He is cross because his feet are dirty. He tells his adviser to get rid of all the dust in India. His adviser asks the villagers to help him. First, they try to sweep away the dust (*'sweep, sweep'*), then they try to wash away the dust with water (*'slosh, slosh'*), and finally the townspeople help him sew together (*'stitch, stitch'*) a carpet made from leather pieces. The adviser spreads the carpet across India. The dust does disappear underneath the carpet, but a wise sage points out, 'Now the plants and crops will die.' The wise person fixes everything by asking the Rajah to stand on the leather carpet where the sage cuts around both of the Rajah's feet with a scissors and then with a piece of twine ties the ruler's feet to the two pieces of carpet. When the Rajah's pulls his feet from the carpet, he finds that he is wearing the first sandals. Now everyone is happy. The Rajah has new shoes, the adviser stays in the ruler's favour, and the carpet is rolled up so the people can plant their crops again. The children should be happy, too, because they have learned the story of how sandals first came into the world.

Dramatisation

Drama enables children to participate directly in the story as it is told and later by means of follow-up action and reflection to experience it from different perspectives.

PERSPECTIVE 1

As the story is told, children play the roles of villagers who '*sweep, sweep*' with their brooms; '*slosh, slosh*' with their buckets; and '*stitch, stitch*' with their needles.

PERSPECTIVE 2

Following the telling of the story, children explore the action from the perspective of dust being swept; the water turning to mud; and the carpet unrolling.

PERSPECTIVE 3

Who was the wise person, the sage, who dared to challenge the Rajah? In a small group, children construct his life story. Then they choose the three most 'significant' moments to present as still photographs. As a 'this–is–your-life reporter', one of the group narrates the sage's story as the others change the photographs to suit the account. (Suggestion: Photographs stay 'frozen' in the previous pose, until the reporter reaches the next event.) This idea is similar to A Day in the Life where participants work backwards from an important event to develop scenes that show the previous 24 hours leading up to this event (Neelands 1990, p. 27).

Student Response: *A Gift for the Rajah* (From the Classroom 10.1) demonstrates how storytelling can stimulate children to imagine story characters and events that they then portray in their own unique ways.

From the Classroom 10.1

Student Response: *A Gift for the Rajah*

A Gift for the Rajah (Story and Script Box 10.4) was shared with Year 2 students who actively participated during the storytelling session. They mimed each of the suggested activities and contributed vocal sound effects (e.g. 'sweep, sweep'; 'slosh, slosh'; 'stitch, stitch'). These drawings show two children's responses to the question: 'What was your favourite part of the story?'

a   b

Figure 10.9 What was your favourite part of the story? (a) Bob's servant and king—the servant thinks he'll lose his head. (b) Bradley's leather carpet made from squares stitched together.

Dramatic activities following the sharing of the traditional tale, *The Three Little Pigs* (Story and Script Box 10.5), are used to reinforce the message of cooperation to overcome hardships and achieve goals.

Story and Script Box **10.5**

The Three Little Pigs

Background

This is an adaptation of the well-known traditional tale.

Story summary

The three little pigs each decide to build a house. One builds a house from straw, one from wood, and the third from bricks. When the wolf comes calling, he blows down the houses of straw and wood, but the house of bricks stands firm.

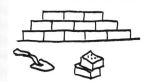

Figure 10.10 Bricks make the strongest house

Dramatisation

Encourage children to cooperate in groups to reinforce a main story theme. Tell the story. Follow up the telling with emphasis on the story theme of cooperation and working together.

1   Introduce the concept of: action–reaction.
    In partners (A-B) demonstrate the following without touching each other:
    –   A turns on a light switch; B is the light being illuminated;
    –   A pushes a box; B is the box being pushed;
    –   A is heat on the stove top; B is water boiling;
    –   A is an artist drawing; B is the picture taking shape;
    –   A is an egg cracking; B is the baby chicken hatching; and
    –   A is the wind blowing; B is the tree bending.
2   Relate the concept of action–reaction to the story of *The Three Little Pigs*. Divide the class into three groups with each group assigned to make one of the houses in the story (i.e. straw, wood, brick) using their hands, arms and bodies. The wolf (teacher-in-role) will try to blow down each house in turn (straw, wood, brick). Work to coordinate the movement of the house with the puffs of the wolf; the first two houses fall to the ground in slow motion. As each house is blown down it joins the house of brick. When all three groups join the brick house, have them consider whether there are 'renovations' they could make to make it as strong as possible. Reshape the brick house using all three groups.

(Suggestion: Consider the drama concepts of: contrast in level and use of space in reshaping the house.) This time, although the wolf huffs and puffs, the house of brick stands.

The various approaches to dramatising stories actively involve children with the structure and elements of story, including character, setting and theme. This hands-on approach that uses visualisation, participation and reflection helps students identify with characters and their situations, while at the same time enhances their understanding of underlying relationships, themes and issues that may have relevance beyond the story.

Applications for middle school students

For storytelling to be accepted by adolescents, the stories shared need to be seen by the group as relevant and meaningful. When students create their own stories, this goal is usually achievable. Likewise, enabling stories to grow naturally out of other drama work cuts down any resistance older students may initially have to 'telling stories'. For instance, the following examples can be turned into dramatic monologues that tell a story: students in role as the first passengers to travel by rail on the Ghan from Adelaide to Alice Springs record their impressions and share them with other passengers in the tradition of Chaucer's *Canterbury Tales* (1986); or written diary entries composed by students in role, such as construction workers on the Harbour Bridge or rebellious miners at Eureka Stockade. Student participation in role with situations that stimulate them to reflect empathetically on the human condition gives the stories they generate in the process a current reality, even though the actual events are distant in time.

When the students or the mentor (as storyteller) choose tales from others to tell, there are several main considerations. First, although many stories are timeless, even a 'good' story may not 'work' for every group. One of the main criteria for judging the appropriateness of a story in a particular situation is to know the group—their needs, interests and concerns. When this is not possible (as when a professional storyteller visits schools to share stories with a range of classes), understanding the theories behind young people's cognitive, affective and emotional development at different stages is another helpful strategy (e.g. Erikson [1959, 1950], Havighurst [1952], Kohlberg [1963], Maslow [1970], Piaget [1966]). Despite the general insight that this investigation can provide, when possible it is still advisable to reflect on the particular group and their interests. This is particularly crucial when sharing with adolescents who may perceive that they are 'past it' when it comes to storytelling.

Storytelling strategies with young adults, in particular, involve capturing and keeping their interest, such as intriguing them with new twists on familiar tales (e.g. *The Wedding Ghost* [Garfield 1985], a haunting story about Jack, who follows a map to Sleeping Beauty's chamber only to find footprints in the dust of the others who have arrived before him, but changed their minds about waking the princess). Gregory Maguire's retellings of classic tales, too, play with traditional perspectives because they are told from the viewpoint of a secondary character in a well-known story or folktale. Two of these are: *Wicked: The Life and Times of the Wicked Witch of the West* (1995), derived from Lyman Frank Baum's *The Wonderful Wizard of Oz* (2000, 1900), and now also a stage musical, and *Confessions of an Ugly Stepsister* (1999), derived from the fairytale of *Cinderella*. The appeal of such works for adolescents is that the original story lines are known by most of them and the character and plot twists enable them to enjoy what they hear (or read) in light of what they already know. Outlandish humour and surprising perspectives are also two reasons why stories by Morris Gleitzman (e.g. *Bumface* [1998]); Roald Dahl (e.g. *Revolting Rhymes* [2001, 1982]); and Paul Jennings (e.g. *Uncovered* [2002, 2000]) have ongoing appeal for upper primary and early middle school students.

The macabre, too, has its appeal for young people as shown by the popularity of the **steampunk** Lemony Snicket A Series of Unfortunate Events books starting with *The Bad Beginning* (1999) and concluding with *The End* (2006). Both a film and a video game are also based on this series with its eccentric characters and calamitous situations. The appeal of these works for young people is how the young protagonists, who continually find themselves in life-threatening circumstances, still manage to fight against the anarchistic elements of a 19th century dystopian society. These books provide a motivating stimulus for storytelling and other drama-based activities because they treat compelling problems (e.g. loss of family, fortune) while, at the same time, distancing them through a fictitious frame. The endless allusions to other novels, historical people and situations also challenge the detective skills of older students to pursue these inter-textual links in order to enrich both the literacy and drama experiences.

One particular story type that gives older students opportunities to collect, share and dramatise stories is the urban legend, also known as the urban myth. This type of story sounds plausible (maybe even did happen once) but has been embellished by its continual retelling; for example, the mystery black panther of the Kangaroo Valley; tales of Yeti or Bigfoot; or 'the fact' that alligators crawl through the sewers of Paris (Scott 1996). Exaggerated, sometimes even ghoulish in their content (e.g. the poisonous spider in the lady's hairdo), these tales have a certain 'shock' appeal and are, what de Vos (1991, p. 20) calls, 'an immediate hook' for young adults. If chosen carefully, these stories can motivate them to engage in storytelling and story dramatisation as well as serve as the impetus for finding out more about their origins and how they are transmitted (e.g. by word of mouth, the media, and photocopy and fax machines). Bill Scott's *Pelicans & Chihuahuas and Other Urban Legends* (1996) and Jan Brunvand's *The Baby Train & Other Lusty Urban Legends* (1993) are two collections of this type of tale. In a similar vein is the astonishing collection of Australian tales, *Red Dog* by Louis de Bernières (2002) that tells the exploits of a real dog who became a legend in Western Australia from 1971 to 1979. The appeal of urban legends motivates older students to collect variations of a tale, share these aloud as 'rip-snorting' yarns, and dramatise them through improvisation and playbuilt scripts.

Summary

This chapter demonstrated how storytelling is a form of drama that involves the making, telling and dramatising of stories. Detailed examples were provided of individual and group approaches to 'storying'. There are many ways to share and dramatise stories and equally as many strategies for doing it. For this reason, it is useful to find opportunities to watch other storytellers in action. As Stephanie, one beginning storyteller reported, 'watching a technique performed gives you tips about how to approach it' and 'ideas in how to improve' (Poston-Anderson & Potter 2002).

Story and Script Box 10.6

Ready, Set, Go!

Background

Ready, Set, Go! tells the story of a race in Vanuatu between a hermit crab and a bird called a kingfisher. This story has child appeal because the exploits of Hermit Crab and Kingfisher have similarities to the tale of 'Tortoise and Hare' that most of them will know. There are some key differences; however, they can be revealed through reflection on the story's message.

Story summary

Kingfisher challenges Hermit Crab to a race. Kingfisher is very boastful, so Hermit Crab decides to trick him. He crawls around the island to all of his relatives and asks them to help him during the race on the following day. He wants them to rub their shells against a stone. In this way, when Kingfisher looks down from the sky as he flies overhead, he will see a hermit crab rubbing its shell against a stone and think Hermit Crab has arrived at the spot first.

The next day each of his relatives helps Hermit Crab who stays hidden during the race only to appear at the finish line. Kingfisher thinks he has lost the race. He is so cross he flies up into the sky and then dives down deep into the sea.

Several days later a rock formation comes to the surface of the water that looks just like Kingfisher. People say he's still there waiting to race another day. They also say this is how one of the islands in Vanuatu was formed.

Story source

The story summary is based on *How the Hermit Crab Tricked the Kingfisher* (Roberts, 1980).

For further study

1 Read the background and story summary for *Ready, Set, Go!* (Story and Script Box 10.6) or select your own story. Discuss what makes this story an appropriate choice to share aloud.

2 Develop the summary for *Ready, Set, Go!* or your own selection into a story to tell aloud. Consider:
   (a) What is the story's central theme(s)?
   (b) What is the story's basic structure?
   (c) How many characters are there? (Add dialogue for these characters.)
   (d) How can each one be differentiated using voice and movement?
   (e) How does the story begin and end?

3 Develop dramatisation approaches for *Ready, Set, Go!* or your own story. Consider:
   (a) What drama activities can introduce the story?
   (b) How can listeners participate as the story is told?
   (c) What follow-up drama activities can be developed?
   (d) How can this story be 'cracked open' to explore the themes and/or characters?

For reflection

Discuss the statement: 'Our reality is made up of an interconnecting web of stories' (Cockett 1997). Provide examples from your own experience to illustrate your points.

Preview

Chapter 11: Puppet Making, Operating and Presenting considers these three aspects of puppetry collectively as a form of drama and provides an introduction to the types of puppets, how to operate them, and guidelines for developing scripts for puppet plays and presenting them.

Puppet Making, Operating and Presenting

'The true values of the puppet only appear when one accepts it for what it is … ' (Arnott 1964).

Introducing puppets

Throughout history and across cultures puppets of various sizes and shapes have passed down cultural knowledge from one generation to the next, entertained people in diverse locations from fairgrounds to pubs, assisted learning in schools and other educational environments, and been regarded as an art form in their own right. Today in education puppets are valuable learning resources across the curriculum and are used for teaching basic literacy and numeracy skills, as aids in second language learning, and in helping children overcome learning difficulties as well as for the enjoyment they give (Fisler 2003, Cattanach 1996, Renfro 1984).

Defining what a **puppet** is, however, is not straightforward because new technologies have blurred the boundaries between puppets and other forms of animation. Even so, the traditional definition of the puppet as 'an inanimate figure' that 'moves under human control' in front of an audience provides a useful starting point (Baird 1965, McPharlin 1969, 1949). Tillis (1992) extends this definition by describing puppets as 'objects that are given design, movement and frequently speech, in such a way that the audience imagines them to have life' (p. 28).

Whether the puppet is a coloured cardboard cut-out glued to a paddle pop stick or a sophisticated multi-stringed marionette, the puppeteer's task is to use movement and voice to breathe 'life' into the figure for an audience. The three essential elements of puppetry then are: the inanimate figure (i.e. the puppet); the movement and voice bestowed on this figure by the puppeteer; and the audience who suspends disbelief in order to accept that the puppet has a separate 'persona' (Tillis 1992, p. 7). All three of these elements combine in performance to give the puppet the illusion of having 'a life apart' from the puppeteer and 'a character of its own' (Tillis 1992, p. 19). As Lorrefico (2003) states, 'The puppet and the puppeteer share the same heart, the same mind but must exist in different bodies' (p. 19).

The medium of puppetry complements and extends drama for children by integrating the arts. During the process of designing and making a puppet, students develop and apply visual arts and design skills. When role playing and improvising with a puppet, children learn how to develop a puppet character, giving it voice and movement. During a puppet play production students also learn about how to integrate music, lighting and sound effects. Through creating a puppet show, young people experience a theatrical medium over which they have complete control from scripting to performance.

There are many ways to use puppets with children. As an important starting point, the types of puppets and their characteristic movements need to be understood. This knowledge enables mentors to help facilitate children's choices when it comes to puppet making for specific purposes. For this reason the following sections of this chapter focus on making puppets, operating them, and performing with them for an audience. Guidelines are also provided for developing scripts for puppet plays.

Making puppets

For educational purposes it is useful to describe puppets in terms of their types. Some of the main categories are **finger puppets**; **hand puppets**; **character puppets**; **rod puppets**; **shadow puppets** and **marionettes**. Each of these types has distinctive features that will be discussed in turn.

Finger puppets

As their name suggests these small puppets are made to sit on top of fingers or are drawn directly on the fingers or hands with washable ink. Paper puppets with reinforced holes cut in them enable fingers to form a puppet's arms or legs. Thimbles make a workable base on which to paste paper character faces or figures. When a tiny puppet is glued onto a magnet, it can be moved around a mini-puppet stage by another magnet moving underneath the stage. These finger puppet types are shown in Finger Puppets (Concept Box 11.1).

Concept Box 11.1

Finger puppets

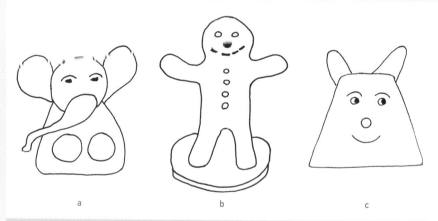

Figure 11.1 Finger puppets (a) Paper elephant puppet: Stick fingers through holes and watch it walk. (b) Gingerbread boy glued to a magnet: Place puppet on thick cardboard, move a second magnet under the cardboard and watch the puppet move. (c) Thimble puppet: Draw a face on a thimble and attach ears.

Finger puppets can be used to focus children's attention as a story is read or told in a small group. Because they are easy to make, children can create their own set of finger puppets to re-enact the story as the teller shares it or after it is told. Puppets in Action (From the Classroom 11.1) shows how absorbing finger puppets can be for young children.

From the Classroom 11.1

Puppets in action

While on student teacher placement, Barbara observed her supervising teacher using puppets with a Kindergarten class:

> The teacher shared the story, *Tikki Tikki Tembo* (Mosel 1989, 1969), about a little boy with an impossibly long name, who falls into a well and is eventually rescued by a man with a ladder. With the Kindergarten class seated on the floor in front of her, she used a bucket as the well and finger puppets made from clothes pegs to represent the story characters (the mother, her two sons, and the old man with the ladder). The teacher had just finished telling the story when she was called away to the office. The children sat quietly for a minute and then spontaneously took turns retelling the story using the finger puppets until the teacher returned. Of this experience, Barbara writes: 'I was amazed at how naturally the children responded to the puppets and how they were able to use them to retell the story without any prompting.'

Telling a story with finger puppets is also a positive way for older students to interact with younger ones on a one-to-one basis. The older student chooses an appropriate story to tell, makes the puppets, and then shares the story with the younger child. This strategy serves to increase the **oracy** skills of the older student, enhance the younger child's listening skills and, at the same time, provide a positive interaction for both students.

Hand puppets

Hand puppets, also called **glove puppets**, are created so that they can be slipped onto the hand and operated either with the hand moving the mouth or with the fingers in the arms of the puppet. Fur animals with moveable mouths have instant appeal for children. Such puppets are easy to use, not too heavy and are particularly useful when characters talk a lot or need to pick things up. Moveable mouth puppets can also be easily crafted from paper bags or a sock. Socks are extremely versatile with the addition of different ears, mouths and eyes changing it from a caterpillar to a rabbit to a dog. Arnott (1964, p. 58) suggests that the various types of hand or glove puppet are 'ideal' as a first introduction to puppet construction and control. Several different types of hand puppet are shown in Hand Puppets (Concept Box 11.2).

Concept Box 11.2

Hand puppets

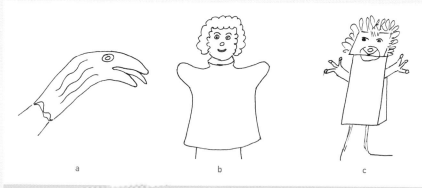

Figure 11.2 Hand puppets: (a) sock puppet (b) glove puppet (c) paper bag puppet

Hand puppets are adaptable to many educational purposes. A teacher may use them to tell stories, get student attention and as a motivational teaching aid. Glove puppets can be as simple (i.e. shapes cut from felt and glued around the edges) or as elaborate (i.e. costumed bodies with papier mâché heads) as the puppet maker desires, while **sock puppets** and **paper bag puppets** are easy for even the youngest children to make in a minimum of time.

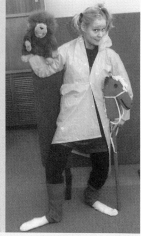

Figure 11.3 Mr Nelson, a glove puppet, on the hand of a student playing the part of Pippi Longstocking

Character puppets

A character puppet, also called a **host puppet**, functions as an intermediary between the audience and the puppeteer (Champlin & Renfro 1985). This 'solo' puppet, designed with child appeal in mind, may be in the form of a person (e.g. Jeff with his puppeteer, Jono) or an animal (e.g. a bear, dog or rabbit). As a team, the puppet and the puppeteer interact together and with the children. If the puppet has a voice, it may ask children questions, convey messages from them to the puppeteer, introduce a story, or even teach basic concepts such as letters and numbers. This requires vocal skills on the part of the puppeteer (akin to **ventriloquism**) in order to distinguish between puppet and puppeteer.

On the other hand, a character puppet can be silent. In this case, the puppeteer interprets for the audience the puppet's feelings and requests (i.e. *He's sad because you are so noisy; She's just told me a secret, would you like to know what it is?*).

The final option for the puppeteer is to act 'invisible' when operating the puppet. This means that the puppet does not interact with the puppeteer at all, only with the children in the audience.

Character Puppets (Concept Box 11.3) shows student puppeteer Jono as Il Capitano with his character puppet, Jeff, as they performed in the children's theatre production, *A Cultural Celebration of Italian Folktales* (Poston-Anderson 1999a).

Concept Box 11.3

Character puppets

Figure 11.4 Student puppeteer Jono as Il Capitano with his character puppet Jeff

Mentor note

Pre-loved stuffed toys make the ideal base for constructing a large animal character puppet. Remove the arms of the toy and add a hollow tube of fake fur for each arm. Wearing gloves, push your arms through the fur tubes. Your fingers become the animal paws. Hold the puppet in your lap and have your 'host' puppet introduce you to the children.

Children relate to character puppets and develop a rapport with them. When the puppet calls for attention, tells them to sit down or asks them to be quiet, they are likely to follow its directions because children respond to a character puppet as a personality in its own right.

Rod puppets

Rod puppets, also called stick puppets, can be as simple to make as putting an orange with a face drawn on to it onto a short length of dowel, or pasting a cut-out of a face onto a Paddle Pop stick. The construction may also be as complex as a handcrafted character fastened to a rod with thin wires attached to its hands or legs in order to make the puppet's limbs move. In Rod Puppets from Wooden Spoons (Concept Box 11.4), three rod puppets, each crafted on top of a wooden spoon, are shown.

Concept Box 11.4

Rod puppets from wooden spoons

Mentor note

The key feature of all rod puppets is a central rod around which the puppet is constructed. At its most basic, these puppets are easy and quick for children to make. They are also simple for the youngest children to use because they can be easily held and manipulated.

Figure 11.5 Crafted rod puppets with wooden spoon bases on which the puppets (from left) Witch, Pirate and Old Mother Hubbard are fashioned

Shadow puppets

A shadow puppet is a 'flat two-dimensional figure held against a translucent screen' that is illuminated with light from behind (Arnott 1964, p. 59). Although traditional shadow puppets, such as those in Indonesia and Turkey, are constructed from leather pounded thin, shadow puppets can be as simple as having children use their hands to cast shadows on a screen. However, a workable alternative for children is for them to make their shadow puppets by cutting figures from cardboard and attaching them to light-weight dowels. Colours can be added to the puppets by cutting out the insides of the puppet and inserting cellophane. When light is projected from behind them, these puppets cast shadows with colourful features onto the screen as shown in Shadow Puppets (Concept Box 11.5).

Concept Box 11.5

Shadow puppets

Figure 11.6 The visual affect of the shadow puppet queen, who is made of cardboard, can be enhanced by using coloured cellophane inserts for the veil and gown.

Shadow puppet show

Place the light behind the puppet so that it casts its shadow on the translucent screen. The audience sits on the other side of the screen and sees the image as a projected shadow. Use coloured plastic to enhance the visual affect as in the queen's veil and gown in this image that can be made from cardboard with blue cellophane inserts.

Another way to create a shadow puppet show is to place the puppets on top of an overhead projector and then project the shadows onto a white wall. Regardless of how the shadows are projected, however, Arnott (1964, p. 59) suggests that shadow puppetry is well suited for illustrating stories that are read or told by a narrator, with the overall effect being like a 'moving picture book'.

Shadow Shapes (From the Classroom 11.2) shows how even basic shapes can be used to make shadow puppets.

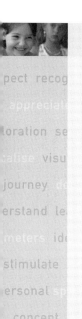

From the Classroom 11.2

Shadow shapes

While on student teacher placement, B.J. observed a shadow puppet show.

The teacher cut simple shapes (i.e. circle, heart, triangle, square, rectangle) from thick paper, placed them on an overhead projector and projected the shadow images onto the wall. Each shape represented a different character in the story of *Little Red Riding Hood* (i.e. girl, mother, grandmother, wolf, woodcutter). After the teacher told the story using the shadow puppets, each child was given a set of shapes. As the teacher retold the story, the children participated by moving their shapes on the floor in front of them. At the end of the session, the children were encouraged to take the shapes with them and share the story with someone at home. B.J. writes: 'As the students moved the shapes during the story retelling, they were totally engaged and actively involved. They became co-storytellers with the teacher.'

Whether they are simple shapes or intricate artistic creations, shadow puppets cannot escape their two-dimensional constraints. In order to maximise the potential of this puppetry form, then, puppeteers are well advised to choose stories that are less boisterous and more dignified (e.g. traditional fairytales or myths) and to take advantage of the unique opportunities that shadow puppetry provides for artistic design in the puppets and the projected set.

Marionettes

A marionette is a distinct type of puppet that is manipulated by pulling strings (or sometimes wires). Philpott (1969, p. 147) indicates that 'operation from above' is a key distinction of this type of puppet. With regard to the number of strings, Kaplin (1999, p. 34) indicates they can vary from several in a basic marionette to ten or eleven strings in more complex figures, such as the European-style marionette. Some Chinese examples have more than thirty strings. The act of animating the figure rather than the level of its design complexity is the defining characteristic. Basic movements include walking, sitting and head movement (Arnott 1964, p. 60).

Marionettes (Concept Box 11.6) shows marionettes from the Griffiths Marionette Company collection performing with student actors in a children's theatre production.

Concept Box 11.6

Marionettes

Figure 11.7 Captain Hook (left) and the Never Birds are marionettes from the Griffiths Marionette Company that feature in the children's theatre production *Second Star on the Right: The Adventures of Peter Pan*

These traditional marionettes are from a collection of 125 figures that were created by Rayburn and Freda Griffiths during their lifelong careers as **marionettists**, first in New Zealand and then in Australia (Poston-Anderson 2007). This collection is currently housed at the Centre for Research and Education in the Arts (CREA) in the Faculty of Education at the University of Technology, Sydney.

In Staging *The Tempest* as a Puppet Show (From the Classroom 11.3) two student teachers describe their experiences as novice marionettists.

From the Classroom 11.3

Staging *The Tempest* as a puppet show

Lisa and Karen participated as puppeteers in a marionette workshop production of Shakespeare's *The Tempest*, using Griffiths Marionette Company characters. In this adaptation, readers provided the dialogue while the puppeteers stood behind a curtain and operated the marionettes from above the stage. Both student puppeteers provide insight into this experience.

1. What we did

- 'We puppeteers dressed in black and removed all jewellery to blend in with the curtain. We worked our marionettes from above the stage. It was a tiny stage with the puppeteers trying to pass puppets around each other, ten puppets in all' (Lisa).
- 'One rule we applied in our performance was that the puppet that was speaking moved, while the other puppets were frozen in position' (Karen).

2. What we learned

- 'Marionette puppetry is a difficult skill to master because the puppets need to convey meaning by their movements and gestures without the range of facial expression that actors have' (Karen).
- 'During the six hours of rehearsals and performance, I learned that puppetry is not just about moving the puppet. Any acting skills I had had to be transferred to the puppet' (Karen).
- 'Tape the characters' voices so the puppeteers can rehearse using the tape and get used to the verbal cues. Practise specific movements to accompany the dialogue' (Karen).
- 'Puppets are better suited to shorter, rather than longer plays' (Karen).
- 'The mistakes we made were usually from moving the puppets off or on the stage at the wrong cue. This emphasised for me the need to know the script well enough to know all the entrance and exit cues' (Lisa).
- 'To further our puppetry skills I believe each puppeteer needs to work with their puppet in front of a mirror, or another person, to further discover all of the puppet's possibilities' (Karen).

3. What we felt

- 'It is unexplainable how the puppeteers become so involved with their puppets that an emotional connection grows' (Lisa).

5. Why we think puppets are important

- 'Working with the puppets has enabled me to see their benefit in a classroom situation. Puppets are an excellent tool for use in discussing and resolving important issues that affect children [because] the children can be distanced from the situation [through the use of puppets]' (Lisa).

In summary, when children make their own puppets, they have a diversity of puppet types from which to choose. Their design and construction decisions may be based on pragmatic factors, such as the availability of materials or even imposed time frames for completion. However, when possible, it is important to encourage children to choose a design that will support the purpose to which the puppet will be put. This requires them to have a further knowledge of how a puppeteer operates puppets.

Operating puppets

People animate puppets by the ways in which they move their hands (e.g. hand puppets), manipulate the rods (e.g. rod puppets) or pull the puppet strings (marionettes). Puppet on a String (Activity Box 11.1) gives children the opportunity to 'get the feel' of what it's like to 'be in control' before they actually operate a puppet.

Activity Box 11.1

Puppet on a string

Description

Work with a partner. One of you sits on a chair, the other stands behind the chair. If you are on the chair, you are the puppet. If you are standing behind it, you are the puppeteer. The puppet has imaginary strings attached to its hands; then its feet. The puppeteer leans over the top of the chair (so the puppet can see the hands that are pulling the imaginary strings). First start with each hand separately. As the puppeteer moves the imaginary string, the puppet responds. Now move the hands together as the puppeteer pulls the strings. Work with your partner to ensure that the puppet's moves match the puppeteer's pulling of the strings.

Next move to the feet. The puppeteer now has strings attached to each of them. Start with each foot separately and then move them together.

Mentor note

Before starting the exercise, ask the children: 'What is a puppet?' and 'What are its characteristics?' Ask them: 'What is the person called who operates a puppet?'

(e.g. puppeteer, marionettist). Stress the interrelationship that exists between the puppet and the puppeteer and point out that the goal in this exercise is to cooperate with each other so the puppet's moves match the ways in which the puppeteer pulls the strings.

Change roles so that each child has the opportunity to be both the puppet and the puppeteer.

Extensions

Share excerpts from the classic book about a puppet, Collodi's *The Adventures of Pinocchio* (1988, 1944) or share with younger children Patricia Lee Gauch's *Poppy's Puppet* (1999). Both of these stories feature puppets that have minds of their own.

Puppets have appeal for children because they have control over the total medium. One person or a small group can do everything from creating the puppets to making the scenery and staging the play. A puppeteer can be 'a single, all-controlling artist' (Tillis 1992, p. 30). This is easily demonstrated by having children create their own **cup theatres** where they are the puppet maker, scene designer and performer all in one as in Make a Cup Theatre (Activity Box 11.2).

Activity Box 11.2

Make a cup theatre

Description

- Choose a nursery rhyme or simple folktale, for example *Humpty Dumpty* or *The Three Little Pigs*. Make a cup theatre to share the rhyme or story.
- Take a paper cup and decorate it. Cut out the bottom. Make your puppets from thick paper and colour them. Stick them to pencils or Paddle Pop sticks. Use the cup as your theatre, pushing the puppets up from the bottom to perform the nursery rhyme. You may wish to make scenery and stick it on the back inside of the cup. Alternatively, make puppets from wooden clothes pegs and attach them to the cup's edge.

Figure 11.8 Cup theatre

Mentor note

Here is a cup theatre for *The Three Little Pigs* with clothes peg puppets.

Encourage young children to share their puppet shows with others in small groups.

Variation

Cup and Container Theatres: Examples are provided in Champlin and Renfro's *Storytelling with Puppets* (1985, pp. 190–95).

For older students

Encourage older children to develop their own stories for cup theatre performances with the goal of sharing these with younger children. Guidelines: Keep the stories short based on a single main incident involving only two or three main characters.

Puppets can be used as a stimulus for improvisation, as animated props in storytelling, as actors in their own play, and as motivational devices in a wide range of drama activities. When children use puppets, their interaction and response is enhanced when they spend time getting to know their puppet. Since a puppet's personality is enhanced by its name, deciding on a name merits careful consideration. A puppet's name can suggest its physical characteristics (e.g. Lanky Len), personality (e.g. Bubbles), interests (e.g. Hot Rod Harry), geographical origin (e.g. City Mouse, Country Mouse), personal qualities (e.g. Sparkle the Star), or energy levels (e.g. Dog Tired). Not only does a name give the puppet an identity, but 'name dynamics' between characters can be a 'source of humour' (Mattson 1997, p. 29); for example, a chase scene during which Dog Tired tries to catch Dog Gone. Introducing … (Activity Box 11.3) is an exercise that helps children get to know their own puppets as a first step in introducing them to others.

Activity Box 11.3

Introducing ...

Description

Make a **character profile** for your puppet:

- Photo (draw a picture of your puppet)
- Name
- Nickname
- Age
- Occupation
- Education
- Hobbies and interests
- Characteristic behaviours or mannerisms
- Favourite colour
- Likes and dislikes

Use this information to develop a first-person monologue for your puppet in which it introduces itself to others (e.g. Hello! My name is Marvellous Marvin—I'm a magician. Call me Marv for short ...).

Following this brief introduction, your puppet is hot seated and is questioned by the group. Make your puppet answer these questions in the first person ('I') using its own voice.

Mentor note

Encourage children to focus on the puppet as it speaks, not on the puppeteer.

For older students

Understand the 'complex' relationship between the puppeteer and puppet by emphasising that they are 'connected' but at the same time 'separate' entities. To reinforce this point use the following visualisations (Lorrefico 2003):

- You and your puppet breathe different types of air (e.g. the puppeteer breathes crisp and icy air; the puppet breathes thick-like-honey air).
- You and your puppet live in 'different but connected' worlds (e.g. the puppeteer lives on the seashore; the puppet lives in the sea).

Once the puppets have been introduced to each other, have them participate in a group situation where they interact together. Seen Moving (Activity
Box 11.4) enables children to explore the movement potential of their puppets
as they engage with others. The aim is to extend puppeteers' skills so that the
puppets they operate perform with more complex and diverse movements.

Activity Box 11.4

Seen moving

Description

1 Teach your puppet to move by taking it to movement classes. Choose one of
the puppets in the class to be the leader who calls out the moves.

   Here are some possibilities for puppet moves: Puppet points to itself, points
to another puppet, waves, claps, turns to the right, to the left, to the back, to
the front, looks up, looks down, nods, shakes its head 'no', hops, turns, runs,
floats, sits, jumps, shivers, dances, sneaks, falls, stands still.

2 Have your puppet join others and create a movement scene. One puppet
narrates the story, while the other puppets move. Here is an example.

   Rain Storm

   Narrator Puppet: Look at those people waiting for the bus (*puppets stand in a
   queue*). OH, NO! it has started to rain! (*puppets look up*). They're getting wet.
   Now the wind is blowing so hard, they can hardly stand up (*puppets nearly fall*).
   How cold they must be. Look! They're shivering (*puppets shake*). Hear that
   thunder? Oh, what a big clap that was! They're all jumping with fright (*puppets
   jump*); they're running away (*puppets run*).

   Develop your own puppet movement story that includes different types
of movement. Make the story active, such as a crowd watching fireworks and
responding, runners in a marathon, dancers in a competition.

Mentor note

Puppets can become heavy for young hands. For this reason, sock puppets, paper
bag puppets and other puppets made from light-weight materials are suggested
options for the youngest puppeteers.

When bringing a puppet to life, which is called 'animating' it, it is necessary to decide whether or not the puppet will speak. Some hand puppets communicate by whispering to their operators who then convey the message to the audience; some animal characters converse using squeaks or growls, while other puppets may remain silent (e.g. shadow puppets that move to illustrate a narrated story). However, if a puppet does speak it is important that its voice reflects its character. As a puppeteer works with a puppet and gets to know it, a character voice emerges. Puppet, Speak Up! (Activity Box 11.5) encourages students to create a character voice for a puppet.

Activity Box 11.5

Puppet, speak up!

Description

- Warm up your own voice.
- Now look at this drawing of a kangaroo puppet and give it a name. How do you think it would speak? Consider how this puppet could express itself in relation to pitch, volume, pace, inflection, tone and vocal quality (see Activity Box 6.16: Express Yourself Vocally).
- Create this kangaroo's character voice and use it to say the following verse.

I have a little joey
and it likes to hop.
It likes to hop
and never stop.
But when I scratch its ears
and pat its head,
it hops into my pouch
and goes to bed.

As you say the poem, project your puppet voice to various parts of the room.

Figure 11.9 How would this kangaroo puppet speak?

Extension

- For another puppet that you have (or make), create a puppet voice, experimenting with vocal characteristics until you are satisfied with the result.

Tape record and play back the various voices to help you make the final decision.

- Find a poem (or make one up) and have your puppet recite that poem in character. Add appropriate actions for your puppet and have it perform the poem for others. Project your puppet voice so everyone in the room can hear you.

Mentor note

- Ensure that students complete a vocal warm-up before they begin creating puppet voices. Remind them to breathe properly and not to strain their voices.
- Discuss how the voices that different children created for the puppet kangaroo vary. How are they alike? How are they different? Why might they vary?
- When children are each working with their own puppet, have them explain why they developed the character voice the way they did.

Puppeteers need practice, not only in manipulating their own puppet, but in making their puppet interact with others that share the same space. In Putting It Together (Activity Box 11.6) the focus is on improvised speech and puppet 'body language' (Mattson 1997, p 27). As one puppet announces a range of situations, the other puppets respond.

Activity Box 11.6

Putting it together

Description
One puppet makes an announcement and the others respond with improvised movement and speech.

ANNOUNCEMENTS:
- Today is a holiday!
- The blowflies here are awful!
- We must sneak out so we're not heard.
- We're falling through space.
- Oh, it is so hot!
- Look at that mountain over there.

- Let's go for a swim.
- Let's do the jive!
- I'm freezing!

Mentor note

Encourage children to develop other announcements to which the puppets can respond.

Putting It Together (Activity Box 11.6) involves a several stage process. First, the puppeteer must understand the situation and know what type of response is appropriate. Then, within the design constraints of the puppet, the puppeteer must relay this response through skilful manipulation to the puppet so it can move accordingly. Depending on the puppet's complexity, this is not always as straightforward as it sounds. Yet the operator needs to regard the puppet as 'an extension' of himself or herself, not as a separate entity (Arnott 1964, p. 99). For this reason, puppeteers benefit from knowledge of drama's elements and forms, building their own skill in order to enhance the performances of the puppets they operate. If a puppet presentation is to be effective, puppeteers must first make their puppets move convincingly themselves and then have them interact believably with other puppets.

Presenting with puppets

Puppets can enhance many drama settings. *Wooden Maid* (Story and Script Box 11.1) demonstrates how a puppet can be used as a story character when a storyteller shares a traditional tale. During the telling of this story, the storyteller constructs a wooden spoon puppet in front of an audience. They then watch as it is transformed.

Story and Script Box 11.1

Wooden Maid

Background

Versions of this tale are known around the world from the Middle East to the Inuit people of North America.

Story summary

In olden times, four men go to the market. One buys wood, another buys cloth, the third buys ribbons and laces, and the fourth, a holy man, goes along with the others to see the countryside. On the way back home they spend the night in the open and build a fire. Each one watches in turn. The first gets bored and takes out a piece of wood and with a knife whittles a doll. The second man, when he watches, adds some cloth to make a dress for the doll. The third man, when he watches, adds some ribbon and lace. The fourth man, when he watches, breathes on the doll three times and she becomes a real live little girl. Instead of going home with any of the men to be a companion for their children, she decides to see the world for herself.

Figure 11.10 Wooden Maid: The wooden-spoon doll (left) is transformed like magic into a 'little girl' hand puppet

Suggestions for telling

Use the props of a wooden spoon, cloth and lace and ribbons to make a doll that is kept in the bag. When the holy man breathes into the bag bring out a hand puppet that is made of the same cloth as the wooden spoon figure.

Mentor note

This story works well with young children because they actually believe the wooden figure has changed into the little girl.

Sources

- A picture book version of this story is Fiona French's *Maid of the Wood* (1985).
- More suggestions for using puppets in storytelling, when singing children's songs and sharing children's literature, can be found in Jan M. VanSchuyver's *Storytelling Made Easy with Puppets* (1993).

For older students

Encourage older students to revisit stories they enjoyed when they were younger and to adapt these stories as puppet plays for younger children. Scripting, designing and making puppets, and producing the play all enhance their drama and related arts skills.

A Magic Moment (From the Classroom 11.4) recounts one storyteller's experience in sharing *Wooden Maid* with young children.

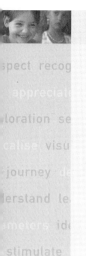

From the Classroom 11.4

A magic moment

Heather says: 'I told *Wooden Maid* (Story and Script Box 11.1) to a Kindergarten class using puppets as suggested. The students were mesmerised when I (in the role of the holy man) blew into the bag. They stared at the bag—not moving, not making a sound, wondering what was going to happen next. When the little girl puppet peeked over the edge of the bag, they were surprised. One verbalised for the rest what had happened. "It was magic!" she said. Later, during recess, another child, who obviously was still thinking about the story, sought me out and asked me if I were magic!'

Here are illustrations three of these children made of the story characters from *Wooden Maid*.

a   b   c

Figure 11.11 (a) Sienn's maid (b) Joshua's view of the four men at the market (c) Katie's maid

Another option for using puppets in storytelling is to wear an apron, shirt or carry a bag to which pockets are sewn as shown in Storytelling Garments (Concept Box 11.7). From these pockets, the puppeteer draws small finger puppets to tell simple stories or nursery rhymes. If the pockets are decorated with colours, shapes, numbers and letters, the young children can request a particular pocket by name, thus reinforcing their basic concept development.

Concept Box 11.7

Storytelling garments

Figure 11.12 A puppet bag

Mentor note

After children choose small puppets from the pockets, the puppeteer-storyteller can use these to create mini-puppet plays or to tell a story.

The advantage of presenting with puppets in front of an audience is the direct relationship that can be established with the listeners. The physical presence of the puppeteer-storyteller enables direct eye contact to be made with individuals in the audience. Interactivity is at its peak when the story narration and pace of the action are adjusted to take into consideration the audience response. Older students can learn many presentational skills first-hand when they take on the role of a storyteller-puppeteer for younger children.

In addition to being a character in a story narrated by a puppeteer-storyteller, puppets can perform in their own plays. There are several ways to find a puppet play. First, there are published puppet plays that can be performed (e.g. Mattson 1997). Students can also playbuild (see Chapter 9), developing improvisations they have done with their puppets into a scripted puppet play. Teachers and their students can also adapt folktales and other copyright-free materials into puppet plays.

No matter what the story source is, there are important principles to keep in mind. First, the playwrights need to recognise the special features and constraints of the puppetry medium. Although puppets can do many things that humans cannot (e.g. fly, disappear, jump continuously), they also have their limitations. The basic features of a puppet cannot change (unless it is a 'trick' puppet that can be transformed into another shape). Once a smile is painted on a puppet face, it remains. Puppet types also differ from each other in their key characteristics; for example, hand puppets with moveable mouths can be synchronised with speech; marionettes demand a humanistic type of movement; shadow puppets interact in two-dimensional space; while finger puppets, although easy for children to manipulate, are difficult to see from a distance. When developing a play for puppets, characteristics and constraints such as these affect how the script is constructed. Puppet Play Guidelines (Concept Box 11.8) provides some points to remember when choosing a story or developing an original one to adapt into a puppet play.

Concept Box 11.8

Puppet play guidelines

In a puppet play:

- *Action* needs to be:
    - Driven by characters with a goal they want to reach, which they either achieve or do not achieve during the play;
    - Simple, avoiding complicated sub-plots; and
    - Direct, resolving quickly once the climax has been reached.
- *Characters* need to be:
    - Clearly developed, avoiding subtlety; and
    - Limited in number, using how each puppet looks, what they say and how they act to distinguish it from the others.
- *Scenes* need to be:
    - Limited in number; and
    - Not too long with a limited number of puppets in any one scene.
- *Transitions between scenes* need to be:
    - Limited in number;
    - Brief, using sound or music when appropriate; and
    - Easy to manage.

Mentor note

Detailed guidelines for scripting puppet plays are provided in Jean M. Mattson's book, *Playwriting for the Puppet Theatre* (1997).

Father Anansi and His Children (Story and Script Box 11.2), an African folktale, is presented here as an example of a puppet play. As the play begins, Anansi enters and introduces himself and his children, doing away with the need for a separate narrator. The action develops quickly with Father Anansi's journey ending in disaster. Each of his six children employs special skills to save him. Suspense is built into the play structure as the rescued Father Anansi is carried away again—this time by a bird. Snappy dialogue and repetitive lines contribute to the fast-paced, forward movement that culminates in a fitting resolution that brings the action full circle (i.e. to another adventure).

Story and Script Box 11.2

Father Anansi and His Children

FATHER ANANSI

My name is Father Anansi. I'm a spider—a hero to the Ashanti people in Africa. I always get into trouble, but I always get out again. Sometimes my special children help me. (*Calls to children*) Come, children, introduce yourselves.

SEE TROUBLE

I'm See Trouble. I see trouble a long way away (*says, 'Look there!'*).

ROAD BUILDER

I'm Road Builder. I make well-built roads (*says, 'Pound, pound'*).

RIVER DRINKER

I'm River Drinker. I drink rivers in a single gulp *(says, 'Slurp, slurp')*.

FEARLESS HUNTER

I'm Fearless Hunter. I cut open anything I catch for dinner with my little knife (*says 'Swish, swish'*).

STONE THROWER

I'm Stone Thrower. I throw stones (*says, 'Ooooh, ouch!'*).

PILLOW

I'm Pillow. I'm soft (*says, 'Squish, squish'*).

FATHER ANANSI

Children, today I'm going on an adventure. Goodbye!

CHILDREN

Goodbye!

(*Father Anansi moves across the stage as See Trouble watches. A big fish rises and swallows Father Anansi.*)

FATHER ANANSI

Help! Help!

SEE TROUBLE

Look, there! (*to other spiders*) Come quickly!

OTHER CHILDREN

What's wrong, See Trouble?

SEE TROUBLE

Father fell into a river. A big fish swallowed him.

CHILDREN

We must save him.

ROAD BUILDER

I will build a road to get us there. (*'Pound, pound'*) All finished!

CHILDREN

Let's go! (*Spiders cross to other side of stage.*) What now?

RIVER DRINKER

Don't worry. I will drink the river (*'Slurp, slurp'*).

SEE TROUBLE

(*Fish rises and dives.*) Look, there! I see the fish that swallowed Father.

CHILDREN

What now?

FEARLESS HUNTER

Don't worry. I'll dive down and cut open the fish (*dives, then says, 'Swish, swish'; Father Anansi and Fearless Hunter appear; spiders cheer*).

FATHER ANANSI

Thank you, children. (*Bird swoops and carries Father Anansi away.*) Help! Help!

SEE TROUBLE

Look, there! A bird has carried our Father away.

CHILDREN

We must do something!

STONE THROWER

Don't worry. I will hit the bird with a stone so he will drop Father. 1.2.3! (*says, 'Oooh, ouch!'; sound of squawk*).

SEE TROUBLE

Look, there! The bird has dropped Father. He is falling through the air.

CHILDREN

We must do something!

PILLOW

Don't worry. I will save him. (*Looks up and calls*) Father, you must fall on my back (*sound of a downward slide whistle; Pillow says 'Squish, squish' as Father Anansi lands on Pillow's back*).

FATHER ANANSI

Children, thank you for saving my life!

CHILDREN

You're welcome!

FATHER ANANSI

Now let's all go on another adventure!

CHILDREN

Hooray!

FATHER ANANSI

Goodbye! (*Waves and exits.*)

CHILDREN

Goodbye! (*Wave and exit following Father Anansi.*)

Source: *Anansi the Spider, A tale from the Ashanti* by Gerald McDermott (1972).

The puppets for *Father Anansi and His Children* (Story and Script Box 11.2) can be simply constructed. Anansi can be made from a single black glove, the fingers his legs with a pom-pom attached for his body. The smaller spider puppets are attached to or made from the fingers of the second glove, with the exception of Pillow, the sixth son, who is made separately and pinned to the back of the glove. Small props can be attached to the spiders to enhance audience identification with them (e.g. glasses for See Trouble, little cup for River Drinker, miniature knife for Fearless Hunter, tiny stone for Rock Thrower, and tiny cushion for Pillow). The fish and the bird can either be two painted paper rod puppets, or hand puppets with moveable mouths to swallow Father Anansi.

When producing a puppet play, there are a number of options for staging. In addition to the traditional constructed puppet stage with a **proscenium arch**, curtains can be strung across doorways above which (or in the case of marionettes, under which) the puppets perform or a table can be turned on its side with hand and rod puppets performing above the upper edge. A puppeteer may decide to do away with the stage completely and perform directly in front of the audience picking up the puppets from a tabletop or from the floor as they are needed. Children soon forget the puppeteer and concentrate on the puppets and their actions. As previously mentioned, the advantage of working in front of the audience is the immediacy of the situation, enabling the puppeteer to respond instantly to the audience's reactions.

When introducing children to puppetry as a drama form, simplicity is the criterion on which to base puppet construction and production, for as Arnott (1964) suggests, the '[p]uppet's power derives from its own simplicity of stripping away unessentials and leading the spectator to the very heart of the drama' (p. 74). To achieve an effective puppet play then, the aim is to introduce 'broad sweeping effects and to avoid subtlety' (Arnott 1964, p. 62).

Applications for middle school students

Puppetry, as a drama form, has a long theatrical tradition. Even today marionette companies perform plays for children and adults in many places in the world. Several exquisite productions by the Salzburg Marionette Theatre are available on DVD. Two of these are the Mozart operas, *Cosi fan tutte* (2005) and *The Magic Flute* (2005). In addition to the productions themselves, special features provide insights about the marionettes and how the marionettists operated them during the performances. When adolescents view quality marionette productions such as these, they come to realise the skill, expertise, artistic talent and dedication needed to become a professional puppeteer. They see that puppets are works of art, not only intended for young children, but for people of all ages.

Puppetry provides adolescents with opportunities to realise their own imaginative worlds through the design and creation of puppets and puppet shows. Students develop their playwriting skills by authoring puppet scripts; employ their artistic and design skills in the development of puppet figures; use their production skills in set design and staging; increase their technical skills in the use of lighting and sound; and utilise acting skills in the development of characterisations for their puppets. When students write their own music and design dance movements for their puppets, composing and choreographic skills are also developed. In all these ways, a puppet production mirrors what happens in a theatrical production, yet its miniaturisation means that students have more control over the total process from design to performance than they would have in a full-scale production. For this reason, producing a puppet performance offers students an integrated, holistic artistic experience in which they can participate at every stage.

Older students, who have more well developed fine motor skills than younger children, can undertake the more difficult challenges of making and manipulating complex puppets, such as marionettes with strings or large puppets controlled by more than one operator. For example, based on the idea of traditional Japanese **Bunraku puppets** (i.e. three-quarter life-sized figures each manipulated by several operators), older students have the skills to fashion large puppets using broom handles as the base on which puppet bodies and costumes are constructed. In order to operate the arms, legs and head of such a puppet, several students must cooperate to coordinate the puppet's movements. To operate the puppet successfully, student puppeteers must work as a team. Move it, Mother Goose! (From the Classroom 11.5) describes how a novice puppeteer worked together with a friend to create a life-sized puppet.

From the Classroom 11.5

Move it, Mother Goose!

Joy writes of her experience with a life-sized puppet:

My friend and I made a life-sized Mother Goose puppet from a broomstick, old clothes and odds-and-ends. We both were needed to operate it. I wore old-fashioned boots and stepped through a slit in the back of the puppet's long skirt to make her legs, and, at the same time, with my right hand I worked Mother Goose's sock mouth through an opening in the back of the puppet's head, while slipping my left arm through the back of the puppet's left sleeve at the elbow to be the hand that held the body of a large puppet goose. (We also made that!)

My friend held the pole on Mother Goose's back to hold her upright with her left hand and she put her right arm through Mother Goose's right sleeve at the elbow that became Mother Goose's hand going into the neck of the goose puppet so she could move its beak as it honked.

I was the voice of Mother Goose; my friend did the goose's honk. It took a lot of planning and practise to get Mother Goose and her goose moving well. It was worth all the effort, however, when we used Mother Goose to tell nursery rhymes to the younger children.

Making a life-sized puppet and planning the logistics of how to operate it is a challenging, yet rewarding task for older students. This process demonstrates for them that puppetry is more than 'child's play'.

How puppetry is used in film and theatre can be appreciated through an examination of contemporary examples such as: Tim Burton's animated puppet film, *The Corpse Bride* (2005), now in DVD format (that includes a special feature on how the puppets were made); the musical theatre production of *The Lion King* (Capitol Theatre, Sydney 2003) with its spectacular use of rod and shadow puppetry; and the Sydney Festival production of May Gibbs's *Snugglepot and Cuddlepie* (2007) where shadow puppetry was used to show birds in flight helping the Gumnut Babies escape from the clutches of the Banksia Men. Outstanding examples such as these demonstrate for adolescents the ongoing relevance of puppetry as a drama form and the innovative ways it can be adapted for film and the stage.

Summary

Puppets can enhance drama activities in many ways from providing the stimulus for storytelling or improvisation to being the impetus for developing children's vocal and production skills. When children make and operate their own puppets, they engage with the puppetry medium on multiple levels as they design puppets, plays, props, and sets; experiment with voice to create and project a character; synchronise puppet movement with speech; and cooperate with others to perform a puppet show. In short, puppetry provides students with a multidimensional aesthetic experience that not only gives them enjoyment, but also enriches their learning.

For further study

1   Respond to the statement: Puppetry has value because it is 'an integration of all arts', involves 'multiple areas of learning (creative, intellectual and technical)', and is 'a means to develop community' (Fisler 2003, p. 30). To help you fully explore this statement, see a staged puppet show and provide examples from this experience to back up your points.

2   Investigate forms of puppetry from different cultures; for example, Wayang Kulit shadow puppetry, Vietnamese water puppets, Japanese Bunraku puppet theatre, or the Salzburg Marionette Theatre. Prepare a PowerPoint presentation to inform others about this medium.

3   Adapt the story, *A Letter for Anansi* (Appendix 2.1), into a puppet play for three characters using the following guidelines.

SCRIPT DEVELOPMENT

1   How will you treat the narrative? One option is to delete the narrative passages altogether, using a combination of the following strategies:

   (a) create dialogue from them (e.g. I'm so worried! At this rate I'll be bitten to pieces);

   (b) use them as stage directions for how to say a line of dialogue (e.g. annoyed, hissed, screamed, shouted) or how to do the actions (e.g. slithered, crawled, hopped); or

   (c) use them as a guide to puppet placement (e.g. behind the door, in a high corner).

   Another option is to use the story narration but give it to one of the puppets already in the play (e.g. Rabbit), who then serves as both a narrator and a character.

2   How many scenes will you need? Collapse the scenes into as few as possible, yet still keeping the plot line easy to follow.

PUPPET DEVELOPMENT

1   What type of puppets best fit the needs of the script?

2   How will you construct these puppets?

3   Do any of them need special features? (e.g. a snake puppet with a mouth to carry letters, Snake's removable fangs).

STAGING THE PUPPET PLAY

1   How will you stage the puppet play (e.g. with puppeteers behind a puppet stage or in front of audience)?

2   How will you show the different spaces (e.g. inside and outside of Anansi's house at the same time)?

3   What props will you need (e.g. copper pot, letters, snake fangs)?

4   What are the features of the set needed for each scene (e.g. a door that opens)?

5   How will you show the transitions between scenes? (e.g. scenes collapsed with no transitions, music, pulling a curtain, raising and lowering lights)?

6   How will you show the passage of time from morning, to afternoon, to the next day? (E.g. insert dialogue which indicates passage of time, use a set piece such as a circle with the sun on one side and the moon on the other, which is flipped during the presentation to show time passing).

For reflection

As a group, share the experiences you have had with puppetry as a child, young adult, or adult. Based on your discussion, what do you believe are the main benefits of puppetry as a drama and art form or as a vehicle for social development in young people? What other benefits can you suggest?

Review of Part Four

Part Four: Activating Alternatives: Shaping Drama Experiences focused on selected forms of drama, including: improvising, role playing, playbuilding; story making, telling, dramatising; and puppet making, operating and presenting. For each drama form, descriptions, explanations, examples and exercises were provided to enable students to gain experience in working with these drama forms.

Preview

Part Five: Appreciating Drama: Performance Perspectives consists of Chapters 12, 13 and 14.

Chapter 12: Readers' Theatre: Scripting and Staging considers readers' theatre as a form of drama and presents guidelines for adapting scripts and staging them, including an extended script example.

Appreciating Drama: Performance Perspectives

Objectives

At the end of this section, you should be able to:

- Develop a readers' theatre script and stage it;
- Understand and apply the principles of children's theatre production; and
- Appreciate and respond to theatrical traditions applying them in script development and in performance.

Part Five examines ways to help children develop an appreciation for theatre tradition and performance. In Chapter 12, strategies for developing readers' theatre scripts from text, workshopping these scripts through drama sessions, and staging them in readers' theatre form are presented. In Chapter 13, an introduction to children's theatre production is given with suggestions for how to develop scripts for children's plays and prepare them for performance. In Chapter 14, ways to integrate historical and cultural traditions into drama sessions and productions for children are explored.

PART FIVE

Readers' Theatre: Scripting and Staging

'Readers Theatre is not a critical analysis of a text but an aesthetic experience' (Coger & White, 1982).

Introducing readers' theatre

The name readers' theatre provides a clear indication of how this performance medium works. Basically, readers share text using modified theatrical conventions to draw attention to the words and ideas being shared. An oral reading becomes a readers' theatre presentation when a group of readers share a poem, story, chapter from a book, picture storybook text, or other material aloud using suggested characterisation and action, usually with script in hand. Because the aim of readers' theatre is to help listeners visualise the action of a story in their own minds, it is sometimes known as 'theatre of the mind' (Coger & White 1982, p. 2). (Note that readers' theatre is written both as readers' theatre with the apostrophe and readers theatre without the apostrophe, depending on the source. Both are acceptable. This book uses readers' theatre, unless quoting a source that uses the other alternative.)

'Adapting' text to script

The outstanding feature of the readers' theatre medium is the way in which it brings a written text to life. Sharing literary material aloud enhances children's appreciation of it. In choosing material to present in readers' theatre form, it is important to select items that have child appeal. Characters who are memorable, a storyline that is active and vivid language are elements that contribute to a successful readers' theatre **script.**

Once the text is chosen, the preparation of a readers' theatre script is governed by several important principles. First, the text remains exactly the same as the author wrote it. No substantive changes are made, the exception being the elimination of superfluous speech identification phrases, such as 'he said' and 'she said', which interrupt or slow down the flow of dialogue. Although a readers' theatre script is called an 'adaptation', this refers not to the changing of an author's text, but rather to the way in which the text is divided into parts for sharing. Sometimes more than one text (e.g. poem, story or a mixture of these) is combined, linked through music and/or movement to a theme.

Most readers' theatre scripts have both narration and dialogue. Readers can handle these elements in various ways. First, a reader or several readers may be assigned to read all the **narration** (i.e. descriptive lines or sections) in the story. Other readers are then assigned to take the characters. A characteristic of readers' theatre is that one reader can change parts within the presentation; for example, the reader may start as a narrator and later read the role of one or more characters. Another way to handle the narration and dialogue is to have a reader take the narration that refers to his or her character. The opening lines of the folktale *Little Red Riding Hood* in Scripting: Dividing the Parts: Options 1–3 (Story and Script Boxes 12.1–12.3) are used to demonstrate each of these ways.

Story and Script Box 12.1

Scripting: Dividing the parts: Option 1

Little Red Riding Hood

CHARACTERS AND ONE NARRATOR
(1) Narrator   (2) Mother   (3) Little Red Riding Hood

> (1) Once long ago in a cottage near the forest lived a girl known as Little Red Riding Hood. One afternoon her mother said to her,

(2) 'Little Red Riding Hood, I have baked some currant buns for Grandma. Will you take them to her, please?'

(1) Mother held out the straw basket filled to the brim with delicious buns covered by a yellow cloth.

(3) 'Of course, I will!'

(1) exclaimed Little Red Riding Hood, who loved her grandmother and took any opportunity to visit her. Grandma's house was across the clearing, down the path and through the forest. She would have to hurry if she wanted to be home by nightfall.

Mentor note

In this option there is a separate division between the narrator and the characters. The narrator looks directly at the audience, while the characters use **offstage focus** to interact with one another.

Story and Script Box 12.2

Scripting: Dividing the parts: Option 2

Little Red Riding Hood

CHARACTERS AND SEVERAL NARRATORS

(1) Narrator   (3) Narrator   (5) Little Red Riding Hood
(2) Narrator   (4) Mother

(1) Once long ago in a cottage near the forest lived a girl known as Little Red Riding Hood.

(2) One afternoon her mother said to her,

(4) 'Little Red Riding Hood, I have baked some currant buns for Grandma. Will you take them to her, please?'

(2) Mother held out the straw basket filled to the brim with delicious buns covered by a yellow cloth.

(5) 'Of course, I will!'

(1) exclaimed Little Red Riding Hood, who loved her grandmother and took any opportunity to visit her.

(3) Grandma's house was across the clearing, down the path and through the trees.

(1) Little Red Riding Hood would have to hurry if she wanted to be home by nightfall.

Mentor note

Reader 1 takes the narration related to Little Red Riding Hood; Reader 2 takes the narration for Mother; while Reader 3 takes narration related to Grandma. Later in the story there would be a separate Narrator for the Wolf and another for the Woodsman. This means five narrators in total, to match the number of characters. Option 2 provides an opportunity for more readers to participate than Option 1 where there was only one narrator. If the number of narrators and characters becomes too unwieldy, however, each narrator can take several characters; for example, one for Little Red Riding Hood; one for the Wolf; and one for Mother, Grandma and the Woodsman.

Story and Script Box 12.3

Scripting: Dividing the parts: Option 3

Little Red Riding Hood

EACH CHARACTER TAKES HER OWN NARRATION
(1) Mother   (2) Little Red Riding Hood   (3) Grandma

(2) Once long ago in a cottage near the forest lived a girl known as Little Red Riding Hood.

(1) One afternoon her mother said to her, 'Little Red Riding Hood, I have baked some currant buns for Grandma. Will you take them to her, please?' Mother held out the straw basket filled to the brim with delicious buns and covered by a yellow cloth.

(2) 'Of course, I will!' exclaimed Little Red Riding Hood, who loved her grandmother and took every opportunity to visit her.

(3) Grandma's house was across the clearing, down the path and through the forest.

(2) Little Red Riding Hood would have to hurry if she wanted to be home by nightfall.*

Mentor note

- *You might want to consider giving this line to the Wolf for ironic effect.
- When a character takes his or her own narration, the character says the dialogue in character and says the narration in a normal voice speaking directly to the audience.

Options 1, 2 and 3 for dividing a text into parts are only suggestions. The nature of the script itself can suggest what strategies to use. The eeriness of a ghost story may benefit from an atmospheric soundscape of squeaky doors and groans to underscore the text (see Activity Box 8.11: Mood Makers), while repetitive stanzas of a poem, such as: 'Australia is an old land,/a bright land of sun/ Hold hands across Australia./Let us be as one', may sound more effective when read together by a chorus of voices.

From Text To Readers' Theatre Script (Concept Box 12.1) provides a suggested procedure for readers' theatre script development.

Concept Box 12.1

From text to readers' theatre script

1   Read through the text. Ask: How many characters and how many narrators will I have?
2   Divide the text into parts. Do not change the author's words.
    Use units of meaning to guide you in breaking up the text into lines and phrases. Remember that it is difficult for a group, particularly of younger children, to synchronise a series of one or two word phrases. It works better for each child to have a line or, at least, a complete phrase to say.

3 Read through the script. Ask: Has each part been numbered clearly on the script?

4 Create an attention-getting introduction to the script that identifies the text, the author, and also motivates the audience to listen.

5 Consider the script in relation to the group who will share it.
   - Ask: Will everyone in the group be involved in some way?
   - If there are not enough reading parts, have some children mime action (e.g. wind blowing), become props (e.g. basket, broom) or pieces of the set (e.g. door frame, window opening), and suggest locations (e.g. trees in the forest, people in the marketplace). These are all ways to have a large group participate during the oral sharing of the readers' theatre script.
   - Also, if there are not enough readers, remember that in readers' theatre one person may read more than one part.

Preparing a text for readers to present as a staged script is a creative process that engages the adapter, whether that person is an adult or a child. To turn a literary text into a script, the adapter must imagine how the written words on the page will sound when shared aloud and how, through simple staging, the poem or story can be brought to life.

Another way to develop a script is to have children first create their own story, edit it, and then write it down in final form. Then this story can be adapted into a readers' theatre script. Developing Stories for Readers' Theatre (Concept Box 12.2) provides a framework for helping children create their own stories that can be transformed into readers' theatre scripts for presentation.

Concept Box 12.2

Developing stories for readers' theatre

The process

1 Take the children on an imaginative journey, such as the one described in Balloon Trip (Activity Box 6.5). On a flight over a remote island (e.g. in a

balloon, as a bird, in a plane), they look down and appreciate the many natural features of the landscape. When they return from the trip, ask children to describe the natural feature they liked the most (e.g. flowers, a waterfall, trees).

2   Use defining the space (Neelands 1990) to map the island's features onto the real space available for drama. In other words, make the space in the room represent the island.

3   Students are directed to go to the place in the room where their favourite natural phenomenon was on the island. Each child creates a still photograph of it and then indicates what feature they represent.

4   The mentor directs the children to find others in the room who have similar or related features, then form a group (e.g. rock, mountain, volcano; waterfall, river, pool). If one group is too large (e.g. more than six children), split this group into two smaller groups. If there are features that do not seem to fit anywhere, group them together (e.g. shell, rainbow).

5   Each group develops a pourquoi story which tells how these features of the landscape came to exist (e.g. how the rock became a volcano or how waterfalls began).

6   Each group shares their story in two different ways. First, they show the story with movement and sound effects only; then the group tells the story aloud as they move it.

7   Finally, all the groups move their stories with sound effects at the same time in different parts of the space. Collectively, these stories become tales of the island's origin.

8   Next each group writes down their story and edits it in final form.

9   Children then learn about how to create a readers' theatre script and put their stories into readers' theatre format for sharing.

(This approach was inspired by a workshop developed and run by storyteller Moses Aaron.)

Readers' Theatre Script Development (Story and Script Box 12.4) provides an example of a story created by upper primary children and adapted into a readers' theatre script using the workshop process in Developing Stories for Readers' Theatre (Concept Box 12.2).

Story and Script Box 12.4

Readers' theatre script development

How the Flower got its Yellow Centre

STORY AND READERS' THEATRE ADAPTATION BY EDWINA, REBEKAH, BELINDA, ANTHONY, BEN AND JUSTINE

(1) Narrator	(4) Second Gnome
(2) Goddess	(5) Giant
(3) First Gnome	(6) Forgotten Flower

(1)   At one stage the world was in total darkness, so the Goddess decided to do something about it.

(2)   'I think the world needs some brightness. Let there be flowers!' (*waves hand*)

(1)   Even though the flowers were all pink, the little gnomes decided to make them even brighter.

(3)   'These flowers are a bit dull. What can we do about it?'

(4)   'Why don't we paint them different colours?'

(1)   So the little gnomes scurried home, got some paint, and painted the flowers. (*gnomes mime painting*)—but they forgot one.

(6)   'What about me?'

(1)   screamed the forgotten flower

(3)(4) but the little gnomes didn't hear.

(1)   Then the Goddess called upon the Giant to do his part in making the world brighter.

(2)   'Please paint the sun a fiery yellow, Giant. The world is not yet bright enough.'

(5)   'As you wish, oh Goddess!'

(1)   So the Giant painted the sun yellow (*mimes painting sun*).

(5)   'This looks brighter!'

(1)   Unfortunately some of the paint dripped into the centre of the forgotten flower.

(6)   (*angrily*) 'Look what you've done to me, you clumsy old giant! (*thinking*) Actually, I like it!'

(1)   But the Goddess didn't!

(2)   'I don't like the yellow centre! You are disgraced, Giant!'

(All)   That's how the flower got its yellow centre.

Staging the script

When staging a readers' theatre script, nothing should be done to detract from the audience's own visualisation. Vocal expression and movement are used in ways to encourage listeners to see the story in their own minds as it unfolds. This means that suggestion rather than realistic representation is the rule.

Placement of readers

Readers can be positioned in the presentation space to show the relationship among the characters and their place within the setting; for example, Hansel and Gretel, children in the German folktale, are left to their fate in the woods where they discover a gingerbread house and eventually overcome a wicked witch. At the beginning of the story, the readers can be placed within the different settings as appropriate as shown in Staging *Hansel and Gretel* (Concept Box 12.3)

Concept Box 12.3

Staging *Hansel and Gretel*

(Children as Cottage)	(Children as trees)	(Children as Gingerbread House)
Hansel and Gretel		Witch (with back to the audience)
(Space 1) Cottage	*(Space 2) Woods*	*(Space 3) Gingerbread House*

Hansel and Gretel are at home in their cottage (Space 1); while the Witch, on the opposite side of the presentation space, sits on a stool inside her gingerbread house (Space 3). At the start of the story, the Witch is **out of scene** with her back to the audience until Hansel and Gretel wander through the woods (Space 2) to arrive at her gingerbread house. Later in the story, Hansel and Gretel must again wend their way back through the woods (Space 2) to return to their cottage (Space 1).

Rather than using sets to represent the different locations, groups of children can use their bodies to form the frame of the humble cottage, menacing trees in the woods, and the gingerbread house covered with sweet treats. Other groups could form the cage in which Hansel is trapped by the witch and the oven into which she is eventually pushed. This approach encourages the audience to picture for themselves the colours, shapes and textures of the set, while at the same time involving a larger number of children who use movement, mime and even sound effects, such as forest sounds and a squeaky cage door, to enhance the readers' theatre presentation.

Focus

The focus of the readers (i.e. where they look when they are reading) can be either **onstage**, offstage or a combination of both. Onstage focus involves readers looking directly at each other as they speak. This is what actors in a play usually do on stage when they are performing. Offstage focus, on the other hand, means that readers look towards the audience and not at each other (Robertson & Poston-Anderson 1986).

Focus Options (Concept Box 12.4) shows examples of onstage and offstage focus as used in several different children's theatre performances. (Note: These were children's theatre performances not readers' theatre presentations.)

Concept Box 12.4

Focus options

In traditional readers' theatre, the use of offstage focus has been a convention or characteristic. This means that instead of looking at the other readers, a narrator shares his or her lines directly with the audience, telling them the story. The

Figure 12.1 Onstage focus: In this scene from *Second Star on the Right: The Adventures of Peter Pan,* the Darling family's attention is focused on what they are doing on stage.

Figure 12.2 Offstage focus: The characters in *Fair, Brown and Trembling* look towards the audience as if they were speaking with another character.

characters, too, look towards the audience, but if they are speaking with another character, they look to the point in the audience where their own focus would cross with the other character if there were a large mirror across the back of the presentation space. They also change the level of their focus to reflect the relative height of the characters to whom they speak; for example, a tree talking to an ant would look out and down, whereas the ant would look out and up. Offstage Focus (Concept Box 12.5) explains this process through diagrams.

Concept Box 12.5

Offstage focus

This diagram shows how three different characters would interact with each other. The shaded area indicates where the audience is seated and the dotted line is the back wall of the room.

When Character A talks to Character B, each looks towards the back wall where the other character would be reflected; their focus crosses at the point AB.

When Character B talks to Character C, each looks towards where the other character would be reflected; their focus crosses at the point BC.

When Character A talks to Character C, each looks towards where the other character would be reflected; their focus crosses at the point AC.

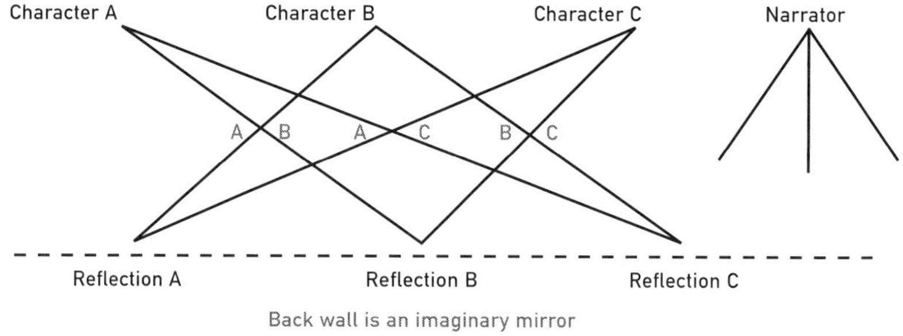

Back wall is an imaginary mirror

Figure 12.3 Interaction between characters using offstage focus

When offstage focus is used, the focal points cross in the audience, making the listeners feel that the words are directed to them, yet the readers can still establish to which character they are speaking by where they direct the dialogue. Narrators, in contrast to characters, speak their lines directly to the audience trying to include as many of them as possible within their gaze.

Characterisation through voice and suggested movement

VOICE
In readers' theatre, a reader's voice is the main tool used to project the words of the text to the audience. Vocal tone, quality, pitch, volume and the pace at which the words are said create word pictures for the listeners. Voices may blend or contrast; be in sync or purposefully out of sync; be soft and lulling or strident and confronting. These vocal elements, together with suggested movement, signal changes in character, mood and location. In this way, a reader's voice becomes an expressive instrument through which the text is filtered. The success of a readers' theatre presentation, then, to a large extent depends on how effectively readers use their voices individually and as a group (Robertson & Poston-Anderson 1995).

MOVEMENT
Just as the principle of suggestion governs the overall staging of a readers' theatre script, so, too, does it affect the nature and amount of movement. Coger and White (1982) indicate that readers' theatre can be presented in

several different styles, two of which are particularly relevant in the classroom. The first is the traditional form where readers use little movement and the second is staged where facial expression, gestures and movement are used to suggest the characters, their interactions and their placements within the presentation space.

Traditional readers' theatre, also called conventional readers' theatre (Coger & White 1982, p. 10), is most frequently staged with readers sitting on stools or standing so that all readers can be seen. For example, in a story set on a mountain, the readers can arrange themselves in a mountain shape with readers at the back on higher stools and those in the front on lower stools; all readers use offstage focus and scripts, the covers of which may be decorated to emphasise the mountain setting, to suggest their characters, or to emphasise a main theme.

Staged readers' theatre, also called free readers' theatre (Coger & White 1982, p. 10), uses more action than a traditional approach, but the movement is still suggested rather than fully realistic. For example, a character going on a journey walks in place, one who dies turns her back and lowers her head, while a timid character cowers behind his script. The arrangement of readers and movement in this style may also be used to suggest relationships among the characters. In addition, there may be more variation in the ways in which offstage focus and onstage focus are used, or whether all or only some of the readers carry scripts. The nature of the text being shared may help to determine what conventions are selected. Readers' Theatre Moves (Activity Box 12.1) provides practice in how to suggest movements that are consistent with offstage focus.

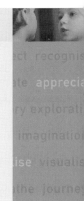

Activity Box 12.1

Readers' theatre moves

Description
Show the following movements using suggested action:
- As individuals:
  - Run a race
  - Write a letter

- – Climb up stairs
- – Practise ballet dancing
- – Ride a horse
- – Hit a cricket ball
- – Light a candle
- With a partner
  (One of you is A, the other is B.)
  - – Practise passing a crown back and forth using offstage focus (i.e. A hands the imaginary crown out towards B, B takes the crown from where A hands it and places it on his or her head. Then the crown passes back again from B to A).
  - – Plan a three-stroke sword fight. First use onstage focus to establish what strokes you will use, then shift the focus offstage—so that you, as sword fighters, look out towards the audience. Have your swords cross where the two characters' focus crosses in the audience. (Note: Your swords do not actually cross.)

Mentor note

Have participants hold a script in one hand as they do the above actions. This reinforces the idea that the movement is only suggested, not fully realistic.

Suggested costumes and props

When it comes to costumes and props, the temptation is to use too much of everything. In fact, the saying that 'less is more' is particularly apt in this presentation medium. Since the goal of readers' theatre is to encourage listeners to use their imaginations, anything that detracts from this is to be avoided. This includes full-scale costumes and make-up that transform readers into characters and draw attention away from the words being said. For this reason, a simple scarf, hat, or pair of ears is enough to suggest a character. Sometimes all readers choose to dress in the same way (e.g. all in one colour or in one style) to emphasise that attention is not on them personally. This reinforces the point that readers are the medium through which the words of the text come alive.

Use of mimed props rather than real objects also emphasises that the action takes place in the minds of the audience not on stage. Often the script, which it is usual for each reader to hold, can be used as a prop; for example, a script can become a letter to read, a book to open, a wall to hide behind, a covering for one's head during a rainstorm, a sandwich to eat, or a package to untie. The possibilities are limitless. Staging Tips for Readers' Theatre (Concept Box 12.6) provides answers to some frequently asked questions about staging scripts.

Concept Box 12.6

Staging tips for readers' theatre

1 How are the readers arranged in the presentation space?
All readers must be seen; use grouping of readers or different levels to achieve this.
   Avoid standing readers in straight lines. Either work for an aesthetically pleasing picture or arrange characters to show their relationships.

2 Where should the narrators be placed in relation to the characters?
Often narrators are placed closer to the sides of the presentation space and the characters arranged in the centre.
   Keep in mind that, during the course of a readers' theatre presentation, a narrator may become a character or a character a narrator; likewise, a reader may become more than one character. Feel free to have the characters and narrators move to different spots in the presentation space as is appropriate.

3 How are characters differentiated?
Use suggested action and movement to help establish a character. Facial expression, gestures, and bodily stance provide a visual indication of 'who is who'.
   Also, use voice to differentiate the characters. Vary the elements of voice (e.g. volume, pace, pitch, tone, vocal quality) to develop a vocal pattern for each character.
   When a reader takes more than one part, this person uses voice and bodily movement to portray each one differently.

During the presentation, characters shift offstage focus to establish to whom they are speaking.

4   How do I create different locations that are in the text?

Readers can move from spot to spot in the space or use a combination of light-weight stools, chairs, steps, ladders, which they move to show a change of location.

Consider also using children to form the shapes that are needed to suggest different places (e.g. trees in the forest, skyscrapers in the city, waves at the seashore).

Steps in Preparing a Readers' Theatre Presentation (Concept Box 12.7) summarises the process for developing a readers' theatre script from a text and how to stage it.

Concept Box 12.7

Steps in preparing a readers' theatre presentation

- Prepare the script
  - Choose a text, usually one with descriptive narration and dialogue.
  - Break the text into parts for sharing, using narrators and characters as is appropriate.
  - Prepare an introduction to the script that identifies the source of the text and any other relevant background information.
- Prepare the readers
  - Engage in drama exercises that focus on:
    - movement and mime;
    - vocal characterisation through tone, pitch, volume, pace, quality; and
    - working together as a group.
  - Adapt the exercises to reflect the content, moods and characters in the reading; for example, use Imaginary Object Pass (Activity Box 6.4), but pass objects that appear in the readers' theatre script or use Mood Makers (Activity Box 8.11) to create background sound as atmosphere for the story.

- Stage the script
  - Plan how the readers will enter the presentation space and leave it **in character** or in a way that suggests the setting, mood, and/or time period of the text.
  - Place the readers in the space to create an aesthetic picture or to suggest their character relationships.
  - Add suggested movement, involving mime and offstage focus.
  - When presenting an adaptation from a longer work, decide whether there will be musical transitions between the scenes or prior to and after the presentation.
  - Will sound effects be used? If so, how will they be made (e.g. vocally, body percussion, musical instruments)?
  - Consider whether costume pieces or minimal props will be used.
  - Practise the script aloud with the movement and staging until the group feels confident.
  - Present the script aloud for others and enjoy their feedback.

Preparing a readers' theatre script for presentation

This section provides an in-depth examination of how readers' theatre in combination with storytelling and drama workshops can be used to introduce children to a remarkable person from Australian history. In this extended example, the career of balloonist Vincent Patrick Taylor (1874–1930), also known as the Australian daredevil aeronaut, Captain Penfold, is the focus. His exceptional skill at operating and performing from hot air balloons was legendary in the early 1900s before aviation was common. 'At 3000 feet he would set off firecrackers, do acrobatic tricks, take photos of the crowd below, distribute advertising brochures and then detach himself from the balloon and float back to earth by parachute' (Webber 1997).

The preparation stage for readers' theatre involves introducing children to true stories from the aeronaut's life and then workshopping them through process drama (see Appendix 3 for this readers' theatre preparation workshop). The drama sessions culminate in the presentation of a readers' theatre script.

Presenting a readers' theatre script: An extended example

Picture Perfect (Story and Script Box 12.5) is a readers' theatre script adapted for seven readers. However, more mimed roles may be added (e.g. the camera, doors on Bert's studio and the fruit shop, the fruit and vegetables in the boxes, the crowd waiting to see the publicity shot). In this way an entire class can be engaged in the presentation.

INITIAL READ-THROUGH

Before the initial read-through, show the format of the script, *Picture Perfect*, to the students and discuss with them the difference between a story and a script. Show them how the lines have been assigned to different readers. This script has four narrators and three main characters: Captain Penfold, Bert, and the Fruit Shop Owner. Reader 7 is the Fruit Shop Owner and also the narrator who introduces the story. Sit in a circle and read the story aloud, going around the circle with each person taking a line.

Story and Script Box 12.5

Picture Perfect

(Story and readers' theatre adaptation by Barbara Poston-Anderson)

(1) Narrator   (3) Narrator   (5) Captain Penfold   (7) Fruit Shop Owner
                                                                   and Narrator

(2) Narrator   (4) Narrator   (6) Bert

(7)   Captain Taylor Penfold, whose real name was Vincent Patrick Taylor, was born in 1874. He called himself the 'Aussie Aeronaut' because he enjoyed entertaining people with his daring balloon flights. Barbara Poston-Anderson, who wrote this story, called *Picture Perfect*, based it on a real incident in this amazing Australian's life.

(*Scene 1: Bert's photography studio*)

(1)   Jaunty Captain Penfold,

(5)   (*proudly*) Australian aeronaut and daredevil extraordinaire,

(1)   strode down King Street whistling a cheerful tune. (*Reader 5 whistles*)

(2)   His polished white shoes shone.

(3)   The brass buttons on his navy blue jacket sparkled.

(4)   His wiry moustache glistened

(5)   (*twirling moustache*) with an extra dab of glossy wax!

(1, 2, 3, 4)   Today was a big day!

(1)   He was to have his official photograph taken—

(2)   the one he would use for all his publicity.

(3)   As he walked through the door of the studio the Captain called,

(5)   'Good day, Bert.'

(6)   (*calls*) 'Be with you in a minute,'

(4)   replied the excited photographer,

(6)   (*busily*) positioning the camera, then carefully aiming the lights.

(3)   It wasn't every day that someone as famous as Captain Taylor Penfold came to see him.

(4)   Everything had to be perfect.

(6)   'Ah, Captain, now I'm ready for you. Right this way, please.'

(4)   Bert guided him into the studio and placed him in front of a full cloth backdrop of fluffy white clouds.

(1)   He adjusted it once,

(2)   then twice,

(3)   then again, before he finally said,

(6)   'That looks perfect!'

(2)   What better setting than clouds for this daring balloonist who made his living by rising from the ground seated on a trapeze with a parachute on his back?

(1)   Once he was airborne he would shoot off firecrackers then drop back to earth to the amazement of the crowd watching below.

(3)   Bert was certain this photograph would be special.

(6)   'Say, cheese!'

(4)   called Bert ready to take the picture.

(1)   The Captain took a deep breath,

(2)   turned to the camera

(5)   and smiled.

(6)   'Hold on a minute!'

(4)   cried Bert.

(5)   'What's wrong?'

(6)   'Something isn't right.'

(5)   'Is my hair out of place?'

(4)   asked the Captain.

(6)   'No, but something isn't right.'

(4)   replied Bert staring at the Captain.

(5)   'Do I have too much wax on my moustache?'

(6)   'No, your moustache curls perfectly, but something isn't right.'

(1, 2) Together the Captain

(3, 4) and Bert

(1, 2) crossed to the full-length mirror

(3, 4) for a closer look.

(5)   'Is my smile too big?'

(6)   'NO.'

(5)   'Are my buttons too shiny?'

(6)   'NO.'

(5)   'What is it then?'

(6)   'I don't know!'

(1,3)   They both stared at the Captain's reflection in the mirror.

(6)   'It's the cap!'

(4)   cried Bert.

(5)   'What's wrong with my cap?'

(2)   questioned the Captain.

(1)   It was his favourite.

(6)   'Something is missing,'

(4)   replied Bert.

(5)   'What?'

(6)   'An emblem.'

(3)   Bert was definite.

(6)   'You need an emblem to show you're a balloonist. Otherwise, how will people know what you do?'

(5)   'I never thought of that!'

(2)   mused the Captain, seeing Bert's point.

(5)   'I must find an emblem for my cap—now!'

(Scene 2: The fruit shop next door)

(1)   Out the door raced jaunty Captain Penfold

(2)   in his polished white shoes

(3)   with his brass buttons shining

(1)   and into the fruit shop next door.

(7)   'How may I help you?'

(1)   asked the startled owner.

(5)   'I'll tell you when I know,'

(2)   answered the Captain,

(4)   his wiry moustache twitching.

(7)   His sharp eyes wandered over boxes filled with

(1)   red tomatoes,

(2)   ripened peaches,

(3)   and sturdy avocados.

(7)   For a long moment his glance lingered on a spiky pineapple before moving on to a basket filled with walnuts.

(5)   'A knife! Hand me that knife, mate!'

(1)   demanded the Captain.

(2)   The owner, concerned with his customer's odd behaviour, tried to control his trembling as he handed over his little slicing knife.

(7)   'Here you are, sir.'

(3)   Then he put his hands in front of his face and peeked nervously through his fingers.

(4)   The Captain raised the sharp blade and let it fall.

(All)   WHACK!

(7)   With one clear blow, the walnut was split in two.

(5)   'Bonza!'

(1)   the Captain cried.

(7)   'Bravo!'

(3)   echoed the fruit shop owner who knew a good slice when he saw one.

(5)   'Now I have an emblem for my cap!'

(1)   the delighted Captain laughed tossing the relieved shopkeeper a coin.

(Scene 3: Bert's photography studio)

(2)   Back inside the studio, the Captain attached the half walnut to his cap band.

(6)   'What a great emblem!'

(3)   declared Bert.

(6)   'That walnut looks just like a balloon. Now say cheese!'

(1)   The shutter opened.

(6)   Hold it!

(All)   FLASH!

(2)   The bulbs popped.

(3)   The shutter closed.

(All)   Picture perfect!—

(5)   *(pleased)* walnut, cap and all.

CHARACTER DEVELOPMENT

Once the reading is finished, reflect on the personalities of the three characters. What motivates each one? How do they speak and move? How do they interact with each other? Have students draw portraits of the characters to show how they visualise them as shown in Student Response: Captain Penfold Drawings (From the Classroom 12.1).

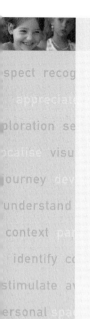

From the Classroom 12.1

Student response: Captain Penfold drawings

A Year 5 class preparing for a readers' theatre presentation of *Picture Perfect* created visualisations of Captain Penfold and key events in the story. Here are two of the drawings that resulted from this preparation work.

Figure 12.4 Year 5 students' visualisations of *Picture Perfect* (a) Luke shows the Captain as he finds the walnut, chops it and attaches it to his hat. (b) Hannah captures the moment when Captain Penfold poses for his photograph.

Ask children how they could differentiate the three main characters (e.g. the Captain, Bert and the Fruit Shop Owner) in a readers' theatre presentation. Some options could be: having them speak and move differently; dressing each in a different colour; using small costume pieces such as a cap, vest or apron; or decorating the script covers to show who each character is. Have children consider the advantages and disadvantages of using 'real' props for the knife and the camera. Can they think of ways to make these items through movement and mime without using actual props? The half walnut is of particular importance to the story. Will they use a real one to attach to a cap for the Captain or are there other options?

STAGING THE SCRIPT

Take time to review the basics of readers' theatre, particularly offstage focus and suggested movement. Also, remind students that when they share *Picture Perfect* they will hold a script. The exercises in Readers' Theatre Warm-ups

(Activity Box 12.2) reinforce the concepts of offstage focus and suggested movement.

Activity Box 12.2

Readers' theatre warm-ups

Description

Find a partner. One of you is A, the other is B. Use offstage focus.

- Captain (A) hands Bert (B) his cap.
- Bert (B) hands the Captain (A) back his hat.
- Fruit Shop Owner (B) hands the Captain (A) his knife.
- Captain (A) hands the Fruit Shop Owner (B) back his knife.
- Captain talks to Bert who is sitting on the floor.
- Bert talks to Captain on chair from the floor.
- Bert climbs a ladder to see how the photo looks from above.
- Captain talks to Bert who is perched near the top of a ladder.
- Captain races into shop.
- Fruit Shop Owner is frightened and hides.

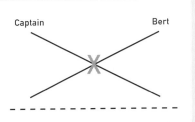

Figure 12.5 Offstage location approach: The imaginary cap is passed to and taken from the spot labelled X.

Mentor note

Remind the students to use offstage focus. Also, demonstrate for them how to hand mimed objects to each other using the offstage location approach (i.e. Captain hands cap out towards where Bert is reflected in the imaginary mirror; Bert takes cap from Captain by reaching out towards him where he is reflected in the imaginary mirror).

When staging this script, consider keeping the narrators to either side of the space with the characters in the centre. As shown in Reader Placement in *Picture Perfect* (Concept Box 12.8), divide the centre space into two locations, Bert's photographic studio and the fruit shop. The Captain, who is in the middle, can interact with Bert in the photographic studio or with the Fruit Shop Owner in his fruit shop.

Concept Box 12.8

Reader placement in *Picture Perfect*

Figure 12.6 Reader placement

When the children have decided on the staging and have considered how they will read their parts with suggested characterisation and movement, rehearse the script and then share it with others. Following the presentation discuss with children what they thought went well and their perceptions of how the audience responded to the performance of a readers' theatre script.

Children can be encouraged to adapt and stage their own scripts, or existing scripts can be used. Two sources that contain scripts appropriate for use with primary school students are: *Readers' Theatre: A Practical Guide* (Robertson & Poston-Anderson 1986) and *Imagine This: A Readers' Theatre Source Book* (Robertson & Poston-Anderson 1995).

Applications for middle school students

One of the benefits of readers' theatre for older students is that this medium reinforces visualisation and abstract-thinking skills as students convert a written text to an oral presentation that uses suggested movement and staging. To achieve this, students use only their voices, facial expressions and bodily movements supported by a handheld script and a few, if any, costume and set pieces (e.g. stools, chairs, ladder, box). This minimalist approach presents readers with artistic challenges for which they must find creative solutions, such as: how to 'energise the demolition beams' in *The Hitch Hiker's Guide to the Galaxy* (Adams 1979); how to show Lockie Leonard on his surfboard (Winton 1997); how to depict simultaneously King Arthur's fifth-century Britain and the twelfth century of the crusades in *The Seeing Stone* (Crossley-Holland 2000); or how to suggest the death of the lion, Aslan, in *The Lion, The Witch and The Wardrobe* (Lewis 2005, 1950). Developing creative solutions through movement, focus and stage positioning that fall within the parameters of readers' theatre, challenges older students' thinking and develops their knowledge of how to work within this drama form.

From the shorter poems and stories appropriate for readers' theatre adaptation for younger children (usually presented in full), older students can begin with longer works, preparing excerpts from novels or linking a series of shorter stories and poems by theme. Readers' theatre programs can be created from a diverse range of fiction, poetry and non-fiction that are combined with music and visuals to form an integrated arts performance. Students may also use their own stories or ones that they collect; for example, family 'origin' stories (Concept Box 10.1: Story Types) can be combined into a composite program representing the diversity of the class.

A major advantage of readers' theatre for adolescents (as for students of all ages) is that script preparation and presentation encourage the development of literacy skills. Even students with less developed reading skills can participate in readers' theatre and find success. As part of the group sharing process, they discover literary works that they might not have chosen or been able to read by themselves, yet find accessible through readers' theatre. This can be an important motivation for script development as was the case with Latrobe and Lauglin's book (1989), *Readers Theatre for Young Adults: Scripts and Script Development*, the aim of which was to introduce young people to classic works of English and American fiction through readers' theatre. Short scripts from novel excerpts and guidelines for adapting scripts from forty other young adult novels selected for their literary quality and popular appeal with young people are provided.

Using a similar approach, older students can choose and adapt readers' theatre scripts based on excerpts from their favourite Australian novels. This 'educational use' of another's work is within copyright regulations as long as the work is attributed to the author and the resulting readers' theatre performances are done to 'promote' the original book within a school 'not for profit' context. If there is any doubt, check with the copyright holder for permission (e.g. particularly if you want to publish and sell the scripts or perform them in public as opposed to within a school or educational context).

Readers' theatre presents innovative challenges for older students as they use their creative and dramatic skills to develop and stage their own presentations based on literary sources and/or personal stories. Even when resources, space, and time are limited, readers' theatre is a workable drama form because such constraints challenge students to be even more creative in the decisions they make about what to stage and how to stage it.

Summary

As a performance medium, readers' theatre has many benefits for the classroom. First, a readers' theatre script can be adapted to involve as many students as required. There can be narrators, characters, a chorus of readers, and children who use mime and bodily movement to create the scenery and set pieces. Another advantage of readers' theatre is that students do not need to memorise their lines because a script is an expected convention of this drama form. Finally, readers' theatre encourages both the readers and the listeners to use their imaginations to bring the script to life. As Robertson and Poston-Anderson (1995, pp. 13–14) conclude:

> Readers' Theatre encourages the development of the relationship between language and imagination and places the responsibility for creating the mind pictures squarely on the shoulders of the readers and the audience. These qualities make Readers' Theatre one of the most exciting, entertaining and rewarding ways to encourage children to explore literature from picture books to novels.

For further study

1 Develop a readers' theatre script for the story, *Anansi's Party Trick* (Appendix 2.2). Divide the story into parts keeping both the narration and dialogue as they appear in the story. Integrate audience participation as indicated in the story. If you prefer, choose your own text on which to base a readers' theatre script.

2 Use readers' theatre principles, including offstage focus and suggested movement, to stage the script you created for *Anansi's Party Trick* or your own text.

3 Choose a theme (e.g. friendship). For this theme develop a readers' theatre script integrating different types of text (e.g. poetry, stories, song lyrics, newspaper accounts). Decide how you will link these elements to make them into a coherent script (e.g. through use of a narrator, music, movement). Stage your readers' theatre script for an audience.

For reflection

One of the benefits claimed for readers' theatre is that it encourages students' literacy development, particularly in reading and speaking. Explore this statement providing examples and reasons for your views. What other benefits can you suggest for this drama form?

Preview

Chapter 13: Children's Theatre: Playwriting and Performing considers children's theatre as a form of drama with particular emphasis on selecting and writing plays for children; the team effort required in producing a play; and the nature of the child audience.

Children's Theatre: Playwriting and Performing

'The imagination of the actor adorns the text of the playwright with fanciful patterns and colors from his own invisible palette' (Stanislavski 1988, 1961).

Introducing children's theatre

Children's theatre refers to a 'formal theatrical experience in which a play is presented for an audience of children' (Goldberg 1974, p. 5). In this book, the term 'children's theatre' can refer both to a performance acted by adults for children and to a rehearsed play presented by children for others. This theatrical event may be an end of year school play performed on the school stage, a children's play presented by a professional company at a local theatre, or a play performed by a combined cast of adults and children at a festival or other community event. (A related term is **theatre-in-education** that most frequently refers to companies composed of [professional] actors that perform in schools, using issues-based approaches that encourage child participation.)

Viewing Children's Theatre (Concept Box 13.1) depicts three different ways in which plays can be performed for children.

Concept Box 13.1

Viewing children's theatre

(1) Adults perform a play for children on a stage.

Figure 13.1 *A Cultural Celebration of Italian Folktales*

Figure 13.2 *Sense and Sustainability*

Figure 13.3 *Rumplestiltskin*

(2) Children perform with adults in an outdoor community setting.

(3) Children perform for younger children in a drama studio.

Despite the fact that it takes time and a coordinated effort from a team of people, staging a children's theatre production is worthwhile. One group of tertiary pre-service teachers who staged a children's play for primary schools reported some of the advantages (Poston-Anderson 2002). They experienced self-growth and awareness of themselves as performers, they learned how to work together as a team, and they developed acting and performance skills, such as 'staying in character' and 'knowing your part and how it fits into the whole production'.

Children, too, benefit from the experience of 'putting on' a play. As actors, they learn about: projecting their voices and moving in a performance space; the responsibilities of being a cast member in a play (e.g. memorising lines, supporting each other); and the necessity for cast and crew to work together to achieve a theatrical outcome. As members of a design, technical, production or publicity team for a show, children develop specialised skills (e.g. costume making, make-up design, how to operate lighting and sound, set and prop construction, and promotional skills); learn about the need to meet deadlines; and discover how artistic and technical elements fit together to form a unified production. The following discussion explores children's theatre from the perspective of the play, the play production team, the actors, the child audience, and the performance space.

The play

The text of a play is called a script. Although a performance can be developed without one (i.e. playbuilt from improvisation), the advantage of a written script is that it provides 'direction, development, and focus' for the play, as well as giving actors a 'fixed base' from which to develop their characters (Hornby 1995, 1977 p. 98). Scripts may be developed and written by children, by the teacher, or by professional writers who make their plays commercially available for purchase through publishers. The writer of a play is called a **playwright**.

Selecting a play

The selection of an appropriate play for children is essential to a production's success. The script chosen must have 'respect for children' as well as 'entertainment' value (Goldberg 1974). The main characters need to be ones with whom the child audience can empathise, while the themes and issues dealt with in the play need to be relevant to children's interests and their levels of development. This does not mean, however, that important issues and challenging ideas should be avoided or treated 'simplistically' (Wood 1999, p. 20); instead these issues need to be approached with sensitivity at an appropriate level for the child audience.

Action, which involves 'showing' rather than 'telling', is another essential play ingredient that is needed to keep audience attention and to forward the plot in ways that invite child response. Active plays with humorous characters or situations have particular appeal for youngsters. No matter what the theme or tone of the play, however, quality needs to be the keynote (Wood 1999). Plays for children need to be well written with believable characters and situations.

When seeking an appropriate children's play to produce, it is helpful for the selector to try to identify the playwright's assumptions, what Stanislavski (1988, 1961) calls 'the angle of vision' as revealed in the script (p. 5). These underlying premises will affect how the subject matter and themes are treated. Does a particular script for *Cinderella* give a traditional, feminist or social justice slant to the story? Does a specific version of *The Pied Piper* lend itself to a realistic 'stranger danger' or a light-hearted musical treatment? Usually the language, themes, dialogue and character interactions will provide valuable clues to the 'voice' and orientation of the play. Identifying the playwright's underlying intent is a useful strategy for teachers who need to select appropriate script material for an assembly program or a play for an all-school production.

Writing a play

The initial idea for a play script can come from anywhere (e.g. conversations, personal incidents, quirky people, newspaper and media reports, pictures, or children's stories). Once the idea is chosen, a playwright draws on knowledge of children and insight into the subject matter to create a script. An important principle to remember when sorting and selecting possible ideas is the fact that children's plays must 'capture children's interest' (Johnston 2003, p. 137).

One popular starting place for playwrights is the genre of the folktale because of its 'universal' themes (e.g. good versus evil), recognisable characters (e.g. brave hero), and familiar structures (e.g. happily-ever-after endings). The advantage of working with a folktale is that the pre-existing story structure can serve as the frame on which to construct a script (Wood 1999). Folktales have the added appeal that many of them are already familiar to children through picture books and fairytale collections.

Some playwrights choose to take traditional story themes and update them by placing them in contemporary contexts, what Wood calls putting 'age old themes' in 'new packaging' (Wood 1999, p. 32). What happens when the

Tortoise and the Hare enter the marathon at the Olympics? What if Cindy (i.e. Cinderella) couldn't go to her Year 12 formal? What if a Year 5 student in your school had the King Midas touch and everything he touched turned to gold or everything he wished for came true?

When playwrights choose existing stories, whether they are traditional or contemporary, they must adapt them to meet the theatrical conventions of the stage. Unlike readers' theatre, where the author's words are retained and 'to adapt' means to divide the text into parts and to decide how the literary work will be staged, when adapting a story into a children's play it is usual for dialogue and dramatic action to replace narration. 'Changing, altering, modifying, cutting, and simplifying' are all features characteristic of the kinds of adaptation used when creating a play for the stage (Rosenthal 1995, p. 166). Whether to follow the tale slavishly or to use it as a starting point, and how best to remain faithful to the spirit of the story while making the necessary changes to the text to make it work as a play script are challenges playwrights face.

A survey of playwrights who adapt folktales into children's plays (Poston-Anderson & McCrae 2002) showed that these writers had no hesitation in adding or cutting down the number of characters, changing the sequence of events, altering the number of settings, modifying the language, and simplifying the theme to make the story work on the stage. Their main goal was to create a workable children's play that young people found meaningful. Modifications such as these are possible with a traditional folktale because there are no copyright restrictions. However, when a playwright uses a story published by an identifiable author, permission must be sought from the copyright holder to adapt the text into a play for performance to a fee-paying audience.

When playwriting for children, societal concerns, such as multicultural representation, gender equity and inclusiveness need to be kept in mind. In a diverse society it is important that plays not over-represent any one group, that they do not always reinforce the active male, passive female stereotype, and that they are inclusive, stressing what characters can do rather than what they cannot. Since plays, like other literature for children, reflect the time and culture in which they are written, playwrights need to tune in to such concerns and take them into consideration in their own writing.

Kids' Playwriting Workshop (From the Classroom 13.1) provides guide-lines for working with young people who want to write their own scripts.

From the Classroom 13.1

Kids' playwriting workshop

At a CREA playwriting workshop for upper primary students entitled 'So You Want to Be a Playwright?', students developed their own scripts that were performed for an invited audience and then videotaped as a record of the performance.

Figure 13.4 Young playwrights at a playwriting workshop explore character voice through improvised dialogue.

Playwriting workshop guidelines

Where to begin:

1 Start with the children's own interests that will provide them with the motivation to persevere with the script.
2 Write with the end product in mind—a script. Show participants examples of scripts and how they are set out. Read and discuss several short scripts together.
3 When learning how to write a play, it is sometimes best to start with a short one-act play.

How to proceed:

4 Some playwrights first write a synopsis of each scene, and then turn each one into dialogue; the advantage of this is that the play has a clear structure. Other playwrights start with characters and put them into interesting settings. Still

others start with an idea or a central question they want to solve. Explore each of these ways to see what works best for individual playwrights.

5   What makes a play attention grabbing is conflict or dramatic tension (see Chapter 8); this need not always be physical conflict, tension can also be created by characters with different goals pulling against one another.

6   Encourage the writers to use visualisation and the 'movie camera technique' (see Chapter 10) to play the scenes in their heads as they write them.

7   Have playwrights distinguish between the script and the performance. The script divides the action into acts and scenes with descriptions of where each scene is set, provides the character dialogue, and gives some brief instructions in brackets for how lines are to be said. On the other hand, the detail of how the script will ultimately be performed on the stage is the responsibility of a director who will block the script during rehearsals.

How to refine the script:

8   When working with a group, have them read aloud each other's work at draft stage so the writers can hear how the dialogue sounds aloud.

9   Emphasise that each character has a voice that is unique; the writer tries to capture this by the way in which they write the dialogue.

10 Reinforce that playwriting is a creative process and, like any other form of writing, involves the steps of drafting and revision in order to reach a final product.

Playwriting is one option for developing a script, particularly when children already enjoy writing in other literary genres (i.e. short story, poems). Writing a play gives them the opportunity to conceptualise their ideas through another form, the script, which hopefully will lead to a theatrical performance.

The play production team

When children are involved in the play production process, they become part of a team. Within this team, they may play any number of roles. The What's What of Theatrical Production (Concept Box 13.2) provides an overview of some of these roles.

Concept Box 13.2

The what's what of theatrical production

Directors

- *The Director:* selects the play and makes decisions about how to stage it.
- *Musical Director:* in a musical, the person who is in charge of the music and who may also conduct the singers and musicians during the performance.
- *Choreographer:* the person who develops the dances and teaches them to the cast.

Designers

- *The Designer:* uses line, colour, space, shape, scale to develop the visual concept for the play.
- *Lighting Designer:* creates the concept for the stage lighting and visual effects.
- *Costume Designer:* creates the concept for the costumes (i.e. what the actors wear).

Depending on the complexity of the show, there may also be people who design: the make-up, sound effects or soundscapes, and the set (i.e. large stage pieces and backgrounds) and/or props.

The construction teams (e.g. sets, props, costumes) make or find all the items once they have been designed. Everyone works together with the designer, who is in ongoing consultation with the director, to bring the show to life.

Performers

- *Actors:* play the roles in the play.
- *Dancers:* may be the same as the actors or separate from them (i.e. soloist or part of a dance ensemble).
- *Singers:* may be the same as the actors or separate from them (i.e. soloist or part of a choir).
- *Other Musicians:* includes the band, orchestra or musical ensemble.

Production team

- *The Production Manager:* in a large show, the person who organises and ensures that the overall work schedule is on track and calls production meetings with the director, the designer, and the stage manager.

- *Stage Manager:* creates the **prompt copy** (i.e. master script) for the play that includes all the cues (sound, lighting, actors' entrances and exits); helps with rehearsals, and runs the show during performance.
- *Stage Crew:* make the show happen during performance (e.g. change of sets).
- *The Sound and Lighting Technicians* and the stage crew, under the management of the stage manager, support the actors in making the performance happen.

Others

- *Front of House Staff:* manage the audience before the performance starts (e.g. checking tickets, handing out programs).
- *Publicity Team:* ensure that people know that the show is happening (e.g. media reports, posters).

This information was adapted from various sources (Wood 1999; Perry 1997; Rodgers & Rodgers 1995).

Putting on a play is a joint effort that involves commitment and dedication from every team member. In addition to learning how to complete their assigned job(s), children learn from play production how to communicate with others, be organised, and work towards common goals.

The actors

When children perform in a play, the particular roles may be assigned to them by the director, or may be parts for which they have auditioned. The **audition** is a specified time when the director meets with all those who wish to 'try out' for the play. At the audition, participants engage in vocal and physical warm-ups, do exercises in characterisation and movement, and read aloud from the script in role. On the basis of this, the director makes a decision about whom to **cast** in the show.

Once a person is chosen for a role, the next step is to prepare the part. According to Stanislavski (1988, 1961), this involves: 'studying it, establishing the life of the role, and putting it into physical form' (p. 3). First, actors read the script with other cast members to get a feeling for their part and how it fits within the context of the entire play. From this initial read-through, actors gain first impressions of their characters, the 'seeds' from which a full characterisation will develop during the rehearsal period (Stanislavski 1988, 1961, p. 3).

Studying the role means that actors consider the various levels in the script, what Stanislavski (1988, 1961) calls **planes**, and how the character they play fits within them. These planes are: 'external (i.e. facts, events, plot, form); social situation (i.e. class, nationality, historic setting); literary (i.e. ideas, style); aesthetic (i.e. theatrical, artistic relating to scenery and production); psychological (i.e. inner action, feelings, inner characterisation); physical (i.e. external characterisation); and personal creative feelings (i.e. those of the actor)' (Stanislavski 1988, 1961, p. 11). To study a part thoroughly means to understand how each of these factors is important to characterisation. The actor gradually peels away the layers moving towards the central core (i.e. heart, soul, essence) of a character. When taken seriously, this process can help actors avoid stereotypical characterisations. Each character is different, even when two characters are labelled in the same way; for example, both Robin Hood and Ned Kelly are considered to be outlaws but each had his own personality and motivation for what he did. Likewise onstage, even in a crowd scene, each character needs a personality and motivation for being there. Be-Witching Characters (Activity Box 13.1) provides an opportunity for students to apply Stanislavski's planes to show how two characters, both labelled as witches, can be dramatically different.

Activity Box 13.1

Be-witching characters

1 Use the novel and the fairytale as source materials for finding out about each of these witches. When reading the stories, pay close attention to what each does and says and to what other characters say about them.

2 Create a character profile based on Stanislavski's planes that identifies each witch's biographical history,

Figure 13.5 The Wicked Witch from *Snow White and the Seven Dwarves*

social situation, physical characteristics and psychological make-up. Justify your profile with reference to the texts.

3 Use this profile to develop a characterisation for each witch. How does each one sound vocally? Move physically? Interact and react to others? As an actor how would you use space, focus, mood and the other drama elements to portray each character?

4 Create a short monologue for the witch of your choice and perform it for others.

Mentor note

After several actors present their monologues, reflect as a group on the following questions:

1 How are the witches alike and/or different?

2 How can the character of each witch be portrayed emotionally, physically and aesthetically using voice and movement?

3 How can costuming and make-up enhance the believability of the characterisation?

4 Why is it important for actors to take time to 'get to know' their characters?

Actors bring a character to life and give it physical form through use of their imaginations as they visualise the character's persona and as they experiment with voice and movement searching for the most appropriate elements to make this character 'believable'. Actors attempt to get 'inside' their characters to find answers to the questions: What motivates them? Why do they do the things they do? Developing a character profile, as demonstrated in Getting into Character (From the Classroom 13.2), is a useful place to start this process.

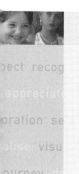

From the Classroom 13.2

Getting into character

Student teacher Simon was cast as the shoemaker, Cob, in a production of *The Elves and the Shoemaker* performed for primary school children. After an initial read-through of the script, he began his actor's preparation by visualising Cob's background, personality and physical characteristics.

Cob and Dora in *The Elves and the Shoemaker*

Figure 13.6 Student teachers play the parts of Cob and Dora in a production of *The Elves and the Shoemaker*.

BACKGROUND

Cob, the local shoemaker in the town, is a middle-aged man who is beginning to show his age. Born into a family of shoemakers, he has never led an extravagant life and does not dream of one. He enjoys nothing more than turning a simple piece of leather into a shoe for people to enjoy.

RELATIONSHIPS

Cob lives with his wife, Dora. Although the two of them have been unable to have children, they have learned to be content with all that comes with life. Mild-mannered and gentle, Cob is well liked by everyone in the village.

PERSONALITY

Cob is down-to-earth and does not have any aspirations or dreams of being more than who he is. He is a cobbler—that is all he knows and desires. As long as he can provide bread for the table, he is happy.

Cob is also a faithful husband who will do anything for his wife. Others may perceive that Dora controls him, however, this is not the case. Cob can be stubborn with a stubbornness that is only matched by his wife's.

PHYSICAL CHARACTERISTICS

- Appearance: Since Cob is poor, he is often seen wearing odds and ends. He prefers bright colours to match his normally jovial personality. He has a beard, as do all cobblers.
- Walk: Cob's walk is normally a slow gait to accompany his slow pace of life. However, when happy or excited, he can move quickly with a bounce.
- Voice: Cob, depending on his mood, can either have a booming voice or a gently quiet one. When happy, he can be heard throughout the village singing as he works. When meeting a friend, the rest of the villagers are likely to hear his warm welcoming exclamations. However, when he is tired or depressed, Cob becomes sullen and doesn't speak much. When he does speak, it sounds more like a string of sighs.

During the rehearsal process actors continue to find out more about their characters while memorising their lines, learning their **blocking** and practising their scenes. To help actors fine-tune their characterisations, the play's director may employ process drama techniques, such as hot seating and thought tracking. To assist in unifying the cast, the director may use role plays, improvisations, and cooperative teambuilding activities. Process drama activities are invaluable within the rehearsal period as vocal and physical warm-ups to begin each session, as skill building devices to improve actors' abilities to observe and to imagine, and as vehicles for enhancing the cast's ability to work together.

Character Considerations (Concept Box 13.3) provides some insights from student actors about characterisation.

Concept Box 13.3

Character considerations

Student teachers who acted in a play performed for children share what they learned from this experience about the 'characters' they played.

- 'Each character has an important place in the play' (Heather).
- 'I get into my character best through putting on the make-up and costume [during] that quiet time of getting ready' (Bec).
- '[During the performance], you need to be in character all the time' (Bec).
- 'Kids respond to characters as characters. Adults know it is a real person' (Mandy).
- 'Don't be afraid of making a fool of yourself. In order to be a successful actor for children's plays you have to put yourself out there' (Matt).

Figure 13.7 Rat overhears a secret in *The Peter Piper Pickled Pepper Mystery*.

In summary, actors breathe life into a playwright's words. Through their creative realisation, they take a script's two-dimensional characters on the page and make them three-dimensional on the stage.

The child audience

In a school setting, the audience for a play may include the young kindergarten child as well as the adolescent in the upper primary years. As challenging as this is for performers, this age range may be even greater in a theatre or community setting. However, in a school situation, plays are often staged for designated grades (e.g. K–2 or 3–6) because the characters, subject matter, and play presentation style are perceived to match one group's interests and developmental levels more closely than another's. Regardless of age, however, humour, music, dance and colour have been identified as performance elements that appeal to children (Wood 1999). Likewise, believable characters and an active plot contribute to their enjoyment.

Because by nature a child audience is responsive, performers need to be prepared for spontaneous participation at any time during a performance in the form of laughter, calling out of warnings, or even volunteering to take part in action on stage. Students performing *A Web for Wilbur*, student teacher Melanie Wong's adaptation of the children's classic *Charlotte's Web*, experienced this when Charlotte, the spider, plaintively asked Wilbur, the pig, 'Who will look after my babies when I am gone?' A little girl in the audience enthusiastically waved her hand crying, 'I will! I will'. Another unexpected response from the audience was when Wilbur started to sing and a little boy grimaced and covered his ears with his hands.

Usually actors need to ignore isolated interjections in order to keep the show on track and not slow the pace. However, when a character on stage directly asks for the audience's help (e.g. 'Have you seen my friend?' or 'Which way did he go?'), he or she needs to listen closely to the advice given or run the risk of frustrating the audience, causing them to call out even more loudly. Actors need to be ready for any eventuality, for as Wood (1999) points out, 'children enjoy being active participants rather than passive spectators' (p. 16). They 'lack self consciousness' and their responses often show 'uninhibited exuberance' (p. 17). In Children as an Audience (Concept Box 13.4), student teachers who performed a play for primary aged children reflect on the nature of a child audience.

Concept Box 13.4

Children as an audience

Student teacher actors said:

- 'Children are honest. They tell you when they are bored or excited' (Jacqui).
- 'Playing to children is different than to adults because their perception is different ... Children laugh [at different places] to the adults [so] watch the children, not the teachers' (Bec).
- 'Children respond to people in costume as characters not as actors—even when they speak in their own voice' (Mandy).
- 'The audience was very responsive today which works in our best interest so we can then bounce off them' (Jill).
- 'Be careful when you try to get the audience involved. Sometimes it is too much. [When this occurs], move back and focus on the show' (Matt).
- '[As an actor] the real learning is knowing when to encourage their excitement and when to pull back' (Bec).

Many of these same points apply when children perform for other children. Also, when this occurs, there is the added element of excitement (and possible distraction) that children may experience when seeing other children perform in costume and in role. For this reason, teachers may find it worthwhile to discuss with children what it means to be a 'good' audience member before the children see the show.

In summary, the nature of the child audience needs to be understood by those who perform for young people. In particular, actors should not 'talk down' to children but regard their reactions as honest reflections of their responses to the stage action. As performers for children, actors need to be flexible and develop skills for managing audience participation in order to ensure that the performance flows smoothly, yet at the same time gives children opportunities to respond in active ways.

The performance space

Consideration of the performance space is a critical factor when staging a children's theatre performance. There are many options, although not all of them will be available in every situation. The most usual spaces are on the stage behind the picture frame formed by the proscenium arch; on the floor below the stage using the curtain as a backdrop (appropriate in some school hall situations); on a **thrust stage** (also called an open stage or apron stage) where the stage extends into the audience who see the action from three sides; and **in-the-round** (also called an arena stage) where the actors are in the middle of the space and the audience encircles them (Rodgers & Rodgers 1995).

The director has the responsibility for blocking the show; in other words, telling the actors how to move around the performance space. Stage Terminology (Concept Box 13.5) provides some of the terminology directors use to communicate with actors during rehearsals.

Concept Box 13.5

Stage terminology

Parts of the stage
- **Offstage**: areas not seen by the audience.
- **Onstage**: the space where the performance occurs.
- **Opposite prompt**: the opposite side of the stage from the prompt corner.
- **Prompt corner**: (also known as the stage manager's desk) from where the stage manager 'calls' the show (i.e. gives the cues).
- **Wings**: offstage areas to the stage right and stage left; the usual places from where actors enter or exit.

Stage directions
- **Centre stage**: in the middle of the stage.
- **Downstage**: towards the front of the stage.
- **Stage left**: the left side of the stage from an actor's perspective facing the audience.

- **Stage right**: the right side of the stage from an actor's perspective facing the audience.
- **Upstage**: towards the back of the stage.

(This terminology is particularly relevant for a proscenium arch stage as seen in this drawing.)

UR upstage right
UC upstage centre
UL upstage left
CR centre stage right
C centre stage
CL centre stage left
DR downstage right
DC downstage centre
DL downstage left

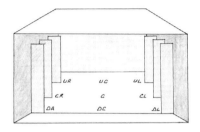

Figure 13.8 A proscenium arch stage showing the parts of the stage

This box includes information from the *Encyclopedia of Acting Techniques* (Perry 1997) and the *Play Director's Survival Kit* (Rodgers & Rodgers 1995).

In summary, the type of performance space, its shape and size, have an impact on the overall production. These factors can affect: the nature of the actor/audience interaction; whether amplification is needed; if there is an orchestra, where it will be placed; whether scenery not in use can be 'flown' into the **fly loft** or needs to be shifted offstage into the wings; and how many seats are available for the audience—to give a few examples. Directors, designers and performers all need to take into consideration the strengths and limitations of the space and work within these constraints in order to produce an effective children's theatre production.

Performing a children's play

Each time a play is performed it varies because there are different children and, as a result, the actors' interactions with the audience change. Actors soon come to realise that each performance is unique. In Performance Reflections (Concept Box 13.6), student teachers who performed the same children's play a number of times in different situations reflect on their experiences.

Concept Box 13.6

Performance reflections

What I learned about performing:

Figure 13.9 Young people meet the cast of *Tales from the Golden Chair*

- 'Warm-ups are essential' (Matt); 'Warm-ups focus your mind on the character' (Linda).
- 'One thing that is hard to do is when you make a mistake to keep going—to not let the audience know' (Jill).
- 'Even when you do forget lines, energy is the essential element; it will carry the show' (Bec).

What I learned about interacting with the audience:

- 'Exaggerating reactions and lines really involved the audience as well as making them stay focused' (Jacqui).
- 'Actors need to stop and wait until the audience has finished laughing or clapping [before they continue] so the story isn't lost halfway through' (Jacqui).
- 'Children love the interaction as we "walk through" the audience in character' (Matt).

What I learned overall:

- 'Working with a group helps develop a team dynamic' (David).
- 'It is important to have consistency in a performance and to regard each performance as a new one' (Jill).
- 'I found it interesting how teachers say, "Thank you—I've never seen my students sit still for so long"' (Jill).

An extended example of a children's theatre script with accompanying drama workshops is provided in Appendix 4. The script, *All in Good Time*, was adapted for younger children from the well-known Hans Christian Andersen story, *The Ugly Duckling* and performed by student teachers for children. Costumes for *All in Good Time* (Concept Box 13.7) shows the adaptable costume design used in a student teacher performance for children that enabled a quick transformation of Baby from cygnet to swan.

Concept Box 13.7

Costumes for *All in Good Time*

Baby is transformed from a cygnet to a swan by adding a white feather boa and hood to the original costume. (Costume design by Annabel Robinson.)

Figure 13.10 (a) (From left) Fluffy, Baby and Duffy (b) Baby as a swan

The script, *All in Good Time,* is divided into six parts with an introductory drama workshop for each one. These workshops focus on developing characterisations, exploring movement and learning the songs in the play, as well as building children's confidence as actors. The script and workshops as presented in Appendix 4 suggest a process that can be used by the teacher (as a beginning director) to work with children (as beginning actors) to produce a children's theatre production.

Preparing *All in Good Time* (From the Classroom 13.3) recounts one teacher's experience with the first workshop and script section.

From the Classroom 13.3

Preparing *All in Good Time*

A teacher's perspective

The twenty-one third graders sat in a circle as I explained that we were going to do a play called *All in Good Time,* based on the story of *The Ugly Duckling*. When I asked how many of them had heard this story, most of them had. Specifically, they remembered how the animals were mean to the ugly duckling and how he finally changed into a swan.

During Drama Workshop No. 1, the children enjoyed being little ducklings waiting to hatch. They accompanied their hatching with appropriate movements and sounds. This activity requires enough space to enable each child to have enough room to spread out.

We then read Scene 1 going around in a circle with each child reading one line. Most children read softly. (Working on projection and vocal expression would be a productive next step for these children.) Because of time constraints, I told the rest of the story to them using different voices for the various characters, which they enjoyed because they were asked to contribute actions and sounds when appropriate.

Figure 13.11 In this drawing Rebecca brought her own experience to the story by colouring the swan black rather than white.

When asked to draw the favourite part of the session, twelve of the children's drawings focused on the transformation of Baby into a swan.

Rebecca's picture demonstrates the power of her own visualisation of the story. Although I showed the children pictures of white swans, characteristic of Denmark where the story originated, she chose to colour her swan black, the colour of swans more commonly seen in Australia. In this way Rebecca brought her own experience to the story.

This imaginative drawing (unsigned) depicts Baby as a swan with elaborate silken-feathered wings. The student effectively captures the transformation that has occurred.

Figure 13.12 The caption in the drawing reads: 'When the swan went in the air happily with the other lovely swans.'

The children enjoyed revisiting a story most of them already knew. They participated in the workshop actively and related what they had learned to the script as they read and performed it.

In summary, putting on a play is a holistic way to engage children, build their drama skills, and enhance their talents in the performing and related arts. When the preparation for a performance is accompanied by drama workshops, the depth of visualisation and characterisation is enhanced and students gain a more in-depth understanding of the play and its possibilities.

Applications for middle school students

Consistent with the middle school aim of developing collaboratively organised learning is a theatre company approach to drama. Having students organise themselves into a theatre company gives them a structure within which to achieve common goals that this community sets together. Within the framework, participants choose flexible roles (e.g. actor, director, stage manager, designer) that change with each production so students experience theatre from a wide range of perspectives. Students learn about the audition, rehearsal, performance and production processes while working towards a performance or a series of performances. The advantage of a 'company' approach to drama is that it enables students to learn within an authentic context (e.g. simulated theatre context), gives them a voice in how this learning occurs, and introduces them to a team environment through which they achieve shared goals.

Older students may wish to extend their theatrical knowledge by developing directing skills. These skills require an understanding of how to apply drama elements to performance and a willingness to work with actors to block a play. In addition, the director consults the various designers (i.e. costume, set, lighting) to create a unified concept for the production. Directing a play gives older students an opportunity to fulfil their visualisations for a play by assuming the role of group leader, thus fulfilling one of Maslow's basic human needs (i.e. being a group member and having a valued role within the group).

In learning how to direct a play, adolescents may benefit from a **cognitive apprenticeship** approach (Poston-Anderson & Potter 2003, 2002; Merriam & Caffarella 1999, p. 243). This involves first working with a director who already has these skills, perhaps as an assistant director. As the novice gains confidence, over time the mentor withdraws until the student performs the role alone. Brandt, Farmer and Buckmaster (1993) have divided the cognitive apprenticeship process into five phases: 'modelling', where the learner observes the expert; 'approximating', where the learner reflects on the model and tries the skill with guidance from the mentor; 'fading', where the mentor decreases the coaching and scaffolding of the learner; 'self-directed learning', where the learner practises what has been learned; and 'generalizing', where the learner applies what has been learned in different situations.

Unlike novels, short stories or essays written for individual reading, plays are meant to be shared aloud and performed. This point has important implications for older students, in particular, who are often introduced to play scripts as a 'genre of literature' and as literary artefacts for analysis. Privileging the play 'as literature' over the play 'as theatre' overlooks the fact that a play is more than words on a page and that it is through performance that it 'lives'. For this reason, as students read plays they need ample opportunities to engage with the characters and the action of a script through role play, improvisation and performance.

What scripts to select for performance is a worthwhile question to consider when working with adolescents. At school, older students often read and perform scripts that are chosen for them to extend their thinking and life experience. While this is a worthwhile goal, adolescents also benefit from producing plays for children. Performing plays based on stories they enjoyed at a younger age heightens their enjoyment while at the same time developing skills needed to perform for a younger age group. The point here is not to limit the selection of plays to those that only challenge the student, but to extend the choice to a wide range of plays from those based on children's stories to those that deal with more mature themes. Giving adolescents a choice in the plays they read and perform empowers them.

Summary

When children participate in a children's theatre production or attend one produced for them by others, they gain insight into the artistry and team effort that is required. These experiences give children the opportunity to increase their appreciation of performance as an art form. To this end, Goldberg (1974) contends that 'the goal of children's theatre is to provide the best possible theatrical experience for the audience ... using all the techniques and principles of the theatre'.

For further study

1   Develop a play script for children based on a folktale. Write several versions. First, write the script from a traditional viewpoint that is close to the original tale. Second, update the story, writing it from one of the following orientations: a feminist main character, a social justice theme, a realistic tone, a futuristic setting, or a perspective of your own choosing.

2   Choose one of the pictured characters (or a character from a play you know) and develop a character profile; then develop and present a brief monologue through which you demonstrate your understanding of this character's personal history, social situation, physical characteristics, mannerisms and psychological state.

Refer to the 'story' in which each character appears as source material.

- Queen Mother (i.e. Queen Dowager) in Hans Christian Andersen's *The Princess and the Pea* (1974, 1835).
- The Mouse Family in *Mouse's Marriage* (1987, 1985), retold by Anne Ingram.
- Crocodile in J.M. Barrie's *Peter Pan* (2000, 1911).

Figure 13.13 (a) Queen Mother (b) Mouse Family (c) Crocodile

1   Attend a children's theatre performance at a school, theatre or community venue. Use the following questions to guide your analysis of this production.

   (a) What was the name of the play and what were its themes? Was it an appropriate choice as a production for children? Explain.

   (b) What types of characters were in the play? Did the children relate to them? Explain.

   (c) What responses did the children make during the performance? Do you think these reactions were appropriate? Explain.

   (d) How did the actors interact with the children? Did they handle this interaction effectively? Explain.

   (e) What suggestions would you make to improve the actor/audience relationship in this performance?

(f) How would you rate this performance as a children's theatre production? Consider the acting, directing, costumes, sets, lighting and sound, including music. Rate each component using this scale:

1 (poor)   2 (fair)   3 (average)   4 (good)   5 (excellent)

Explain the reasons for your evaluation.

- What rating would you give this performance overall? Explain.

For reflection

Teachers, particularly those with some drama background or experience, are often asked to direct a school play. What skills (e.g. theatrical, organisational, other) would be required to do this? Which of these skills do you currently have? What skills would you need to acquire? What strategies can you use to gain the skills you need to direct a children's play at school?

Preview

Chapter 14: Theatrical Traditions: Appreciating and Responding considers some of the rich theatre traditions that contribute to the understanding and appreciation of drama as an art form. Examples show how to draw on these traditions in drama work with young people.

Theatrical Traditions: Appreciating and Responding

'Theatre is not words on a page. Theatre is performance' (Fortier 2002).

Introduction

Making time for children to respond to drama through 'viewing, talking, reading, and writing' (Boyle et al 2002) is important for their aesthetic growth. When students 'describe, reflect, and analyse their own drama work and that of others' (Board of Studies NSW 2000), they undertake a process of critical engagement that deepens perspective, heightens appreciation, and, ultimately, enhances learning. Such critical engagement requires that they develop **multi-literacies** in order to think critically, interpret text and visuals perceptively, speak about issues convincingly, and effectively use the media of print, photography, video and computer graphics to respond to dramatic works, whether they be from the past or the present.

When students act as audience members, drama critics and theatre researchers, they extend their own personal experience to embrace the broader social, cultural and historical meanings embedded within dramatic works and their performances. For this reason, an understanding of historical and cultural drama traditions, albeit at an introductory level, can enrich both students' understandings and their own drama experiences. This chapter examines ways to draw on this rich theatrical tradition when working with primary school students using the themes: rituals and processions; mysteries and miracles; humour and spontaneity; and language and spectacle. Under each heading a particular theatre period or cultural tradition will be highlighted.

Rituals and processions

Rituals and processions linked to religious rites were an important part of the theatrical tradition for ancient Greeks. In fact, the origin of theatre is associated with ritualistic ceremonies honouring the gods, particularly Dionysus. As early as 534BC, a contest for dramatists was held, won by the playwright, actor, director and producer, Thespis. This prize earned him a place in history because modern actors still call themselves 'Thespians' in his honour (Nagler 1952).

For the ancient Greeks, theatre was connected to life. Plays taught them about human frailty and fallibility, how even the greatest among them could be brought low by 'hubris' (i.e. overweening pride). Tragedies (drawn from well-known stories about heroes and their relationships with the gods and goddesses) and comedies (with their political satire) were enacted in open-air amphitheatres at festival time and performed by a limited number of actors (traditionally three) wearing masks. A chorus supported these actors through words and movement that commented on the action, advised the characters, responded emotionally and physically to what was happening, and provided a bridge between scenes.

The performance space, called the **orchestra** (i.e. 'dancing place'), originally had an altar in the centre. Later, a **skene** or stage building to which actors could retire or from which they could enter was added and formed a background for the orchestra on the side away from the seating (i.e. **theatron,** the 'seeing place'). The side wings of the skene were called the **paraskenia** and the space between these and the seating space formed passageways, the **parodoi,** which served as entrances for the chorus and actors as they processed into the orchestra (Brocket 1979). Gradually over time, what began as rituals and processions in honour of the gods developed into the 'formalised acting out of myths' (Waters 2001).

Still today ritual and procession are powerful concepts that add depth and significance to drama work. In modern plays, when ritual (defined as a formal procedure or ceremony) is used, a pattern becomes recognisable for the audience. The effect can be one of awe (e.g. a religious procession), grandeur (e.g. a coronation ceremony), anticipating action (e.g. a clown applies make-up in front of the audience as a prelude to performing), and even impending doom (e.g. a warrior farewells his comrades before battle). Create a Ceremony (Activity Box 8.15) provided an opportunity for children to explore everyday rituals and to develop ceremonies of their own. Revisiting this exercise can provide children with a basis for understanding what a ritual is and why it is important.

On the stage, as in real life, processions suggest that something worth watching is happening; for example, the pageantry of courtiers entering by rank into a king's throne room or the disheartenment of convicts linked together in a chain gang. When a procession occurs within a play, it attracts the audience's attention because a group of characters (e.g. people, animals, animated objects), even though they are separate individuals, join together for a common purpose. Processions can entertain, as when circus performers parade energetically through the aisles, or can confront, as when weeping mourners solemnly follow a funeral cortege across the stage. The overall effect depends on how well the procession is integrated into the play and portrayed through stage action.

Many Greek myths and other traditional stories from early times, such as Aesop's fables (see Story and Script Box 5.1: Who is Responsible?: *The Ant and the Grasshopper*), remain meaningful today because they convey values and lessons that transcend their own time and place. Many of these tales adapt well for drama work with children. Snakes Alive! (Story and Script Box 14.1) uses an incident from the Greek myth of Perseus to explore ritual and procession as well as to highlight a hero who overcomes impossible odds to achieve his goals.

Story and Script Box 14.1

Snakes alive! (theatre-in-the-round)

Task

Improvise a play from the following four scenes that tell the story of how Perseus defeats the snake-haired monster, Medusa.

Figure 14.1 The head of Medusa

Scene 1

At his court in Seriphos, evil King Polydectês challenges the hero Perseus to journey to the land of darkness and bring him back the head of Medusa, a fearful Gorgon (i.e. monster) who has snakes for hair. Perseus accepts the test; then, with ceremony, sets off on his quest.

Scene 2

The goddess Athena appears to Perseus. After he greets her with ritual reverence, she discloses a dreadful secret. Whoever gazes directly at Medusa will turn into stone. Athena gives Perseus a leather bag and a shiny shield. She instructs him to approach Medusa walking backwards and to look only at the monster's reflection in the shield in order to escape being turned into stone. Only then will Perseus be able to overcome the Gorgon. Athena disappears and Perseus practises the procedures he will use when he meets Medusa.

Scene 3

Perseus locates Medusa in the land of darkness and, with his shield and sword in readiness, walks backward, sneaking up on her. When she turns her fiery eyes on him, his back is turned and he sees only her reflection in the shield. He strikes the death blow, secures her head, and puts it in the leather bag. Then he ceremoniously gives thanks to Athena for her support.

Scene 4

Perseus arrives unexpectedly back at the court of evil King Polydectês. The wicked King demands to see Medusa's head, so Perseus obligingly pulls it from the leather bag. The King gazes at it in terror and is instantly turned into stone. Then the goddess Athena appears to reclaim her shield and leather bag. She takes Medusa's head and fastens it to her shield, so that whenever she meets enemies in battle, she can turn them to stone. The court celebrates with rituals and a grand procession to celebrate their deliverance from wicked King Polydectês.

Put the following elements into the play:

1 The main characters:
   - Perseus, a brave hero who goes on a quest;
   - Athena, a clever, war-like goddess;

- Medusa, a vicious Gorgon whose gaze turns people into stone; and
- King Polydectês, an evil ruler who plots against Perseus.

2 A chorus. Divide the chorus into two sections (A and B) that respond to each other, the characters and the audience. This response may use voice and/or movement and may comment on the action, provide advice to Perseus, react emotionally, or be used to provide scene transitions.

3 Include at least one procession. For example, the chorus become supplicants who appear one by one before the King; or the grand procession to celebrate the downfall of the wicked king.

4 Include at least one ritual. For example, what are the standard preparation procedures that Perseus uses to ready himself for his fight with Medusa? Or, alternatively, what is the ritual that Medusa follows to enchant people when they gaze at her?

Present the improvised play in-the-round to suggest that it is taking place in the orchestra of an ancient Greek amphitheatre. If possible, take students outside and seat the audience on a hillside while the actors perform below.

Mentor note

- Divide into small groups to develop ideas for the processions and rituals.
- Try out the procession ideas as one large group.
- With rituals, have one group teach the others. After workshopping the ideas, decide as a large group which ones you will use in the improvised play.
- You may wish to use instrumental music to accompany the processions because it helps to create an appropriate mood and keep the participants in character.
- Costume the play, dressing the main characters and chorus in either traditional (e.g. robes) or contemporary clothes (e.g. contrasting colours to differentiate main characters from the chorus).
- Show students the drama masks for comedy and tragedy. Have children create masks in keeping with the traditions of ancient Greek tragedies for their characters.

Extension

Introduce children to the ideas of Aristotle, who lived in Greece in the fourth century BC, and wrote a book called *Poetics,* which is still regarded as 'the most fundamental study of the art of drama' (Fergusson 1961). In it, he discusses the characteristics of tragedy and comedy as he experienced them in his day.

Sources
Be aware that the Perseus myth summary presented in this Story and Script Box is in abbreviated form. Find the story of Perseus (Hutton 1993) and read about all the trials he faced when defeating Medusa.

Appreciating and responding
- Have you ever faced an impossible task? Did you achieve your goal? What help did you receive from others? Tell the story.
- Read other stories from Greek mythology, such as: How Troy was defeated (i.e. 'The Trojan Horse') or How the Seasons came to be ('The story of Persephone'). Develop a 'one-minute' play that shows the main events.
- Storytellers in times past, called **bards**, preserved the tales of mighty heroes in song. Create a **ballad** (i.e. a story-based song) about the brave deeds of Perseus or another hero you know. Perform your ballad for others.

In summary, drawing on elements of ancient Greek theatre can add dignity, grandeur, and significance to a performance. The pattern of a ritual repeated at key turning points in the plot can provide emphasis and structure, while a procession can focus audience attention and add spectacle, hilarity, or solemnity, depending on its purpose.

Mysteries and miracles

In medieval times, there was no universal literacy, so priests, with the help of their assistants, chanted the liturgy as a means of sharing Bible 'mysteries and miracles' with their flock of worshippers (Wickham 1987). Later, as re-enactments became more elaborate and secular elements were added, these early religious plays were moved from the church sanctuary into the courtyard. Eventually, with the rise of trade guilds, the plays were staged on **pageant wagons** that were rolled through the city streets. Each guild, comprised of individuals in the same trade (e.g weavers, tanners), was responsible for one part of the **play cycle**. If spectators had the stamina to stand in one of the designated spots around town on the chosen day(s), they would see Bible stories from Creation to the Final Judgment re-enacted. These dramatisations ensured that all people, from commoner to the privileged few, had access to the religious message. Later these plays were collected into what became known as cycles of **mystery and miracle plays** (e.g. York, Wakefield), often named for the city in which they were performed (Beadle & King 1984; Rose 1961).

Simulate this style of drama presentation by placing a platform in the classroom and decorating it as a pageant wagon (whether or not it has wheels). With the children, choose a traditional or contemporary story to develop into a play cycle. (The story does not need to have religious content, although it helps if it is episodic.) Divide the story into segments and assign one segment to each group of four to six students. Each group then develops, rehearses and performs its segment as part of the overall story sequence.

During the performance, seat everyone around the raised platform (i.e. pageant wagon) that becomes the players' performance space. Have each small group start its segment in a still photograph that comes to life and then returns to a picture at the end of the scene. As an added challenge, assign each group an occupation to advertise within its segment; for example, in *Rain, Rain, Go Away!* (Story and Script Box 14.2), the weavers' guild, who present the first segment, advertise their trade by making Noah too busy supervising his family's weaving to pay attention to God's warning. Consider linking the episodes using a song or chant that those around the perimeter of the performance space sing as one group leaves the platform and another assumes its opening position.

Story and Script Box 14.2

Rain, Rain, Go Away! (pageant wagon theatre)

Refrain

Voices 1: Noah, Noah,
built an ark.

Voices 2: Noah, Noah,
built an ark.

Figure 14.2 Noah's ark

Voices 1: Then the rain came tumbling, tumbling down.

Voices 2: Then the rain came tumbling, tumbling down.

Everyone: The rain came tumbling down!

1   *The Weavers' Guild*: Noah works in the fields with his family. The Lord appears telling him the big rains are coming and he should build an ark. A too-busy-to-listen Noah ignores the warning.

Refrain

2   *The Carpenters' Guild*: When it starts to rain, Noah remembers that the Lord told him to build an ark. Noah's wife is displeased that Noah has waited so long to begin. Together they call their friends asking them to help build the ark, but they mock Noah and his wife, saying they are foolish. When they leave, Noah and his wife build the ark themselves.

Refrain

3   *The Harness Makers' Guild*: Noah herds the animals into the ark, two by two with the help of his wife. He tries to make sure that every species is represented. Some of the elephants have trouble getting up the gangplank.

Refrain

4   *The Pot Makers' Guild*: The rain pelts down. The ship rocks back and forth. Noah and his wife get seasick. Noah decides to send a dove out of the window reasoning that if the water is receding, the bird will not return. To their disappointment, the dove comes back. Now they really do feel sick.

Refrain

5   *The Tanners' Guild*: The animals in the ark are getting tired of being cooped up. At first, they are only noisy, but then they begin to rampage. Noah and his wife need all their energy to keep them from rocking the boat and sinking it. Finally, they get them under control.

Refrain

6   *The Rope Makers' Guild*: Noah and his wife are bored. They know every cubit of the ark. They've paced it for forty days and forty nights! Suddenly, the rain stops. Noah and his wife can't believe it. Noah sends out the dove again. This time it does not return.

Refrain

7   *The Brick Layer's Guild:* Noah and his wife joyfully lower the gangplank and the animals return to land. Up in the sky is a beautiful rainbow, the Lord's promise that never again will there be such a flood to destroy the earth. Noah and his wife build an altar of thanksgiving.

Refrain

Voices 1: Noah, Noah built an ark.

Voices 2: Noah, Noah built an ark.

Voices 1: When the rain stopped tumbling, tumbling down.

Voices 2: When the rain stopped tumbling, tumbling down.

Everyone: Noah thanked and praised his Lord.

Source
A written text for *Noah's Flood*, performed by the Fishers and Mariners, as part of the York cycle, can be found in Beadle and King's *York Mystery Plays* (1984).

Appreciating and responding
Use this same strategy to turn any story that contains a series of episodes into pageant wagon theatre or, as an alternative, find a collection of stories about the same character and present them as a play cycle; for example, the African 'Anansi' stories (see Story and Script Box 11.2 and Appendix 2.) Sequence the stories using music, body percussion and movement as appropriate.

When performing this style of theatre, a performance platform in the classroom has advantages because it raises the actors above the audience giving them prominence. When placed in the centre of the room with the audience sitting around it on the floor, this stage enables everyone to see the action.

Humour and spontaneity

Humour and spontaneity add sparkle to a drama performance. Italian street theatre of the sixteenth century, called **commedia dell' arte** (i.e. 'comedy of artists'), was lively and boisterous with its comic **stock characters**, known by such names as Arlecchino or Harlequin, Il Capitano, Panatalone, Pulcinella,

Isabella and Colombina—to name a few. These exaggerated character types, called 'masks', traded insults, were involved in subterfuge and intrigue, and romped their way through the sketchy scenarios that guided their performances. Each character had a unique voice and movement as well as 'lazzi' or stage business (e.g. sneezing, tripping, dropping a handkerchief or fluttering a fan), 'burle' (character interactions), 'battute' (stock banter and wordplay) and 'concetti' (stock speeches and monologues) (Rudlin 1994, p. 55). To construct each performance, actors drew on these elements and their knowledge of the character and how he or she would be likely to interact with the other 'masks'. These troupes of actors, expert at improvising, singing, dancing, miming and juggling, travelled from town to town performing in marketplaces and at village fairs.

The element of broad comedy, based on exaggerated characters and lively action, and the **street theatre** interactivity make this performance style accessible to children. Stories with madcap characters and outlandish plots can be readily adapted to this style; for example, the riotous tale of *Gammer Gurton's Needle*. The original comedy, thought to be one of the earliest plays recorded in English, dates back to 1533. The scenario in *Gammer Gurton's Needle* (Improvised Street Theatre) (Story and Script Box 14.3) is an abbreviated children's version that focuses on a limited number of characters engaged in slapstick humour and melodramatic action.

Story and Script Box 14.3

Gammer Gurton's Needle (improvised street theatre)

Figure 14.3 Gammer Gurton with her cat Gib

Task

Develop a performance based on this scenario. Emphasise the comic nature of the characters and the situations enhancing them through exaggerated voice and movement.

Characters

- Gammer Gurton, a busybody and gossip
- Hodge, her dim-witted servant

- Gib the cat, a stalker and milk-drinker
- Diccon, the prankster
- Dame Chat, another busybody and gossip
- Rat, the arresting officer
- Townspeople

Scenario

1 *A stitch in time saves nine*
   Gammer Gurton, a fearsome Dame, mends her servant Hodge's trousers with her favourite needle. She cautions him to hold still; he tells her to hurry and be careful with the needle.

2 *Crying over spilt milk*
   The cat Gib stalks the milk on the stove and pounces on it. As she starts to lap it up, the distracted Gammer Gurton loses the needle. She screams at the cat, chasing it around the kitchen and out the door.

3 *Like searching for a needle in a haystack*
   'I can't find my needle!' cries Gammer Gurton. 'Hodge, find my needle for me!' Hodge looks up; Hodge looks down; Hodge looks everywhere, but the needle cannot be found. 'Oh, fie! Oh, woe!' cries Gammer Gurton. 'It was my favourite needle!' Huge tears roll down her cheeks as she sobs loudly.

4 *The untruth*
   Diccon, the prankster, overhears the commotion at Gammer Gurton's cottage, and goes to Dame Chat, her neighbour, announcing, 'I've got news for you!' Dame Chat tells him to go away because she is caring for her chickens. Diccon persists. 'Gammer Gurton lost her needle and says YOU stole it!' 'What?' screams Dame Chat so loudly that her chickens fly the coop. Now she's so angry she throws things around the room, before racing out the door to find Gammer Gurton.

5 *The fight*
   Dame Chat is angry. 'You said I stole your needle!'
   At first Gammer Gurton protests. 'I did not!' Then she sneers, 'I bet you did!'
   The argument begins: Did not! Did! Did not! Did! Next the furious fight begins. What hits! What kicks! What knocks! Finally Dame Chat gets in one big hit. Down goes Gammer Gurton—out cold!

6 *The arrest*
   Rat comes to arrest Dame Chat, but he fears her ferocious temper, so he crawls down the chimney to surprise her. When Dame Chat sees him covered

in chimney dust, she thinks he's a burglar who has come to steal her chickens. She screams and grabs her broom. 'Take that, thief! And that! And that!' Rat scurries away.

7   *All's well that ends well*

Diccon confesses to spreading the unfounded rumour. He is in trouble with everyone until he distracts them by pretending to find the needle. He says, 'I see the needle!' 'Where?' demands Hodge bending over to take a closer look where Diccon points. The prankster brings his hand down with a SMACK on Hodge's backside. 'Ow!' cries Hodge. 'Why did you stick a pin in me?' He pulls it out. In truth, he has found Gammer Gurton's needle where she left it—in his trousers.

8   *Oh happy day!*

Everyone in the town square buzzes with the news that Gammer Gurton, who lost her needle, now has found it.

Performance notes

PREPARATION

Begin by dividing the group into pairs (A and B) who work in shared space together and do not intrude on the space of other pairs.

Share each scenario in turn and have all the pairs improvise with sound and movement at the same time. Encourage them to exaggerate the action. Have them do the scene and then ask them to do it again 50 per cent larger than the first time. Remind them to make their movements simple and clear. Every movement needs purpose. This entire process will be lively, animated and noisy, so together agree on a signal to regain the students' attention.

Because the scenario contains a 'humorous' stage fight, teach the students in partners how to do a 'stage slap' in which no physical contact is made between actors and the sound of the slap is made by the 'slapper' or 'slappee' hitting another part of their bodies (e.g. leg). Also, practise creating a fight in slow motion where no contact is made between the antagonists.

PERFORM A STREET THEATRE IMPROVISATION

Assign one pair to take each scenario (1–7). This means that everyone is a main character in one scene and is a townsperson when other groups perform. (The mentor may need to repeat the process and perform the play twice if there are more than fourteen students.)

Designate an identifiable space as the town square. Have students enter the space one at a time until it is filled with townspeople. Accompany their walking with appropriate medieval or early Renaissance music. When the mentor stops the music, the first scene begins. Everyone stops where they are and watches the actors in scene 1 perform. When this scene finishes, the mentor starts the music again and the townspeople continue to walk around the square until the music stops again. Then the actors in scene 2 present it as townspeople watch from all sides. This continues until scene 7 finishes. When the music stops for scene 8, everyone interacts with each other until the music begins again. Then one by one the townspeople leave the square until it is empty again.

EXTENSIONS

Share with children part of The Prologue from the 1533 play of *Gammer Gurton's Needle,* written in middle English. Have them see if they can decipher what the words mean. (Read the words aloud, because some of them sound similar to modern English even though they are spelled differently.)

Gammer Gurton's Needle

(1533)

The Prologue

As Gammer Gurton with manye a wyde styche

Sal pesynge & patching of Hodg her mans briche

By chance of misfortune as shee her geare tost

In Hodge lether bryches her needle shee lost.

When Diccon the bedlem had hard by report

That good Gammer Gurton was robde in thyssorte,

He quietly perswaded with her in that stound

Dame Chather deare gossip this needle had found.

GLOSSARY

bedlem	'madcap' or zany person
Dame Chather	Dame Chat
hard by report	heard by report
lether bryches	leather trousers (britches)

mans briche	man's trousers (britches)
manye a wyde styche	many a wide stitch
perswaded	persuaded
pesynge	piecing
robde in thyssorte	robbed in this way
shee her geare tost	she her gear tossed
stound	situation

Sources

The full play script of this play in middle English can be found at 'The E Server Drama Collection' at the website <http://www.drama.server.org/plays/medieval/gammer-gurton.txt>.

A colourful picture book version of Gammer Gurton's Needle entitled *The Ridiculous Story of Gammer Gurton's Needle* (1987), is retold by David Llyod and illustrated by Charlotte Voake.

For older students

Learn more about commedia dell' arte as a theatre form and its stock characters. Develop scenarios for performance. An in-depth resource for the mentor in this process is Rudlin's *Commedia dell' Arte: An Actor's Handbook* (1994).

What student teachers said

- 'I thought it was a great way to introduce the commedia dell' arte style because "Gammer Gurton's Needle" gives a general impression of its characteristics' (Elisa).
- 'The Gammer Gurton play started very small and was manageable with pairs acting out each scene. Then when it was all put together it was entertaining, challenging and rewarding for everyone' (Nickola).
- 'I really liked going through each scene separately before putting it all together. [It's] good for students who don't have confidence, giving them time to think and explore ideas. Music was also helpful in setting the mood' (Julie).
- 'Putting together the Gammer Gurton scenes with the crowd stopping to watch is an activity you could do with the class or even as an assembly item. [It is]

something different, rather than the standard stage production—enjoyable to act as well as to watch' (Tracy).
- 'I loved the street theatre idea, acting in pairs amongst the rest of the class. There was a lovely feeling to it' (Katrina).
- 'This idea is definitely suitable for a primary class that can be used for any story' (Carly).

This interactive performance approach captures the excitement and thrill of street theatre where performers and audience mingle together with no barriers to separate them. In fact, it is not uncommon in this performance medium for those watching to become involved in the action.

Once familiar with the commedia dell' arte style of performance, children become attuned to modern day counterparts, such as the Punch and Judy puppet show and the various types of clown (Newton 1958, p. 39). The English hand puppet called Mr Punch is a version of the pugilistic commedia character, Pulcinella; while clowns, like the commedia 'masks', are one of a range of stock characters, such as the graceful white-face clowns or the foolish Augustes (Newton 1958, p. 12). Clowns develop stage business for their acts, similar to the 'lazzi' of the commedia, and the humour, slapstick antics and buffoonery they use are part of the tradition they inherited from their commedia dell' arte ancestors.

Language and spectacle

The dramatic works of the playwright, William Shakespeare (1564–1616), are admired worldwide for their rich language, memorable characters and compelling plots. Although the subtleties and nuances of Shakespeare's plays are most fully appreciated by adults, the problems and dilemmas that his characters confront are ones that most children can understand. Rebelling against one's parents (*Romeo & Juliet*), doing anything to get what one wants (*Macbeth*), and suffering the consequences of a malicious prank (*A Midsummer Night's Dream*) are not so far removed from everyday situations.

In Shakespeare's time, select companies of actors were named for those in high places from whom they received patronage (e.g. The Chamberlain's Men and The Queen's Men). These companies performed at court or in purpose-built theatres, such as The Swan and The Globe, which were located in London. Theatre during the reigns of Queen Elizabeth I (1558–1603) and her successor James I (1603–1625) was rich in music, dance and spectacle. At court elaborate **masques** were performed, while in the popular theatre, songs, dance sequences and instrumental music added to the dramatic entertainment (Brockett 1979).

Educationally, there is ongoing discussion about the most appropriate ways to introduce Shakespeare and his works to primary school children—or even whether it is appropriate at all. Certainly, as Winston (2003, p. 39) suggests, any involvement of younger children with Shakespeare's works will involve 'selections, choices, decisions, and interpretations with a keen eye on the audience as well as the material'.

In 'Shake it!' with Shakespeare (Story and Script Box 14.4) and continued in Appendix 5, the playlets aim to motivate children to find out more about Shakespeare and his plays by introducing them to some of his memorable characters and a few selected speeches from his plays. Each segment is presented as a mini-musical in the spirit of Elizabethan theatre with its popular music, dance and spectacle. These playlets are taken from 'With Will There's a Way' (Poston-Anderson 1999b), a children's play written as a commemoration of Shakespeare's birthday on April 23rd. In addition to the scripts and music (included in Appendix 5), each playlet has a section that encourages children 'to appreciate and to respond'.

Story and Script Box 14.4

'Shake it!' with Shakespeare (musical playlet)

Overview
The mini-musicals in this Story and Script Box and in Appendix 5 are based on scenes from three of Shakespeare's most famous plays. When direct quotations from the plays are used, they appear in **_bold italics_**.

Mentor note
Although this playlet includes lines from several scenes, it was inspired by Act 2, Scene 2 of _Romeo and Juliet_, set in the Capulet orchard.

Playlet 1: Balcony Blues (*Romeo and Juliet*)

Setting: In the Capulet Orchard, Verona, Italy
Characters: Juliet, Nurse, Romeo, his Friends, Lord Capulet and the Household Guards

(As scene opens Juliet and her Nurse are on a balcony; Romeo enters on the street below with Swordsmen.)

JULIET

(*Juliet looks down from the balcony and calls.*)

Romeo, Romeo, wherefore art thou, Romeo?

ROMEO

(*Romeo sees her and sings*)

['Sunshine Girl']

(*spoken*) **But soft!**

WHAT LIGHT THROUGH YONDER WINDOW BREAKS?

(*spoken*) **It is the east!**

AND JULIET IS THE SUN!'

JULIET IS THE SUN!

FRIENDS

THE SUN!

ROMEO

JULIET IS THE SUN!

FRIENDS

THE SUN!

FIRST HALF FRIENDS

JULIET!

                    SECOND HALF FRIENDS

JULIET!

                    FIRST HALF FRIENDS

JULIET!

                    SECOND HALF FRIENDS

JULIET!

                    ROMEO AND FRIENDS

JULIET IS THE SUN!

                         ROMEO

WHAT LIGHT THROUGH YONDER WINDOW BREAKS?

                         FRIENDS

(*spoken*) The East!

                         ROMEO

AND JULIET IS THE SUN!

                         FRIENDS

THE SUN! THE SUN!

                         ROMEO

THE SHINING SUN!

                    ROMEO AND FRIENDS

JULIET IS THE SHINING SUN!

                         NURSE

What ARE they on about, girl? You're no son—you're a daughter!

                         JULIET

Oh, Nurse! He means I'm the sun—*that celestial orb that warms the heavens and brightens the sky!*

NURSE

Nonsense! You're a girl, nothing more—nothing less! Who does that young man think he is anyway?

JULIET

He's son of Lord Montague—Romeo, my own true love.

NURSE

Not likely! He's hardly out of nappies. (*Romeo tries to climb trellis*) Fie! He'll break your father's trellis. (*to Romeo*) Shoo, you! Go before I set the guards on you. (*to Juliet*) He'll break your heart, too, my lady. Nothing good ever came of a Montague.

JULIET

What's in a name?—that which we call a rose by any other name would smell as sweet.

NURSE

Rubbish! Mark my words, my lady. That boy is trouble. He'll be the death of you!

JULIET

Don't worry, Nurse! I know what I'm doing. I'm in love!

NURSE

(*calls offstage*) Lord Capulet, come here at once!

LORD CAPULET

(*enters with household guard*) What is it?

NURSE

(*points to Romeo*) A Montague!

LORD CAPULET

(*to household guards*) After him! (*Household guards engage Romeo and his friends in swordplay with the reprise of 'Sunshine Girl' in the background. Before Romeo and Friends exit, Romeo picks a rose from the trellis and throws it to Juliet who sighs. Lord Capulet and Nurse shake their heads in dismay.*)

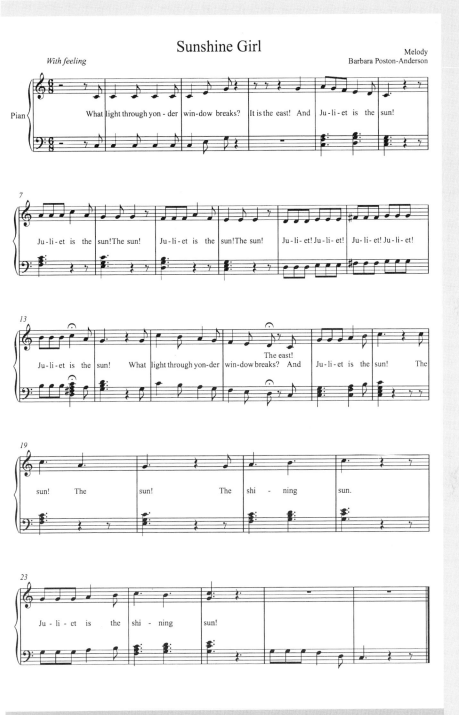

Figure 14.5 Sunshine Girl: Words and music

Appreciating and responding

Shakespeare's plays are rich in **figurative language**. Consider Romeo's line: 'What light through yonder window breaks? It is the east and Juliet is the sun.' In this metaphor, Shakespeare directly compares Juliet to the sun that rises in the east at daybreak.

Have children reflect on what this line means. Then have them develop their own metaphors for each of the other characters. Review the playlet to see what each character says and does and use these insights as a basis. Here are some examples:

- Romeo is *a branch on the Montague tree* (because he is the next generation).
- Romeo's friends are *a flock of noisy galahs* (because they are loud and boisterous).
- The Nurse is *a wet blanket* (because she tries to dampen Juliet's feelings for Romeo).
- Lord Capulet is *an angry bee* (because he buzzes at Romeo's intrusion).
- The Household Guards are *faithful dogs* (because they follow Lord Capulet, doing his bidding without question).
- Note: Additional playlets are found in Appendix 5. These are Playlet 2: King Duncan's Downfall (*Macbeth*) and Playlet 3: Tricky Business (*A Midsummer Night's Dream*).

Theatre traditions from various times and places provide children with a fascinating insight into their own culture and that of others. For this reason they offer a satisfying avenue for research, learning and enjoyment. In addition to written material, web resources, videos and films can bring these past and present theatre traditions to life. Whether it be the lively Spanish traditional musical play the **zarzuela**, the Caribbean carnival with its colourful costumes and street dancing, the Oberammergau Passion Play performed as a village tradition in Germany every ten years since 1634, or the classic Bunraku puppet theatre of Japan that uses three-quarter life-sized puppets operated by puppeteers in black, the range of type and form of performance is limitless.

Of course, theatre is at its best when it is 'live'. Taking children to see performances gives them first-hand experience of the actor-audience relationship, performance styles and techniques and stagecraft. It is through experiencing their own work and responding to that of others that children develop an appreciation of the role that drama plays in history and culture and begin to understand the contribution that the dramatic and performing arts have made and continue to make to humankind.

Applications for middle school students

One strategy for encouraging adolescents to appreciate the traditions and variations of theatrical forms is to start in the present with pop culture examples and trace their antecedents. Many contemporary artistic works are considered to be **pastiche**, meaning they are creative works that borrow, imitate or satirise another work or artistic style; for example, comic books of Shakespeare's works that put play text into cartoon blurbs (e.g. Shakespeare Graphic Library versions of *King Lear* [2006] and *Macbeth* [2005]) or computer games where characters from popular books, such as Harry Potter and the Hobbit, interact in computer-generated landscapes. Eclectic, contemporary, often technology-based or generated and drawing on 'whatever works', a pastiche is a creative synthesis that results in new artistic expressions.

Pastiche has appeal for adolescents because such works have a contemporary mixed-media 'feel' that relies on zany juxtaposition of ideas, an unabashed use of technology, and often breathtaking invention upon traditional forms and materials. Consider, for example, the performances of Cirque du Soleil, where the clowning, acrobatics and high-wire acts of the traditional circus are transformed by skilled performers into thought-provoking, visually spectacular vignettes involving colourful costumes, intricate movements and indefinite images that symbolise different things for different people.

Starting with contemporary versions of dramatic works can motivate students to return to traditional sources. For example, comparing the BBC 2006 version of Shakespeare's *A Midsummer Night's Dream* set in a local park with recognisable character-types in modern dress with contemporary problems (i.e. a broken engagement, drug-induced dreams, love lost and found) with the visually captivating and musically rich 1999 20th Century Fox movie version (starring Kevin Kline, Calista Flockhart and Michelle Pfeiffer) reveals similarities but also striking contrasts (e.g. how much of Shakespeare's language is used, portrayal of the fairies). Knowing about theatre traditions can enrich such investigations and help students see how the same theatrical conventions (e.g. script, lighting, sound, costume, set, make-up) can be treated in different ways depending on the drama form.

Adolescents can also benefit from learning about the different theatrical styles in which plays can be performed and produced. Some of these styles are: classic (i.e. formal presentation with stately movement); naturalistic (i.e. a 'slice of life' with 'warts and all'); realistic (i.e. a selective showing of life, yet true to characters' psychological motivations); melodramatic (i.e. exaggerated action with stereotyped characters, such as in traditional 'pantomime'); symbolic (i.e. with meaning conveyed by symbols); and surrealistic (i.e. dream-like quality, unreal, even 'absurd') (Gadaloff 1998, 1991). Students can increase their appreciation of the interrelatedness of the arts by comparing theatrical styles to corresponding visual arts styles. Designing a production where acting, costuming, make-up and set design all represent a consistent style is a challenging exercise for older students; for example, how can the musical, *Annie*, be produced using naturalism, realism, melodrama or surrealism? Or how could this same musical be produced as a pastiche? When older students are grounded in theatre traditions and have knowledge of theatrical styles, they are able to use these understandings to build depth into the plays that they write (or select), direct, design and produce.

Summary

Chapter 14: Theatrical Traditions: Appreciating and Responding brings this book full circle. Every age and culture has contributed to making dramatic traditions what they are today. The magnitude of the contribution that drama and the other arts have made to the wellbeing of people over time should not be underestimated. Providing entertainment, probing the great questions of life, pointing out the foibles of human nature, serving as a medium for learning and a vehicle for protest and change are all ways that drama serves humanity. Teachers who work with children in drama have the responsibility for introducing young people to drama's traditions, elements and forms and for encouraging them to make, perform, appreciate and respond to drama within the contexts of the learning environment and the broader society.

For further study

1   Examine folktales, fables and nursery rhymes. Identify ones that could be shared as: theatre in-the-round using processions and rituals, pageant wagon theatre, improvised street theatre or as a mini-musical. Choose one and develop a plan for involving children in sharing it by means of your chosen performance style.

2   In the library and on the Internet, investigate drama practice during a particular historical period or within a particular culture. (Consider choosing a non-western drama tradition from Japan, Indonesia, India or an Australian Aboriginal culture.) Develop an approach for sharing this tradition or form with primary school children.

3   Discuss how drama helps children develop multi-literacies. Provide specific examples.

For reflection

Attend a play performance and analyse the production. How does this play reflect historical and/or cultural traditions? What is the overall style of the production? Provide examples to justify your views.

Review of Part Five

Part Five: Appreciating Drama: Performance Perspectives focused on how to develop scripts for the drama forms of readers' theatre and children's theatre and stage them. In addition, theatre appreciation was encouraged through discussion of selected theatre traditions with suggestions for ways to adapt them for drama with young people.

Appendix 1

Figure A1.1 *Sense and Sustainability*: Words and music

410

Appendix 2
Anansi Stories

2.1 A Letter for Anansi

(*A traditional tale retold by B. Poston-Anderson*)

Anansi, the spider, was annoyed. 'Why does everyone receive mail, except me!' He thought until he knew the reason. 'I have no one to deliver letters to me.'

He hurried to find Snake who owed him a favour. 'Snake, will you be my postman?'

'Certainly,' hissed snake. 'What must I do?'

'Oh, it's very easy. Every day you bring me a letter.'

Crafty Snake replied, 'Yes, I will do this on one condition.'

'What is that?' asked Anansi.

'Every day you must let me bite you,' grinned Snake snapping his fangs.

Anansi thought a bite was a small price to pay for receiving a daily letter so he agreed.

The next day, Snake slithered to Anansi's door. 'Anansi!' he called. 'Here is your letter. I wrote it myself.'

Anansi was thrilled—his first letter! He grabbed it.

'Wait!' Snake reminded him. 'We have an agreement.'

'Oh, that!' Anansi lowered his head. Snake bared his fangs then bit Anansi on the top of his head.

'Yeeeow! That hurt!' cried Anansi as Snake glided away.

The next day Snake came early to Anansi's door. 'Anansi! Here is your second letter. I signed it myself.'

Anansi called from inside. 'Slip it under the door, Snake.'

'No! Open the door,' demanded Snake.

Anansi opened the door a crack and tried to grab the letter, but Snake was too fast. He bared his fangs then bit Anansi on the nearest of his eight legs.

'Yeeeow! That really hurt!' screamed Anansi. 'Don't bother to come tomorrow, Snake.'

'A deal is a deal,' hissed Snake. 'At sunrise I'll be here with another letter.'

Anansi was worried. At this rate he would be bitten to pieces.

That afternoon Rabbit hopped past Anansi's house.

'Come inside, Rabbit,' called Anansi who had a clever idea.

First Rabbit and Anansi had a chat.

Then Rabbit and Anansi sang a song.

Next Rabbit and Anansi had something to eat from a copper pot.

Finally Rabbit said to Anansi, 'It's time for me to hop along!'

'Oh, NO!' cried Anansi. 'Stay until tomorrow. I'm expecting an important letter. You can help me read it.'

'All right,' agreed Rabbit thinking what good company Anansi was.

So Anansi and Rabbit had another chat.

Then Anansi and Rabbit sang another song.

Next Anansi and Rabbit had something more to eat from a copper pot.

Finally Anansi chuckled as Rabbit fell asleep. 'When Snake comes tomorrow, Rabbit will answer the door. Snake will bite him instead of me!'

Anansi crawled into a high corner to hide and fell asleep, too.

A little later Rabbit woke with a start. 'Why am I at spider's house when I could be snug at home?' Rabbit hopped out the door and down the path.

Morning came. Snake arrived at Anansi's door with another letter.

'Anansi! Your mail is here,' Snake called.

There was no answer.

Snake shouted a little louder.

'Anansi! I have a letter for you. I licked the stamp myself.'

Still there was no answer.

Snake banged his head on the door, softly at first—then very loudly.

Anansi peered out from his hiding place. When he saw that Rabbit was gone, he cried, 'What will I do now?' He crawled frantically across the room until he reached the copper pot. He took it and put it securely on his head.

'Here I am,' called Anansi.

By this time furious Snake had fully bared his fangs. As soon as Anansi opened the door, he struck without warning. Instead of soft spider, however, his fangs bit into the hard copper of the pot on Anansi's head.

'You tricked me!' screamed Snake, spitting out his broken fangs. 'I don't want to be your postman, anymore,' he hissed as he swiftly disappeared into the bushes.

Anansi waited until Snake was well out of sight. Then he removed the pot from his head, sat in the sun, and sighed with relief, 'No more mail for me!'

Variation

Williams-Ellis 1981, 'Anansi and the snake-postman' in *The Story Spirits and Other Tales from Around the World*, pp. 81–85, Heinemann, London.

2.2 Anansi's Party Trick

(*A traditional tale retold by B. Poston-Anderson*)
Once in Africa there was a spider.

'I am Anansi. This is my drum *(beats drum)*. *(to audience)* You are ALL my children. You're drummers, too. Can you drum with me? *(everyone uses body percussion to play drums)* Can you play them loudly? Can you play them softly? What a sound! Can you play them quickly? Can you play them slowly? What a tempo! I'm counting on you to help me with this story.'

One fine day in the jungle, Lion asked Elephant, 'Would you like to come to my party?'

'Oh, yes, Lion,' trumpeted Elephant. 'I would.'

'Fine,' Lion replied, 'but don't tell Father Anansi and his children.'

'Why not?' asked Elephant.

'They eat too much.'

(to audience) 'Eat too much!' cried Anansi. 'Did you hear that? Do you think we eat too much? Of course not!'

Lion soon saw monkey swinging high above him from the branches.

'Monkey, would you like to come to my party?'

'Oh, yes, Lion,' Monkey chattered. 'I would.'

'Fine,' replied Lion. 'But don't tell Father Anansi and his children.'

'Why not?' asked Monkey.

'Because they are too noisy.'

(*to audience*) 'Too noisy!' cried Anansi. 'Did you hear that? Do you think we're too noisy? Of course not!'

A little later, Lion passed Giraffe who was stretching his neck to reach juicy leaves.

'Giraffe, would you like to come to my party?'

'Oh, yes, Lion,' Giraffe responded. 'I would.'

'Fine,' replied Lion. 'But don't tell Father Anansi and his children.'

'Why not?' inquired Giraffe.

'Because there are too many of them.'

(*to audience*) 'Too many of us!' cried Anansi. 'Did you hear that? Do you think there are too many of us? Of course not!'

When Lion roared the signal, Elephant, Monkey and Giraffe all headed toward Lion's house.

'A party! We're not invited,' grumbled Anansi. 'Don't worry—We'll use our special drums to get an invitation. Do you remember how to play them? Let me hear you. (*children play*) We'll get an invitation yet.'

At Lion's house, the party began. Lion needed water from the river to cook the food. 'Who will get some water?' asked Lion.

'I will, Lion,' Elephant replied. 'Water fits easily into my trunk.'

Elephant plodded down to the river, near where Father Anansi and his children were hiding with their drums in the tall grass.

(*to audience*) 'Come, will you help me drum?' whispered Anansi (*drumming*).

Elephant waded into the water, then stopped, 'Are those drums I hear?'

'Hello, Elephant,' called Anansi.

'Oh, hello, Father Anansi. Your drums make me want to dance. Make them stop, I have work to do.'

'When we stop—you stop,' said Anansi as the drums suddenly stopped (*drumming stops*).

There stood Elephant, his trunk lowered in the water, still as a statue.

Back at the party, Lion was annoyed. 'I wonder where Elephant is.'

'I'll find him,' volunteered Monkey.

Down Monkey came to the water and called, 'Elephant! Elephant! Where are you?'

(*to audience*) 'Help me drum slowly, now,' whispered Anansi (*drumming slowly*).

'Hello, Monkey,' called Anansi.

'Oh, hello, Father Anansi. Your drums beat slowly today.'

'We can play them faster. (*to audience*) Can't we?' (*drumming faster*)

'Stop, stop, Father Anansi. I must find Elephant.'

'When we stop, you stop,' said Anansi as the drums suddenly stopped (*drumming stops*).

There stood Monkey with his tail in the air. He couldn't move it no matter how hard he tried.

Lion roared, 'What is keeping them? If we don't cook soon, the party will be over!'

'Don't worry, Lion,' Giraffe calmed him. 'I have a long neck. I will see them wherever they are.'

Giraffe ambled down to the water, stretching her neck as far as she could. 'Elephant! Monkey!'

(*to audience*) 'Can you drum with me now quietly?' (*drumming quietly*)

'Hello, Giraffe,' called Anansi.

'Oh, hello, Father Anansi. You and your family are good musicians.'

'Yes, we can play softly like this! (*drumming softly*) Loudly like this.' (*drumming loudly*)

'Stop, stop! It's much too loud!' cried Giraffe in distress.

'When we stop, you stop,' said Anansi as the drums suddenly stopped. (*drumming stops*)

Giraffe stood still, his neck stretched out across the water.

By this time, Lion, King of the Jungle, was upset. 'Where is everyone? Elephant! Monkey! Giraffe!' he roared as he prowled toward the river.

'Hello, Lion,' called Anansi.

'Oh, hello, Father Anansi,' roared Lion in return.

'Why are you roaring?' asked Anansi.

'I'm upset. Monkey and Giraffe came to find Elephant who was sent to get water for *my party* … Oh, dear,' sighed Lion, '*You* weren't supposed to know about it.'

'Never mind, my children and I are partying here on our own by the river with Elephant, Monkey, and Giraffe.'

Lion saw his three friends, standing still like rocks—held fast by the powerful beat of Anansi's drums.

'Anansi, please, free my friends!' pleaded Lion.

'That depends!' Anansi replied.

Shaking his mane, Lion apologised. 'I'm sorry, Anansi. If you promise not to be too noisy and not to eat too much, you may come to my party.'

'Hoorah!' cheered Father Anansi and all his children. 'Thank you, Lion. We would all like to come. (*to audience*) Children, help me free the animals, then we're going to Lion's party. When I signal, drum with me. Elephant, (*drumming*) you are free. Monkey, (*drumming*) you are free. Giraffe, (*drumming*) you are free. Now we are all free to go to Lion's party!' (*Everyone drums enthusiastically until Anansi signals them to stop*).

Variation

Graff, F. 1989, 'Spider the Drummer' in H. East (comp.), *The Singing Sack*, pp. 10–12, A & C Black, London.

Appendix 3
Readers' Theatre Preparation
Workshop for *Picture Perfect*

3.1 Sharing stories

The following vignettes present incidents from Vincent Patrick Taylor's amazing career as a balloonist in Australia in the late nineteenth and early twentieth centuries. Share these vignetters with children.

What a Life!

Story 1: *Captain and the Sharks*

One day Captain Penfold went up in a balloon over Sydney. When he parachuted back to earth, he was blown off course and landed in Sydney Harbour. He was swimming around calling for help when a fishing boat rescued him. The fishermen were worried because they had recently seen sharks swimming near by. They quickly made for shore. In this way, the Captain was saved from the sharks to 'fly' another day.

Story 2: *Captain and the Train*

One day the Captain launched his balloon from a Sydney park. As he floated over the train line, the wind stopped blowing. His balloon stalled in the air over the railway tracks. When it came down, it landed right on the main train line

---

stretching from Central Station to the Western suburbs. A train approached. The train driver didn't see him! The Captain scrambled from the line just as the train sped across his balloon and tore it to shreds. Captain Penfold was safe, but that balloon never flew again.

Story 3: *Captain's Christmas Caper*

One Christmas when the Captain was visiting London, he was asked by the Sandow Chocolate Factory to dress up as Santa Claus, ascend in a balloon, and later parachute out over a nearby park to distribute chocolates to the children who would be waiting there for him. He agreed to do it. Up he went accompanied by a film crew sent to record his exploits, but then disaster struck. The fog rolled in. He couldn't see a thing! He was lost high in the air dressed as Santa Claus. Far off course, he finally parachuted to the ground, landing in a farmer's yard. There he handed out chocolates to a farmer's delighted children. They couldn't believe their luck! Christmas had come early. Santa had jumped from the clouds to bring them Christmas treats.

Story 4: *Picture Perfect*

The Captain entered a photographic studio to get his publicity photo taken, but Bert, the photographer, told him he needed an emblem for his cap to indicate his profession. The Captain raced to the fruit shop next door, cracked open a walnut, and attached one half to his cap. He thought it looked exactly like a balloon! Now the Captain had his emblem and was ready to have his photo taken.

Source: These summaries are based on accounts of the life of Captain Penfold found in the archival collections of the Mitchell Library, New South Wales State Library, Sydney.

3.2 Doing drama

Once the daring exploits of Captain Penfold found in Appendix 3.1 have been shared with children, use them as the stimulus for creating still photographs and developing improvisations.

Still life

Description

STEP 1

With four other students, choose one of the stories to create as a tableau. Caption your tableau, then share it. First your group says the caption. While everyone else closes their eyes, your group gets into position. Then the others open their eyes again to see your tableau.

STEP 2

Once this is done, with your group create the still photograph that goes before and the one that comes after the central photo. Replay the tableau in sequence (e.g. photo 1, 2, 3).

STEP 3

Link the pictures using slow motion. Start with a still photograph, then move in slow motion to the second picture, freeze, then move again to the third picture, then freeze.

STEP 4

Start in a still photograph, improvise the sound and action to accompany photo 1 to photo 3 and then end in a still photograph.

Mentor note

Introduce Still Life by constructing a **flip book**. Have children make several different line drawings of Captain Penfold in an action sequence with small variations between each picture. Put the pictures in order (i.e. what happened first to what happened last). Flip the pages of the book quickly and watch the figures animate. Indicate to the children that they will be making still photographs that change into a 'live action' sequence.

3.3 Classroom experiences: Still life captions and photographs

Here is what happened when the readers' theatre preparation workshop was run for a group of upper primary school children.

The teacher said:

'I used these ideas with a 5th Grade Class, a group of nineteen students, in a session that lasted thirty minutes. In a cleared space in the corner of the school library, I told the group the first three Captain Penfold stories. The students were impressed that the stories were 'real'.

First, the students made still photographs of incidents from the stories; then they were divided into small groups. Each selected their favourite incident within one of the stories to prepare as a tableau. Captions ranged from 'The Lucky Escape' to 'Shark Tale'. Each group in turn told the others their caption and then presented their tableau. The rest of the group closed their eyes while the presenting group set their photograph. This actually took some time as the small group adjusted their position. When the group was ready, I instructed the rest of the class to open their eyes.

The most popular tale was the story of the sharks, followed by the train incident. The students were focused on the task and each group presented a tableau, although not all groups were able to think of captions.

There was not time in this short session to do a three shot sequence. At least two more sessions would have been necessary to introduce readers' theatre and to prepare and present the readers' theatre script, *Picture Perfect*. As the students were not used to learning through drama, preparation work in movement, voice, and the characteristics of readers' theatre will be necessary before preparing and presenting the script.

Students drew their favourite moment from the stories. Here are some of their responses.'

Story 1: *Captain and the Sharks*

Figure A3.1 Students depict the incident where Captain Penfold drops in to Sydney Harbour.

Story 2: *Captain and the Train*

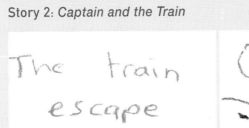

Figure A3.2 Students depict the incident where Captain Penfold lands on the train line and his balloon is run over by a train.

Story Combination

Figure A3.3 One student combined elements from two stories—depicting the film crew who went with Captain Penfold on his Santa flight (Story 3), but showing them filming the rescue from the sharks (Story 1).

Appendix 4
All in Good Time

4.1 Drama workshop and script

What follows is one example of how to integrate process drama into the preparation for a children's theatre production where students are the actors. Use it as a starting point for developing other ways of approaching the presentation of plays with and for children.

All in Good Time

(Adapted by Barbara Poston-Anderson [2000b] from Hans Christian Andersen's story, *The Ugly Duckling*)

Part 1: The barnyard

DRAMA WORKSHOP NO. 1

Mime and movement

1   Introduce the control device (e.g. drum, sound effect). Say to the children: 'When you hear this sound, freeze in place.' Have children move 'on the spot' and respond to the signal until everyone understands and is able to follow directions.

Figure A4.1 Baby with Sheep, Cow and Cat played by puppets.

---

2 Introduce the story. In their own personal space, have children explore movement as a duck. How will they waddle with webbed feet? How will they move their wings? Have children fill the space and waddle as ducks (regular speed, slow motion, quick time). Also have them change direction and level (forward, sideways, backward, down low, up high).

Voice and meaning

1 How do ducks communicate? Find a partner; one is Fluffy (A), the other is Duffy (B). Quack the following messages using only the word: Quack!
   A to B: I'm so happy to be hatched.
   B to A: I'm afraid of the cat.
   A to B: I wonder what the world is like.
   B to A: Will you be my friend?
   A to B: Yes I will.
2 A and B carry out a conversation using the word 'Quack' and their wings to communicate. They quack about:
   - The other animals in the barnyard,
   - How lovely their mother is,
   - What it's like to hatch from an egg.

Visualisation and enactment

1 Say to the children: 'Close your eyes and imagine. You are a duckling waiting to hatch curled up inside your eggshell. It is warm and safe there. Suddenly your shell begins to crack! What's happening? A draft of cold air comes inside the eggshell. You shiver. Then you start to explore. You push at the egg with your beak, then with one little wing and then with the other. You push and push and then peck at it again with your beak. Finally the egg cracks and falls apart. You start to uncurl as you breathe fresh air. You stretch out your little wings. You put one tiny webbed foot out and then the other. Stand up. Move out of the broken eggshell! Stand tall. Give one big quack. You've hatched!'
2 Have the children find their own personal space. Read the scenario about the duck hatching again. This time have the children enact it through mime.

Script reading

Before reading the script aloud, show children how to read it.

1 The character's name is centred on the page and the lines following this name are to be read by the person playing this part. If there are two names, the line is said by both characters together.

2 The words in brackets, for example, (*softly*) or (*jumps*), are directions for the actor and are not meant to be read aloud. These directions help the person playing the part know how to interpret the lines and what actions to do.

3 What is an **aside**? This is when an actor in character talks directly to the audience or to someone else onstage but the other actors purposely do not hear what he or she says. Have children experience this technique for themselves. First, establish with them where the audience is sitting. Then, form partners with one of them as Fluffy, the other as Duffy. Have them improvise a conversation about the transformation of Baby into a swan. When the mentor signals, both Fluffy and Duffy turn toward the audience and talk directly to them about the change in Baby, until the mentor signals again and they return to their original conversation with each other. Tell the children to be alert for asides in Scene 1 and throughout the script.

The script

SCENE 1: THE BARNYARD
(Characters: Mother, Fluffy, Duffy, Baby)

MOTHER

(*waddles around three unhatched eggs, fussing*) (*aside to audience*) They'll hatch any moment now. Watch and see. (*two eggs creak, groan, and hatch*) Oh! At last! Aren't they beautiful? (*to ducklings*) Little ducklings, I am your Mother. Now what shall I call you? I know! (*to Fluffy*) You are Fluffy.

FLUFFY

Quack! Quack! Quack!

MOTHER

(*to Duffy*) You are Duffy.

DUFFY

Quack, Quack, Quack!

MOTHER

Oh! Happy day!

DUFFY

(*amazed*) What a big world it is, Mother!

FLUFFY

(*unsure*) Very big!

MOTHER

Now, my dears, don't think this is everything. The world stretches far beyond the garden, far beyond the pond—then faraway across the hill.

FLUFFY, DUFFY

Have you been there, Mother?

MOTHER

No, not even I have been everywhere. Now, stay close. Don't wander or the cat will get you.

FLUFFY, DUFFY

The CAT? (*Mother nods*) OHHHHHHH

MOTHER

Follow me.

DUFFY

Where are we going, Mother?

MOTHER

To the pond for your first swim. Webbed feet out—yellow beaks up—

FLUFFY, DUFFY

Quack, quack, quack, quack, quack!

MOTHER

WAIT!

FLUFFY, DUFFY

WHAT?

MOTHER

We can't go yet!

FLUFFY, DUFFY

Why NOT?

MOTHER

My last egg is yet to hatch.

FLUFFY

How long will we wait?

MOTHER

As long as it takes.

DUFFY

That long?

FLUFFY

That egg is SO big—it will take forever.

DUFFY

(*worried*) Probably longer.

MOTHER

Be patient, little ducklings—all things happen in their own good time (*last egg quivers*).

FLUFFY

Look.

DUFFY

LOOK!

FLUFFY, DUFFY

L*O*O*K! (*Baby hatches*) OOOOHH ....

DUFFY

(*to Fluffy*) I think it's a turkey!

FLUFFY

What's a turkey?

DUFFY

(*puzzled*) I don't know.

MOTHER

(*to Baby*) Welcome to the world, Baby! We've been waiting for you.

Part 2: On the way to the pond

DRAMA WORKSHOP NO. 2

Chant

1   Children repeat the chant after the mentor, line by line.
    QUACK, QUACK, QUACK!
    RIGHT WING UP
    LEFT WING UP
    FEET OUT WIDE
    HEADS UP HIGH
    SLIDE TO THE RIGHT
    SLIDE TO THE LEFT
    SLIDE, SLIDE, SLIDE, SLIDE
2   Once the chant is learned, children stand and add duck movements. Repeat
    the verse and movements several times until the children know them.

The script

SCENE 2: ON THE WAY TO THE POND
(Characters: Mother, Fluffy, Duffy, Baby)

MOTHER

Come to the pond, my ducklings.

Quack, quack, quack! Webbed feet out, yellow beaks up!

FLUFFY, DUFFY, BABY

Quack, quack, quack! Webbed feet out, yellow beaks up!

MOTHER

QUACK, QUACK, QUACK!

RIGHT WING UP

LEFT WING UP

FEET OUT WIDE

HEADS UP HIGH

SLIDE TO THE RIGHT

SLIDE TO THE LEFT

ALL

SLIDE, SLIDE, SLIDE, SLIDE

FLUFFY

(*aside to audience*) I'm Fluffy!

DUFFY

(*aside to audience*) I'm Duffy!

BABY

Who am I?

FLUFFY, DUFFY

(*to Baby*) You're a turkey.

BABY

No, I'm not!

MOTHER

(*scolds Fluffy, Duffy*) Quack, quack, quack.

MOTHER, FLUFFY, DUFFY, BABY

QUACK, QUACK, QUACK.
RIGHT WING UP
LEFT WING UP
FEET OUT WIDE
HEADS UP HIGH
SLIDE TO THE RIGHT
SLIDE TO THE LEFT
SLIDE, SLIDE, SLIDE, SLIDE

FLUFFY

(*to Baby*) You don't look like one of us.

DUFFY

You're different.

FLUFFY, DUFFY

You MUST be a turkey!

BABY

No, I'm not.

FLUFFY, DUFFY

Yes, you are!

BABY

(*cries*) NO! I'm not!

MOTHER

(*scolds Duffy, Fluffy*) Quack, quack, quack! You two ducklings, wait at the edge of the pond. Off you go—now!

FLUFFY, DUFFY

Quack, quack, quack, quack, quack ... (*exit*)

MOTHER

(*calls*) Watch out for the cat!

Part 3: Still on the way to the pond

DRAMA WORKSHOP NO. 3

Feelings

1 Have children show with their facial expressions using a 'face wipe': sad, happy, relaxed, worried, brave, afraid.
2 Have children show with their facial expressions *and* bodies: sad, happy, relaxed, worried, brave, afraid.
3 Transformations: Have children change from happy to sad, relaxed to worried, and brave to afraid. Count to six. On each number children make a small change so that by the time they reach six they have totally transformed from one emotion to the other. Move back and forth between the emotions several times. Remind them to use their whole bodies as they transform. Also, encourage them to be as expressive as possible (see Activity Box 6.18: How do You Feel?).

Exploring voice and movement

1 What sounds does each of these animals make: cow, sheep, cat? The mentor says the animal names as children make the sounds. Move back and forth between the names several times. Have children provide different qualities to the sounds, such as a cow that's stuck in the mud or a contented cow chewing its cud.
2 Children sit in groups of six to eight and make sounds of the barnyard. The mentor beats a steady rhythm. Children choose one of the animals from the story so far (duck, cat, cow, sheep). Go around the circle, each one adding

a sound on top of the one before and making it complement the beat. When it is his or her turn, each child tries to say the chosen sound differently from others who have chosen the same animal (see Activity Box 8.16: Keep the Beat).

1 How would each of these animals move: cow, sheep, cat?
2 Each child chooses an animal. In common space they move as their animals until the mentor beats a drum. Then they change animals and move as that animal until the next time they hear the drum beat, when they change again.

The script

SCENE 3: STILL ON THE WAY TO THE POND
(Characters: Baby, Mother, Cow, Sheep, Cat)

BABY

(*sadly*) Am I a turkey, Mother?

MOTHER

No, dear, you're NOT a turkey. While it's true, you look a bit unusual for a duck, always remember you are my Baby. I love you.

COW

MOOOO—Mother duck, what do you have there?

MOTHER

One of my new ducklings, Cow. (*to Baby*) Introduce yourself, dear.

BABY

Quack.

COW

Good day. (*to Mother*) Bit strange for a baby duck, isn't he?

MOTHER

Never you mind. He'll amount to something one day.

SHEEP

Where did the ugly duckling come from?

COW

One of Mother duck's new brood.

SHEEP

BAAAAAd news, if you ask me.

BABY

(*starts to cry*)

COW

MOOOOve along, Sheep. Now you've hurt its feelings!

SHEEP

Have I? I'll cheer him up then. (*to Baby*) Say, little Fluff-face! Do you know what ducks eat for breakfast?

BABY

No.

SHEEP

Quackers! (*Sheep & Cow laugh*)

BABY

(*cries*) I don't think that's funny!

COW

(*aside to Sheep*) Oh, dear ... (*aside to audience*) MOOOdy, isn't he?

SHEEP

(*to Cow*) Now I've REALLY hurt its feelings—BAAADLY!

COW

Let's MOOOOve on, Sheep!

(*Sheep and Cow exit*)

MOTHER

Don't sniff, dear. What's important is what you are—not how you look. You wait here while I find the others.

(*Mother exits*)

CAT

(*enters, aside to audience*) Ah, ha! What is that? A tasty morsel for my breakfast. SHHHHHHHH (*sneaks up on Baby*) … Got ya! (*pounces, Baby moves, Cat misses and falls*) OOOF!

BABY

(*noticing Cat, brightly*) Good morning! Will you be my friend? (*Cat hisses*) Oh dear, you're not the cat, are you?

CAT

Me? NO! I'm a kitten!

BABY

That's all right then!

CAT

YEOWW! What are *you*?

BABY

I'm a duckling.

CAT

Really? You look like a dog's breakfast to me! (aside *to audience*) He looks so bad, who knows how he'd taste!

BABY

(*proudly*) I'll amount to something one day—Mother says.

CAT

Really? Tell me ... Can you arch your back, like this? (*demonstrates*)

BABY

No ...

CAT

Can you purr, like this? (*demonstrates*)

BABY

No ...

CAT

Can you yowl at the moon, like this? (*demonstrates*)

BABY

No ...

CAT

Not even a little?

BABY

Maybe ... I'll try! (*tries*) Quack, quack, quack, quack, quack. How's that?

CAT

(*covers ears*) MEEOOOOW! Cat-astrophic! (*Cat exits*)

BABY

Come back! Come back!

Part 4: Still on the way to the pond

DRAMA WORKSHOP NO. 4

Song

Teach the song, *So Lonely*, in Scene 4 to children line by line. (The melody is in this Appendix 4.2) Divide into two groups: Baby and the Animal Chorus. Have them sing the song through several times.

The script

SCENE 4: STILL ON THE WAY TO THE POND
(Characters: Baby, Cow, Sheep, Cat, Mother, Fluffy, Duffy)

BABY

Oh, I'm so lonely!

I'M SO LONELY, I COULD CRY!
EVERYONE JUST PASSES BY,
I'M LONELY,
SO VERY LONELY.
I'M LONELY AS ALONE CAN BE.

COW, SHEEP, CAT

(enter, sing, [Use 'he' or 'she' as is appropriate to the gender of the actor])

HE'S SO LONELY, HE COULD CRY!
EVERYONE JUST PASSES BY,
HE'S LONELY,
SO VERY LONELY.
HE'S LONELY AS ALONE CAN BE.

BABY

I LONG TO FLY LIKE THE BIRDS ABOVE ME,
LONG TO SOAR ON THE BREEZE.
I LONG TO FIND FRIENDS TO MAKE ME HAPPY.
WON'T SOMEBODY HELP ME, PLEASE?

                              COW, SHEEP, CAT

HE'S LONELY,
SO LONELY ALL ALONE.

                                    BABY

I'M LONELY,
SO LONELY ALL ALONE.

                              COW, SHEEP, CAT

HE'S SO LONELY, HE COULD CRY!
EVERYONE JUST PASSES BY.
HE'S LONELY,

                                    BABY

Quack! Quack!

                              COW, SHEEP, CAT

SO VERY LONELY.

                                    BABY

Quack! Quack!

                              COW, SHEEP, CAT

HE'S LONELY AS ALONE CAN BE.

                                    BABY

I LONG TO FLY LIKE THE BIRDS ABOVE ME.

                              COW, SHEEP, CAT

HE LONGS TO SOAR ON THE BREEZE.

                                    BABY

I LONG TO FIND FRIENDS TO MAKE ME HAPPY.

                              COW, SHEEP, CAT

WON'T SOMEBODY HELP HIM, PLEASE?

BABY

I'M LONELY, SO LONELY ALL ALONE.

COW, SHEEP, CAT

HE'S LONELY, SO LONELY ALL ALONE.

COW

See you! (*exits*)

SHEEP

So long! (*exits*)

CAT

Bye! (*exits*)

BABY

I'M ALL ALONE. (*sighs*) I'm not staying HERE any longer. I'm going into the wide, wide world. Surely someone THERE will be my friend. (*exits*)

MOTHER

(*enters followed by Fluffy and Duffy*) Baby, we're back!

FLUFFY

Where is he?

DUFFY

Maybe the cat got him!

MOTHER

Oh, no! Don't say that! I won't rest until we find him. (*To audience*) Have you seen my baby? Which way did he go? (*audience response*) Thank you! (*Mother exits.*)

FLUFFY, DUFFY

(*exit following Mother*) Quack, quack, quack, quack, quack.

Part 5: At the pond

DRAMA WORKSHOP NO. 5

Movement

1   What words could describe the movement of a swan (graceful, gliding, smooth)? You are a swan. Move your right wing gracefully; add your left wing; move your wings together. As your wings go up, move your head up; as your wings come down, move your head down. Move around the space slowly and lightly. On each step move your wings up, then on the next step down, moving your head in the same way.

2   Swans move one at a time in succession. The first swan moves and watches carefully so that when the next swan begins to move, the first swan will stop (see Activity Box 7.9: Feathered Friends).

3   Birds fly in a V formation. Children become a group of swans flying in V formation. The mentor chooses the first swan for the tip of the V. When the first swan is in place, another swan joins on the right and another on the left, until the V is formed. Swans fly in place in V formation until the sound of the drum beat. Have birds fly well enough apart so they can extend their wings and still not bump into one another.

Transformation

1   Have children take a position in personal space and assume the role of Baby. On a count of six have them transform themselves from an awkward duckling to a graceful swan.

2   Have children find a partner—one is Baby, the other is Baby's reflection in the pond. Baby looks at his/her reflection and begins to move. First, Baby is the little duckling, but gradually she/he grows into a beautiful swan, all of which is reflected in the pond. Children change places. The pond reflection becomes Baby and Baby becomes the pond reflection. Do the transformation again.

The script

SCENE 5: AT THE POND

(Characters: Baby, Swan, Mother, Duffy, Fluffy)

BABY

(*enters, sees pond*) What a lovely pond! I'll have a swim. (*jumps in*) I like the feel of water running down my feathers *(shakes feathers, then sees swan)*. Oh, look! Up there! What a beautiful bird I see—all feathery with a long graceful neck and a colourful beak. Oh, how I wish I could be like that.

SWAN

(*enters*) Why wish for something you already are?

BABY

What do you mean?

SWAN

You're a swan—like me.

BABY

I am?

SWAN

You'll see. Close your eyes. Let time pass. Seasons will follow one after the other. All in good time you will be a swan, stretching your wings and soaring high in the sky (*exits*).

BABY

Wait! Don't go! Come back! (*exits after swan*)

FLUFFY

(*enters with Duffy behind Mother*) Mother, we should give up. He's gone for good.

DUFFY

(*aside to audience*) I bet the cat got him!

MOTHER

Remember this, young ones. A mother never gives up on her children. (*To Fluffy*) You look over there! (*To Duffy*) You look over there. I'll look over here.

BABY

(*enters as swan*)

FLUFFY

(*notices swan, aside to audience*) I'll ask that pretty bird there. (*to Baby*) Hello.

BABY

Hello, Fluffy.

FLUFFY

You know my name!

BABY

Of course I do! It's me! Baby!

FLUFFY

(*amazed to audience*) It's the turkey!—but he's not a turkey anymore! (*calls to Duffy*) Duffy!

DUFFY

What?

FLUFFY

Look!

DUFFY

Where?

BABY

Here I am, Duffy!

DUFFY

(*calls*) Mother, this beautiful bird knows us.

MOTHER

That's a swan, dear.

BABY

Mother, don't you recognise me?

MOTHER

Oh, my goodness, little one, how you've changed—from a cygnet to a stately swan!

BABY

Have I?

MOTHER

Look at yourself! (*Baby looks at reflection in pond*) Your wings are feathery, silky and long. Your beak is bright.

BABY

I'm special!

MOTHER

You always were. (*pause*) Now, my dear, your time has finally come. Go! Fly with the swans. You are the most magnificent of them all.

BABY

I'm so happy! (*hugs Fluffy, Duffy, and Mother*) Goodbye!

FLUFFY, DUFFY

Goodbye, Baby.

BABY

(*Calls out to swans*) Swans! Wait for me! Here I come! (*exits*)

MOTHER

Goodbye, my child. May fortune favour your flight.

Part 6: Finale

DRAMA WORKSHOP NO. 6

1 Have each child choose one of the characters from the script. In small groups of the *same* character, create a 'happy' still photograph (i.e. groups of Baby, Fluffy, Duffy, Mother, Cat, Sheep, Cow, Swan). Have each group look at the photographs of the other groups, then reflect together on how a character can be portrayed in different ways.

2 Divide into groups with one of *each type* of character in every group. Create another 'happy' still photograph. Rework each still photograph until it makes an effective stage picture.

3 Have characters in (2) focus on the swans flying overhead from left to right. Wave goodbye to the swans and call out farewells as they fly past (see Activity Box 8.9: At the Race as a preparatory exercise).

The script

FINALE

THE ENTIRE CAST

[*All swans fly in formation with Baby at the point of the V. Mother, Fluffy and Duffy wave goodbye*]

ALL (EXCEPT BABY)

(*sing. Melody is in Appendix 4.2*)

HE WAS LONELY ONCE BEFORE,
HE'S NOT LONELY ANYMORE.
HE'S HAPPY,
SO VERY HAPPY.
HE'S HAPPY AS A SWAN CAN BE.

MOTHER, FLUFFY, DUFFY

NOW HE FLIES WITH THE BIRDS ABOVE US.
NOW HE SOARS ON THE BREEZE.
NOW HE'S FOUND FRIENDS TO MAKE HIM HAPPY.
WHAT A CHEERFUL SWAN IS HE!

BABY

I'M HAPPY,

NOT LONELY ANYMORE!

ALL (EXCEPT BABY)

I'M/HE'S HAPPY,

NOT LONELY ANYMORE.

(*Curtain Call: Everyone bows*)

Figure A4.2 *So Lonely*: Words and music

Figure A4.2 *So Lonely:* Words and music (continued)

Figure A4.3 *So Lonely: Reprise*

Appendix 5
'Shake it!' with Shakespeare: Playlets 2 and 3

- 5.1 Playlet 2: King Duncan's Downfall (*Macbeth*)
- 5.2 Playlet 3: Tricky Business (*A Midsummer Night's Dream*)
- These two playlets can be used in conjunction with 'Shake it!' with Shakespeare (Musical Playlet) (Story and Script Box 14.4).
  (Note that direct quotes from the plays are in bold italic.)

Playlet 2: King Duncan's Downfall (*Macbeth*)

Setting: A long time ago in Scotland

Characters: Three witches, King Duncan, Macbeth, and Lady Macbeth.

(Witches enter cackling)

WITCH 1

When shall we three meet again?
In thunder, lightning or in rain?

Figure A5.1 Witches with King Duncan (left), Macbeth and Lady Macbeth

WITCH 2

When the hurlyburly's done?
When the battle's lost and won?

WITCH 3

That will be ere set of sun.

WITCH 1

Where the place?

WITCH 2

Upon the heath—

WITCH 3

There to meet with—

ALL

Macbeth!

WITCHES

WAAAAHHHHHHHH (*feeling thumbs*)

(*sing*) ['Something Wicked'—see Figure A5.2 *Something Wicked*: Words and Music]

BY THE PRICKING OF MY THUMBS,
SOMETHING WICKED THIS WAY COMES.
FEEL IT!
IT'S IN THE AIR.
FEEL IT
CREEPING EVERYWHERE.
FEEL IT!
IT'S IN THE AIR.
FEEL IT
CREEPING EVERYWHERE---
WAHHHHHHHHHHHHHHHHHH—
HAIL, MACBETH,
THANE OF CAWDOR.
HAIL, MACBETH,
KING HEREAFTER,

WITH YOUR LEGACY OF BLOOD AND DEATH,
YOU WICKED THING! YOU VILLAIN, YOU!
BY THE PRICKING OF MY THUMBS
SOMETHING WICKED THIS WAY COMES.
FEEL IT!
IT'S IN THE AIR.
FEEL IT
CREEPING EVERYWHERE.
FEEL IT!
BEWARE! BEWARE!

WITCH 1

(*To audience*) Look! THERE! (*Macbeth enters*)

WITCHES

ALL HAIL, MACBETH!
WAAAHHHHHHHHHHHHHH (*hissing*) Macbeth!

WITCH 2

A nasty thing who would be King.

WITCH 3

An evil man with an evil plan!

WITCH 1

Look! THERE! (*Lady Macbeth enters with knife.*)

WITCH 2

His wicked wife with a wicked knife. (*Lady Macbeth gives knife to Macbeth.*)

WITCHES

WAAAAAHHHHHHHHHH...

(*Sound of trumpets; King Duncan enters*)

WITCH 1

(*To audience*) Look! THERE! (*points to King Duncan*)

WITCH 2

A royal sire ...

WITCH 3

Soon to expire!

MACBETH

King Duncan. (*bows*)

LADY MACBETH

Welcome, my lord. (*curtseys*)

WITCHES

(*hissing*) Lies ...

MACBETH

We give you hospitality.

WITCHES

(*hissing*) Lies ...

MACBETH

Sire, you are weary. Rest safe with us.

WITCHES

(*Hissing*) More lies ... (*King Duncan exits behind screen*)

MACBETH

If it were done when 'tis done, then 'twere well it were done quickly ... (*Macbeth goes to side of screen*)

WITCHES

The King shuts his eyes, then a wicked surprise—

WITCH 1

A stab in the back with a whack, whack, whack.

WITCH 2

King Duncan tumbles down, down, down.

(*crown rolls out from behind screen*)

WITCH 3

Here it comes! Grab that crown! (*Macbeth does.*)

ALL WITCHES

Murder! Murder! Foul and base!
Everything is out of place.

WITCH 1

Hear the cries?

WITCHES

King Duncan dies!

WITCH 2

Now Macbeth becomes the King (*Macbeth puts on crown*)—yet cannot sleep for anything!

MACBETH

Methought I heard a voice cry, 'Sleep no more. Macbeth does murder sleep ... Macbeth shall sleep no more!'

(*Lady Macbeth goes behind the screen, enters with knife, gives it to Macbeth*)

WITCH 3

Before him sees a dagger turning, guilt inside him churning—churning!

WITCH 2

The lady tries to cleanse her stains, but nightmares haunt her for her pains.

LADY MACBETH

(*wringing hands*) **Out! Out I say! Who would have thought the old man had so much blood in him. Oh, Oh, OH! All the perfumes of Arabia will not sweeten this little hand. OOOOhhhhhhh.**

MACBETH

Out, out brief candle. Life's but a walking shadow, a poor player that struts and frets his hour upon the stage and then is heard no more. It is a tale told by an idiot, full of sound and fury, signifying nothing.

WITCHES

(*whisper*)To kill a King, a wicked, wicked thing.

(*Macbeth and Lady Macbeth exit to sounds of thunder and flashes of lightning*)

WITCH 1

I come graymalkin ...(exits)

WITCH 2

Paddock calls. (exits)

WITCH 3

Anon. (exits)

Notes

This playlet includes lines from several places in *Macbeth*, including, Act 1, Scene 1; Act 1, Scene 7; Act 2, Scene 2; Act 5, Scene 1; Act 5, Scene 5.

Appreciating and responding

- Have children think of something they really wanted. Did they or didn't they get it? What did they do? How did they feel?
- What does Macbeth want more than anything? What does he do to get it? Is he happy when he becomes King? Why not?

Figure A5.2 *Something Wicked*: Words and music

- Consider Macbeth's speech:

  'Out, out brief candle. Life's but a walking shadow, a poor player that struts
  and frets his hour upon the stage and then is heard no more. It is a tale told by
  an idiot, full of sound and fury, signifying nothing.'

- Ask children:
  - What do you think this speech means? Why do you suppose Macbeth says it?
  - What figurative language does Shakespeare use for 'life' (e.g. brief candle, walking shadow, poor player, tale told by an idiot)?
  - Consider the words: graymalkin (i.e. a grey cat), paddock (i.e. a word here meaning a toad), and anon (i.e. at once). What do they mean? Why would witches say these things?
- Create a television crime documentary about the murder of King Duncan. Interview students in role as suspects, witnesses and psychiatrists to try to understand why this tragedy occurred. How could it have been prevented?

Playlet 3: Tricky Business (*A Midsummer Night's Dream*)

Setting: The Fairy Bower in a woods near Athens

Characters: King Oberon—Fairy King, Robin Goodfellow, Titania—Fairy Queen, Donkey, fairies and other assorted creatures.

(Titania and her fairy court yawn and fall asleep. King Oberon enters stealthily; sprinkles flower juice in Titania's eyes.)

KING OBERON

Flower of this purple dye,

Hit with Cupid's archery! (*Magic sound*) *What thou seest when thou wakes ... it is they dear. Wake when some foul thing is near.* (*Donkey enters and brays; King Oberon laughs and exits.*)

Figure A5.3 Robin Goodfellow

DONKEY

HEE HAW!

TITANIA

What angel wakes me from my flowery bed?

DONKEY

HEE HAW!

TITANIA

Robin, look! (*Robin sniggers.*) **Come, wait you on him. Lead him to my bower.**

ROBIN

(*protests*) But, my Queen, that's a donkey!

TITANIA

At once! (*Robin and fairies lead Donkey to Titania*) (*to Donkey*) **Wilt thou hear some music, my sweet love?**

DONKEY

HEE HAW!

ROBIN

(*sings as fairies dance; Titania listens with Donkey at her side*)

[Sing 'Sweet Lullaby'—see Figure A5.4 *Sing Sweet Lullaby*: Words and Music]

YOU SPOTTED SNAKES WITH DOUBLE TONGUE,
THORNY HEDGEHOGS, BE NOT SEEN;
NEWTS AND BLIND-WORMS, DO NO WRONG,
COME NOT NEAR OUR FAIRY QUEEN.

TITANIA

PHILOMEL, WITH MELODY
SING IN OUR SWEET LULLABY
LULLA, LULLA, LULLABY.

FAIRIES

LULLA, LULLA, LULABY.

ROBIN

NEVER HARM

NOR SPELL NOR CHARM,
COME OUR LOVELY LADY NIGH;

ALL

SO GOOD NIGHT, GOOD NIGHT, WITH LULLABY. (*Fairies dance keeping away unwanted creatures*)

ROBIN

WEAVING SPIDERS, COME NOT HERE;
HENCE, YOU LONG-LEGG'D SPINNERS, HENCE!
BEETLES BLACK, APPROACH NOT NEAR;
WORM NOR SNAIL, DO NO OFFENCE.

FAIRIES

PHILOMEL, WITH MELODY
SING IN OUR SWEET LULLABY;

ROBIN

LULLA, LULLA, LULLABY.

FAIRIES

LULLA, LULLA, LULLABY.

ROBIN

NEVER HARM,
NOR SPELL NOR CHARM
COME OUR LOVELY LADY NIGH.

ROBIN/FAIRIES

SO, GOOD NIGHT,
GOOD NIGHT, WITH LULLABY.

(*Everyone falls gently asleep*)

DONKEY

(*quietly*) HEE HAW (*changes into gentle Hee Haw snores*)

Figure A5.4 *Sing Sweet Lullaby*: Words and music

Notes

This playlet is based on the beginning of Act 2, Scene 2 of *A Midsummer Night's Dream*.

- During the song, fairies dance. Also, choreograph movement for snakes, hedgehogs, newts, spiders, beetles and worms. Workshop how these creatures might move alone and together.
- Develop a movement spell used by fairies to keep unwanted creatures away from Titania. Workshop how the creatures respond when the spell takes effect (e.g. scuttle away, fall asleep).

Appreciating and responding

Challenge children to become 'theatre' researchers.

- What is a 'fairy bower'?
- Who is Cupid? Why does King Oberon mention Cupid's archery?
- Why does King Oberon play a trick on Queen Titania? (Use the play to find your answer.)
- Who is Robin Goodfellow?
- What are these creatures: Hedgehog? Newt? Philomel? Can you find pictures of them?

King Oberon plays a prank on Queen Titania by dropping 'love' juice into her eyes so the first thing she sees when she wakes, she loves. This happens to be a donkey!

Hot seat different characters (King Oberon, Robin Goodfellow, a fairy, a newt, a snake, Queen Titania, the Donkey) to find out what they really think about this 'joke'.

Discuss the question: 'When is a joke or prank not funny?'

Glossary

(Most terms in the glossary, with several exceptions, are given in the singular and in the present tense. The meanings provided are those that are most relevant for understanding how the terms are used in this book.)

aesthetic engagement
A state of in-depth involvement with an artistic product or process.

allegory
The name for a text or art work in which the characters and/or events stand for other things at a deeper, more symbolic level.

analogy
A comparison between two things that have similarities, usually to make a point or to help explain something more clearly.

as if
A term that refers to the ways in which drama participants interact within an imaginary world.

aside
When an actor in character talks directly to the audience or to someone else on stage unbeknown to other actors.

assessment
Formal evaluation of student progress usually represented as a grade, mark or a narrative learning profile.

assumption
Something believed to be true without actual proof; something taken for granted.

asymmetrical
When two halves of an object, shape or picture are not the same (i.e. unmatched).

audition
A time set aside for a director to meet those who wish to try out for a part in a play where decisions are made about who will be cast in the show.

authentic learning
Learning that is relevant and useful for the student in real-life contexts.

ballad
A story-based song.

bard
A medieval term for a storyteller.

blocking
Planned stage movement of actors set in consultation with the play's director.

body percussion
Using hands and feet to make claps, snaps or taps in a rhythmic pattern.

bounded space
An area that has definite physical boundaries; the type of space recommended for drama.

Bunraku puppets
Traditional Japanese puppets that are three-quarter life-sized and are operated by several puppeteers, usually dressed in black, that remain visible to the audience.

cast
(1) A collective term for the group of individuals (i.e. actors) chosen to act the parts in a play; (2) The process of selecting actors for a play by means of an audition (i.e. 'to cast a play').

cautionary tale
A story that includes a warning, often against engaging in certain types of behaviour.

centre stage
The middle of the acting area.

character profile
An actor's study of the role being played including an examination of the character's personal history, social situation, physical characteristics, mannerisms and psychological state; this approach can also be used to develop a puppet character.

character puppet
A solo figure that functions as an intermediary between the audience and the puppeteer; also called a host puppet.

children's theatre
A formal theatrical experience in which a play is presented for an audience of children, either by other children, by adults, or by a combination of children and adults.

choreograph
To plan and teach the movements for a dance or dance drama to others.

closed question
An enquiry that results in a limited response, such as 'yes' or 'no'.

cognitive apprenticeship
A scaffolding technique where a novice works with an expert who, over time, withdraws the coaching as the novice learns the necessary skills.

cognitive development
Stages of mental development through which humans progress. Piaget, a developmental psychologist, identifies these as sensori-motor (in infancy), pre-operational (in early childhood), concrete operational (in primary and early adolescence) and formal operational (in adolescence and adulthood).

commedia dell' arte
An improvised theatre form prevalent in sixteenth-century Italy with stock characters, called 'masks', and improvised action around a scenario.

common space
The area where drama participants work together without interacting.

consensus
Reaching agreement within a group; the process of achieving this is called consensus building.

conspectus
A collective view that recognises different opinions within the group.

contextual frame
A term used for the physical setting in which the drama takes place.

contrast

A drama element based on the concept of sameness or difference, such as opposites and symmetrical or asymmetrical.

cool down period

A time set aside, usually at the end of a drama session, to make the transition from the drama 'as if' world back into the actual world assisted by physical exercises and other debriefing strategies.

crystallisation

The process of viewing a phenomenon from a number of perspectives when there is no expectation that all perspectives will coalesce.

cup theatre

A mini-puppet theatre constructed from a paper cup that is held in one hand and tiny rod puppets enter and exit through the hole in the bottom of the cup; also called cup and container theatre.

dance drama

A story told through movement, mime and/or formalised dance steps.

de-role

To make the transition from playing a character in an 'as if' context to being oneself in the here-and-now; a process often undertaken as part of a debriefing session.

decision walk

A technique for objectifying a decision and identifying the reasoning behind it where the decision-maker walks between two lines of people who give him contrary advice. At the end, the person makes a decision and explains the reasons for the choice.

deconstruct

To analyse text in order to understand the underlying meanings as perceived by those conducting the analysis.

defining the space

This process involves mapping the imaginary space in drama onto an actual space.

description

A non-evaluative comment and/or account.

descriptive critique
The evaluator provides comments related to what they have received from the work so its creator can assess whether the work has conveyed what was intended.

developmental critique
A written or oral appraisal where the focus is on the development of the artistic product from one draft to the next.

dichotomy
Where two concepts are set at opposite poles (e.g. love versus hate); also called a binary opposition.

diction
The clarity of how a person speaks or sings.

docudrama
A dramatisation based on a reality-based story; also called a drama-doc or a fact-fiction drama.

doubling
When two participants do the same thing or each do part of a process (e.g. one the thoughts the other the actions); a broader term that includes thought tracking.

downstage
A position toward the front of the acting area.

drama
Also called creative drama, educational drama, process drama; depending on the definition used, it can refer to the process of creating drama only, to products of drama such as performances, or to both drama process and products.

drama game
Fast-paced and motivational activity often used as a warm-up exercise for drama.

dramatic retelling
As this term applies to drama, it means re-enacting a story using drama elements and forms; also called story dramatisation and/or story drama.

embodiment
Knowing through physical awareness; the resulting knowledge is described as somatic.

emotional intelligence
The ability to know one's own emotions and manage them and to recognise emotions in others and empathise with them.

emotional memory
The process of thinking back to certain events that enables a person to recapture the feelings of that time.

empathy
The ability to see things from another person's point of view.

ESL
English as a Second Language.

etymological dictionary
A dictionary that provides word origins and the development of the word over time.

evaluation
When a judgment is made about something (e.g. its worth, value, effectiveness, importance).

fable
A short story with a message, e.g. Aesop's fables.

family story
A narrative about events or people in a family, either current event or passed down from one generation to the next.

feedback
Comments given in response; either descriptive or evaluative.

figurative language
Using a non-literal sense of words as in similes and metaphors.

fill the space
Participants spread out to occupy the total space available for drama.

finger puppet
Small figures designed to sit on top of fingers or drawn directly on hands with washable ink.

flashback
Interrupting the forward flow of the action to return to an earlier point in the narrative; the opposite is flashforward, where action is projected into the future.

flip book
A series of attached pages on which figures are drawn so that when the pages are turned quickly the figures appear to move.

fly loft
An area above the stage into which backdrops and scenery can be lifted by pulling ropes or using technological means.

focus
An element of drama that relates to where attention is given in a tableau or scene.

focus group
A number of people who meet together to give feedback to a person who asks them questions, such as a researcher.

folktale
A traditional story originally circulating in oral form before being written down.

formative evaluation
Evaluation that occurs during a process.

forum theatre
A type of feedback theatre in which participants watch a scene, then, when it is played a second time, audience members can stop the scene and take the place of those enacting it to find a different pathway through the action.

freeze
An instruction given that means participants immediately stop what they are doing and remain silent and still.

glove puppet
See hand puppet.

hand puppet
A figure that fits over the hand; fingers either fit into the mouth and move it or are distributed among the head and arms of the figure; also called a glove puppet.

hegemony
Control or domination by one person or group over another person or group.

host puppet
A figure (i.e. doll-like or animal) that serves as an intermediary between the puppeteer and the audience; a synonym for a character puppet.

hot seat
A technique in which a person in role is asked questions by other group members.

hypertext fiction
A story composed of text and/or images that uses computer technology to enable multiple pathways through the story allowing readers to choose which links to follow in which order.

hypothetical question
A type of question that requires listeners to ponder 'what if'.

improvisation
A form of drama that involves spontaneous interaction using voice and/or movement.

in character
A term meaning the drama participant is portraying a part; often thought of in relation to a staged play.

in role
When drama participates take on or play different parts; the term used in improvisation and role play.

in-the-round
A type of performance space where there is no front to the acting area and the performers are surrounded by the audience.

inflection
Voice modulation accomplished by a change in tone or pitch.

integrated
An approach to curriculum in which subject boundaries blur and activities chosen contribute to a central learning core related to a theme or issue.

integrated learning

A phrase that implies a connection between previously separated content or skills areas.

key learning area (KLA)

A term used in some curriculum documents for subject areas (e.g. mathematics); in the plural it can refer to separate subjects or to clustered subjects (e.g. creative arts); also known as KLAs.

learning spiral

See spiral principle.

legend

(1) The symbols and their meanings as listed on a story map; (2) A story that may once have had its basis in fact; *see also* urban legend.

Likert scale

An instrument for measuring the degree of agreement or disagreement among a group of people by means of their response to a statement, usually on a three, five, or seven point scale.

locogram

A sociodramatic technique for identifying the opinions or attitudes of a group of people; also known as an opinion map.

locus of control

A psychological term that refers to whether a person perceives that the control for a situation is external (i.e. other people in control) or internal (i.e. inner control).

mantle of the expert

An improvisational strategy devised by Dorothy Heathcote where participants are empowered by being given the role of a person with expertise; this expertise can be gained through research or experiencing the character during enactment.

marionette

A puppet operated by strings attached to its limbs.

marionettist

The official name for the puppeteer who works with marionettes.

masque
In Renaissance theatre (sixteenth-seventeenth centuries) a form of court entertainment with music and dance in which masked performers often represented mythological or allegorical characters.

melt
A process through which participants make the transition from a freeze position to bringing a still photograph to life.

mentor
The person, usually a teacher, who facilitates the drama session.

metacognition
The state of actively thinking about your own thinking and what influences it.

metaphor
A figure of speech that makes a direct comparison, for example 'The sun is a yellow balloon'; *see also* simile.

metaxis
The state in drama in which participants belong to two different worlds at the same time, the imaginary and the actual here-and-now world.

mime
Meaningful movement without words, using gesture, facial expression and the body.

mirroring
(1) In partners, when one person moves and the other follows the movement as a reflection in a mirror; (2) Playing back through feedback theatre forms (e.g. talk back theatre, forum theatre) a person or group's ideas to them, usually as a basis for discussion and reflection.

monologue
An uninterrupted speech by one actor in character.

montage
Assembling and overlapping many different segments to form a whole art work.

mood
(1) A drama element that refers to emotional states expressed through feelings and actions; (2) The emotional atmosphere in a dramatic scene.

moral development
Growth in the ability to make ethical choices and decisions based on reasoning and understanding consequences; Kohlberg's theory suggests that a person's moral reasoning develops in stages into adulthood.

movie camera technique
A strategy for remembering a story by visualising it as a film playing back in your head.

multi-literacies
Involve the ability to think critically, interpret text and visuals perceptively, speak about issues convincingly, and effectively use the media of print, photography, video and computer-based technologies.

multiple intelligences
A term used to refer to a person's problem-solving or creating processes. Gardner identifies these as: linguistic, logical-mathematical, musical, visual/spatial, bodily kinaesthetic, interpersonal, intrapersonal, naturalistic and existential abilities.

mystery and miracle plays
In medieval times these plays were based on Bible stories, a number of which were associated with the miracles of Jesus.

narration
In a story, the descriptive lines or sections, not the dialogue.

narrator
A person outside the action that introduces a script or provides descriptive links for the audience, or tells what is happening.

nested
An approach to curriculum within a subject area where social, thinking and content skills are developed together.

offstage
(1) The areas not seen by the audience during a performance; (2) In readers' theatre, **offstage focus** refers to where the readers place their character focus and direct their suggested action (i.e. towards the audience).

on the spot
Drama participants move in place in their own personal space.

onstage

(1) The parts of the stage or acting area that are used for performance; (2) In a readers' theatre presentation, onstage focus occurs when readers look at and direct their suggested action towards each other.

open question

When an enquiry is phrased in a way to enable an unrestricted response.

opportunity class

One name for a classroom of students (usually upper primary) identified as gifted and talented and grouped together for this reason.

opposite prompt

The opposite side of the stage from the prompt corner.

oracy

Verbal literacy that involves speaking fluently, articulating to be understood, and communicating effectively.

orchestra

In an ancient Greek theatre, the performance space, originally called the 'dancing place'.

outcomes-based

When syllabi are based on a developmental framework that indicates what students are to know and do at different stages or levels.

out of scene

A term in readers' theatre that means a character suggests that they are offstage by lowering their head, turning their back, or turning focus away from the audience.

pace

The rate or speed of speaking.

pageant wagon

In medieval times, a moveable cart on which a play was staged.

pantomime

(1) Sometimes used as a synonym for mime; gesture and movement that tell a story; (2) A style of play including songs, dancing, jokes and melodrama (e.g. British Christmas pantomime); often based on a children's story or folktale.

paper bag puppet
A figure made from a paper bag that fits on the hand and is animated by it.

paradigm
An orientation or 'world view' that has associated with it specific vocabulary, assumptions, values and ways of doing things.

paradigmatic
A term in linguistics that refers to analysis based on themes and/or other textual elements.

paraskenia
In ancient Greek theatre, the side wings of the skene or stage building.

parodoi
The passageways between the seating and the stage building in an ancient Greek amphitheatre.

pastiche
A drama, text, or piece of art composed of a mixture of styles or ideas borrowed from other works; may satirise the works upon which it draws.

performativity
A theory that holds that all aspects of life involve performance.

personal incident story
A narrative about an event that actually happened to the storyteller.

personal space
In drama, the area around each participant into which others do not enter.

pitch
Where a tone is located within the range of sound from the lowest to the highest note you can make.

planes
A term used by Stanislavski to refer to the various levels at which a play script can be analysed (i.e. external, social situation, literary, aesthetic, psychological, physical, actor's personal creative feelings) and how an actor uses these to develop a character.

play cycle
In medieval times, a collection of plays from the Bible that told the story of the world from creation to doomsday.

playbuild
A process that uses improvisation and role play to develop a dramatisation that is often presented for an audience.

playlet
A short play.

playwright
A person who writes a play.

pourquoi story
An origin tale that tells how something came to be the way it is.

praxis
The practical side of a subject; often seen as the application of a theory.

pre-text
Preparatory work for a drama session that may involve presenting a stimulus (e.g. a story, poem) or setting up the drama in some way.

prescriptive critique
A critic-centred evaluation that indicates the strengths and weakness of a dramatic product from the assessor's point of view.

probe
A question that digs below the surface of a participant's response with the aim of deepening students' thinking (e.g. Can you tell me more?).

programming
In drama, the specific written plan the teacher develops for working with drama in the classroom over a designated period of time (e.g. a term).

projection
When referring to vocal production, this term means saying the words loudly enough to be heard in any given situation.

prompt
(1) A question that aims to remind participants of something they already know or to encourage them to speak (e.g. Do you remember when … ?; (2) A theatre term meaning to provide actors with their lines when they forget them during a performance; the person who does this is the prompter.

prompt copy
The master copy of a play script with all the cues for lighting, sound and the actors' entrances and exits marked.

prompt corner
The place on the stage where the stage manager calls the show (i.e. gives the cues); also known as the 'stage manager's desk'.

proscenium arch
The frame around a traditional stage through which the audience looks to view the play.

puppet
An inanimate figure that moves under human control.

readers' theatre
A drama form where a group shares a text aloud using suggested characterisation and action in order to stimulate the imaginations of the listeners.

reflection
Thinking back over what has occurred in order to deepen understanding.

reflection-in-action
Stopping to consider what is happening in drama as it happens.

reflection-on-action
Individuals look back on what they have done to reinforce, consolidate, challenge and evaluate their learning.

rod puppet
A figure designed around a central rod, stick or dowel with thin wires to move its limbs; also called a stick puppet.

role
The part played by someone in an 'as if' drama world or a social context; one of the starting points for improvisation.

role on the wall
When drama participants choose a part from those listed or pictured on a wall or when the picture of a central character is placed on the wall so participants may refer back to it during the drama.

role play
Improvisation in which children respond as if they are someone else in the 'as if' drama world.

role reversal
When partners in an improvisation change places and role play from the other person's point of view; often used to have participants experience situations from contrasting perspectives.

role theory
Holds that in everyday life each person plays parts governed by certain rules or norms that serve as a blueprint for behaviour.

scaffold
When a mentor assists students to achieve more than they could achieve on their own.

science drama
(1) The application of drama elements and forms to science learning; (2) Sometimes used more particularly to relate to using playlets or readers' theatre scripts to dramatise scientific principles.

scope and sequence document (chart)
A planning document (usually in a school) that organises learning outcomes and activities sequentially across the grades to avoid overlap and repetition.

script
The text of a play (or readers' theatre text) that includes the lines which characters say, and some indication of how these lines are to be said.

sculpting
A drama technique where individuals or groups mould each other into tableaux to represent different characters or situations.

self-reflexivity
Thinking back on one's actions to gain insight about oneself.

sensorimotor stage
The first stage in Piaget's theory of cognitive development where the infant learns through the senses.

separate subject
An approach to curriculum where outcomes in each subject or KLA are kept distinct.

shadow puppet
A flat two-dimensional figure held against a translucent screen and illuminated from behind to cast a shadow on the screen.

shared (between subjects)
An approach to curriculum where the outcomes in several subjects are met through activities that are relevant to both.

shared space
When more than one person occupies the same area and interacts within it.

simile
A figure of speech that makes a comparison between two different concepts using 'like' or 'as', for example 'The child ran like a rabbit'.

simulation
One way to begin improvisation by using a situation that approximates a real-life one (e.g. practice for a fire drill).

situated context
When learning occurs in a situation that has features of a real-life situation.

skene
In ancient Greek theatre, a stage building to which actors could retire or from which they could enter.

skit
A short scenario, sometimes comic and improvised.

sociodrama
An approach to drama where the subject of the drama is the group itself and its development.

sock puppet
A figure made from a sock often with a moveable mouth; a type of hand or glove puppet.

somatic knowledge
A term that relates to knowing by means of 'doing'.

sound story
A story to which sounds and movements are added so that the whole group can participate as the story is told; one structure presents a sequence of events that is

resolved; another structure is a series of events that leads to a climax after which the action reverses until the characters return to the story's beginning.

soundscape
A composition created through body percussion and/or vocalisation to suggest the atmosphere of a particular place and/or time.

space
A drama element that participants use to show the relationship between themselves and others; described as individual or personal, common and/or shared.

spectrogram
A sociodramatic technique that requires participants to show what position they hold on a subject or issue by moving to a designated place in the room that indicates their degree or intensity of response.

spiral principle
When a concept is revisited at different times during students' learning careers with increasing levels of complexity as their understandings increase.

stage business
Planned action undertaken by an actor in the acting area.

stage left
The left side of the stage from an actor's perspective facing the audience.

stage picture
Placing actors in the performance space to show relationships or provide an aesthetic grouping.

stage right
The right side of the stage from an actor's perspective facing the audience.

staged readers' theatre
This drama form uses more action than a traditional approach to readers' theatre, but the movement is still suggested rather than realistic; also called free readers' theatre.

steampunk
A genre of speculative fiction set in the era of the steam engine (i.e. nineteenth century) but using elements of science fiction and fantasy; characters confront anarchistic situations.

stereotyping
Involves classifying objects, events and people without regard for their individual qualities or situations.

still photograph
A form of depiction where drama participants shape themselves into a picture with no sound or movement; also known as a tableau.

stock characters
In commedia dell' arte, these are the traditional characters associated with the form who have identifiable personalities, movements and typical ways of interacting with other characters.

story
(1) Traditionally defined as a narrative with a beginning, middle and end involving characters who overcome obstacles to reach a goal; (2) Contemporary definitions allow for a less-structured, more open-ended structure characteristic of hypertext fiction and computer games.

story drama
A technique that can involve re-enacting a story or exploring it through its themes, characters and settings. This can involve story dramatisation.

story dramatisation
Re-enacting a story.

story making
Participants use the elements of story (i.e. characters, actions, settings) to create their own stories that may take a range of forms (e.g. tangram tales, sound stories, circle stories).

story map
A technique for remembering the structure and characters in a story by charting or graphing the action.

story rattle
A musical instrument that symbolises that the person holding it is the storyteller; often passed around in a group to encourage different people to tell stories.

story stick
Fulfils the same function as the story rattle; the person holding it is the one who speaks and others listen.

storyboard
The sequential plan for a film or video shown in diagrams in which each box shows the words/script, and the images and camera shots/artwork that accompany it.

storytelling
When an individual and/or a group shares a narrative aloud with others, bringing it to life through voice and movement.

storytelling apron
An apron onto which decorative pockets have been sewn, and each pocket contains a small finger puppet or object that can be used to tell a story.

storytelling shirt
A shirt that has a similar function to a storytelling apron.

street theatre
Refers to a play, often partially improvised and interactive, which takes place in the street or anywhere that people gather where there is no separate distinction between the actors and the audience.

suddenly
A drama technique that indicates an unexpected event that changes the direction of what is happening in a scene.

summative evaluation
When a judgment occurs at the end of a process.

sustainability
In relation to the environment, this term means to develop a frame of mind that leads to developing personal values, attitudes and actions that relate to maintaining the balance of nature or an eco-system.

symbol
(1) A drama element, sometimes referred to as symbolisation; (2) An object, person, event, action or place that can stand for something else (e.g flag, dove).

symmetrical
A state that exists when the halves of an object, shape or picture are the same (i.e. matched).

syntagmatic
A term in linguistics that refers to textual analysis based on story sequence.

talk back theatre
A technique that involves developing and presenting scenarios that focus on a problem that can then be discussed by the group.

tangram picture
Visuals made from a tangram (i.e. a square cut into seven pieces in a defined way) where pieces can be combined in different ways to form shapes and figures (e.g. cat, house, boat, person).

teacher-in-role
When the mentor takes part in the improvisation—usually as a secondary character—in order to give support and prompt the group to provide the reasons behind their decisions.

tension
An element of drama; tension results when participants in a problem-solving situation strive to reach a goal, but are blocked in some way; also called 'dramatic' tension.

theatre-in-education
A type of theatre experience in which a small company of (professional) actors tour schools presenting issues-based plays/scenarios, often involving student participation and discussion.

Theatresports
The improvisational theatre form developed by Keith Johnstone in which competing teams challenge each other to complete tasks and the 'best' team for each event is awarded points by judges.

theatron
In ancient Greek theatre, the seating for the audience, called the 'seeing place'.

thought tracking
A form of doubling where the first person speaks and the second person reveals the inner thoughts of the first person.

thrust stage
Where the stage extends into the audience who sit on three sides; also called an open stage or apron stage.

time
(1) A drama element that refers to the dimension in which drama events occur, i.e. the passage of time; time can be conceptualised in different ways, for example as sequential or cyclical; (2) the concept of beat, tempo or pulse related to rhythm; (3) controlling the pace of the action (i.e. timing).

told story
A term that indicates when a story is shared aloud rather than read.

tone
The way words are said to show the intent or feelings behind what is said.

tongue twisters
Words or phrases said in sequence that require a participant to enunciate clearly (example: red leather, yellow leather).

traditional readers' theatre
A form of drama where scripts are read and staged with readers sitting on stools or standing so that all readers can be seen; also called conventional readers' theatre.

triangulation
A term associated with data verification that uses multiple sources and/or methods to illuminate a phenomenon.

triggering device
An action or event that serves to mark the transition between the actual and imagined worlds in drama (e.g. dimming the lights, or putting on a certain costume piece such as a hat).

upstage
Toward the back of the stage.

urban legend
Contemporary stories that are repeated so often that they take on a folklore quality; also called an urban myth.

ventriloquism
Projection of the voice in such a way that it sounds as though it is coming from someone or somewhere other than the source.

vignette
An abbreviated incident or story often used as a discussion starter.

vocal projection

Relates to a person's ability to cast (i.e. throw) vocal sounds over varying distances.

vocal quality

The nature of the sound made when a person speaks (e.g. husky, shrill).

volume

The loudness or softness of a vocal tone.

warm-up

(1) Involves exercises such as stretches, jumping, hopping, skipping, running that prepare participants for drama by helping them focus and relax; (2) These may be exercises that involve visualisation and other preparatory activities such as drama games.

webbed

An approach to curriculum where a theme is treated in relevant ways within a range of subjects simultaneously.

wings

Offstage areas to the stage right and stage left; the usual places from where actors enter or exit.

zarzuela

Spanish musical theatre, often comic, that integrates dialogue, music and dance.

zone of proximal development

Vygotsky's term for the level at which a child can reach with the help of a mentor that goes beyond what the child could do alone.

References

Aaron, M. 1998, *Storytelling workshop*, personal communication, Sydney.

Abbs, P. 1982, *English Within the Arts*, Hodder and Stoughton, London.

Abbs, P. (ed.) 1989, *The Symbolic Order: A Contemporary Reader on the Arts Debate*, Falmer Press, London.

Ackroyd-Pilkington, J. 2001, 'Acting, representation and role', *Research in Drama Education*, vol. 6, no. 1, pp. 9-22.

Amatruda, M. 2006, 'Conflict resolution and social skill development with children', *Journal of Group Psychotherapy, Psychodrama & Sociometry*, vol. 58, no. 4, pp. 168-81.

Andersen, C. 2004, 'Learning in "As-if" worlds: Cognition in drama in education', *Theory into Practice*, vol. 43, no. 4, pp. 281-87.

Aristotle 1961, *Poetics*, S.H. Butcher (transl.), Hill and Wang, New York.

Arnold, R. & Taylor, P. 1995, 'Drama in education: Assuming centre stage', *Forum of Education*, vol. 50, no. 2, pp. 19-27.

Arnott, P. 1964, *Plays without People: Puppetry and Serious Drama*, Indiana University Press, Bloomington.

Baird, B. 1965, *The Art of the Puppet*, Macmillan, New York.

Bany-Winters, L. 1997, *On Stage: Theatre Games and Activities for Kids*, Chicago Review Press, Chicago.

Bayliss, P. & Dodwell, C. 2002, 'Building relationships through drama: The Action Track Project (1)', *Research in Drama Education*, vol. 7, no. 1, pp. 43-60.

Beadle, R. & King, P. 1984, *York Mystery Plays*, Clarendon Press, Oxford.

Benjamin, W. 1968, 'The storyteller', in H. Zohn (transl.), *Illuminations*, pp. 83-107, Fontana Press, London.

Berghammer, G. et al n.d., *Developmental Drama: The Curricular Process for Prekindergarten-Grade 6*, Iowa Arts Council/National Endowment for the Arts, Iowa State Department of Education, Iowa Alliance for Arts Education, Des Moines and Iowa City.

Bloom, B.S. 1956, *Taxonomy of Educational Objectives: The Classification of Educational Goals: Handbook I: Cognitive Domain*, David McKay, New York.

Boal, A. 1995, *The Rainbow of Desire*, Routledge, London.

Board of Studies NSW 1999, *Science and Technology K-6 Outcomes and Indicators*, The Board, Sydney.

Board of Studies NSW 2000, *Creative Arts K-6: Syllabus*, The Board, Sydney.

Bohannan, P. & van der Elst, D. 1998, *Asking and Listening: Ethnography as Personal Adaptation*, Waveland Press, Prospect Heights, IL.

Bolton, G. 1979, *Towards a Theory of Drama in Education*, Longman, Harlow, Essex.

Bolton, G. 1984, *Drama as Education: An Argument for Placing Drama at the Centre of the Curriculum*, Longman, Harlow, Essex.

Bolton, G. 1985, 'Changes in thinking about drama in education', *Theory into Practice*, vol. 24, no. 3, pp. 151-57.

Bolton, G. 1986, *Gavin Bolton: Selected Writings*, D. Davis & C. Lawrence (eds), Longman, London.

Bolton, G. 1996, 'Afterword: Drama as research', in P. Taylor, *Researching Drama and Arts Education: Paradigms and Possibilities*, pp. 187-94, Falmer Press, Bristol, PA.

Bolton, G. & Heathcote, D. 1999, *So You Want to Use Role-Play? A New Approach in How to Plan*, Trentham Books, London.

Bonnett, M. 1999, 'Education for sustainable development: A coherent philosophy for environmental education?', Special Issue: Environmental education, sustainability, and the transformation of schooling, *Cambridge Journal of Education*, vol. 29, no. 3, pp. 313-24.

Boyle, M., Ward, H., Wedge, D. & Woods, M. 2002, 'Taking the mystery out of drama responding', *Drama Queensland Says*, vol. 25, no. 2, pp. 22-25.

Brady, L. 2006, *Collaborative Learning in Action*, Pearson Education Australia, Frenchs Forest, NSW.

Brandt, B., Farmer, J. & Buckmaster, A. 1993, 'Cognitive apprenticeship approach to helping adults learn', in D. D. Flannery (ed.), *Applying Cognitive Learning Theory to Adult Learning*, New Directions for Adult and Continuing Education, n. 59, Jossey-Bass, San Francisco.

Brockett, O. 1979, *The Theatre: An Introduction*, 2nd edn, Holt, Rinehart & Winston, New York.

Buchanan, M. n.d., Artist-centred Evaluation: An approach to the objective grading of creative work <http://www.childdrama.com/mainframe.html>10 September 2006.

Bundy, P. 2005, 'Asking the right questions: Accessing children's experience of aesthetic engagement', *Applied Theatre Researcher*, vol. 6, article no. 12, 18p. <www.gu.edu.au/centre/cpci/atr/journal/volume6_article12.htm> 10 September 2006.

Butt, A. 1999, *Embodiment and memory*, personal communication, Freelance Dance Company, Sydney.

Carey, J. 1995, 'Drama conventions: A quick reference guide', *Drama*, vol. 4, no. 1, pp. 29-32.

Carlson, M. 1996, *Performance: A Critical Introduction*, Routledge, New York.

Carlsson, B. 2003, 'Dramatic potosynthesis [sic]', *Australian Science Teachers' Journal*, vol. 49, no. 1, pp. 26-35.

Carroll, J. 1996, 'Escaping the information abattoir: Critical and transformative research in the drama classroom', in P. Taylor (ed.), *Researching Drama and Arts Education*, pp. 72-84, Falmer Press, London.

Cassady, M. 1993, *Acting Games: Improvisations and Exercises*, Meriwether Publishing, Colorado Springs.

Cattanach, A. 1996, *Drama for People with Special Needs*, A & C Black, London.

Champlin, C. & Renfro, N. 1985, *Storytelling with Puppets*, ALA, Chicago.

Cockett, S. 1997, 'Drama, myth and parable: Problem-solving and problem-knowing', *Research in Drama Education*, vol. 2, no. 1, pp. 7-20.

Coger, L. & White, W. 1982, *Readers Theatre Handbook: A Dramatic Approach to Literature*, 3rd ed., Scott, Foresman and Company, Glenview, IL.

Coleman, D. 1995, *Emotional Intelligence*, Bantam Books, New York.

Commonwealth of Australia 2005a, Nine Values for Australian Schooling <http://www.valueseducation.edu.au/values> 13 September 2006.

Commonwealth of Australia 2005b, Status and Quality of Teaching and Learning of Science in Australian Schools <http://www.dest.gov.au/sectors/school_education/publications_resources/science_in_australian_schools> 2 September 2006.

Connelly, F. M. & Clandinin, D. J. 1990, 'Stories of experience and narrative inquiry', *Educational Researcher*, vol. 19, no. 5, pp. 2-14.

Conrad, D. 2004, 'Exploring risky youth experiences: Popular theatre as a participatory, performative research method', *International Journal of Qualitative Methods*, vol. 3, no. 1 <http://www.ualberta.ca/~dhconrad/publications.html> 20 December 2005.

Cossa, M. 2006, 'How rude!: Using sociodrama in the investigation of bullying and harassing behavior and in teaching civility in educational communities', *Journal of Group Psychotherapy, Psychodrama & Sociometry*, vol. 58, no. 4, pp. 182-94.

Courtney, R. 1990, *Drama and Intelligence: A Cognitive Theory*, McGill-Queen's University Press, Montreal & Kingston.

Covey, S.R. 1990, 1989, 'Six paradigms of human interaction' in *The Seven Habits of Highly Effective People: Restoring the Character Ethic*, Simon & Schuster, New York.

Crain, W.C. 1985, 'Chapter 7: Kohlberg's stages of moral development', in *Theories of Development*, pp. 118-36, Prentice-Hall, Englewood Cliffs, NJ.

Cremin, M. 1998, 'Identifying some imaginative processes in the drama work of primary school children as they use three different kinds of drama structures for learning', *Research in Drama Education*, vol. 3, no. 2, pp. 211-24.

de Bono, E. 1999, *Six Thinking Hats*, rev. edn, Penguin Books, London.

de Vos, G. 1991, *Storytelling for Young Adults: Techniques and Treasury*, Libraries Unlimited, Englewood, CO.

de Vries, P. & Poston-Anderson, B. 2000, 'The Peter Piper Pickled Pepper Mystery: Arts educators collaborate to create a musical play for pre-schoolers', *International Journal of Education & the Arts*, vol. 1, no. 5, 11p. <http://ijea.asu.edu/v1n5 > 15 October 2006.

de Vries, P. & Poston-Anderson, B. 2001, '"If the shoe fits, share it!": Approaches to arts-based integration', *Curriculum Perspectives*, vol. 21, no. 3, pp. 25-30.

Denzin, N.K. & Lincoln, Y.S. (eds) 1994, *Handbook of Qualitative Research*, Sage, Thousand Oaks.

Dodd, P. 1998, 'Using improvisation to foster team learning', in *Pushing the Boundaries: Learning Organization Lessons from the Field*, Kennedy Press, Ann Arbor, MI.

Drabble, M. 2004, *The Red Queen: A Transcultural Tragicomedy*, Penguin, London.

Dunn, J. 2005, 'Practising the art of forensic assessment', *Drama Queensland Says*, vol. 28, no. 2, pp. 2-5.

Erikson, E. 1950, *Children and Society*, Norton, New York.

Erikson, E. 1959, *Identity and the Life Cycle*, International Universities Press, New York.

Fergusson 1961, 'Introduction', in *Aristotle*, Poetics, S.H. Butcher (transl.), Hill and Wang, New York.

Fisler, B. 2003, 'Quantifiable evidence, reading pedagogy and puppets', *Research in Drama Education*, vol. 8, no. 1, pp. 25-38.

Fleming, M. 2000, 'Wittgenstein and the teaching of drama', *Research in Drama Education*, vol. 5, no. 1, pp. 33-44.

Fogarty, R. 1991,'Ten ways to integrate curriculum', *Educational Leadership*, vol. 49, no. 2, pp. 61-65.

Fortier, M. 2002, *Theory/Theatre: An Introduction*, 2nd edn, Routledge, London.

Freire, P. 1993, 1970, *Pedagogy of the Oppressed*, M.B. Ramos (transl.), Penguin Books, London.

Gadaloff, J. 1998, 1991, *Australian Drama*, Jacaranda Press, Milton, Qld.

Gardner, H. 1983, *Frames of Mind: The Theory of Multiple Intelligences*, Basic Books, New York.

Gardner, H. 1985, *Reintroducing Frames of Mind*, Basic Books, New York.

Gardner, H. 1993, *Multiple Intelligences: The Theory in Practice*, Basic Books, New York.

Gardner, H. 1999, *Intelligence Reframed: Multiple Intelligences for the 21st Century*, Basic Books, New York.

Gleeson, L. 2000, 'The Great Bear V the school reader', Libby Gleeson's biography <http://www.libbygleeson.com.au/great_bear_vs_school_reader.html> 10 December 2006.

Goldberg, M. 1974, *Children's Theatre: A Philosophy and a Method*, Prentice-Hall, Englewood Cliffs, NJ.

Grady, S. 1996, 'Chapter 2. Toward the practice of theory in practice', in P. Taylor, *Researching Drama and Arts Education: Paradigms and Possibilities*, pp. 59-71, Falmer Press, Bristol, PA.

Graham, D. 1972, *Moral Learning and Development: Theory and Research*, Angus & Robertson, Sydney.

Halley, S. 2006, 'Playback theatre and social change (a work in progress)', *Interplay Journal* <http:www.playbacknet.org/interplay/journal/halley.html> 20 September 2006.

Havighurst, R.J. 1952, *Developmental Tasks and Education*, David McKay, New York.

Heathcote, D. 1975, 'Drama as education', in N. McCaslin, *Children and Drama*, pp. 93-108, David McKay, New York.

Heathcote, D. 1984, *Collected Writings on Education and Drama*, L. Johnson & C. O'Neill (eds), Northwestern University Press, Evanston, IL.

Henig, R. and Stillwell, L. 1974, *Creative Dramatics for the Classroom Teacher*, Prentice-Hall, Englewood Cliffs, NJ.

Henry, M. 2000, 'Drama's ways of learning', *Research in Drama Education*, vol. 5, no. 1, pp. 45-62.

Hornby, R. 1995, 1977, *Script into Performance: A Structuralist Approach*, Applause Books, New York.

Hoyt, L. 1992, 'Many ways of knowing: Using drama, oral interactions, and the visual arts to enhance reading comprehension', *The Reading Teacher*, vol. 45, no. 8, pp. 580-84.

Innes, I., Moss, T. & Smigiel, H. 2001, 'What do children say? The importance of student voice', *Research in Drama Education*, vol. 6, no. 2, pp. 207-21.

Izzo, G. 1998, *Acting Interactive Theatre: A Handbook*, Heinemann, Portsmouth, NH.

Jacobs, G. & Cleveland, H. 1999, Social Development Theory <http://www.icpd.org/development_theory/SocialDevTheory.htm> 13 September 2006.

Jamieson, N. 1981, *Clowning Around: The Great Medici's Handbook of Clowning*, Arrow Books, London.

Janesick, V. 1998, 'Observation exercises', in *'Stretching' Exercises for Qualitative Researchers*, pp. 14-18, Sage Publications, Thousand Oaks.

Johnston, R.R. 2003, 'Carnivals, the Carnivalesque, *The Magic Puddin'*, and David Almond's *Wild Girl, Wild Boy*: Toward a theorizing of children's plays', *Children's Literature in Education*, vol. 34, no. 2, pp. 131-46.

Johnstone, K. 1979, *Impro: Improvisation and the Theatre*, Theatre Arts Books, New York.

Johnstone, K. 1999, *Impro for Storytellers: Theatresports and the Art of Making Things Happen*, Faber & Faber, London.

Kaplin, S. 1999, 'A puppet tree: A model for the field of puppet theatre', *The Drama Review*, vol. 43, no. 3, pp. 28-35.

Kemp, A. 2002, Implications of diverse meanings for 'scientific literacy' <http://www.ed.psu.edu/ci/Journals/2002/aets/s3kemp.rtf> 27 August 2006.

Kohlberg, L. 1963, 'The Development of Children's Orientation Toward a Moral Order. 1. Sequence in the development of Moral Thought', *Vita Humana*.

Kruper, K. 1973, *Communication Games*, Free Press, New York.

Krusic, V. 1999, 'Between the metaphors: Selected papers IDEA '98', *NADIE Journal (NJ)*, vol. 23, no. 1 & *IDEA Journal*, vol. 1, no. 1, pp. 17-22.

Kysilka, M. 1998, 'Understanding integrated curriculum', *The Curriculum Journal*, vol. 9, no. 2, pp. 197-209.

Lakoff, G. & Johnson, M. 1980, *Metaphors We Live By*, University of Chicago Press, Chicago.

Latrobe, K. & Laughlin, M. 1989, *Readers Theatre for Young Adults: Scripts and Script Development*, Teacher Ideas Press, Englewood, CO.

Lawrence-Lightfoot, S. & Davis, J.H. 1997, *The Art and Science of Portraiture*, Jossey-Bass, San Francisco.

Livo, N. & Rietz, S. 1986, *Storytelling: Process & Practice*, Libraries Unlimited, Littleton, CO.

Lorrefico, T. 2003, 'Warm up exercise: Same heart, same mind, different body', *Australian Puppeteer*, Winter, p. 19.

McCaslin, N. 1974, *Creative Dramatics in the Classroom*, 2nd ed., David McKay, New York.

McCullough, C. 1998, 'Building a dramatic vocabulary', in D. Hornbrook (ed.), *On the Subject of Drama*, pp. 169-84, Routledge, London.

McKone, F. 1997, 'Engagement and assessment in drama', Viewpoints, *Research in Drama Education*, vol. 2, no. 2, pp. 215-16.

McLean, J. 1994, *An Aesthetic Framework in Drama: Issues and Implications*, in C. Hoepper (ed.), NADIE Research Monograph Series, no. 2, National Association for Drama in Education (Australia), Melbourne.

McLuhan, M. 1967, *The Medium is the Massage*, Bantam, New York.

McPharlin, P. 1969, 1949, *The Puppet Theatre in American, A History: 1524 to 1948*, with a supplement, 'Puppets in America since 1948' by M.B. McPharlin, Plays, Boston.

Maslow, A. 1970, *Motivation and Personality*, 2nd edn, Harper & Row, New York.

Mattson, J. 1997, *Playwriting for the Puppet Theatre*, Scarecrow Press, London.

Merriam, S. & Caffarella, R. 1999, *Learning in Adulthood*, 2nd edn, Jossey-Bass, San Francisco.

Millar, R. & Osborne, J. (eds) 1998, *Beyond 2000: Science Education for the Future*, School of Education, King's College, London.

Moore, P. 1988, *When Are We Going to Have More Drama?*, Thomas Nelson, South Melbourne.

Moore, R. 1991, *Awakening the Hidden Storyteller: How to Build a Storytelling Tradition in Your Family*, Shamabhala, Boston.

Moreno, J. 1978, *Who Shall Survive? Foundations of Sociometry, Group Psychotherapy, and Sociodrama*, 3rd edn, Beacon House, Beacon, New York.

Morgan, N. & Saxton, J. 1994, *Teaching Drama—A Mind of Many Wonders*, Stanley-Thomes, Cheltenham.

Morningside Center for Teaching Social Responsibility (New York), Teachable Moment, 'Two lessons for grades 3-5: Be strong, be mean, or give in?' <www.teach ablemoment.org/elementary/strong_mean_giving_in.html> 15 February 2007.

Murray, I. 2006, 'Drama and student voice', Workshop, Ph.D. Research, University of Technology, Sydney.

Nagler, A.M. 1952, *A Source Book in Theatrical History (Sources of Theatrical History)*, Dover Publications, New York.

Neelands, J. 1984, *Making Sense of Drama*, Heinemann Educational, London.

Neelands, J. 1990, *Structuring Drama Work: A Handbook of Available Forms*, T. Goode (ed.), Cambridge University Press, Cambridge.

New South Wales, Department of Education & Training 2003, 'Cooling Conflicts' Program, Multicultural Programs Unit <www.racismnoway.com.au/strategies/ programs/nsw >28 February 2007.

Newton, D. 1958, *Clowns*, George G. Harrap, London.

Nicholson, H. 1995, 'Drama education, gender and identity', *Forum of Education*, vol. 50, no. 2, pp. 28-37.

Norris, J. 1999, Living citizenship through popular theatre, process drama and play-building <http://www.quasar.ualberta.ca/css/Css_35_3/ARliving_citizenship.htm> 28 February 2007.

Novelly, M. 1985, *Theatre Games for Young Performers*, Meriwether Publishing, Colorado Springs, CO.

O'Neill, C. & Lambert, A. 1982, *Drama Structures: A Practical Handbook for Teachers*, Heinemann, Portsmouth, NH.

O'Toole, J. 1992, *The Process of Drama: Negotiating Art and Meaning*, Routledge, New York.

O'Toole, J. & Burton, B. 2005, 'Acting against conflict and bullying, The Brisbane DRACON project 1996-2004—emergent findings and outcomes', *Research in Drama Education*, vol. 10, no. 3, pp. 269-83.

Pascoe, R. 1999, 'New literacies/old literacies for a new millennium: Drama and the arts as necessary languages for all students', *NJ (Drama Australia Journal)*, vol. 23, no. 1, pp. 121-36.

Perry, J. 1997, *Encyclopedia of Acting*, Quarto, Cincinnati.

Philpott, A.R. 1969, *A Dictionary of Puppetry*, Macdonald, London.

Piaget, J. 1966, *The Origins of Intelligence in Children*, M. Cook (transl.), International University Press, New York.

Pierce, P. 1999, *The Country of Lost Children: An Australian Anxiety*, Cambridge University Press, Melbourne.

Poston-Anderson, B. 1994, *Storytelling: An Idea Book*, Faculty of Humanities and Social Sciences, UTS, Sydney (unpublished booklet).

Poston-Anderson, B. 1996, 'The place of story in the Internet age', NSW Schools Section A.L.I.A. Conference, Sydney.

Poston-Anderson, B. 2000a, 'Story as a way of knowing: A methodological review', *CREArTA*, vol. 1, no. 1, pp. 84-91.

Poston-Anderson, B. 2002, '*With Will There's a Way*: Performing a children's play—A way of learning', *CREArTA*, vol. 2, no. 2, pp. 20-29.

Poston-Anderson, B. 2004, 'Storytelling with young children', UTS, Lindfield, NSW (unpublished workshop notes).

Poston-Anderson, B. 2007, *Living with Marionettes: The Story of the Griffiths Marionette Theatre*, OZ Tales, Sydney (in press).

Poston-Anderson, B. & Bathgate, K. 1997, 'Communicating with string figures', Research funded by UTS Summer Scholarship Program, *Play and Folklore*, no. 32, pp. 2-8.

Poston-Anderson, B. & McCrae, M. 2002, 'From story to script: Adapting traditional tales for the stage', Research funded by UTS, Faculty of Education, UTS, Lindfield, NSW (unpublished paper).

Poston-Anderson, B. & Potter, J. 2002, 'Cognitive apprenticeship as a model for professional development of children's services staff: Developing storytelling expertise', UTS, Lindfield, NSW (unpublished paper).

Poston-Anderson, B. & Potter, J. 2003, 'Storytellers' journeys: Apprenticeship as a pathway to learning', *Orana*, vol. 39, no. 2 < http:// www.alia.org.au/publishing/ orana/39.2/poston-anderson.potter.html> 3 March 2007.

Poston-Anderson, B. & Redfern, L. 1996, 'Once upon our time: Research into the value of told story today', Research funded by UTS Summer Scholarship Program, *Orana*, vol. 32, no. 4, pp. 241-47.

Prior, R. 2001, 'Tension, power and control: Creating effective participatory drama', *NJ (Drama Australia Journal)*, vol. 25, no. 2, pp. 23-33.

Queensland Studies Authority 2004, *The Arts, Years 1-10 Syllabus*, The Authority, Spring Hill, Qld.

Reason, P. & Hawkins, P. 1988, 'Storytelling as inquiry', in P. Reason (ed.), *Human Inquiry in Action: Developments in New Paradigm Research*, pp. 79-101, Sage, London.

Relan, A. & Kimpston, R. 1993, 'Curriculum integration: A critical analysis of practical and conceptual issues', in Fogarty (ed.), *Integrating the Curricula: A Collection*, Hawker Brownlow Education, Melbourne.

Renfro, N. 1984, *Puppetry, Language and the Special Child*, N. Renfro Studios, Austin, TX.

Robertson, M. & Poston-Anderson, B. 1986, *Readers Theatre: A Practical Guide*, Hodder and Stoughton, Sydney.

Robertson, M. & Poston-Anderson, B. 1995, *Imagine This: A Readers' Theatre Source Book*, Hodder Headline Australia, Rydalmere, NSW.

Rodgers, J. & Rodgers, W. 1995, *Play Directors' Survival Kit: A Complete Step-by-Step Guide to Producing Theater in Any School or Community Setting*, The Center for Applied Research in Education, West Nyack, New York.

Rose, M. (ed.) 1961, *The Wakefield Mystery Plays*, W.W. Norton, New York.

Rosenthal, A. 1995, *Writing Docudrama: Dramatizing Reality for Film and TV*, Focal Press, Boston.

Rudlin, J. 1994, *Commedia dell' Arte: An Actor's Handbook*, Routledge, New York.

Saatchi and Saatchi Australia 2000, *Australians and the Arts: What do the arts mean to Australians?*, Australia Council, Surry Hills.

Sabatine, J. 1995, *Movement Training for the Stage and Screen: The Organic Connection between Mind, Spirit, and Body*, Back Stage Books, New York.

Schiller, W. & Veale, A. 1989, *An Integrated Expressive Arts Program, Drama, Dance, Art, Music*, Resource Booklet no. 4, Australian Early Childhood Association, Watson, ACT.

Schön, D. 1983, *The Reflective Practitioner: How Professionals Think in Action*, Basic Books, New York.

Schotz, A. 1998, *Theatre Games and Beyond: A Creative Approach for Performers*, Meriwether Publishing, Colorado Springs.

Science WOW Factory <http://www.gvc03c32.virtualclassroom.org> 12 December 2006.

Scott, P. 1985, 'Storytelling: A guide to the art', *Primary English Notes*, no. 49, Primary English Teaching Association, Rozelle, NSW.

Scott, W. & Oulton, C. 1998, 'Environmental values education: An exploration of its role in the school curriculum', *Journal of Moral Education*, vol. 27, no. 2, pp. 209-25.

Shoemaker, B. 1989, *Integrative Education: A Curriculum for the Twenty-First Century*, Oregon School Study Council 33/2.

Simons, J. 1992, 'Bridging the gap: Adolescent plays,' *NADIE Journal*, vol. 16, no. 3, pp. 31-4.

Singer, M. 1959, *Traditional India: Structure and Change*, American Folklore Society, Philadelphia.

Skeat, W. 2004, *An Etymological Dictionary of the English Language*, Oxford University Press, Oxford.

Slade, P. 1954, *Child Drama*, Hodder and Stoughton, London.

Smith, A. 2006, 'Science drama for everyone', *Teaching Science: The Journal of the Australian Science Teachers' Association*, vol. 52, no. 1, pp. 36-38.

Stanislavski, K. 1988, 1961, *Creating a Role*, Methuen Drama, London.

Stanislavski, K. 1995, 1937, *An Actor Prepares*, Methuen Drama, London.

Staveley, R. 2000, Drama movement workshop, Faculty of Education, UTS, Lindfield, NSW.

Stephens, J. & Waterhouse, R. 1990, *Literature, Language and Change: From Chaucer to the Present*, The Interface Series, Routledge, London.

Stinson, M. 2000, 'Don't throw the baby out with the bathwater! Assessment using an outcomes approach', *QADIE says*, vol. 23, no. 1, pp. 15-17.

Taylor, P. 1990, 'Thoughts on narrative, positivism, and ethnography, Part 1', NADIE, National Association for Drama in Education, Autumn, pp. 2-5.

Taylor, P. (ed.) 1995, *Pre-text & Storydrama: The Artistry of Cecily O'Neill & David Booth*, National Association for Drama in Education, Brisbane.

Taylor, P. (ed.) 1996, *Researching Drama and Arts Education: Paradigms and Possibilities*, Falmer Press, Bristol, PA.

Tillis, S. 1992, *Toward an Aesthetics of the Puppet: Puppetry as a Theatrical Art*, Contributions in Drama and Theatre Studies, no. 47, Greenwood Press, New York.

Turner, V. 1982, *From Ritual to Theatre*, Performing Arts Journal Publications, New York.

VanSchuyver, J. 1993, *Storytelling Made Easy with Puppets*, Oryx Press, Phoenix, AZ.

Vygotsky, L. 1978, *Mind in Society: The Development of Higher Psychological Processes*, M. Cole (transl.), Harvard University Press, Cambridge, MA.

Wagner, B.J. 1976, *Dorothy Heathcote: Drama as a Learning Medium*, National Education Association, Washington, D.C.

Walker, D. 1995, 'Integrative Education', ERIC Digest 101 <http://www.eric.uregon.edu/publications/digests/digest101.html> 10 May 2006.

Warner, C. 1997, 'The edging in of engagement', *Research in Drama Education*, vol. 2, no. 1, pp. 21-42.

Warren, K. 1992, *Hooked on Drama: The Theory and Practice of Drama in Early Childhood*, Institute of Early Childhood, Macquarie University, Sydney.

Warren, K. 1993, 'Drama for young children', *Drama*, vol. 1, no. 3, pp. 7-10.

Waters, I. 2001, 'Ancient Greek tales for today', *Contemporary Review*, vol. 278, no. 1625, pp. 356-64.

Watson, I. 2000, 'Ways of understanding the culture: Re-examining the performance paradigm', *New Theatre Quarterly*, vol. 16, no. 64, pp. 333-47.

Way, B. 1967, *Development Through Drama*, Longman, London.

Webber, N. 1997, 'Extraordinary life of Aussie folk hero' in 'My World', *Parramatta Advertiser* (April 23).

Weigler, W. 2001, *Strategies for Playbuilding—Helping Groups Translate Issues into Theatre*, Heincmann, Portsmouth, NH.

Whitmore, J. 1994, *Directing Postmodern Theatre: Shaping Signification in Performance*, University of Michigan Press, Ann Arbor.

Wickham, G. 1987, *The Medieval Theatre*, Cambridge University Press, Cambridge.

Winch, G. & Poston-Anderson, B. 1993, *Now for a Story: Sharing Stories with Young Children*, Phoenix Education, Albert Park, Vic.

Winston, J. 2002, 'Drama, spirituality and the curriculum', *International Journal of Children's Spirituality*, vol. 7, no. 3, pp. 241-55.

Winston, J. 2003, 'This is the logbook of the Starship "Tempest"—Drama, Shakespeare and "multiple cultural competence"', *NJ (Drama Australia Journal)*, vol. 27, no. 2, pp. 37-51.

Witkin, R. 1974, *The Intelligence of Feeling*, Heinemann Educational Books, London.

Wolford, L. 1996, *Grotowski's Objective Drama Research*, University Press of Mississippi, Jackson.

Wood, D. 1999, *Theatre for Children: A Guide to Writing, Adapting, Directing and Acting*, with J. Grant, Faber & Faber, London.

Woods, P. 1993, 'Critical events in education,' *British Journal of Sociology in Education*, vol. 14, no. 4, pp. 355-71.

Young, D. 2000, 'Theatrical channel surfing: Reflections on the nature of improvisation and competition in the drama classroom', *NJ (Drama Australia Journal)*, vol. 24, no. 2, pp. 73-85.

Zachariah, M. & Moreno, R. 2006, 'Finding my place: The use of sociometric choice and sociodrama for building community in the school classroom', *Journal of Group Psychotherapy, Psychodrama & Sociometry*, vol. 58, no. 4, pp. 157-67.

Resources for Young People: Books and Media

Adams, D. 1979, *The Hitch Hiker's Guide to the Galaxy*, Pan Books, London.

Adrenium Games 2004, *Lemony Snicket's A Series of Unfortunate Events* (video game), Activision, Santa Monica, CA.

Alberti, L. & Alberti, G. 1987, *The Red Parcel*, A. Sage (transl.), Hutchinson, London.

Andersen, H.C. 1974, 1835, 'The Princess and the Pea', in I. Opie & P. Opie, *The Classic Fairy Tales*, pp. 216-18, Oxford University Press, London.

Andersen, H.C. 1997, 'The Ugly Duckling', in M. Ashley (ed.), *The Mammoth Book of Fairy Tales*, pp. 523–531, Robinson, London.

Anonymous n.d., *Gammer Gurton's Needle*, The E Server Drama Collection <http://www.drama.eserver.org/plays/medieval/gammer-gurton.txt> 3 January 2006.

Arkin, A. 1976, *The Lemming Condition*, Harper & Row, New York.

Ashcroft, J. 1960, 'Little Boy Lost' (song), Sydney Leeds Music, Sydney.

Ashley, M. (ed.) 1997, *The Mammoth Book of Fairy Tales*, Robinson, London.

Baker, J. 1987, *Where the Forest Meets the Sea*, Walker Books, London.

Barrie, J.M. 2000, 1911, *Peter Pan*, A Classic Illustrated Edition, C. Edens (comp.), Blue Lantern Studio, Raincoast Books, Vancouver, BC.

Baum, L.F. 2000, 1900, *The Wonderful Wizard of Oz: 100th Anniversary Edition*, W.W. Denslow (illus.), HarperCollins and Books of Wonder, London.

Bishop, G. 1984, *Chicken Licken*, Oxford University Press, Auckland.

Bowker, P. 2005, *Shakespeare's A Midsummer Night's Dream* (DVD), BBC in association with Horsebridge Productions.

Brunvand, J. 1993, *The Baby Train & Other Lusty Urban Legends*, W.W. Norton & Company, New York.

Burton, T. 2005, *The Corpse Bride* (DVD), Warner Bros. Entertainment [Rated PG].

Cameron, W. 1972, *A Tangram Tale*, Brockhampton Press, Leicester.

Carle, E. 1970, *The Very Hungry Caterpillar*, Penguin Putnam, New York.

Chaucer, G. 1986, *The Canterbury Tales*, An Illustrated Edition, N. Coghill (transl.), Century Hutchinson, London.

Choose Your Own Adventure Series 1979–1998, Bantam Books, New York, and 1999⁺, Chooseco, Waistfield, VT.

Climo, S. 1989, *The Egyptian Cinderella*, R. Heller (illus.), HarperCollins, New York.

Coburn, J.R. 2000, *Domitila: A Cinderella Tale from the Mexican Tradition*, C. McLennan (illus.), Shen's Books, Auburn, CA.

Coerr, E. 1981, *Sadako and the Thousand Paper Cranes*, M. Yamaguchi (illus.), Hodder and Stoughton, Sydney.

Coerr, E. 1995, 1993, *Sadako*, E. Young (illus.), Margaret Hamilton Books, Sydney.

Collodi, C. 1988, 1944, *The Adventures of Pinocchio*, E. Harden (transl.), R. Innocenti (illus.), Alfred A. Knopf, New York.

Corrin, S. & Corrin, S. (eds), 1964, *Stories for Seven-Year-Olds and Other Young Readers*, Faber & Faber, London.

Craft, R. 1975, *Pieter Brueghel's 'The Fair'*, J.B. Lippincott, New York.

Crew, G. 1999, *Memorial*, S. Tan (illus.), Thomas C. Lothian, Port Melbourne.

Crossley-Holland, K. 2000, *The Seeing Stone*, Orion Children's Books, London.

Dahl, R. 2001, 1982, *Revolting Rhymes*, Q. Blake (illus.), Picture Puffins, New York.

de Bernières 2002, *The Red Dog*, A. Baker (illus.), Vintage, Milsons Point, NSW.

de Paola, T. 1983, *The Legend of the Blue Bonnet*, Putnam, New York.

Ellis, J. 1991, 'The Giant Frog', in *From the Dreamtime: Australian Aboriginal Legends*, pp. 54-58, Collins Dove, Melbourne.

French, F. 1985, *Maid of the Wood*, Oxford University Press, Oxford.

Garfield, L. 1985, *The Wedding Ghost*, C. Keeping (illus.), Oxford University Press, Oxford.

Gauch, P.L. 1999, *Poppy's Puppet*, D. Christiana (illus.), Scholastic, Sydney.

Gibbs, M. 2007, *Snugglepot and Cuddlepie* (Musical), J. Clarke with D. Macleod (scriptwriter), produced at Sydney Festival, Sydney.

Gleeson, L. 1999, *The Great Bear*, A Greder (illus.), Scholastic, Sydney.

Gleitzman, M. 1998, *Bumface*, Puffin, Ringwood, Vic.

Gordon, R. (screenwriter) 2005, 2004, *Lemony Snicket's A Series of Unfortunate Events* (DVD), Paramount Home Entertainment.

Graff, F. 1989, 'Spider the Drummer', in H. East (comp.), *The Singing Sack*, pp. 10-12, A & C Black, London.

Hamanaka, S. 1995, *The Peace Crane*, Morrow Junior Books, New York.

Hathorn, L. 1995, *The Wonder Thing*, P. Gouldthorpe (illus.), Viking/Penguin Books, Australia, Ringwood, Vic.

Hutton, W. 1993, *Perseus,* Margaret K. McElderry Books, Macmillan, New York.

Ingram, A.B. 1987, 1985, *Mouse's Marriage*, J. Morimoto (illus.), Fontana Picture Lions, William Collins, Sydney.

Jennings, P. 2002, 2000, *Uncovered*, Viking, Camberwell, Vic.

John, E. and Rice, T. 2003, *The Lion King* (Musical), Disney Productions, Produced at the Capitol Theatre, Sydney.

Johnston, R. R. & Poston-Anderson, B. 2002, *Tales from the Golden Chair*, CREA Production, UTS, Sydney.

Jorgensen, N. & Harrison-Lever, B. 2002, *In Flanders Fields*, Sandcastle Books, Fremantle.

Kelly, J. 1995, *Everyday Machines: Amazing Devices We Take For Granted*, D. Burnie and Obin (illus.), Turner, Atlanta.

Lambert-Potter n.d., 'One Tin Soldier' <http://www.niehs.nih.gov/kids/lyrics/tin.htm> 13 September 2006.

LaPrise, R.L. n.d., 'Hokey Pokey' <http://www.niehs.nih.gov/kids/lyrics/hokey.htm> 2 February 2007.

Lewis, C.S. 2005, 1950, *The Lion, The Witch and the Wardrobe*, in *The Chronicles of Narnia*, HarperCollins, London.

Llyod, D. 1987, *The Ridiculous Story of Gammer Gurton's Needle*, C Voake (illus.), Walker Books, London.

Lum, D. 1994, *The Golden Slipper: A Vietnamese Legend*, M. Nagano (illus.), Legends of the World, Troll Associates, Mahwah, NJ.

McDermott, G. 1972, *Anansi the Spider: A Tale from the Ashanti*, Henry Holt and Company, New York.

McNaughton, C. 1994, *Suddenly!*, Collins Picture Lions, HarperCollins, London.

Maguire G. 1995, *Wicked: The Life and Times of the Wicked Witch of the West*, ReganBooks, HarperCollins, New York.

Maguire, G. 1999, *Confessions of an Ugly Stepsister*, ReganBooks, HarperCollins, New York.

Marin, G. 2007, *A True Person*, New Frontier, Epping, NSW.

Marsden, J. 1998, *The Rabbits*, S. Tan (illus.), Lothian, Melbourne.

Mayhew, J. 1997, *Katie Meets the Impressionists*, Orchard Books, Lane Cove, NSW.

Mosel, A. 1989, 1969, *Tikki, Tikki, Tembo*, B. Lent (illus.), Henry Holt, New York.

Mozart, W.A. 2005, *Cosi Fan Tutte* (DVD), Salzburg Marionette Theatre, HHO Multimedia Australasia.

Mozart, W.A. 2005, *The Magic Flute* (DVD), Salzburg Marionette Theatre, HHO Multimedia Australasia.

Pollock, P. 1996, *The Turkey Girl: A Zuni Cinderella Story*, E. Young (illus.), Little, Brown and Company, Boston.

Popov, N. 1998, *Why?*, North-South Books, New York.

Poston-Anderson, B. 1999a, 'Bella Venezia: The Italian Snow White', in *A Cultural Celebration of Italian Folktales*, CREA Production, Centre for Research & Education in the Arts, UTS, Lindfield, NSW.

Poston-Anderson, B. 1999b, *With Will There's A Way*, CREA Production, Centre for Research & Education in the Arts, UTS, Lindfield, NSW.

Poston-Anderson, B. 2000b, 'All in Good Time', in *Tales from Hans Christian Andersen*, CREA Production, Centre for Research & Education in the Arts, UTS, Lindfield, NSW.

Poston-Anderson, B. 2000c, *Asian Folktales* (script), Children's Theatre Series, no. 1, CREA Publication, UTS, Lindfield, NSW.

Poston-Anderson, B. 2001a, *A Cultural Celebration of Irish Folktales* ('The Adventures of Finn McCoul'; 'Fair, Brown & Trembling'), CREA Production, Centre for Research & Education in the Arts, UTS, Lindfield, NSW.

Poston-Anderson, B. 2001b, *Sense and Sustainability*, CREA Production, Funded by a UTS Sustainability Grant with R. R. Johnston (1999-2000), Centre for Research & Education in the Arts, UTS, Lindfield, NSW.

Poston-Anderson 2001c, *Second Star on the Right*, Tour to Primary Schools, CREA Production, Centre for Research & Education in the Arts, UTS, Lindfield, NSW.

Poston-Anderson, B. 2004, *The Elves and the Shoemaker*, CREA Production, Centre for Research & Education in the Arts, UTS, Lindfield, NSW.

Poston-Anderson, B. & de Vries, P. 2000, *The Peter Piper Pickled Pepper Mystery*, CREA Production, Centre for Research & Education in the Arts, UTS, Lindfield, NSW.

Roberts, W.A. (ed.) 1980, *How the Hermit Crab Tricked the Kingfisher*, Custom Stories of Our Islands (Series 1), Ministry of Education, Vanuatu, Port Vila.

Romeril, J. & Perkins, R. 2001, *One Night the Moon* (Film), MusicArtsDance Production, Dendy Films Release [Rated M 15+].

Rosen, M. 1989, *We're Going on a Bear Hunt*, H. Oxenbury (illus.), Walker Books, London.

Saxe, J.G. 1963, *The Blind Men and the Elephant*, P. Galdone (illus.), Whittlesey House, New York.

Say, A. 1993, *Grandpa's Journey*, Houghton Mifflin, Boston.

Scott, B. 1996, *Pelicans & Chihuahua's and Other Urban Legends*, Queensland University Press, St. Lucia.

Shakespeare, W. 2005, *Macbeth*, Shakespeare Graphic Library, Puffin Books, New York.

Shakespeare, W. 2006, *King Lear*, Shakespeare Graphic Library, Puffin Books, New York.

Shakespeare, W. 2005, *Romeo and Juliet* in Play Script—Text, Romeo and Juliet <http://www.william-shakespeare.info/shakespeare-play-romeo-and-juliet.htm> 28 February 2007.

Snicket, L. (a.k.a Daniel Handler) 1999, *The Bad Beginning*, HarperCollins Children's Books, London.

Snicket, L. (a.k.a Daniel Handler) 2006, *The End*, HarperCollins Children's Books, London.

Sophocles 1999, 'Antigone', in *Fall of the House of Oedipus*, R.R. Johnston & B. Poston-Anderson (adaptors), CREA Production, Centre for Research & Education in the Arts, UTS, Lindfield, NSW.

Southey, R. 1837, 'The Three Bears', in *The Doctor*, vol. 4, Longman, London.

Troughton, J. 1977, *What Made Tiddalik Laugh*, Thomas Nelson (Australia), West Melbourne.

UTS Youth Theatre Company 2000, 'Rumplestiltskin' (playbuilt production), CREA, UTS, Lindfield, NSW.

Uys, J. 1980, *The Gods Must Be Crazy* (Film), 20th Century Fox.

Venn, S. 1992, *Roy & Matilda: The Gallery Mice*, Edwina Publishing, Canterbury, Vic.

Venn, S. 1994, *Roy & Matilda: The Golden Locket*, Edwina Publishing, Canterbury, Vic.

White, E.B. 1952, *Charlotte's Web*, Harper & Row, New York.

Williams-Ellis, A. 1981, *The Story Spirits and Other Tales from around the World*, Heinemann, London.

Winton, T. 1997, *Lockie Leonard, Legend*, Pan Macmillan, Sydney.

Wong, M. 1999, *A Web for Wilbur*, Tour to Schools, UTS, Lindfield, NSW.

Index